Readings
in Calvin's
Theology

Readings inCalvin's Theology

DONALD K. McKIM
EDITOR

BAKER BOOK HOUSE
Grand Rapids, Michigan 49506

ISBN: 0-8010-6150-4

Library of Congress Catalog Card Number: 83-73010

Printed in the United States of America

To my sons
Stephen Ernest McKim,
who could recognize and say
"John Calvin" at age two,
and
Karl Andrew McKim,
who attended his first Calvin
conference at seven months —
may they learn appreciatively
from John Calvin

Contents

Introduction

Now we are to conceive the Christian faith as no bare knowledge of God or understanding of Scripture which rattles around the brain and affects the heart not at all. . . . But it is a firm and staunch confidence of the heart by which we securely repose in God's mercy promised us through the Gospel.[1]

The theology of John Calvin (1509–1564) has had a significant impact on Western Christianity since the sixteenth century. It has been the foundation for the Reformed theological tradition, helping to shape the faith and personal beliefs of men and women of Reformed churches.

There is no substitute for the study of the primary writings of Calvin himself. In his theological works, biblical commentaries, sermons, and letters we have Calvin the scholar, the churchman, the pastor, the preacher, and friend. The range of his knowledge was outstanding, the insights he offered were penetrating, and the true piety he evinced shows a Christian genuinely struggling in faith to understand and live God's will for his life.

The essays offered here present many of the leading aspects of Calvin's thought. They seek to draw together Calvin's thinking on various topics to present an overview of his teachings. The leading scholars represented provide in this one volume a wealth of material *from* Calvin for the interpretation *of* Calvin. This book may thus act as a supplement to the reading of Calvin as a way to broaden and reflect further on one's understanding of the Genevan Reformer.

1. *John Calvin: Catechism 1538,* translated and annotated by Ford Lewis Battles (Pittsburgh: Pittsburgh Theological Seminary, 1972), pp. 17–18.

Abbreviations

1

John Calvin: Doctor Ecclesiae

John T. McNeill

In Ephesians 4:11 we are told of the gifts of Christ to the church in the ministry, in the ranks of which are apostles, prophets, evangelists, pastors, and teachers. If you look this up in Beza's Latin text, you will read:

> Is igitur dedit alios quidem apostolos, alios vero prophetas, alios autem evangelistas, alios autem pastores et doctores.

Those who know the Greek better than the Latin will recognize that the word here used for teachers is *didaskaloi*. Calvin himself uses the expression *doctor ecclesiae*. It appears in the title of *Institutes* 4.3 — "The Doctors and Ministers of the Church." In section 4 of this chapter he distinguishes the functions of pastors and teachers: "Teachers are not put in charge of discipline or administering the sacraments, or warnings and exhortations, but only of scriptural interpretation — to keep doctrine whole and pure among believers." And it is well known that in the Ecclesiastical Ordinances of 1541 Calvin set a distinct place for the ministry of "doctors."

Robert W. Henderson, in *The Teaching Office in the Reformed Tradition: A History of the Doctoral Ministry,* has followed the difficult course of Calvin's "doctor" through history. There has always been a tendency to combine in one person the doctor or teacher, who with academic learning declares the doctrine or teaching, and the

Reprinted from *The Heritage of John Calvin,* ed. John H. Bratt (Grand Rapids: Eerdmans, 1973), pp. 9–22. Used by permission of Calvin College.

pastor or preacher, who explains and applies it to the people. Calvin indeed did not object to pastors' being called doctors "so long as we know that there is another class of teachers (*alterum doctorum genus*) who preside in the education of pastors, and in the instruction of the whole church" (*Comm. on Eph.* 4:11). The tendency to merge the two offices is nowhere better illustrated than in the case of Calvin himself, who was equally employed in the pulpit and in the academic chair. In both offices, but chiefly as teacher, he vastly extended his impact on mankind through the printed page. In what follows we shall try to confine our attention to his exercise of the doctoral ministry.

In Roman Catholicism the term *Doctor Ecclesiae* is a title applied to about thirty teachers of special distinction. By various popes from Boniface VIII on, these have been named and commended to the schools of the church as guides in theology and ecclesiology. In recent decades numerous Roman Catholic scholars have turned with a new appreciation to Calvin, and there is every reason to think that this trend will continue. We have of course no expectation that he will qualify for the papal accolade; but he has already accredited himself as an eminent teacher to a great part of the Christian church. Not the least remarkable phenomenon of the twentieth-century theological scene has been a new scholarly attention to Calvin's great body of writings. It is no exaggeration to say that during the past half-century the image of John Calvin has grown before the eyes of the entire Christian world of thought to a stature never before reached. His works written — and his work achieved — are coming to be judged more appreciatively, and he is known by those who knew him not. Thus the designation "Doctor of the Church" may be more confidently applied to him today than it could have been formerly.

It is useful to remind ourselves at the outset that Calvin's teaching took its rise from a deep personal experience. Of this Calvin said little; it may not have crossed his mind that readers centuries away would wish to know more of his inner motivation than he incidentally disclosed. But certainly — like Paul, Augustine, Luther, and countless other eminent Christians — he passed through a crisis of conversion, the effect of which gave character to all his later thought and effort. It was long after this happened that he first wrote of it in direct and explicit terms: "God by a sudden conversion subdued my heart to teachableness." In this familiar sentence, have we duly felt the force of his word "teachableness"? Heart and intellect were alike quickened and redirected. Looking back, he declared that before this divine intervention came to draw him out of the mire he had been stubbornly attached to the unreformed papacy and that thereafter he burned with zeal to pursue new studies centered in the Scriptures. He soon began, we know, to put together the materials for the first edition of the *Institutes.* It is clear from this and other autobiographical fragments that Calvin the theologian and teacher of the church came to his office by way of conversion and that this involved a protracted and painful inner conflict. Clearly, too, he was very much aware that it was God who took the initiative. We may regret that he was not more communicative on the details of this transforming experience. He had so much to write about God, God's Word, and God's church that he chose to be reticent about himself.

The man whom God subdued to teachableness and directed to new studies found in Holy Scripture the central documents of his intense intellectual labor. In this task he does not scorn the aid of the church fathers or of the pagan philosophers before them. Indeed, in his vast range of reading he seems to have taken every author as a potential teacher and useful stimulator of his own thought. But he rests his teaching constantly on that of the Bible. The sacred Scriptures were inspired by the Holy Spirit and the devout reader is aided by the Spirit in comprehending their meaning. In this sense, the Bible is the Word of God. Something mystical or sacramental is involved in the Christian use of Scripture. It comes from God the Holy Spirit; and its message is made available by the work of the Spirit whereby it is self-authenticated to the mind obedient to the Spirit, and is not to be subjected to reasoned proof. Superior to all reason is the inner testimony of the Spirit. Yet, if reasons are asked, Calvin will furnish reasons for accepting the divine authority of Scripture. It surpasses the greatest of pagan writings and "is crammed with thoughts that could not be humanly conceived" (*Inst.* 1.7–8).

Calvin is far from regarding all parts of Scripture as of equal value, and nothing could be more erroneous than the notion that he relies on the Old Testament. This is evident from the fact that he wrote commentaries on most of the New Testament books before his first Old Testament commentary appeared in 1551. His references in the *Institutes* to New Testament passages (4340) are almost twice as numerous as those to the Old Testament (2424), despite the disparity in length of the Testaments themselves. He does firmly believe in the continuity of the Old and New Testaments, but he devotes a chapter to the superiority of the New with its fuller light and its range of concern for all mankind in "the calling of the Gentiles." Indeed, the Old Testament receives its significance for him by its anticipations of the New (*Inst.* 2.11). Incidents and rites recorded in the Old Testament are taken as "types" or foreshadowings of what was to be made clear in the New. Moses and the prophets had as their task "to teach a way of reconciliation" leading to the reconciling work of Christ (*Inst.* 1.6.2); and "the inner testimony of the Spirit" needed for an understanding of both Testaments is a testimony to Christ. "The ancient prophets spoke by the spirit of Christ," and it is the passages lending themselves to this interpretation that Calvin cites most frequently. For him the whole Bible is primarily a book about Christ. Still, his commentaries show an extraordinary grasp of historical facts and a power of historical imagination.

The Scriptures are inspired, but Calvin does not make them verbally inerrant in the fashion of modern fundamentalists. When he speaks of the apostolic writers as "authentic amanuenses of the Holy Spirit," the context speaks of doctrine and not of words. Commenting on 2 Timothy 3:16 — "All Scripture is given by the inspiration of God" — he remarks that the law and the gospel are "a doctrine . . . dictated by the Holy Spirit." When it comes to words he does not hesitate to admit errors: Paul, following the LXX, has used a defective rendering of Psalm 51:4, and in repeating the words of Scripture the apostles were *saepe liberiores,* often pretty free, for they were not shackled by a *religio verborum,* a scrupulosity about words. It is the teaching (*doctrina*) that is divine, not the mere words. In his commentaries Calvin treats the words of Scripture often in detail, but as a humanist scholar would treat them, in search of their natural meaning.

No doctor of the church, not even Chrysostom, of whose work he makes much use, was more consistently and effectively than Calvin a doctor of Holy Scripture. He began in Geneva as lecturer in Holy Scripture, and he played this role to the end. Within his works we find embodied the most systematic and penetrating exposition of Scripture that the Reformation produced. Calvin thus gave impetus to the progress of biblical research and interpretation that has continued through the centuries since his time, with its exciting developments in our age. We cannot tell what attitude he would have taken to this or that trend in contemporary biblical criticism. He might have found in some of it a lack of that "piety" and that reliance on the Holy Spirit's guidance which he thought essential. But we should not forget in this connection his warning against the rejection of any truth, even from pagan and secular writers. "If we regard the Spirit of God as the sole fountain of truth, we shall neither reject the truth itself nor despise it wherever it shall appear, unless we wish to dishonor the Spirit of God" (*Inst.* 2.2.15).

Calvin, the doctor of the church, presented a doctrine of the church that remains perpetually challenging. In his last letter, written to his old co-laborer Farel, he takes some satisfaction from the fact that their labors together have been "useful to the Church of God." It is readily inferred from the language he uses in referring to his "sudden conversion" that this experience was difficult because it was a crisis of church attachment. It meant his departure from the papal church to the ranks of the evangelical party. In the *Institutes* and in the Ordinances of Geneva the outlines were drawn of the Reformed church that was beginning to take shape. But for Calvin the church of God was a far more vast and more spiritual entity than any visible church, whether of Rome, Zurich, Wittenberg, Canterbury, or Geneva. It was the "holy catholic church" of the creed; and the phrase that follows — "the communion of saints" — was uniformly taken by the Reformers as a description of the holy catholic church. It implies for Calvin "that the saints are gathered into the society of Christ on the principle that whatever benefits God confers upon them, they should in turn share with one another" (*Inst.* 1.4.3). He excludes here any required community of worldly property but stresses the sharing of spiritual goods, especially of the confident awareness of saving grace.

The distinction between the church which is truly catholic, one, and holy, and the external and visible church, which is found to be defective in holiness, is clearly drawn; but Calvin's great urge, and we may say that of the Reformation, was to bring to the visible church the holiness and the oneness that are the properties posited of the holy catholic church. For that which was reformed in the Reformation was the visible church, which, as the Reformers saw it, had been left in the previous age neither one nor holy nor catholic nor fit to express the communion of saints. Among the Reformers it was Calvin who most clearly and emphatically voiced these concepts.

While Calvin often assails in unmeasured terms the corruption and superstition of the unreformed papal church and urges complete withdrawal from its worship, he nevertheless does not for a moment think of himself and others in the Reformation as presiding over the inception of a church that had not existed before. The church of all God's people has never ceased to exist. It is ageless and indestructible. Even within the confines of the visible unreformed church there have remained vestiges of the true catholic church, like a half-demolished building (*Inst.* 4.2.11–12). Thus "the visible Church which is also Catholic" has an element of continuity through all times. Calvin with Cyprian and Augustine calls the visible church the mother of believers, who, he says, are conceived in her womb, nourished at her breast, guided and instructed by her throughout life. While we recognize that not all who within it make profession of their faith are truly of the faithful, we are to exercise "a judgment of charity" among them.

The marks by which a true church may be discerned are the true preaching of the Word and the right administration of the two scriptural sacraments, together with true discipline, by which the sacraments are protected from profanation. It is sinful to depart from a church showing these proofs of its reality, even though it may embrace members whose lives are scandalous. The churches in Galatia and Corinth had among their members crude offenders, yet they were not sweepingly condemned as false churches. A visible church of perfect saints is excluded by the fact that we believe in the forgiveness of our sins. The visible church is not a community of perfection but a community of forgiveness, whose members daily pray "forgive us our debts" and are daily forgiven (*Inst.* 4.1.21–23). Knowing their imperfections, Christians strive onward, advancing in holiness but not attaining in this life to sinless perfection.

Calvin was indeed jealous for the sanctity of the church and its congregational life. In this spirit he gave attention to the reform of public worship. The forms he introduced and his explanations of worship were calculated to impart a genuine experience of the holy, a sense of common participation in a holy action and in a fellowship of saints. Incidentally, in this connection he strictly enjoined kneeling in common prayer (*Comm. on Acts* 20:36). It should always be remembered that Calvin's whole system of discipline was primarily designed to guard the sanctity of the Lord's Supper, which ought never to be profaned by the presence of scandalous offenders. The Geneva Articles of 1537 already make this clear: "such good discipline that none may present himself at it (i.e. 'the Holy Supper of the Lord') save holily and with singular reverence" (Art. 1).

To nourish and guide the church, God has provided a ministry. We shall not retrace here the steps of Calvin's argument as he tries to establish from Scripture the four orders or offices of ministry that he would see employed: (1) the preaching pastor, corresponding to the presbyter or bishop of the New Testament; (2) the doctor or teacher; (3) the deacon, who serves the sick and the poor; and (4) the elder, who joins the minister in the government of the church and the administration of discipline. Great emphasis is placed on the function of preaching as being primary in the work of the early bishops and presbyters, who were required "to feed the people with the Word of God" (*Inst.* 4.4.3). To this end the minister must be equipped with sound learning. One of Calvin's most memorable sentences occurs in one of his sermons on Deuteronomy (5:23–27). *"Nul ne sera jamais*

bon ministre de la parolle de Dieu sinon qu'il soit premier escolier."
No one will ever be a good minister of the Word of God if he is not
a first-rate scholar (or, perhaps, a competent student). We remember
what zeal and labor Calvin expended in the establishment in Geneva
of that famous Academy, which soon became an international institution of high renown for its work of supplying ministerial leadership
to the Reformed congregations in many lands. The opening of the
Academy in 1559 was the fulfilment of a long-cherished plan; for in
the Ordinances of 1541 Calvin had written of "the need to raise up
seed for the time to come, in order not to leave the Church a desert
to our children" and of "the obligation to prepare youth for the ministry. . . ." These words are echoed, by the way, in the foundation
documents of Harvard University.

I have not cited the entire sentence. The additional words are "and
for civil government." Calvin saw these two functions, that of the
minister and of the political leader, not as being in antagonism but in
balance, and he made provision for both to be prepared by means of
the best possible education. Augustine, Aquinas, and Luther had written on civil government before Calvin. In fact a great deal of the
accumulated literature of political theory had been the work of scholarly clergy. Calvin thought so much and with such deep concern of
things political that he devoted to civil government the final long and
searching chapter of the *Institutes.* And here he finds another "ministry," for the magistrate is a minister of God for the peace and welfare
of the people. Calvin's political concern was intense and had to do
with every part of Europe. But this in no sense means that he entered
a secular realm out of harmony with his religious interests. It is true
that he was a trained lawyer and in an early treatise had shown
familiarity with the classical writers on government. But for Calvin
the churchman and theologian, every man in all circumstances of life,
no less than within the precincts of the church, has a transaction, an
unceasing business, with God (*negotium cum Deo*). So one of his first
official utterances in Geneva states that the rule of kings and magistrates is something holy, *une chose sainte,* and that they are to be
obeyed as God's appointed lieutenants. Men who are not concerned
with "the public good of the country where they live" are unfaithful
to God, and rulers are required to do nothing unworthy of their office
as ministers of God. These ideas were later expanded. The relationship of ruler and ruled is brought within the Christian law of love.
Magistrates on their part are "responsible to God and to men." The
coercive power entrusted to them is to be exercised under God's authority and with the clemency that Seneca praised. In this frame of

motives they may resort to war to protect their people and may levy just taxes, never forgetting that their revenues are the very blood of the people. Even un-Christian and even unjust rulers are to be obeyed, except where they command us to do what God forbids.

Calvin at first showed no preference among the three forms of government discussed by classical writers, monarchy, aristocracy, and democracy. Like Aristotle, he discussed the deviations or perversions of each of these. But he introduced into the *Institutes* in the edition of 1543 a clear statement that in his opinion "aristocracy or aristocracy tempered by democracy far surpasses the others." The aristocracy-democracy pattern was well exemplified in the constitution of .Geneva, which Calvin helped to revise in that same year. It was not an aristocracy of lineal descent. In one of his commentaries (on Mic. 5:5), written in 1560, he views hereditary kingship adversely as out of accord with liberty; and other utterances of his later years seem to show a growing rejection of monarchy. In 1559 he explained his preference for the aristocracy-democracy combination on the ground that kings lack in themselves the ability and justice to meet their duties, so that it is preferable that a number (*plures*) bear rule together, helping and admonishing one another and together restraining rash and aggressive individuals. In different contexts Calvin speaks feelingly of "the inestimable gift of liberty," and liberty is an important ingredient in his picture of good government, a treasure to be prized and defended, indeed "more than the half of life" (*CO* 24.629).

Without sanctioning armed resistance to tyrants by unauthorized individuals, he does from the first hold in view that restraint of kings exemplified by the ephors of Sparta, the demarchs of Athens, and the tribunes of Rome. These ancient functionaries he takes as typical of "popular magistrates" whose responsibility it is to protect the liberties of the people against oppressive rulers. He sees this function properly exercised by the Three Estates of existing realms, an allusion that I take to be, *inter alia,* an appeal for a meeting of the French Estates General (which had not met in his lifetime) to assert authority against the Valois rulers. In these fragments of Calvin's teaching we see some reasons why many of the Calvinist tradition have been contributors to the spread of liberty and of government by and for the people.

If Calvin viewed the function of government as "a holy thing," he wanted likewise to bring a religious and Christian tone to the marketplace. It is very easy to go astray in the interpretation of Calvin's economic ethics, especially when the subject is approached with secular presuppositions. Certainly he does not regard worldly prosperity as a reward for, or a consequence of, a godly life. "We see daily," he notes, "the state of the faithful is more miserable than the state of the despisers of God" (*Comm. on Job* 42:7). The view of Job's monitor Zophar that a man in prosperous ease is in favor with God, Calvin pronounces as "the error of the Sadducees" and the product of "the devilish error that men's souls are mortal" (*Comm. on Job* 21:7). And he explains "Godliness is profitable" by saying that the faithful who are vexed with afflictions are in their extreme poverty happier than the despisers of God, because they are assured that God is with them. Calvin's works abound with such observations, though this is not observed by the school of Weber. We cannot discourse on this tempting theme at this point: suffice it to recall that, among others of his time, Calvin led away from Aristotle's notion of barren money and from the Old Testament literal prohibition of interest and permitted strictly limited interest on loans for production. He would have the whole of economic life controlled by the principle of stewardship. Everyone should consider that "he is a debtor to his neighbors, and that he ought in exercising kindness toward them to set no other limit than the end of his resources," which ought to be expended according to "the rule of love" (*Inst.* 3.7.7). From such passages (and they are numerous) any fruitful study of Calvin's economic ethics must begin.

Calvin warned against that asceticism which would despise the good gifts of God by which our physical life is enriched and rendered pleasurable. Food and drink are given for delight and good cheer, not merely for sustenance. "God has clothed the flowers with the great beauty that greets our eyes, the sweetness of smell that is wafted upon our nostrils. . . . Did he not distinguish colors so as to make some more lovely than others? . . . Did he not endow gold and silver, ivory and marble, with a loveliness that renders them more precious than other stones? Did he not, in short, render many things attractive to us apart from their necessary use?" (*Inst.* 3.10.2). E. Harris Harbison has rightly called attention to "the idea of utility in Calvin's thought." But because of his intense feeling for God's handiwork in the created world, Calvin sets beauty above utility. Calvin was a man fascinated by what he likes to call the "beautiful theater" of the created world in which we do well "to take pious delight," meditating on nature's phenomena as of God's creation (*Inst.* 1.14.20). Even in the animals we may contemplate the majesty of God. He calls attention to the beauty of the horse, the hawk, and the dove, and notes that the lowly ass participated in the splendor of the Son of God. One could take from Calvin an extended anthology of passages eloquent of the world's beauty, always with reference to God, the Author of beauty, often uttered with regret that these tokens of God's majesty are set before sin-blinded eyes (see Léon Wencelius, *L'Esthétique de Calvin,* chapter 11). One is prompted to ask whether the artist or the poet who disclaims the desire to delight us with beauty falls into this mood because he has first lost his sense of God.

It is not required of a *doctor ecclesiae* that he be infallible. But he must be both learned and dedicated, an exemplar of what Calvin's friend John Sturm called *"pietas literata."* "True piety," Calvin wrote in 1537, "does not consist in a fear that would gladly flee the judgment of God [but rather] in a pure and true zeal which loves God altogether as Father . . . and dreads to offend Him more than to die." The first edition of the *Institutes* is described in its subtitle as "worth reading by all persons zealous for piety." Calvin uses the word "piety" with great frequency, and in its ancient, large and generous sense. It is a praiseworthy dutifulness primarily to God, motivated by reverence and love. It was this that was the mainspring of Calvin's life effort.

His labors were the astonishment of his friends. His mental energy seemed inexhaustible. To the heavy schedule of his lectures and sermons, unrelieved by vacations or "sabbaticals," were added his great array of published works, constant attention to the most demanding administrative duties and decisions, conferences with visitors and resident exiles in Geneva, and an extensive correspondence with people of every rank — kings and statesmen, learned friends and fellow-Reformers, and humbler folk in trouble. It is remarkable that in his letters he very rarely alludes to the overwork involved in all this. Despite bodily weakness and pain, he accomplished all this with a certain élan, a characteristic sprightliness of mind, and a promptness that is suggested by his Latin motto, *Prompte et sincere in opere Domini.* His brilliant and rarely matched gifts of quick perception and almost flawless memory continued unimpaired while his bodily strength slowly ebbed away. All his great talents were perpetually stimulated as they were exercised in the context of his piety. His learning and teaching rose to the measure of his devotion. *In opere Domini* nothing was to be withheld. Thus it was that for thirty years John Calvin drove at top speed the high-powered engine of his brain. Thus he became so great a teacher of the church that it is still after four centuries profitable for us to come under his instruction.

2

God Was Accommodating Himself to Human Capacity

Ford Lewis Battles

For Calvin, the understanding of God's accommodation to the limits and needs of the human condition was a central feature of the interpretation of Scripture and of the entire range of his theological work.

Any study of Calvin as scriptural exegete would be incomplete which failed to examine his frequent appeal to the principle of accommodation.[1] Yet, at least in the *Institutes of the Christian Religion* and presumably elsewhere, he never uses the noun *accommodatio*, but always either the verb *accommodare* or *attemperare*, when he has recourse to this principle. Thus, it would be incorrect to entitle this short essay, "Calvin's Use of Accommodation." Our title, therefore, by using the verb instead of the noun, reflects both Calvin's usage and his intent.

Reprinted from *Interpretation* 31 (January 1977): 19–38. Used by permission.

1. I know of only one contemporary study explicitly devoted to accommodation: Clinton Ashley, *John Calvin's Utilization of the Principle of Accommodation and Its Continuing Significance for an Understanding of Biblical Language,* unpub. Ph.D. dissertation, Southwest Baptist Theological Seminary, 1972. It has not been used in preparing this essay. . . . While the evidence of Calvin's biblical commentaries has been examined, this paper rests primarily on the *Institutes,* in which every aspect of accommodation has apparently been set forth; nowhere, however, is it the topic of a separate locus: rather, it is everywhere assumed as a working principle.

In the Battles-Hugo edition of *Calvin's Commentary on Seneca's De Clementia* I have traced the roots of Calvin's rhetoric in the rhetoricians of classical Greece and Rome. The ancient rhetoricians evolved the principles of their art both to clothe in suitable language what they wrote and spoke and also to interpret what had been written and spoken by others. Trained in this school, Calvin served his apprenticeship in commenting on classical texts, notably the *De Clementia* of Lucius Annaeus Seneca. After his conversion, all of Calvin's classical learning was transmuted. In a sense, he exchanged for human rhetoric a divine rhetoric (*Inst.* 1.8.1f.). He saw the task of the theologian no longer as speculative, primarily philosophical, but rather as pastoral, pedagogical (*Inst.* 1.14.4), and making large if guarded use of the rhetorical discipline.[2]

As in human rhetoric there is a gulf between the highly educated and the comparatively unlearned, between the convinced and the unconvinced, a gulf which it is the task of rhetoric to bridge so that through simple, appropriate language the deeps of human thought yield up their treasure, or at least the views of the speaker are persuasively communicated — analogously in divine rhetoric the infinitely greater gulf between God and man, through divine condescension, in word and deed, is bridged. And the divinely appointed human authors and expositors of Scripture express and expound the divine rhetoric under the Spirit's guidance for the benefit of all.

In so espousing the divine rhetoric, Calvin was no innovator; before him went a cloud of patristic witnesses who, in response to the destructive critique of the Scriptures by pagan and heretic alike, had contended that God in revelation was adjusting the portrait of Himself to the capacity of the human mind and heart. But, unlike an Origen, or an Augustine, or a John Chrysostom, or a Hilary of Poitiers, Calvin makes this principle a consistent basis for his handling not only of Scripture but of every avenue of relationship between God and man. Thus, the starkest inconsistencies in Scripture are harmonized through rhetorical analysis, within the frame of divine accommodation to human capacity; but, more than merely serving as an apologetical device, this method unlocks for Calvin God's beneficent tutelage and pedagogy of His wayward children.

Such a method can be little more than an intellectual exercise unless

---

2. Calvin refused to use rhetoric for its own sake or for illegitimate purposes. In *Comm. Sen. De Clem.* 1.1.3, he says: "I have no desire here to indulge in long-winded conceited ostentation; I leave declamation to the rhetoricians." At *Comm. on Ps.* 95:3, he spurns ". . . the lying panegyric with which rhetoricians flatter earthly princes." (See n. 1, Battles/Hugo, *Comm. Sen. De Clem.*, p. 76.)

it be grounded in a firm faith. With Paul, Calvin sees man — even before his fall — as a creature far removed from his Creator. He sees human language as utterly insufficient to leap this gap. Therefore, in Calvin's picture of God three biblical themes especially stand out: God is first and foremost our *Father,* our divine parent exceeding all human parentage. Secondly, He is our *teacher,* who well knows His pupil. Thirdly, He is our *physician,* who skillfully diagnoses our disease. Thus, at the outset we have the three analogies: of parental care, of instruction, and of healing. The weakness and inexperience of childhood, the ignorance of the schoolboy, and the disease of the sick, respectively, correspond to these three divine roles.

But the rhetorician's task is not merely to bridge the gulf of weakness or ignorance. As in the law court the advocate seeks to sway the judge either to mercy or to punishment, so God has to deal not only with inexperience and ignorance but with willful stubbornness and disobedience. The divine rhetoric then becomes a rhetoric of violence, or exaggeration, of unbelievable heightening. Scripture exhibits all shades and moods of divine rhetoric, from the physician's soothing balm to the surgeon's scalpel. We should therefore add to our self-portraits of God that of the judge; and to our figurative institutions of nursery and family, school and hospital, that of the law court.

Here we begin to see that, for Calvin, accommodation has to do not only with the Scriptures and their interpretation, but with the whole of created reality to which, for the Christian, Scripture holds the clue. The entire created universe and all its parts are naught but a grand accommodation on God's part of Himself to the crowning glory (and subsequent shame) of that creation, namely man. The six days of creation bear the message of God's tender care of His human offspring. The unfolding of subsequent history within that universal theater and all the structures of society that mark that history — these, too — decode the message of a just and merciful God to His errant offspring. Here we have in mind preeminently the institutions of state and church whose divinely ordained symbiosis Calvin recognizes.

But more specifically we see in the political sphere, ordered by law however imperfectly and governed by divinely ordained leaders even in their misrule, a reflection of the divine tutelage. Parallelly, in the ecclesiastical sphere we see the God-given realities of Word and sacrament set within a structure of discipline and worship and administered by human functionaries as a prime instance of divine accommodation, of *adminicula* (helps) to salvation.

At the center of God's accommodating Himself to human capacity, however, is His supreme act of condescension, the giving of His only

Son to reconcile a fallen world to Himself. If accommodation is the speech-bridge between the known and the unknown, between the infinitesimal and the infinite, between the apparent and the real, between the human and the divine, the Logos who tented among us is the point from which we must view creation, the fall, and all history, before and since the incarnation. For Calvin, then, in every act of divine accommodating, the whole Trinity — Father, Son, and Holy Spirit — is at work.

Accommodation in Classical Rhetoric

The classical rhetoricians recognized five "offices" in their discipline: invention, disposition, elocution, pronunciation, memory. These are actually stages in the preparation of an oration, or also of other literary forms. *Invention* consists in the finding out or selection of topics to be treated or arguments to be used — the analysis of the topic for discourse and the assembling of materials. *Disposition* is the due arrangement of the parts of an argument or discussion into an ordered discourse. *Elocution* is more or less synonymous with our word "style" — the choice of language appropriate to the topic and the intended audience. *Pronunciation* (cf. Calvin, *Inst.* 2.7.11) is what we would call the delivery of the speech. In each of these stages accommodation takes place; in fact, the whole process of rhetorical construction of discourse is one continuous act of accommodation. This is well brought out in the Pseudo-Ciceronian treatise, *Rhetorica ad Herennium* (1.2.3): "Elocution is the accommodation of suitable words and sentences to invention" (cf. Cicero, *De Inventione Rhetorica,* 1.9). Also, another rhetorician uses the same word in reference to *pronunciation:* "Pronunciation is worthiness of words, accommodation of the voice to the senses, and moderation of body" (Albin., *Rhet.,* 546.12). The corresponding verb *accommodare* is widely found in the Latin rhetoricians in the same sense of fitting, adapting, adjusting language, of building a speech-bridge between the matter of discourse and the intended audience. For example, Cicero (*De Orat.,* 2.159) states that "the oration is to be accommodated to the ears of the multitude." Quintilian (*Inst. Orat.,* 8.2.6; 9.1.15) quotes Livy to the effect that words are to be accommodated to the things to which they refer. Cato speaks of accommodating a fit form of matter, senses, sentences, and words to the use of the reader (cf. *Agr.,* 21.5; 22.1; 135.7). The rhetorical uses of this verb could be multiplied. It was also a technical term among the jurisconsults with reference to legal actions (judicial forms) which were adapted to certain definite cases. Calvin uses also a synonymous verb, *attemperare,* but classical Latin did not apparently employ it as a technical term of rhetoric. The earliest uses of the latter word similar to Calvin's are found in Tertullian.

However *accommodare,* then, was used in Latin rhetoric, it always had to do with the adaptation of the verbal representation of the matter under consideration to the persons being addressed, with full regard to their situation, their character, intelligence, and their emotional makeup. In his reading of the classics, Calvin frequently came across *accommodare* in Cicero, Quintilian, and the minor rhetoricians.

The Use of Accommodation by the Church Fathers

Whenever a religious tradition is translated from one language to another, an enormous act of accommodation takes place. Such accommodation began in the Septuagint version of the Old Testament with the initial restatement of Hebrew religious concepts in Greek, continued in the New Testament itself, and moved (as Christianity became a religion of the Gentile world) into the heterodox and orthodox formulations of the patristic era of the church. The Gnostics and Marcionites in their dehistoricization of the gospel were in fact radical accommodators of Scripture, even though they laid the very same charge of hypocrisy against the apostles (according to Irenaeus): the apostles, they said, were guilty of hypocrisy for they framed their teaching to the capacity of their hearers, tailoring their answers to the opinions and prejudices of their questioners, thus subverting the truth. No, says Irenaeus, the apostles actually taught the true and unaccommodated doctrine that leads to salvation (*Adv. Haer.,* 3.5.2). Yet Irenaeus seems himself to hint at accommodation when he states that ". . . the unmeasurable Father was Himself subjected to measure in the Son, for the Son is the measure of the Father, since He also comprehends Him" (*A.H.,* 4.4.2). Calvin (*Inst.* 2.6.4) interprets this to mean: ". . . the Father, himself infinite, becomes finite in the Son, for he has accommodated himself to our little measure lest our minds be overwhelmed by the immensity of his glory." Irenaeus shows himself a master of scriptural accommodation in his teaching on Christ. Taking a mediating position between the two extremes of Gnostic Docetism and Jewish Ebionism (*A.H.,* 3.16ff.), he emphasizes Christ's human characteristics against the former, and His divine against the latter, with the virgin birth a crucial proof. He denies both the Gnostic doctrine of two Christs and the "pusillanthropous" view of Judaizing Ebionism.

The principle of accommodation seems to emerge more explicitly in the exegetical work of the School of Alexandria, grounded in the prior thought of Philo Judaeus, whose hermeneutical rules included a way of dealing with the anthropomorphisms of Scripture: "The lawgiver talks thus in human terms about God, even though he is not a human being, for the advantage of us who are being educated, as I have often said in other passages" (Philo, commenting on Gen. 11:5). This principle is repeated in Clement of Alexandria (*Strom.*, 2.16.72): "But in as far as it was possible for us to hear, burdened as we were with flesh, so did the prophets speak to us, as the Lord accommodated himself to human weakness for our salvation."

For Origen, accommodation (the Greek term is *symperiphora*) can, through the allegorical senses of Scripture, work in two opposing ways: It can reveal divine truths to the godly; it can conceal them from the godless. The meaning of *symperiphora* is often illustrated by an image later used by Augustine, Calvin, and others. The image is that of an adult stooping to a child: "He condescends and lowers Himself *accommodating Himself* to our weakness, like a schoolmaster talking a 'little language' (*symphellizon*) to his children, like a father caring for his own children and adopting their ways."[3] The same analogy is used by Origen in his reply to Celsus' attacks on the anthropomorphism of the Old Testament:

> Just as when we are talking to very small children we do not assume as the object of our instruction any strong understanding in them, but say what we have to say accommodating it to the small understanding of those whom we have before us, and even do what seems to us useful for the education and bringing up of children, realizing that they are children: so the Word of God seems to have disposed the things which were written, adapting the suitable parts of his message to the capacity of his hearers and to their ultimate profit.[4]

Even more detailed is Origen's use of this analogy when he endeavors to explain how God can be said in the Bible to repent or change His mind:

> But when the providence of God is involved in human affairs, he assumes the human mind and manner and diction. When we talk to a child of two we talk baby-talk because he is a child, for as long as we maintain the character appropriate to an adult age, and speak to

3. Frag. on Deut. 1:21, *PG* 17.24, quoted by R. P. C. Hanson, *Allegory and Event* (Richmond, Va.: John Knox, 1959), p. 226.

4. Hanson, *Allegory and Event,* p. 226, from *Contra Celsum,* 4.71; 5.16.

children without adapting ourselves to their speech, children cannot understand us. Now imagine a similar situation confronting God when he comes to deal with the human race, and particularly with those who are still "babes." Notice too how we who are adults change the names of things for children, and we have a special name for bread with them, and we call drinking by some other word, not using the language of adults. . . . And if we name clothes to children we give other names to them, as if we were inventing a child's name for them. Do we suffer from arrested development when we do this? And if someone hears us talking to children, will he say, "This old man is losing his mind, this man has forgotten that his beard is grown, that he is a grown-up man"? Or is it allowable for the sake of *accommodation,* when we are associating with a child, not to talk the language of older and mature people, but to talk in a child's language?[5]

Origen's chief theological work, *On First Principles,* is really a textbook in accommodation: How Scripture is to be interpreted for human salvation. His system of allegorical senses rests upon the conviction that God, taking cognizance of human limitations, has fashioned Scripture in three levels of meaning, corresponding to the three parts of man: body, soul, and spirit (4.2.4). Spiritual truth finds its vehicle in physical language about God and in the literal crudities of biblical history. In all this, God as our physician and teacher is couching His truths in language we can understand.

The Holy Spirit does not depend on feeble human eloquence. No created mind can by any means possess the capacity to understand all; this is true even of higher beings than man. Let everyone, then, who cares for truth, care little about names and words, for different kinds of speech are customary in different nations. Let him be more anxious about the fact signified, particularly in questions of difficulty and importance. This should be the controlling rule of interpretation: "There are certain things, the meaning of which it is impossible adequately to explain by any human language, but which are made clear rather through simple apprehension than through any power of words" (4.3.14).

The School of Antioch, which developed in reaction to the excessive allegorism of Alexandria, reached its peak in the exegete Theodore of Mopsuestia and the preacher John Chrysostom. Yet, even in this more historically oriented school of interpretation, accommodation was an important principle. One sees it, for example, in their discussion of the varied styles of the biblical writers, or in the pedagogy of our

5. Ibid., p. 227, from *Homilies on Jeremiah,* 18.6.

Lord, especially in the parables. Berkouwer sums up Chrysostom's view of Christ's use of accommodation: "Christ often checked himself for the sake of the weakness of his hearers when he dealt with lofty doctrines and he usually did not choose such words as were in accord with his glory, but rather those which agreed with the capability of men."[6] This is seen in Christ's deliberate delay in performing miracles in order to catch the attention of His hearers and thus heighten the faith-giving force of the miracle.

Since the time of Tertullian, accommodation has frequently been appealed to in the Latin West. Hilary of Poitiers, trained in classical rhetoric, devoted his career largely to the combatting of the Arian heresy. In his chief work, *On the Trinity,* he frequently adverts to the limitations of human speech in handling divine truth and eloquently portrays God's supreme act of condescension in Christ. Actually, against the crass literalism of Arius ("There was a time before the creation of the Son when God was not yet Father") accommodation of the scriptural language was a powerful weapon. Hilary in his *Tractates on the Psalms* (Ps. 126:6) explicitly refers to accommodation: "For the divine Word *tempers* (*temperare*) itself to the habit and nature of our understanding, by common words of things adapted to the signification of doctrine and institution."

It is in Augustine, however, and notably in his *On Christian Doctrine,* that the "scaling down" of the divine speech to human capacity is laid out. Augustine, as a teacher of rhetoric, was put off repeatedly by what seemed to him the rude and barbarous style of Scripture. As he portrays his pilgrimage to faith in his *Confessions,* he did not come to full Christian belief until he realized that sublimity of style and depth of truth are very often not found together. This insight is developed at length in *On Christian Doctrine,* the first Christian rhetoric.

In freeing himself from the Manichees, Augustine had early to come to terms with the Christian doctrine of creation and with the Book of Genesis. The Manichees had, like the Gnostics and Marcionites before them, amassed antitheses between the Old and New Testaments. These he endeavors to resolve in his reply to Adimantus, often using accommodation as his means. And in his *Genesis according to the Literal Sense,* he picks up the familiar figure of a mother stooping down to her child to illustrate the way of scriptural language with our weakness. Calvin's reading of Augustine clearly familiarized him with accommodation as a hermeneutical principle; yet he did not accept the

6. G. C. Berkouwer, *Holy Scripture,* trans. and ed. Jack B. Rogers (Grand Rapids: Eerdmans, 1975), pp. 175f.

excessive allegorism which Augustine had bequeathed to the medieval West.

We may conclude our brief survey of the patristic use of accommodation with a reference to Maximus the Confessor, who explained the prime anthropomorphism of the Old Testament, God's "repentance," ". . . as an accommodation of Biblical language to human ways of speaking. Scripture spoke in a way that was not literally accurate, in order to enable its readers to grasp what transcended literal accuracy."[7]

Some Scriptural Inconsistencies Which Calvin Resolves Through Accommodation

Accommodation begins as an apologetical tool against hostile critics of Scripture; it ends as a pastoral instrument for the edification of believers. Both these notes are struck in Calvin's frequent use of accommodation. Let us first illustrate the former use by four examples, taken from book 1 of the *Institutes;* these we shall set out in propositional fashion for the sake of emphasis:

A. God's Nature (*Inst.* 1.13.1)

Apparent teaching of Scripture: God has a mouth, ears, eyes, hands, and feet.

True teaching: God's infinite and spiritual essence.

Accommodation: As nurses commonly do with infants, God speaks "baby talk" to us: thus such forms of speaking do not so much express clearly what God is like as accommodate the knowledge of Him to our slight capacity. To do so He must descend far beneath His loftiness.

B. The Creation of the Angels (1.14.3)

Apparent teaching of Scripture: The angels are not mentioned in the scriptural account of creation, yet they are afterward introduced as ministers of God.

True teaching: Unquestionably, angels are creatures of God.

Accommodation: Moses, accommodating himself to the rudeness of the common folk, mentions in the history of the creation no other works of God than those which show themselves to our own eyes.

B[1]. The Function of the Angels (1.14.11)

Apparent teaching of Scripture: God uses angels to carry out His commands.

True Teaching: God has no need of angels to carry out His commands; in fact, He sometimes disregards them and acts directly.

Accommodation: God uses angels to accommodate to our feeble capacity and show us more intimately His loving protection for us.

7. *PG* 90.621, 812, cited by Jaroslav J. Pelikan, *The Christian Tradition* (Chicago: University of Chicago, 1974), vol. 2, p. 14.

C. Fate (1.16.9)

Apparent teaching of Scripture: The same fate awaits man and beast, good man and sinner, wise man and fool (cf. Eccles. 2:14f.; 3:19; 9:2–3, 11).

True Teaching: Fate, fortune, chance are pagan terms inadmissible to Christians; nothing is fortuitous, but all things live under God's secret plan.

Accommodation: The sluggishness and limits of the human mind see as fortuitous those things which are actually ordered by God's purpose: Scripture uses "fate" and "fortune" to explain events seemingly contingent, but known to faith to derive from a secret impulse of God.

D. God's Ways with Man: Does He Repent? (1.17.12f.)

Apparent teaching of Scripture: Since God repented of having created man, of having put Saul over the kingdom, and of the evil He determined to inflict upon His people, therefore He has not determined the affairs of men by an eternal decree, but, according to each man's deserts or according as He deems him fair and just, He decrees this or that each year, each day, and each hour.

True teaching: God's ordinance in the managing of human affairs is both everlasting and above all repentance: His plan and will proceed unchangeably from eternity.

Accommodation: God represents Himself to us not as He is in Himself, but as He seems to us, to accommodate to our weak capacity His description of Himself.

In each of these instances, Calvin began as apologist for Scripture, but in his recourse to accommodation he seized upon instruction. Thus the two uses with which we began are actually one.

Scriptural Portraits of God and Man: Ground of Accommodation

God's Self-Portraits

The greatest apparent inconsistencies in Scripture, long recognized by believers and nonbelievers, by Jew and Christian alike, are those between the old and new covenants. Hence a major effort of Christian exegetes has always been, by some means, to harmonize or at least explain such discrepancies. Calvin's appeal to accommodation has therefore very often to do with the differing dispensations of the Old and New Testaments. Building especially upon the apostle Paul (physical/spiritual Israel; law as tutor to Christ) and the author of Hebrews (shadow/reality) as their thought was elaborated by Augustine, Calvin (without explicitly postulating a doctrine of progressive revelation) saw a spiritual growth, an advance toward spiritual maturity, in the pilgrimage of Israel to Christ. Two portraits of God metaphorically share the depiction of this upward movement from childhood to adulthood: God as father and God as teacher. In some Calvinian contexts, it would be difficult to determine which of the two is the ruling metaphor, for both family and school concern themselves with the growth of children.

1. God as Father. Yet the fatherhood of God, so often referred specifically to the history of Israel, has also a universal reference in the creation itself:

> . . . we ought in the very order of things diligently to contemplate God's fatherly love toward mankind, in that He did not create Adam until He had lavished upon the universe all manner of good things. For if He had put him in an earth as yet sterile and empty, if He had given him life before light, He would have seemed to provide insufficiently for his welfare. Now, when He disposed the movements of sun and stars to human uses, filled the earth, waters and air with living things, and brought forth an abundance of fruits to suffice as foods, in thus assuming the responsibility of a foreseeing and diligent father of the family He shows His wonderful goodness toward us (1.14.2).

Summing up his doctrine of creation in the same chapter of the *Institutes,* Calvin adverts once more to the same theme, that by the order of creation God shows that He created all things for man's sake: ". . . the dispensation of all those things which He has made is in His own hand and power and . . . we are indeed His children, whom He has received into His faithful protection, to nourish and educate" (1.14.22).

In taking up the differences between the Old and New Testaments (*Inst.* 2.11), Calvin warns us not to consider God changeable ". . . merely because He accommodated diverse forms to different ages, as He knew would be expedient for each." This Calvin illustrates by the simile of the farmer and of the householder; of the latter he says: ". . . if a householder instructs, rules, and guides, his children one way in infancy, another way in youth, and still another in young manhood, we shall not on this account call him fickle and say that he abandons his purpose. Why, then, do we brand God with the mark of inconstancy when He has with apt and fitting marks distinguished a diversity of times?" (2.11.13). Calvin then relates this comparison to Galatians 4:1ff. where Paul likens the ancient Jews to children, Christians to young men. He sums up with the assertion that such varied dispensation does not show God subject to change. "Rather, He has accommodated Himself to men's capacity which is varied and changeable" (2.11.13).

As we have pointed out in our note to *Institutes* 2.7.2, Calvin

frequently describes the spiritual development of the ancient Hebrews
vis-à-vis Christ as a childhood ". . . that rendered necessary the accommodation of revelation to an elementary mentality in the Old Testament" (cf. 1.11.3; 2.11.2; 2.10.6; *Comm. on Gen.* 1:16; 2:8).

As in the larger sweep of history from ancient Jew to Christian, so
in the personal history of the believer, in his growth in the faith, Calvin
uses the same analogy of Father and child, even as Paul had distinguished between the milk suitable for the childhood of belief and the
strong meat digestible by the mature Christian. Underlying the short
treatise on the Christian life (*Inst.* 3.6–10) which describes the restoration of the image of God in man as a growing process throughout
life is the same sense of God's fatherly accommodation to, and tutelage
of, man's feeble capacity. The cross, for example, which we must bear,
is described as "fatherly chastisement" (3.8.6).

The father of the household also portrays the providence with which
God guides His earthly family. In his commentary on Psalm 11:6,
Calvin states that the metaphor of the householder is used to teach
the carnal mind that calamities and mercies are not chance happenings, but happen according to God's just distribution.

Among the other Calvinian passages that portray accommodation
in terms of a father's care for his children, we can take up here only
Calvin's gloss on the opening words of the Lord's Prayer, "Our Father."
Commenting on the parable of the prodigal son, he says:

> . . . in setting forth this example of great compassion to be seen in
> man, He willed to teach us how much more abundantly we ought to
> expect it of Him. For He is not only a father but by far the best and
> kindest of all fathers, provided we still cast ourselves upon His mercy,
> although we are ungrateful, rebellious, and froward children. And to
> strengthen our assurance that He is this sort of father to us if we are
> Christians, He willed that we call Him not only "Father" but explicitly
> "our Father" (3.20.37).

2. God as Teacher. In discussing the ancient portraits of God as
father and as teacher, our emphasis is not upon Calvin's originality
in using these well-worn figures of speech, but rather upon their functioning as foundation images for his conviction that in all His ways
with man, God is accommodating His infinity to our small measure.
The parabolic method of the prophets and of our Lord often utilizes
a qualitative or quantitative difference between high and low within
human society as the clue to the infinitely greater contrast between
God and man. This is the force of the "How much more . . . ," "How

much greater . . . ," so frequently on Jesus' lips. As the parent stands higher than the infant, so the teacher is above his pupil. But this superiority is not one of tyranny but of tutelage. The instruction fits the pupil where he is. This "scaling down" is at the center of Calvin's appeal to accommodation: For him, the Christian spends his life in the school of Christ.

This metaphor dominated the theology of Alexandria: The second treatise in Clement of Alexandria's great trilogy, *The Instructor,* sees Christ as our tutor unto salvation. For his successor, Origen, the curriculum extends from our earthly life to our future life in heaven, where we shall be educated in ever-new secrets of God. One senses also in the *Confessions* of Augustine a teacher-pupil relationship in his divinely-directed pilgrimage to faith. The insights of the *De Magistro* doubtless draw upon Augustine's awareness of God as teacher.

In the Reformation era, too, Calvin was not alone in picturing the locus of Christian growth as a school. Among other Reformers who employed the analogy was the Silesian nobleman, Caspar Schwenckfeld von Ossig, and the Nuremberg radical Reformer, Hans Denck. The latter used the term "School of the Spirit."[8] Schwenckfeld prefers "School of Christ."[9]

Calvin (*Inst.* 3.21.3) calls Scripture the "School of the Holy Spirit"; in his *Sermons on the Epistle to the Galatians,* 12.26 (*CR* 50.424, 597), the "School of God." Sometimes Christ is called the teacher (*Inst.* 2.15.2; 3.2.4, 6; 3.20.48), or the Holy Spirit is "the inner teacher" (1.9.1; 3.1.4; 3.2.34; 4.14.9) or "the schoolmaster" (4.17.36). Let us content ourselves with but one illustration of this common Calvinian comparison; in searching out scriptural limits to the doctrine of predestination, he says: "For Scripture is the school of the Holy Spirit in which, as nothing is omitted that is both necessary and useful to know, so nothing is taught but what is expedient to know (3.21.3). . . . We are to follow God's lead always in learning, but, when He sets an end to teaching . . . stop trying to be wise."

Calvin attends not only to the teacher, but also to the pupil and to his course of study. The organizing principle of the *Institutes* is not philosophical or even theological (in the traditional scholastic way): It is primarily pedagogical. From his earliest steps after conversion, Calvin was himself marked as a teacher: It is therefore understandable that he has ordered the *Institutes* after the "right order of teaching."

8. From Denck, *Divine Order* 7, in Furcha-Battles, *Selected Writings of Hans Denck* (1976), p. 89.

9. Edward J. Furcha with Battles, *The Piety of Caspar Schwenckfeld* (Pittsburgh: Pittsburgh Theological Seminary, 1969), p. 13.

For him *doctrina* resumes its rightful and root meaning of teaching, *didache*. As one chosen of God to expound the Scriptures, he saw this human task to be a reflection or rather a recapitulation of the divine work of revealing, through scaled down and carefully planned teaching, what is needful of God's nature and purposes for human salvation. That Calvin was sensitive to the limits God the accommodator had set in Scripture to the knowledge of divine things — the parameters of accommodation — is frequently brought to our minds: particularly when boundaries are set to human speculation, notably in his discussion of predestination, as suggested above.

3. God as Physician. The Latin word for salvation (in fact the parent word from which our English term takes its origin) is *salus*. *Salus* has two root meanings: safety and health. Christian salvation partakes of both notions — Christ provides both a safe haven for souls buffeted on the sea of the world and heals our spiritual illnesses. It would be pointless here to amass the countless references, within or without the Judeo-Christian tradition, to the divine healer: The uses of this obvious metaphor are legion. Certainly, from earliest patristic times full use of it was made from biblical sources. One is reminded of the ancient description by Ignatius of Antioch of the Eucharist as the "medicine of immortality." If death was the dread disease brought upon man by his primordial disobedience, the work of Christ was to heal that disease and bring man to *aphtharsia, immortalitas,* deathlessness. God the physician is frequently mentioned by Origen: The divine physician accommodates His treatment to the nature of the sinner's spiritual ailment.

The analogy of physician, as one would expect, is put to good . . . use . . . by Calvin. Even as the two former analogies are used to express the divine accommodation effected in the transition from the old to the new dispensation, so is the portrait of God as physician thus used [though less frequently than the others]. When critics object, in commenting on the contrast between the old and the new covenants, that it is ". . . not fitting for God, always self-consistent, to permit such a great change — afterward disapproving what He had once commanded and commended," Calvin replies: "If a physician cures a young man of disease in the best way, but uses another sort of remedy on the same person when he is old, shall we then say that he has rejected the method of cure that had pleased him before? No — while he perseveres in it, he takes into account the factor of age" (2.11.14). God ought not to be considered changeable merely because He accommodated diverse forms to different ages, as He knew would be expedient for each. What is changeable is man's capacity.

Again, it is the portrait of God the physician which Calvin has in mind when he speaks of election as "God's healing hand": "Therefore, though all of us are by nature suffering from the same disease, only those whom it pleases the Lord to touch with His healing hand will get well. The others, whom He, in His righteous judgment, passes over, waste away in their own rottenness until they are consumed" (2.5.3). The cross of Christ is God's medicine for us: "Some are tried by one kind of cross, others by another. But since the heavenly physician treats some more gently but cleanses others by harsher remedies while He wills to provide for the health of all, He yet leaves no one free and untouched, because He knows that all, to a man, are diseased" (3.8.5).

Man: Portrait of Insufficiency — Vocabulary of Weakness

Over against the scripturally-derived portraits of God as father, teacher, physician, we must of course set mankind as child, schoolboy, sick person. Yet the picture of man in his weakness bursts the bounds of these three sketches. We shall not here itemize the rich vocabulary of weakness Calvin uses to paint man not only in his fallenness but even in the Pauline contrast of creator/creature. Romans 1 provides the key, as has been suggested in my reflections on Calvin's conversion (*Institution 1536,* pp. xvi–xvii). Calvin also affords us a summary of man's insufficiency in the long prayer of confession that begins the Strasbourg/Geneva liturgy.

The key word for Calvin is *captus,* capacity. Frequently (as already noted) the verb *accommodare* or *attemperare* is associated with this noun: "accommodated to our capacity." The same idea is also expressed by *measure.* We try to measure God's immeasurableness by our small measure. But it is God who knows the incalculable difference in measure between His infinity and our finiteness, and accordingly accommodates the one to the other in the way in which He reveals Himself to us.

Our *captus* is described in many and varied ways. Sometimes it is our vision that is singled out; we suffer from *lippitudo,* blearedness. Sometimes it is our *hebetudo,* our sluggishness, that stands in the way. One could multiply the words that bespeak for Calvin our human condition: Let that be the theme of a separate investigation. It is our *captus* that God so well knows. As Calvin, commenting on Psalm 78:60, puts it: "God, it is true, fills both heaven and earth; but as we cannot attain to that infinite height to which He is exalted, in descending among us by the exercise of His power and grace, He approaches as near to us as is needful, and as our limited capacity will bear"

(CTS, Ps. 3.270). The effect of the fall upon human *captus* is concentratedly described in the opening lines of *Institution 1536*, chapter 1 (pp. 20f.).

God's Avenues of Accommodation

Assuming the contrast between creator and creature, between God and man (*Inst.,* book 1), and the even greater gulf between divinity and fallen human nature (*Inst.,* book 2) what bridges has God thrown across that gulf? There is a sense in which the entire visible creation is such a bridge or avenue of revelation, even though for man in his fallenness and insensitivity these clear evidences leave him inexcusable before God. God clothes, so to speak, His invisible, inaccessible nature with the visible, palpable raiment of the universe in which we live (*Inst.* 1.5.1). In these lineaments small or vast — yet still finite — He condescends to our *captus.* And more narrowly, man, the apex of God's creation, also in his own divinely fashioned physical body is an evidence of God's accommodation of Himself to the measure of human understanding (*Inst.* 1.5.2).

Hence if we but look around us at the ordered motion of the heavens, the procession of the seasons, the ordinary and extraordinary miracles of human existence, we see in this theater, in this mirror, accommodated to our creaturely selves, the ways of God to us. For Cicero the universe was a *temple.* Not so for Calvin: With Plutarch he chooses as his ruling metaphor the *theater.* As a stage play is itself an accommodated representation of the playwright's inspiration and insight into human existence to the more limited vision of his audience, so in the vast theater of heaven and earth the divine playwright stages the ongoing drama of creation, alienation, return, and forgiveness for the teeming audience of humanity itself. Or to change the metaphor, God, whose brightness is beyond human seeing, vouchsafes to us a dimmed, reflected image of Himself, accommodated to our creatureliness.

It may be that we have succumbed to the temptation of putting the concept of accommodation too much at the center of Calvin's thought and of trying to organize everything around this notion. Yet, if this be a faithful interpretation, accommodation would seem (even when Calvin does not explicitly advert to it) his fundamental way of explaining how the secret, hidden God reveals Himself to us. Everything of which our senses bring knowledge to us, from our puny bodies to the stars, microcosm and macrocosm, is the work of a beneficent Creator who for our sakes thus shows Himself in these ways, varied, faceted, yet altogether a unity. That, however, we may not give the impression of Calvin as a natural theologian, we must quickly assert that this picture of creation as accommodated revelation of God to us takes its scriptural starting point not in Genesis 1 so much as in Romans 1. The *Institutes* is constructed backward from the incarnation through the law, the fall to the creation, from the second Adam to the first Adam. The theater is built, the stage set, wherein the audience, inexcusable in its blindness, may at last view its true destiny in Christ. Step by step, calculated to our capacity, God moves the drama forward to its heavenly dénouement.

We have spoken of the created universe and of the human body as physical, scaled down, accommodatory avenues between God and man. To a degree a similar reading may be given of the two chief modes in the human ordering of creation — the civil and ecclesiastical structures of society. These are so depicted at the beginning and end of the first book of the *Institutes*. In fact, book 4 in its totality describes God's accommodation to the weakness of His people. The very choice of a human ministry to proclaim the saving message and to nurture us in spiritual growth is in itself an act of accommodation by God to our capacity. And its varied forms throughout times and places are divinely ordained accommodation to varied human needs. To paraphrase Calvin: All the outward helps which the church provides, and in fact is, accommodate to our sluggishness the acceptance of Christ, who becomes ours through faith in the gospel (4.1.1).

Similarly, the peace which a well-ordered civil administration maintains — as necessary to man as sun or air or water or bread — is an accommodatory work of God. It provides a protective form within which spiritual government (which gives us a foretaste of immortal and incorruptible blessedness) can function. We may infer from the six ends that Calvin assigns to civil government and from his general views of the political order that it is to accommodate man's obedience to the King of kings to whom ultimately loyalty is owed. Calvin's particular application of his views to the government of Geneva is a bold effort truly to crown God as the King of His people (4.20.22ff.; cf. 3.20.43; 4.20.32). The great variety of legal and political forms in human history, again, are calculated to the differing capacities of mankind (4.20.8). But beyond the convenience and welfare of men, these civil and churchly structures are, so to speak, a parable of God's. Through them and the economy they represent, God accommodates Himself to us in our weakness.

Scripture as Accommodation

Scriptural Language in General

Classical Christianity affords a number of instances of men who came with great reluctance to the acceptance of the faith. For some of these at least, trained in ancient rhetoric, it was the rude and barbarous language of Scripture which offended their aesthetic sensibilities. Notable among these was (as we have previously noted) Augustine of Hippo. For Calvin, however, there is no thirty-three-year pilgrimage to Christian faith; in his brief but intense sounding of the classics we may rightly read his discovery (painful for a humanist) that sublimity of style and sublimity of thought are not necessarily coterminous. This is the burden of the celebrated passage (at *Inst.* 1.8.1f.) where the finest authors of classic Greece and Rome are found to fall far short of the prophetic eloquence, "far exceeding human measure." The several styles of the scriptural writers are, under the guidance of the Spirit, accommodated to varied human capacities.

As the visible creation itself was the book wherein Adam as yet upright might read his destiny, so in the revealed Scriptures, and preeminently in the law for the ancient Jews, God was accommodating Himself to His fallen creation. Early in his Christian pilgrimage Calvin grasped this essential Pauline reading of the history of salvation. It is rehearsed, from Adam to Christ ("help from another quarter"), first in his French preface of his cousin Robert's translation of the New Testament, then in the compressed initial pages of the first chapter of the *Institution* of 1536. Patiently God, through our history, accommodates His ways of revelation to our condition. Thus, par excellence, the Word made flesh and the written Word from which He speaks are God accommodating Himself to us.

Three Specific Instances of Accommodation

In Scripture, and in the church that flows forth from the Word, we may select for brief analysis three instances wherein God has chosen to accommodate His truth to us. Again we must return to human *captus*. When that *captus* is marked primarily by ignorance, divine accommodation takes the character of "scaled down" language: the mother stooping to her child, God talking the language of babes. When, however, that ignorance is stiffened by stubbornness, the language of accommodation takes on added rhetorical heightening. Let us first look at a single example of this from Psalm 78:65 where God is shockingly depicted as a drunken man. This anthropomorphism is commented on by Calvin in these words: "The figure of a drunken man, although somewhat harsh, has not without reason been put forward, for it is accommodated to the stupidity of the people (*accommodatur ad populi stuporem*)." Only shocking language will sometimes penetrate through our stubborn and perverse stupidity. At such an occasion, as we have said before, the divine rhetoric becomes a rhetoric of violence, of exaggeration, of unbelievable heightening.

It is this point, and not the general observation that for Calvin the law is an instance of accommodation, that is made here. In his reading of the Decalogue, Calvin starts not in Exodus 20 but in Matthew 5–6. The true, interior, spiritual meaning of the law is at last expressly stated by Christ in the Sermon on the Mount. But Moses' pedagogy anticipates Jesus'. There is a divine synecdoche in "thou shalt not kill," or "thou shalt not commit adultery." Of all the instances of one class of sins, the lawgiver has chosen the most heinous instance to be the shocking vehicle of all the rest (*Inst.* 2.8.39, 41). Under the divine inspiration, Moses is singling out the worst crimes in society to stand for all.

God's moral pedagogy is thus accommodated to a stiffnecked people. Yet, before we leave the accommodatory aspect of the law, it is necessary to pit against one another two fundamentally opposed views of wherein it exemplifies God's accommodating to human needs. At issue (in *Inst.* 2.5.6) is the question of whether God's precepts are beyond our strength to keep. Calvin's Roman Catholic opponents, including John Eck,[10] say the law would have been given in vain if it were impossible to observe. Surely God has so accommodated the commandments to our capacities that we are able to fulfill their requirements: What they enjoin is within our power. No, says Calvin. The accommodation God has made in framing the law is, by putting its requirements so far above our power, to show clearly our own weakness and thus point our way, through love, to grace.

Another instance of accommodation is to be seen in the language of the Lord's Prayer. The phrases "Our Father," "in heaven," "hallowed be thy name," to mention only the beginning of the prayer, are interpreted by Calvin so to speak synecdochically in pointing beyond their limited human meaning to the larger sphere of reality to which their accommodated language speaks. "In heaven" does not mean that God "is bound, shut up and surrounded, by the circumference of heaven, as by a barred enclosure . . . but not confined to any particular region [He] is diffused through all things." Yet in the crassness of our mind,

10. See *Enchiridion,* chap. 31, "Concerning Free Will," trans. Battles (Grand Rapids: Baker, 1976), pp. 203ff.

we cannot otherwise conceive His unspeakable glory. The sublimity conjured in our minds by "heaven," the most mighty, lofty, incomprehensible thing we know, raises our thoughts to God, that we may avoid "dreaming up any thing earthly or physical about Him, or try[ing] to measure Him by our small measure or to conform His will to our emotions" (*Inst.* 3.20.40). What is this but the recognition that in the synecdoche on Jesus' lips as He teaches us to pray is accommodation of His Father's greatness to our *captus*? The scriptural language in which we couch prayer, "the chief exercise of faith," is already accommodated speech when we take it up to use it.

Calvin sees in the sacraments a third instance of accommodation. Taking his cue perhaps from Bucer, he applies to them the analogy of the sealed document. As we have souls engrafted in bodies, God imparts spiritual things to us, not in direct incorporeal form, but under visible things, that is, sacraments (4.14.3). God accommodates to our weakness by sealing the "document" of the proclaimed Word with the "seals" of physical sacraments. This is why God gives us Word *and* sacrament. This is why the Pauline marks of the true church are the correct preaching of the Word and the due administration of the sacraments.

To speak of the Lord's Supper: The mystery of Christ's secret union with the devout is incomprehensible, ineffable; therefore God shows it to us — thrusts it before our very eyes — under signs adapted to our small capacity (*Inst.* 4.17.11). By the physical rite of the Supper man's weak mind is helped to rise heavenward that he may apprehend Christ in the Supper (4.17.36). In refuting the papal mass — in Calvin's view a wrong interpretation of Old Testament sacrificial and ceremonial practice to justify the mass's physical character — Calvin proceeds analogically between the Testaments, adverting to the changing form of the divine pedagogy as it proceeds from spiritual infancy to maturity (*Inst.* 4.18.12 – 18). Yet Calvin sees the accommodating character of the Lord's Supper not as exemplifying a completely spiritual reality in mere physical terms, but in the God-given physical lineaments of the Supper in as-if-physical presence of the risen Lord at table with us. The act of accommodating to our weakness is not mere rhetoric clothed with the physical, but divine energy, power, spirit, channeled through the physical. In this the divine rhetoric utterly transcends the rhetoric of the human orator or writer.

The Incarnation as Accommodation

We come now to the most perilous part of this paper. If all the evidence we have sifted so far may be denominated under divine condescension to human weakness, surely the incarnation, to which (for the Christian) all this evidence points and from which it takes its meaning, must be the accommodating act par excellence of our divine Father, Teacher, Physician, Judge, and King. Yet we run the danger, in too glibly inferring this, of making the whole Christian gospel a mere exercise in rhetoric. Let us therefore pause here to take seriously Calvin's warning about theological language.

At two points in the *Institutes* Calvin himself drew back from what might otherwise seem a too easy reliance upon human language. The first passage is at 1.13.5 where Calvin, goaded by the critique of Servetus and others against the use of non-scriptural terms to describe the Trinity (itself a non-scriptural term), stops to comment that it were better to get along without such terms; but when we are called upon in controversy or in teaching to defend orthodoxy, they are not to be rashly repudiated, but to be used with all humility as holding sound scriptural teaching if they concisely express the simple truth of God's Word (1.13.5, 3).

Again, in reluctantly undertaking the writing of his chapter on the Supper, Calvin lays bare the utter inadequacy of his and all human thoughts and words (4.17.7) to deal with this, the greatest mystery of all. Wonder is the only proper response to this life-giving communion. But if we may imperfectly interpret his view: Accommodation, divine accommodation, is at work in the Supper, but (as we have suggested) it is neither accommodation of physical to spiritual nor of spiritual to physical. It is rather accommodation of spiritual *in* physical. Not like Zwingli, should we insufficiently regard the physical signs thus divorcing them from their mysteries, nor like the Roman theologians, should we immoderately extol them, thus obscuring the mysteries themselves (4.17.5).

We are here, cautioned by Calvin's own self-warning, to seek after a definition of divine accommodation which neither repudiates the anthropomorphisms of Scripture in our quest of pure Spirit, nor so clings to the anthropomorphic mode of thought and worship as ourselves, veiled by flesh, to lose sight of our God. In the divine rhetoric accommodation as practiced by the Holy Spirit so empowers the physical, verbal vehicle that it leads us to, not away from, the very truth. Thus accommodating language and the truth to which it points are really a unity. One cannot say this of the tempered speech of human rhetoric.

Thus warned, we can perhaps see in the short but critical chapter 6 of book 2, added in 1559 under the revised organization of the *Institutes* into the "twofold" knowledge of God and of ourselves, an accommodation of the supreme and most substantive character. This chapter links the previous chapters on the fall of man, by way of Christ, to the chapters on the law and on the relation of the old and new covenants; thus we are prepared for the concluding christological chapters of book 2. As Calvin says:

> The natural order was that the frame of the universe should be the school in which we were to learn piety, and from it pass over to eternal life and perfect felicity. But after man's rebellion, our eyes — wherever they turn — encounter God's curse. . . . For even if God wills to manifest his fatherly favor to us in many ways, yet we cannot by contemplating the universe infer that he is Father. . . . This magnificent theater of heaven and earth, crammed with innumerable miracles, Paul calls the "wisdom of God" (1 Cor. 1:21). Contemplating it, we ought in wisdom to have known God. But because we have profited so little by it, he calls us to the faith of Christ, which, because it appears foolish, the unbelievers despise (*Inst.* 2.6.1).

Thus, after the fall of Adam, there is no salvation apart from the Mediator. The accommodatory act of Christ's intermediation is even more expressly stated in Calvin's *Commentary on 1 Peter* (1:20):

> There are two reasons why there can be no faith in God, unless Christ put himself as it were in the middle (*quasi medius interveniat*), for we must first ponder the vastness of the divine glory and at the same time the slenderness of our understanding. Far from certain is it that our keenness could climb so high as to apprehend God. Therefore all thinking about God, apart from Christ, is a bottomless abyss which utterly swallows up all our senses. . . . The other reason is that when faith ought to join us to God, we shy away from and dread all approach, unless the Mediator meets us to free us from fear. . . . Hence it is clear that we cannot trust in God (*Deo credere*) save through Christ. In Christ God so to speak makes himself little (*quodammodo parvum facit*), in order to lower himself to our capacity (*ut se ad captum nostrum submittat*); and Christ alone calms our consciences that they may dare intimately (*familiariter*) approach God.

We may then conclude that all means of divine accommodation — from the vast reaches of the created universe to the characteristic turn of phrase of a prophet calling a stubborn people to repentance (to all of which Scripture holds the clue) — point to the supreme act of God's intermediation in Christ.

3

Calvin's View of Scripture

Donald K. McKim

Calvin devoted his life to the interpretation of Scripture.[1] He authored commentaries on all of the New Testament books except 2 and 3 John and Revelation. He also wrote commentaries on the Pentateuch, Joshua, the Psalms, and Isaiah. These commentaries, together with his lecture-sermons on the other Old Testament prophetical books, fill forty-five volumes in the nineteenth-century English translation made by the Calvin Translation Society. Yet these are only a part of the total output from Calvin's pen. His theological writings, chiefly the *Institutes of the Christian Religion* (published in various editions from 1536 to 1559), his voluminous correspondence with figures throughout Europe, his sermons and polemical writings are all saturated with Scripture.[2]

For Calvin, the calling to ministry in the church was intimately connected with interpretation of Scripture. He stressed, for example, that it was the evangelist Philip and not an angel whom God sent to help the Ethiopian eunuch understand what he read in the holy writings: "Not only is Scripture given to us, but interpreters and teachers

---

1. The literature on Calvin and the Scriptures is immense. A measure of it can be seen in the following essay and also in the section on Calvin in Jack B. Rogers and Donald K. McKim, *The Authority and Interpretation of the Bible: An Historical Approach* (San Francisco: Harper and Row, 1979), pp. 89–116.

2. The standard edition of Calvin's works is *Ioannis Calvini opera quae supersunt omnia,* ed. G. Baum, E. Cunitz, E. Reuss, P. Lobstein, and A. Erichson (Brunswick and Berlin: C. A. Schweiske, 1863–1900). This constitutes vols. 29–87 of the *Corpus Reformatorum* (*CR*). Further volumes titled *Supplementa Calviniana,* ed. E. Mulhaupt et al., have also appeared.

are also added to help us. That is why the Lord chose Philip for the eunuch rather than an angel."[3] The church has been given "the gift of interpretation which sheds light upon the word."[4] God uses human persons to communicate His will and ways. God's purposes are made known through the exposition and preaching of Scripture. As Calvin commented on Amos 8:11–12: "As then the head of a family provides meat and sustenance for his children and servants, so also the Lord supplies us daily with spiritual food by true and faithful teachers, for they are as it were his hands."[5] Calvin himself filled this role vigorously throughout his life.

Background

The past several decades have witnessed a virtual renaissance in Calvin studies. Significant research into all areas of Calvin's thought has stimulated the production of books and articles about Calvin which total into the hundreds yearly.[6]

One of the by-products of this intensive Calvin study has been a new and deeper appreciation of the background of Calvin's thought. Sustained attention has been given to the forces which helped to shape the thought world of the young Calvin.[7] In many cases, these researches have corrected and enriched previous attitudes and understandings.[8]

3. *Comm. on Acts* 8:31 in *Calvin's New Testament Commentaries* (*CNTC*), ed. David W. and Thomas F. Torrance (Grand Rapids: Eerdmans, 1959–1972), vol. 6, p. 247.

4. John Calvin, *Institutes of the Christian Religion,* ed. John T. McNeill, trans. Ford Lewis Battles, Library of Christian Classics (Philadelphia: Westminster, 1960), 4.17.25.

5. *Comm. on Amos* 8:11–12 in the Calvin Translation Society (CTS) edition (*CR* 43.152).

6. See the yearly bibliographies assembled by Peter De Klerk and published in the *Calvin Theological Journal.*

7. Among the significant works in this regard are: Alexandre Ganoczy, *Le jeune Calvin: Genèse et evolution de sa vocation réformatrice* (Wiesbaden: Franz Steiner, 1966); Quirinius Breen, *John Calvin: A Study in French Humanism,* 2nd ed. (Hamden, Conn.: Archon, 1968); Josef Bohatec, *Budé und Calvin: Studien zur Gedankenwelt des französischen Frühhumanismus* (Graz: Hermann Bohlaus, 1950); François Wendel, *Calvin et l'humanisme* (Paris: Presses Universitaires de France, 1976); Ford Lewis Battles and André Malan Hugo, eds., *Calvin's Commentary on Seneca's "De Clementia"* (Leiden: E. J. Brill, 1969); John Calvin, *Institution of the Christian Religion (1536),* trans. Ford Lewis Battles (Atlanta: John Knox, 1975), Introduction; and T. H. L. Parker, *John Calvin: A Biography* (Philadelphia: Westminster, 1975).

8. For example, older studies of Calvin treated him almost solely as a dogmatician with little mention or study of his commentaries on Scripture. So also, treatments of Calvin's view of Scripture have until recently dealt with his statements about Scripture in isolation from such factors as his background, training, and view of language.

Several background influences have surfaced as very important for an appreciation and understanding of Calvin's views on Scripture. One of these is Calvin's training and education as a Christian humanist. Among the areas of his thought most affected by this training were his methods of exegesis, his study of the early Christian theologians, his acceptance of a certain "Christian philosophy," his respect for a number of figures from pagan antiquity, and his strong emphasis on the moral character of the Christian life.[9] The permanent influence of this training was so strong that Calvin, after his conversion to the evangelical faith of the Protestant Reformation, used his classical studies fully and completely but now as tested by the Word of God.[10]

Christian humanism was a branch of Renaissance humanism which in itself was neither Christian nor non-Christian. Instead of being a specific philosophical system, humanism was a cultural and educational approach relating to the curriculum of schools and universities. In the area of studies called the humanities, Renaissance humanists urged a rediscovery of and renewed appreciation for the works of classical antiquity in the original Latin language, and to a smaller extent, in Greek. The *studia humanitatis* included grammar, rhetoric, poetry, history, and moral philosophy.[11]

Christian humanists were Renaissance humanists with a particularly religious bent who wrote on theological topics. They were trained in the classics and the art of rhetoric and approached the ancient texts of the Christian faith from a historical perspective. As such, they attacked the prevailing Scholastic approach to theology which stressed dialectics and sought truth through the method of logical deduction.[12] Instead, Christian humanists wished to return to the classical sources of the faith, particularly the Bible and the early church theologians, to find out what Christ intended Christianity to be. The laws of Aristotelian logic were never to take precedence over the teachings of Scripture. Leading Christian humanists included Erasmus (1469–1536), John Colet (1466?–1519), Jacques Lefèvre d'Étaples (1455?–

9. Ganoczy, *Le jeune Calvin,* p. 195, as cited in Charles B. Partee, *Calvin and Classical Philosophy* (Leiden: E. J. Brill, 1977), p. 13, who notes a number of studies of Calvin and humanism.

10. See Ford Lewis Battles, "The Sources of Calvin's Seneca Commentary," in *John Calvin: A Collection of Essays,* ed. G. E. Duffield (Grand Rapids: Eerdmans, 1966), p. 57.

11. See Paul Oskar Kristeller, *Renaissance Thought: The Classic, Scholastic, and Humanist Strains* (New York: Harper and Row, 1961), p. 10.

12. On the Scholastic approach to theology and the Scriptures see Rogers and McKim, *Authority,* pp. 34ff.

1536), Johann Reuchlin (1455–1522), Guillaume Budaeus (Budé) (1467–1540), and Juan Vives (1492–1540).

Along with the humanist battle-cry *Ad fontes!* ("To the sources!") humanism carried into the Renaissance the strong rhetorical tradition of antiquity. Humanists looked back to Cicero and Plato, who stressed the importance of rhetoric over dialectics (logic). Emphasis was placed on the art of speaking and writing persuasively. Regardless of the truth or falsity of an argument, it must be cast in the best possible *form* in order to make it acceptable to one's hearers.[13]

Augustine, who had been trained as a rhetorician, in book 4 of his *On Christian Doctrine* urged the combination of rhetoric and dialectics. In this respect he echoed Cicero, who had sought a combination of wisdom with rhetoric. Augustine encouraged Christians to particularly study biblical writers who fused wisdom and eloquence.[14] Augustine hoped that by taking this approach people could see both *what* they should communicate as Christians and *how* to communicate it.[15] Augustine, the theologian most used by Calvin,[16] also provided a model of how all Christian humanists could use classical learning for the purposes of Christian theology. Classical wisdom can enrich the church's appreciation of its own literature.[17]

Calvin's roots in the rhetorical tradition of Christian humanism have been amply demonstrated.[18] Cicero's ideal of linking wisdom and eloquence led Calvin to stress the simplicity of truth and the practical problem of how to persuade people. Although Calvin, like Augustine, knew the value of philosophy and logic, both theologians placed primary emphasis not on logical demonstration but on rendering the truth effectively, on making it powerful in human lives.[19] For

13. See E. David Willis, "Rhetoric and Responsibility in Calvin's Theology," in *The Context of Contemporary Theology,* ed. Alexander J. McKelway and E. David Willis (Atlanta: John Knox, 1974), pp. 45–46.

14. On Augustine, see Rogers and McKim, *Authority,* pp. 22ff.

15. Ibid., p. 90.

16. See Luchesius Smits, *Saint Augustin dans l'oeuvre de Calvin,* 2 vols. (Assen: Van Gorcum, 1957).

17. Willis, "Rhetoric," p. 50.

18. For Calvin's rhetorical sources see Battles and Hugo, eds., *"De Clementia,"* pp. 81*–84*; Quirinius Breen, "John Calvin and the Rhetorical Tradition," in *Christianity and Humanism* (Grand Rapids: Eerdmans, 1968), pp. 107–29.

19. See Willis, "Rhetoric," p. 46; Breen, *Christianity and Humanism,* pp. 112–13. Cf. Robert Ayers, "Language, Logic and Reason in Calvin's *Institutes,*" *Religious Studies* 16 (1980): 283–97. Ayers studies Calvin's use of logic and reasoning procedures and also his "pragmatics," his concern to understand an author's intended meaning. Ayers (p. 296) sees Calvin as concerned (in the Augustinian tradition of "faith seeking understanding," on which see Rogers and McKim, *Authority,* pp. 23–25) with both the construction of rational arguments and persuasive speech, that is, saying things fittingly.

Calvin, the gospel was a kind of "divine rhetoric" with an inherent persuasive power: "the apostle rightly contends that the faith of the Corinthians was founded 'upon God's power, not upon human wisdom' [1 Cor. 2:5] because his own preaching among them commended itself 'not in persuasive words of human wisdom but in demonstration of the Spirit and of might' [1 Cor. 2:4]. For truth is cleared of all doubt when, not sustained by external props, it serves as its own support" (*Inst.* 1.8.1). Scripture exhibits its persuasive powers by its effects on its readers:

> Now this power which is peculiar to Scripture is clear from the fact that of human writings, however artfully polished, there is none capable of affecting us at all comparably. Read Demosthenes or Cicero; read Plato, Aristotle, and others of that tribe. They will, I admit, allure you, delight you, move you, enrapture you in wonderful measure. But betake yourself from them to this sacred reading. Then, in spite of yourself, so deeply will it affect you, so penetrate your heart, so fix itself in your very marrow, that, compared with its deep impression, such vigor as the orators and philosophers have will nearly vanish. Consequently, it is easy to see that the Sacred Scriptures, which so far surpass all gifts and graces of human endeavor, breathe something divine. [*Inst.* 1.8.1]

The Scriptures are written in a "rude and unrefined style," said Calvin, yet they are clearly "crammed with thoughts that could not be humanly conceived" (*Inst.* 1.8.2). It is the content of Scripture, not its style, that is persuasive of its truth. With regard to the biblical writers, Calvin said that "the truth cries out openly that these men who, previously contemptible among common folk, suddenly began to discourse so gloriously of the heavenly mysteries must have been instructed by the Spirit" (*Inst.* 1.8.11). Calvin, then, was firmly convinced that there is an innate persuasiveness in God's divine truth.[20]

Calvin's use of the insights of humanism as a Christian theologian was a natural development of his preparatory training. He first applied the methods of humanist scholars in his *Commentary on Seneca's "De Clementia"* (1532).[21] Calvin's life-course had been set toward the study of the law after his father determined that law was a more lucrative profession than the priesthood, the profession toward which he had originally pointed his son.[22] Initially Calvin studied at the University

20. See Partee, *Calvin,* p. 8; Willis, "Rhetoric," pp. 50ff.
21. See Battles and Hugo, eds., *"De Clementia"*; and Battles, "Sources."
22. On Calvin's early life see biographies such as Williston Walker, *John Calvin: The Organiser of Reformed Protestantism* (New York: Schocken, 1969 reprint); François Wendel, *John Calvin: The Origins and Development of His Religious Thought,* trans. Philip Mairet (London: Collins, 1963); and Parker, *John Calvin.*

of Paris (1523–1527) where he received his arts degree in preparation
for theological training. When his father Gérard decreed he should
study law, Calvin enrolled at Orléans, the leading law school of the
day. After a year there (1528–1529), Calvin attended the University
of Bourges (1529–1531) and then went back to the University of
Paris for a year of literary study (1531–1532) and finally again to
Orléans (1532–1533). These educational institutions and his teachers
significantly shaped his intellectual development and his approach to
ancient texts.[23]

In particular Calvin was exposed to new methods of legal research
being developed at that time by humanist scholars. Guillaume Budé
was especially influential in grounding Calvin in legal terminology as
well as in the study of Roman institutions, philosophy (including political philosophy), and literature. The humanist approach stressed
that various scholarly disciplines such as history, law, philosophy, and
rhetoric were necessary background to an understanding of ancient
documents. From Budé's legal commentaries Calvin adopted the tech-
nique of careful word study which was to be a continuing mark of his
later handling of biblical literature.[24] The aim of the "modern" school
of legal study which Calvin emulated was to discover the intent of the
ancient law codes in their original historical contexts instead of relying
on textbooks and traditional commentaries. Thus, in the humanist
view, study of all the contexts of the ancient world was prerequisite
to interpretation of legal documents from early times. These emphases
of the humanists and jurists were applied by Calvin to his study of
Seneca's *De Clementia* and were carried over into his practices of
scriptural exegesis.

Calvin's classical learning was put in service to Christian theology
and his understanding of Scripture. The influence of the modern methods to which he had been exposed is seen most clearly in his developing a contextual rather than atomistic approach to the Bible. Thus
he sought to understand as fully as possible the biblical culture in
which a passage of Scripture is set. The traditional Scholastic approach to theology was closely related to the methods prevailing in
the study of canon law. Canonists collected texts and authorities,
setting them in dialectical relationship to each other. In theology,
Abelard's *Sic et non* and Peter Lombard's *Sentences* adopted this
approach. These were the standard theological textbooks of the time.
In addition, medieval commentators on the Scriptures had added ex-

---

23. For a fuller discussion see Rogers and McKim, *Authority*, pp. 93–96; Battles
and Hugo, eds., "*De Clementia*," chap. 1.
    24. See Battles, "Sources," p. 45.

egetical glosses to the texts. These became in a sense part of the texts themselves and served as data from which further interpretations were drawn.

The humanist movement and Calvin's Christian humanist approach sought a revolutionary change in theological method. As we have observed, humanist legal scholars were seeking direct access to the corpus of Roman law, not via learned authorities or traditions, but through the study of the history and social customs of ancient Rome. Such study gave them a direct understanding of the intentions and meanings of the legal texts. Calvin applied a similar concern for context to his work with Scripture. Circumstances and culture are always main ingredients to be understood as one seeks to interpret the Bible. For these can significantly color the meaning of a text. As Calvin wrote, "there are many statements in Scripture the meaning of which depends upon their context."[25] Sensitivity to this dimension made Calvin a student of the whole fabric of biblical culture; consequently, he felt perfectly free to let his secular studies help interpret Sacred Scripture.

Concern for context led Calvin to seek the divine intention revealed in Scripture. His studies in legal exegesis showed him that the intent of the author is more important than the etymology of words. Calvin called the latter emphasis "syllable-snatching" (*syllabarum aucupiis* — *Inst.* 4.17.14; 4.17.23). Thus he rejected the Anabaptist view that Christ's prescription in the Sermon on the Mount, "Do not swear at all" (Matt. 5:34), prohibits all oath-taking. Calvin said, "Here, however, we shall never attain the truth unless we fix our eyes upon Christ's intention and give heed to what he is driving at in that passage" (*Inst.* 2.8.26). In his sustained treatment against the Anabaptists' position on oath-taking (as it is expressed in their *Schleitheim Confession*), Calvin urged a contextual approach: "In order to understand [Jesus' remarks on swearing] correctly, it is necessary to understand the occasion which prompted Him to speak as He did."[26] In the same way, when interpreting the Ten Commandments, Calvin sought the truth that would be found when "we look into the reason or pur-

25. *Inst.* 4.16.23; cf. 4.15.18. Hans-Joachim Kraus wrote of Calvin: "The real strength of his commentaries lies in his constant concern to discover the distinctive features of the text's environment and the direction in which its message is moving" ("Calvin's Exegetical Principles," *Interpretation* 31 [1977]: 16). Cf. Rogers and McKim, *Authority,* pp. 96ff.

26. John Calvin, *Treatises Against the Anabaptists and Against the Libertines,* ed. and trans. Benjamin Wirt Farley (Grand Rapids: Baker, 1982), p. 97. Farley points out that Calvin's rejection of the theology of the Seven Articles of the *Schleitheim Confession* centered in every case around hermeneutical concerns (p. 28).

pose" for which each was given. The intention of God is to be sought (*Inst.* 2.8.8). Calvin's study of rhetoric had convinced him that rhetorical forms such as figures of speech, metonymies, and synecdoches must be recognized and understood if right interpretation is to take place.[27]

The Need for Scripture

With these background influences in view, we are ready to discuss Calvin's thought on Scripture in general. There are three distinct passages in the 1559 edition of the *Institutes* where Calvin deals formally with the Scriptures. For the fullness of his views to emerge, we must examine these three sections together: Scripture and the knowledge of God (1.6–9), Scripture in the context of the work of the Holy Spirit for salvation (3.2), and the inspiration and authority of Scripture (4.8). Study of his biblical commentaries and sermons provides yet a broader picture of Calvin's conception of the Scriptures. For Calvin, formal statements about the nature of Scripture needed to be implemented by the use of the Bible in the Christian community and in the preaching and pastoral functions of the church.

Initially, Calvin's treatment of the Bible is intimately connected with his views on the knowledge of God. Scripture is needed to reveal God's Word and will, to embody God's revelation or communication of Himself. In Calvin's view, all humans have an innate or inborn knowledge of God. "God has sown a seed of religion in all" (1.4.1). "There is within the human mind, and indeed by natural instinct, an awareness of divinity" (1.3.1).[28] Yet this awareness of the divine did

27. See Battles and Hugo, eds., *"De Clementia,"* chap. 4, "Calvin as Literary Critic and Rhetorician"; Breen, "John Calvin and the Rhetorical Tradition," pp. 114ff. The Lord's Supper is another subject on which Calvin took a contextual approach (*Inst.* 4.17.23).

28. This *divinitatis sensus* and the *semen religionis* ("the seed of religion"— 1.4.1) are discussed in the notes to the Library of Christian Classics edition of the *Institutes* and also extensively in Edward A. Dowey, Jr., *The Knowledge of God in Calvin's Theology* (New York: Columbia University, 1965 reprint), pp. 50ff. Dowey's original publication (1952) was reviewed by T. H. L. Parker in *The Evangelical Quarterly* 26 (1954): 225–29, and further criticized in an appendix to the second printing of Parker's *Doctrine of the Knowledge of God: A Study in the Theology of John Calvin* (Grand Rapids: Eerdmans, 1959). Parker's work had also been published originally in 1952. The 1965 reprint of Dowey's publication responded to Parker. Cf. the earlier interpretation by Benjamin B. Warfield, "Calvin's Doctrine of the Knowledge of God," *The Princeton Theological Review* 7 (1909): 219–325, which has been reprinted in Warfield, *Calvin and Augustine,* ed. Samuel G. Craig (Philadelphia: Presbyterian and Reformed, 1956), pp. 29–130, and in *Calvin and the Reformation,*

not lead humankind to a true knowledge of God. Instead, while humans perceive that there is a God who is "their Maker, they are condemned by their own testimony because they have failed to honor him and to consecrate their lives to his will" (1.3.1). Humans are proud, vain, and obstinate, and "do not therefore apprehend God as he offers himself, but imagine him as they have fashioned him in their own presumption" (1.4.1). This is idolatry and results in the smothering (*suffocari*) and corrupting (*corrumpi*) of the true knowledge of God out of both ignorance and malice.[29] Calvin points out that when we have true knowledge of God, "we not only conceive that there is a God but also grasp what befits us and is proper to his glory, in fine, what is to our advantage to know of him" (1.2.1). A prerequisite to this true knowledge is piety (*pietas*) — "that reverence joined with love of God which the knowledge of his benefits induces" (1.2.1).[30] Calvin observes that true knowledge of God is personal and practical. But sin corrupts this knowledge.

Following in the Augustinian tradition, Calvin regards sin as so pervasive that it affects the totality of humanity's perceptions and orientations. God's revelation of Himself in all of His works through "innumerable evidences both in heaven and on earth" so that humans "cannot open their eyes without being compelled to see him" is rejected by humankind (1.5.1–2).[31] While humans have "within themselves a workshop graced with God's unnumbered works and, at the same time, a storehouse overflowing with inestimable riches," so that they ought "to break forth into praises of him," instead they become "actually puffed up and swollen with all the more pride" (1.5.4). The human mind becomes "like a labyrinth" (1.5.12). The will and the mind both reject a true knowledge of God. Calvin concludes that if humans "were taught only by nature, they would hold to nothing certain or solid or clear-cut, but would be so tied to confused principles as to worship an unknown god" (1.5.12). No natural theology or hu-

ed. William Park Armstrong (Grand Rapids: Baker, 1980 reprint), pp. 131–260. Calvin's agreements with and advances on the concepts of Cicero are examined in Egil Grislis, "Calvin's Use of Cicero in the *Institutes* I:1–5 — A Case Study in Theological Method," *Archiv für Reformationsgeschichte* 62 (1971): 5–37.

29. See Parker, *Doctrine of the Knowledge of God*, pp. 121ff.; Dowey, *Knowledge of God*, pp. 81ff.; and Warfield, *Calvin and Augustine*, pp. 44ff. See also John Platt, *Reformed Thought and Scholasticism: The Arguments for the Existence of God in Dutch Theology, 1575–1650* (Leiden: E. J. Brill, 1982), for an analysis of these concepts in the developing Protestant Scholasticism of the seventeenth century.

30. See Ford Lewis Battles, ed. and trans., *The Piety of John Calvin: An Anthology Illustrative of the Spirituality of the Reformer* (Grand Rapids: Baker, 1978).

31. See Rogers and McKim, *Authority*, p. 101, and the discussion in note 215.

man reasoning in its sinful condition can come to a true knowledge
of God.[32]

The innate knowledge of God in humans has made them responsible for their own sinful condition. "Although we lack the natural
ability to mount up unto the pure and clear knowledge of God, all
excuse is cut off because the fault of dullness is within us" (1.5.15).
Yet God has not left humanity in this state of confusion and ignorance
concerning its Creator. God has met human need for an actual knowledge of Himself by providing "another and better help" to "direct us
aright to the very Creator of the universe" (1.6.1). God provides this
that He might "become known unto salvation." The means God uses
is Scripture. The Scriptures answer human need for "pure knowledge"
of God. Calvin likens the function of Scripture to that of spectacles.

> Just as old or bleary-eyed men and those with weak vision, if you
> thrust before them a most beautiful volume, even if they recognize it
> to be some sort of writing, yet can scarcely construe two words, but
> with the aid of spectacles will begin to read distinctly; so Scripture,
> gathering up the otherwise confused knowledge of God in our minds,
> having dispersed our dullness, clearly shows us the true God.[33]

The Bible is the means God uses to bring people to a true knowledge
of Himself and of salvation. As the Word of God, Scripture is the
crucial source for the knowledge of salvation and a guide for the
Christian life. For "no one can get even the slightest taste of right and
sound doctrine unless he be a pupil of Scripture" (1.6.2).

Scripture is necessary for God's general revelation in nature and
the universe to be made effective. God's special revelation in Scripture
is necessary to communicate what the revelation in creation cannot
because of human sin.[34] As Calvin said:

> Suppose we ponder how slippery is the fall of the human mind into
> forgetfulness of God, how great the tendency to every kind of error,

---

32. Karl Barth and Emil Brunner sharply disagreed on the issue of natural the-
ology in Calvin. See *Natural Theology,* trans. Peter Fraenkel (London: Geoffrey Bles,
1946), for Brunner's *Nature and Grace* and Barth's *No!* Cf. Dowey, *Knowledge of
God,* appendix 3; and G. C. Berkouwer, *General Revelation* (Grand Rapids: Eerd-
mans, 1968), chaps. 2 and 3. Other approaches are found in John Newton Thomas,
"The Place of Natural Theology in the Thought of John Calvin," *Journal of Religious
Thought* 15 (1958): 107–36; and Thomas F. Torrance, "Knowledge of God and Speech
About Him According to John Calvin," in *Theology in Reconstruction* (Grand Rapids:
Eerdmans, 1966), pp. 76–98.

33. *Inst.* 1.6.1. The spectacles metaphor is assessed in differing ways by Dowey,
Parker, and Warfield.

34. See Berkouwer, *General Revelation,* chap. 5.

how great the lust to fashion constantly new and artificial religions. Then we may perceive how necessary was such written proof of the heavenly doctrine, that it should neither perish through forgetfulness nor vanish through error nor be corrupted by the audacity of men. It is therefore clear that God has provided the assistance of the Word for the sake of all those to whom he has been pleased to give useful instruction because he foresaw that his likeness imprinted upon the most beautiful form of the universe would be insufficiently effective. [1.6.3]

Scripture is thus God's gift of grace to fallen creatures, an example of God's provisions for their benefit.

The Nature of Scripture

Calvin's training as a Christian humanist helped shape his perception of the nature of Holy Scripture. As we have just observed, Scripture is the revelation of God, God's way of communicating Himself to sinful humanity. Calvin next approached the highly important issue of the nature of this revelation. He approached it not only as a theologian drawing from the Scriptures themselves, but also as a Christian trained in the humanist methods of studying ancient texts.

Calvin was well aware of the sinful human condition and the need for God to communicate true knowledge of Himself in a special way to humanity. "Since the human mind because of its feebleness can in no way attain to God unless it be aided and assisted by his Sacred Word, all mortals at that time . . . had of necessity to stagger about in vanity and error" (1.6.4). Calvin referred to God's revelation in Scripture as "the Word of God" (1.7.1) which has "flowed to us from the very mouth of God by the ministry of men" (1.7.5). The Sacred Scripture is superior to all human wisdom for in it "the sublime mysteries of the Kingdom of Heaven came to be expressed largely in mean and lowly words" (1.8.1).

As these and numerous other statements in Calvin indicate, Calvin viewed Scripture as God's revelation or Word conveyed to us *by means of* the human words of the biblical writers. To recognize that God has used humans in this way leads us to praise of God and to an enhanced appreciation of the content of His revelation. For Calvin the human form in which Scripture comes to us (i.e., in "uncultivated and almost rude simplicity") "inspires greater reverence for itself than any eloquence." If the Scriptures, Calvin argued, "had been adorned with more shining eloquence, the impious would scoffingly have claimed that its power is in the realm of eloquence alone." But now, given the nature of Holy Scripture — as written by humans in "mean and lowly words" (*contemptibili, humilitate*), "what ought one to conclude except that the force of the truth of Sacred Scripture is manifestly too powerful to need the art of words" (1.8.1)? While Calvin spoke of "the completely heavenly character of its [Scripture's] doctrine, savoring of nothing earthly" (1.8.1), he acknowledged and even stressed that the Holy Spirit at times uses both "eloquence" and "a rude and unrefined style" in Scripture (1.8.2). This is the form in which Scripture comes to us — it was written by human authors.

Calvin's thoughts here include two dimensions. The Scriptures are the Word of God in that they communicate the knowledge of God. Yet the instrument or means of our coming to this knowledge of God is the words of humans. Calvin's humanist training provided him with the concept of "accommodation," which he adopted as a framework to help us understand these two dimensions and, as a matter of fact, every relationship between God and humanity.[35] As ancient rhetoricians "accommodated" the content of their speeches and presentations to the capacities (*captus*) of their audiences, and as lawyers adapted legal principles to specified cases, so God has accommodated (*accommodare*) Himself to human capacity by communicating Himself to sinful humans in a way — through words — adapted to their limited understandings. In Scripture the divine God has bridged the infinite gulf between Himself and humanity by condescending to speak and act in human forms. Human authors, divinely appointed, expressed God's message about Himself in human words and thought forms. Thus, while Scripture may at times be written in less than the most eloquent language by uneducated, simple authors, this is no barrier to God's revelation of Himself; indeed, it is the very *means* of that revelation! For Calvin, Scripture's content or function is more decisive than its language or form (of course we realize all the while that the language and content are not to be found separate from each other). The divine message or doctrine (*doctrina*) of Scripture comes to us through human words. God has condescended to our capacities by giving us the Scriptures. God has accommodated Himself to human weaknesses in Scripture but also, most supremely, in Jesus Christ. This God has done out of His great love for humanity.

35. On accommodation as an important feature of Calvin's understanding see Ford Lewis Battles, "God Was Accommodating Himself to Human Capacity," pp. 21–42 in this volume. Cf. Rogers and McKim, *Authority,* pp. 98ff. On the concept of accommodation in Chrysostom and Augustine with regard to sacrifice as a bond of unity between Old and New Testaments, see Stephen D. Benin, "Sacrifice as Education in Augustine and Chrysostom," *Church History* 52 (1983): 7–20.

The Authority of Scripture

With this perspective, Calvin proceeded to deal with the question, "Who can convince us that these writings came from God?" This question concerns the authority of Scripture. On one level, Calvin dismissed this query by saying that even to ask such a question is "to mock the Holy Spirit" (1.7.1). To seek a proof for the authority of Scripture is the same as asking, "Whence will we learn to distinguish light from darkness, white from black, sweet from bitter?" (1.7.2). These rhetorical flourishes point to his view that the persuasive truth of Scripture is self-evident. "Indeed, Scripture exhibits fully as clear evidence of its own truth as white and black things do of their color, or sweet and bitter things do of their taste" (1.7.2).

Calvin rejected the Roman Catholic position that the authority of Scripture is conferred upon it by the church (1.7.1). He argued that "the church is 'built upon the foundation of the prophets and apostles' (Eph. 2:20). If the teaching of the prophets and apostles is the foundation, this must have had authority before the church began to exist" (1.7.2). Instead, "the Scriptures obtain full authority among believers only when men regard them as having sprung from heaven, as if there the living words of God were heard" (1.7.1). In Scripture, God "opens his own most hallowed lips" (1.6.1). God speaks in Scripture "in his own words," said Calvin (2.8.12). It is "God's Sacred Word" (1.7.4) which is "set down and sealed in writing" (4.8.6). The message or doctrine communicated in Scripture, then, comes fully from God.

In Calvin's view, people come to this conviction about Scripture — that God is its author — by the work of the Holy Spirit. The internal testimony of the Holy Spirit (*testimonium Spiritus sancti internum*) is the means by which we become certain as to the origin and authority of Scripture. "We ought to seek our conviction in a higher place than human reasons, judgments, or conjectures, that is, in the secret testimony of the Spirit."[36] The "highest proof of Scripture derives in general from the fact that God in person speaks in it." The "prophets and apostles" do not "dwell upon rational proofs" as they speak. Nor should we, then, demand rational proof that they spoke divinely. In-

36. *Inst.* 1.7.4; cf. 3.1.1; 3.1.3f.; 3.2.15, 33–36; Dowey, *Knowledge of God,* pp. 106ff.; Wilhelm Niesel, *The Theology of Calvin,* trans. Harold Knight (Philadelphia: Westminster, 1956), pp. 30–39; Warfield, *Calvin and Augustine,* pp. 70–116; and W. H. Neuser, "Theologie des Wortes — Schrift, Verheissung und Evangelium bei Calvin," in *Calvinus Theologus,* ed. W. H. Neuser (Neukirchen-Vluyn: Neukirchener Verlag, 1976), pp. 27ff. Note 12 at *Institutes* 1.7.4 gives further sources.

stead, said Calvin, "the testimony of the Spirit is more excellent than all reason" and "the Word will not find acceptance in men's hearts before it is sealed by the inward testimony of the Spirit." Calvin believed that "the same Spirit, therefore, who has spoken through the mouths of the prophets must penetrate into our hearts to persuade us that they faithfully proclaimed what had been divinely commanded" (1.7.4).

This emphasis on Scripture's self-authenticating authority (Greek, *autopiston*) led Calvin to suggest that it is "not right to subject it to proof and reasoning." For "the certainty it deserves with us, it attains by the testimony of the Spirit." Indeed, "we seek no proofs, no marks of genuineness upon which our judgment may lean; but we subject our judgment and wit to it as to a thing far beyond any guesswork!" "The only true faith" in Scripture, Calvin wrote, "is that which the Spirit of God seals in our hearts." This "each believer experiences within himself" (1.7.5).

Calvin's strongest emphasis, then, was on the work of the Holy Spirit in sealing the testimony to Scripture's divine authority in the hearts of believers. He recognized that there are "human testimonies" which point to Scripture as coming from God. These include such factors as Scripture's unique majesty and impressiveness and its high antiquity (1.8.1–4); miracles and prophecy (sections 5–10); the simplicity, heavenly character, and authority of the New Testament (section 11); and the universal consent of the church and the faithfulness of the martyrs (sections 12–13). Yet for Calvin these "arguments" for the credibility of Scripture are insufficient ("vain") in themselves. Believers need a "certainty, higher and stronger than any human judgment" or than any arguments which are external to the Scriptures and the witness of the Holy Spirit (1.8.1). These external arguments or "human testimonies" do have a place, said Calvin. But they are helpful as "secondary aids to our feebleness" (1.8.13). They are useful to believers who have already accepted Scripture's authority through the internal witness of the Holy Spirit. Once believers have "embraced" Scripture as "devoutly as its dignity deserves, and have recognized it to be above the common sort of things, those arguments — not strong enough before to engraft and fix the certainty of Scripture in our minds — become very useful aids" (1.8.1). External arguments assist faith in Scripture only *after* faith in Christ has become a reality and the Holy Spirit has led one to accept Scripture as God's Word. Rational proofs for the divinity of Scripture encourage believers. But they are never sufficient in themselves to establish faith.[37] As Calvin puts it, "Scripture will ultimately suffice for a saving knowledge of God only when its certainty is founded upon the inward persuasion of the Holy Spirit" (1.8.13).

The faith which the Holy Spirit initiates is a consent or commitment of the whole person to a relationship with God in Jesus Christ. Faith is more than intellectual assent or a feeling. It is instead "a firm and certain knowledge of God's benevolence toward us, founded upon the truth of the freely given promise in Christ, both revealed to our minds and sealed upon our hearts through the Holy Spirit" (3.2.7).[38] There is a rational dimension to faith; but faith is suprarational, concerned with the realm above the human mind (3.2.14). "In understanding faith," wrote Calvin, "it is not merely a question of knowing that God exists, but also — and this especially — of knowing what is his will toward us" (3.2.6; cf. 1.2.2; 1.10.2). Faith is "a knowledge of God's will toward us, perceived from his Word" (3.2.6). Thus faith is personal and relational.[39] There is no need for rational proofs before one can come to faith in Jesus Christ or the Scriptures. For, said Calvin,

37. Warfield argued that in Calvin's "general teaching as to the formation of sound faith in the divinity of Scripture . . . we find . . . indication that he thought of the *indicia* as co-working with the testimony of the Spirit to this result," *Calvin and Augustine,* p. 89. Brian A. Gerrish rightly rejects this reading of Calvin: "Warfield's estimate of the *probationes* (or *indicia,* as he likes to call them) is surely wrong: he exalts them to a status Calvin did not accord them and even tries to argue that Spirit and *indicia* work together as though inseparable." Gerrish goes on to write that "the difficulty is to see why he [Calvin] bothers to mention them at all, for he says that it is improper to subject Scripture to argument (1.7.5)." See Gerrish's essay, "The Word of God and the Words of Scripture: Luther and Calvin on Biblical Authority," in *The Old Protestantism and the New* (Chicago: University of Chicago, 1982), p. 300. This is an expansion of his "Biblical Authority in the Continental Reformation," *Scottish Journal of Theology* 10 (1957): 337–60. J. I. Packer also criticizes Warfield on this point. See J. I. Packer, "Calvin's View of Scripture," in *God's Inerrant Word,* ed. John Warwick Montgomery (Minneapolis: Bethany Fellowship, 1974), p. 108, n. 47. Cf. Rogers and McKim, *Authority,* pp. 103ff.

38. See Wilhelm Balke, "The Word of God and *Experientia* According to Calvin," in *Calvinus Ecclesiae Doctor,* ed. W. H. Neuser (Kampen: Kok, 1979), pp. 19–31.

39. Calvin sees the personal dimensions of faith in its results: certainty, assurance, boldness, and confidence. "There is a far different feeling of full assurance [Greek, *plērophorias*] that in the Scriptures is always attributed to faith. It is this which puts beyond doubt God's goodness clearly manifested for us. But that cannot happen without our truly feeling its sweetness and experiencing it in ourselves. . . . This boldness arises only out of a sure confidence in divine benevolence and salvation" (3.2.15).

believers are "more strengthened by the persuasion of divine truth than instructed by rational proof," and "the knowledge of faith consists in assurance rather than in comprehension" (3.2.14).[40]

The authority of Scripture is established by the inner witness of the Holy Spirit, who testifies to God in Jesus Christ in Scripture through faith. For Calvin, Word and Spirit belong inseparably together. The Spirit does not witness apart from the Word; the Word without the work of the Spirit has no power or efficacy. "The Holy Spirit so inheres in his truth, which he expresses in Scripture, that only when its proper reverence and dignity are given to the Word does the Holy Spirit show forth his power." God has "sent down the same Spirit by whose power he had dispensed the Word, to complete his work by the efficacious confirmation of the Word" (1.9.3). For "faith is the principal work of the Holy Spirit" and "faith itself has no other source than the Spirit" (3.1.4; cf. 3.2.33–35).[41]

In Calvin's view, Jesus Christ is at the center of Scripture. Christ is the object of faith and its goal (scopum fidei — 3.2.6). "True knowledge of Christ" comes "if we receive him as he is offered by the Father: namely, clothed with his gospel" (3.2.6). It is through the Scriptures that this true knowledge comes to us by the work of the Holy Spirit. Thus Christ and the Scriptures are intimately interrelated.[42]

The Inspiration of Scripture

It was Calvin's position that the authority of Scripture springs from the fact that it is God who speaks in and through it. God's revelation of Himself climaxing in Jesus Christ is what the Scriptures convey. The writings gain their authority from the One with whom they orig-

40. G. C. Berkouwer points out that the Reformers used words like *notitia, assensus,* and *fiducia* to describe the nature of faith but "they refused to isolate aspects of faith from one another. 'How could it be *fiducia* without at the same time, and because it is *fiducia,* being *notitia* and *assensus* too?' (Barth, CD I/1, 269). The reformers never talked as if one first accepted and agreed to something and thereafter believed and trusted." Also, "Calvin used the word *cognitio,* but did not reduce faith to intellectual knowledge with it because he insisted that this *cognitio* was directed to 'the benevolence of God toward us' and was more an affair of the heart than of the head"—*A Half Century of Theology: Movements and Motives,* ed. and trans. Lewis B. Smedes (Grand Rapids: Eerdmans, 1977), p. 175.

41. See G. C. Berkouwer, *Holy Scripture,* ed. and trans. Jack B. Rogers (Grand Rapids: Eerdmans, 1975), chap. 2, "The Testimony of the Spirit." This chapter is reprinted in *The Authoritative Word: Essays on the Nature of Scripture,* ed. Donald K. McKim (Grand Rapids: Eerdmans, 1983), pp. 155–81.

42. It is clear that with regard to the authority of Scripture Calvin follows Augustine—"faith leads to understanding." See Rogers and McKim, *Authority,* pp. 100ff.

inate: God. God has communicated Himself to humanity by means of a person, His Son Jesus, and by means of humans who were inspired to communicate the word and will of God in human language.

Calvin's emphasis on the inspiration of Scripture is expressed not only through the terms *inspire* and *inspiration*,[43] but also in other descriptions that stress the divine origin of the writing produced; for example, "the mouth of the Lord," "the school of the Holy Spirit," and "God speaking in Scripture."[44] At some points Calvin seems to indicate that the human writers were so overwhelmed by the Holy Spirit's inspiration that they served as nothing more than "sure and genuine scribes of the Holy Spirit" (*certi et authentici Spiritus sancti amanuenses* — 4.8.9) who composed Scripture "under the Holy Spirit's dictation" (*dictante Spiritu sancto*).[45] Thus Calvin comments on 2 Timothy 3:16: "All those who wish to profit from the Scriptures must first accept this as a settled principle, that the Law and the

43. See, e.g., *Inst.* 1.8.4, 8.

44. See *Comm. on 2 Tim.* 3:16 (*CNTC* 10.330); *Inst.* 3.21.3; 1.7.4.

45. Among those who deal with the references to dictation are: Dowey, *Knowledge of God*, pp. 90ff.; R. S. Wallace, *Calvin's Doctrine of the Word and Sacrament* (Edinburgh: Oliver and Boyd, 1953), pp. 106ff.; Joseph Haroutunian, "Calvin as Biblical Commentator," in *Calvin: Commentaries*, ed. Joseph Haroutunian, Library of Christian Classics (Philadelphia: Westminster, 1958), pp. 33ff.; A. D. R. Polman, "Calvin on the Inspiration of Scripture," in *John Calvin: Contemporary Prophet*, ed. Jacob T. Hoogstra (Grand Rapids: Baker, 1959), pp. 98ff.; Philip Edgcumbe Hughes, "The Inspiration of Scripture in the English Reformers Illuminated by John Calvin," *Westminster Theological Journal* 23 (1960–1961): 140ff.; Warfield, *Calvin and Augustine*, pp. 60ff.; H. Jackson Forstman, *Word and Spirit: Calvin's Doctrine of Biblical Authority* (Stanford: Stanford University, 1962), pp. 50–62; J. I. Packer, "Calvin's View of Scripture," pp. 103ff.; Kenneth S. Kantzer, "Calvin and the Holy Scriptures," in *Inspiration and Interpretation*, ed. John F. Walvoord (Grand Rapids: Eerdmans, 1957), pp. 137ff.; John Murray, *Calvin on Scripture and Divine Sovereignty* (Grand Rapids: Baker, 1978 reprint), chap. 1; J. K. S. Reid, *The Authority of Scripture: A Study of the Reformation and Post-Reformation Understanding of the Bible* (London: Methuen, 1957), chap. 2; John T. McNeill, "The Significance of the Word of God for Calvin," *Church History* 28 (1959): 139–44; Gerrish, "The Word of God and the Words of Scripture," p. 63; Werner Krusche, *Das Wirken des Heiligen Geistes nach Calvin* (Göttingen: Vandenhoeck und Ruprecht, 1957), pp. 161–84; Richard C. Prust, "Was Calvin a Biblical Literalist?" *Scottish Journal of Theology* 10 (1967): 313ff.; A. Mitchell Hunter, *The Teaching of Calvin* (Glasgow: Maclehose, Jackson, 1920), pp. 68ff.

In the older literature there is also: Émile Doumergue, *Jean Calvin: Les hommes et les choses de son temps*, 7 vols. (Paris: Librairie Fischbacher, 1910), vol. 4, pp. 70ff.; Otto Ritschl, *Dogmengeschichte des Protestantismus*, 4 vols. (Göttingen: Vandenhoeck und Ruprecht, 1926), vol. 1, pp. 63ff.; Reinhold Seeberg, *Text-Book of the History of Doctrines*, trans. Charles E. Hay, 2 vols. (Grand Rapids: Baker, 1952), vol. 2, pp. 395–96; J. A. Cramer, *De Heilige Schrift bij Calvin* (Utrecht: A. Oosthoek, 1926); Peter Brunner, *Vom Glauben bei Calvin* (Tübingen: Mohr, 1925), pp. 92ff.; Henri Clavier, *Études sur la Calvinisme* (Paris: Librairie Fischbacher, 1936), pp. 25ff.

prophets are not teachings (*doctrinam*) handed on at the pleasure of men or produced by men's minds as their source, but are dictated (*dictantem*) by the Holy Spirit."[46] Calvin uses the term *dictation* in various other places throughout his commentaries, particularly in his discussions of Jeremiah and Baruch.[47]

Most interpreters of Calvin reject the idea that he conceived of dictation in a mechanical fashion, that is, that he regarded the writers of Scripture as mere puppets or automatons.[48] Various explanations have been advanced to clarify Calvin's language and to relate it to his overall view of the Scriptures. This is necessary in light of the many other statements of Calvin stressing the involvement of the whole personality of a biblical writer in what is written.[49] Adherents of verbal inspiration have argued Calvin meant God selected both the ideas and words of Scripture. He so controlled the minds and personalities of the authors that they wrote exactly the words He willed.[50] This view seeks to avoid the charge that it is tantamount to literal dictation by claiming that Calvin's use of the term *dictation* is figurative, that he is not referring to the mode of inspiration but the result

46. *Comm. on 2 Tim.* 3:16 (*CNTC* 10.330).

47. See Dowey, *Knowledge of God*, pp. 91ff.; Forstman, *Word and Spirit*, p. 53; and Kantzer, "Calvin," pp. 138ff., among others, for examples of usage of the term.

48. In Calvin's view, "the biblical authors, on the human side, were not mere 'typewriters' " (Hughes, "Inspiration," p. 144); "these writers were not involuntary instruments in the hands of the Spirit" (Polman, "Calvin," p. 101); "the writers are not automatons" (McNeill, "Significance," p. 140); the writer "acted throughout as one who really experienced all that he said and who gave forth the message as one coming naturally from his own heart through a process of thought, on a psychological level, no different from that of ordinary human authorship" (Wallace, *Calvin's Doctrine*, p. 108).

49. See Kantzer, "Calvin," p. 139; McNeill, "Significance," pp. 140ff.; and Wallace, *Calvin's Doctrine*, p. 108, for examples of Calvin's statements stressing that the Gospel writers, Paul, David, and the prophets wrote in their own styles from their own experiences. Ezekiel ate the book because "God's servants ought to speak from the inmost affection of their heart" (*Comm. on Ezek.* 3:3 [CTS; *CR* 40.76]; cf. *Comm. on Ezek.* 2:8f. [*CR* 40.72ff.]). So also in the *Comm. on 2 Peter* 1:21 ("holy men moved by the Holy Spirit spoke from God") — Peter "says that they were *moved,* not because they were out of their minds [Greek, *enthousiasmos*] (as the heathen imagine in their prophets), but because they dared nothing by themselves but only in obedience to the guidance of the Spirit who held sway over their lips as in His own temple" (*CNTC* 12.344).

50. Kantzer speaks for the adherents of verbal inspiration when he writes: "By this means, God inspires the writers of Scripture (better breathes out through them as instruments) to speak to man exactly His chosen words which He wills." God is the "ultimate author" of Scripture in that "He sovereignly controls the mind and personality of the men He has chosen to write Scripture" ("Calvin," pp. 141, 140). Among those who believe Calvin subscribed to verbal inspiration are Warfield, Murray, Packer, and Hunter.

of inspiration, namely, that "a pure word of God free from all human admixtures" was produced. The result is "as if it were by dictation."[51]

A second way of understanding Calvin's language has been to stress the role of the biblical writers as witnesses to God's act of incarnation in Jesus Christ. The written Word directs one to the living Word, Jesus Christ. The biblical writers were witnesses to God's revelation in Christ. They possessed a certainty (by the Holy Spirit) of the validity of their experience and consequently bore witness to Christ. When Calvin speaks of dictation, then, he must be seen first of all as stressing (keep in mind the Reformers' historical context vis-à-vis the Roman Church) the subjection of the church to Scripture as God's Word and its primary authority. But secondly this is also a way of stressing the power of the Word of God dwelling in the human words of the biblical writers.[52] Scripture is "verbally inspired" in that God has used the limited language of concrete human words to point humanity to Christ.[53]

A third approach to Calvin's teaching on inspiration is to take into

51. The phrase is Warfield's (*Calvin and Augustine*, p. 64). See Dowey's discussion (*Knowledge of God*, p. viii), and Gerrish's approval ("The Word of God and the Words of Scripture," p. 299, note 74). While noting Calvin's "rather loose usage of the word 'dictate,' " as in "the dictates of nature" and "the natural order dictates," Kantzer does not seem to be fully happy with Warfield's suggestion: "Whether the forcefulness of the reformer's vocabulary can be adequately accounted for by such an interpretation may be open to question." Kantzer then goes on to spell out the verbal-inspiration formula, saying in a footnote that "Calvin employs the word [*dictate*] as the equivalent of produce, affirm, or prescribe" ("Calvin," p. 140).

52. This is the approach of Karl Barth. In citing Calvin's reference to dictation in the *Comm. on 2 Tim.* 3:16f., Barth says neither "a mantico-mechanical nor a docetic conception of biblical inspiration is in the actual sphere of Calvin's thinking" — *Church Dogmatics* 1.2, ed. G. W. Bromiley and T. F. Torrance (Edinburgh: T. and T. Clark, 1956), p. 520. Barth says that, in Calvin's view, inspiration "rests on the relationship of the biblical witnesses to the very definite content of their witness. It is indeed this content which inspires them. . . . But Holy Scripture refuses to know or put before us anything but Christ" (pp. 520–21). Citing Calvin's *Comm. on John* 5:39 (we should read the Scriptures with the purpose of finding Christ in them), Barth says that "according to Calvin it is also part of the equipment of the biblical writers in their speaking and writing of the Word of God that they had a prior *firma certitudo* in their hearts regarding the divine nature of the experiences to which they then speak and write" (p. 521). The witness of Scripture is to Jesus Christ. The words of the Scripture writers are "a human word in the witness of the prophets and apostles as witnesses to His incarnation" (p. 522).

53. This is how Barth understood "verbal inspiration." See Rogers and McKim, *Authority*, pp. 421–23. Barth branded seventeenth-century orthodoxy's view of verbal inspiration, which grounded the authority of Scripture "upon itself apart from the mystery of Christ and the Holy Ghost," as "false doctrine" (*Church Dogmatics* 1.2, p. 525). Among those who stress the Christocentric nature of Calvin's views on Scripture are Dowey, Niesel, Wallace, Reid, and Parker.

consideration Calvin's training as a Christian humanist. His background made him sensitive to the nature of language and of God's communication of Himself to humanity. Of chief importance here is the concept of accommodation. The Scriptures are God's revelation of Himself in a way commensurate with limited human capacities. The divine communication is given to humans as revelation. Through the inspiration of the Holy Spirit the biblical writers used their own thought forms and words adapted to the special situations and capacities of the audiences they were addressing. The divine message came through human thought forms. Calvin's references to inspiration as "dictation" are to be read in this wider sense. The term *dictation* points beyond the writer to remind us that Scripture's ultimate origin is with the God who inspired the writer.

It should also be mentioned here that whenever the *Institutes* speaks of dictation, it is within the context of a discussion of the doctrine or teaching (*doctrina*) which God has given in Scripture. For example:

> But because the Lord was pleased to reveal a clearer and fuller doctrine in order better to satisfy weak consciences, he commanded that the prophecies also be committed to writing and be accounted part of his Word. At the same time, histories were added to these, also the labor of the prophets, but composed under the Holy Spirit's dictation. I include the psalms with the prophecies, since what we attribute to the prophecies is common to them. [4.8.6]

The teaching of Scripture is again the focus when Calvin says of the apostles: "They were to expound the ancient Scripture and to show that what is taught there has been fulfilled in Christ. Yet they were not to do this except from the Lord, that is, with Christ's Spirit as precursor in a certain measure dictating the words" (4.8.8).[54] We can also point to the commentary on 2 Timothy 3:16 and the commentary on Peter 1:11, where Calvin, referring to the prophets, writes:

> At the same time high praise is given to their doctrine, for it was the testimony of the Holy Spirit. Although the preachers and ministers were men, He was the Teacher. He does not say without reason that

54. The note in the Library of Christian Classics edition points out: " '*Verba quodammodo dictante Christi Spiritu.*' The adverb is, however, a deliberate qualification. discounting any doctrine of exact verbal inspiration. The context has reference to teaching, not words merely, showing that Calvin's point is not verbal inerrancy, but the authoritative message of Scripture."

the Spirit of Christ then ruled, and he makes the Spirit, sent from heaven, the Lord of the teachers of the Gospel. He shows that the Gospel has come from God, and that the ancient prophecies were dictated by Christ.[55]

Thus whenever Calvin speaks of dictation, his predominant emphasis is on the divine doctrine or gospel message which humans have expressed in their own words, thought forms, and contexts.[56] God has accommodated His message to human capacities.[57] It is by the power of the Holy Spirit, who both inspired the Scripture and illuminates it for believers in the present, that we recognize the divine authority and thus the inspiration of Scripture. Word and Spirit are bound up inextricably for Calvin (1.9.3). In light of Calvin's overall understanding of the nature of language and of Scripture, and specifically the concept

---

55. *Comm. on 1 Peter* 1:11. Richard A. Muller has noted the trinitarian emphasis of Calvin's view of Scripture. Scripture for Calvin is "the revealing Word of God" which centers on the promise of God made known fully in Jesus Christ by the work of the Holy Spirit. "Rather than deriving the authority of Scripture from a formal doctrine of inspiration, Calvin employs the concepts of inspiration and testimony as correlative aspects of the work of the Spirit mediating in and through Scripture the saving knowledge of God. Scripture is the Word of God because the Spirit of Christ imparted to the ancient authors the wisdom of God directly from its source, the eternal Wisdom or Word which resides in God: 'we see the Word understood as the order or mandate of the Son, who is himself the essential Word of the Father' in the Scriptures given by the 'Spirit of the Word' " (1.13.7). See Richard A. Muller, "The Foundation of Calvin's Theology: Scripture as Revealing God's Word," *The Duke Divinity School Review* 44 (1979): 19.

56. Calvin's emphasis on the divine doctrine or message of Scripture as the focus of inspiration is underlined in *Inst.* 1.6.2: "But whether God became known to the patriarchs through oracles and visions or by the work and ministry of men, he put into their minds what they should then hand down to their posterity. At any rate, there is no doubt that firm certainty of doctrine was engraved in their hearts, so that they were convinced and understood that what they had learned proceeded from God." The Library of Christian Classics edition notes that "Calvin does not here offer an explanation of the manner of inspiration in the origin of the Scriptures. However, the suggestion his language conveys is not of a mechanical verbal dictation, but of an impartation of divine truth that enters the hearts of the Scripture writers."

57. The combination of constant, steadfast doctrine and changing, adaptable forms is reflected in Calvin's discussion of God's constancy in His covenant amidst the various forms of it. "God's constancy shines forth in the fact that he taught the same doctrine to all ages, and has continued to require the same worship of his name that he enjoined from the beginning. In the fact that he has changed the outward form and manner, he does not show himself subject to change. Rather, he has accommodated himself to men's capacity, which is varied and changeable" (2.11.13).

Among those who maintain that Calvin viewed inspiration as God's accommodation of the constant divine doctrine to human capacities are Berkouwer, McNeill, Rogers, McKim, and Battles.

of accommodation, this third perspective seems the best approach
with regard to Calvin's view of inspiration and his references to dictation by the Holy Spirit.[58]

The Interpretation of Scripture

Calvin's work as an interpreter of Holy Scripture is evident in all
of his theological works.[59] Therefore, it is important to assess what
went into his labors as an exegete. His background as a Christian
humanist led him to use the best tools and methods of scholarship

58. Jack B. Rogers has commented on the three positions outlined here (though
without specific reference to Calvin). (1) Verbal inspiration suggests the metaphor of
"the president of the United States dictating a letter to his personal secretary." This
metaphor underscores the complete authority of the divinely inspired Bible. (2) The
Christocentric emphasis suggests the metaphor of editors and columnists reporting
and interpreting the sayings and doings of an incumbent president running for re-
election. The "editors" of the biblical material interpret who God is in Jesus Christ,
recommending that their readers give allegiance to Him. They encourage their readers
to meet the candidate personally and to give their allegiance to this unique person
with saving power. Under this metaphor Scripture is an interpreted record written
by people "who have known and been drawn to commitment to Jesus Christ." (3)
The third position suggests the metaphor of "the president's press secretary speaking
to the public." He has been with the president and knows his inmost thoughts. When
the press secretary speaks, he does so with the authority of the president. But the
press secretary uses his own words, applying and adapting the president's ideas to
the questions asked. This metaphor reminds us that the biblical writers knew God
intimately and that God had revealed to them His mind and will. It also reminds us
that the biblical writers used their own thought forms and words, adapting divine
principles to particular situations and to the capacities of their readers. See Jack B.
Rogers, "Mixed Metaphors, Misunderstood Models, and Puzzling Paradigms: A Contemporary Effort to Correct Some Current Misunderstandings Regarding the Authority and Interpretation of the Bible" (Paper presented at a conference on "Interpreting
an Authoritative Scripture" held at the Institute for Christian Studies, Toronto, On-
tario, June 22–26, 1981), pp. 19–20. Whichever of these positions on inspiration
Calvin may have held, their implications for his view on the matter of inerrancy (is
Scripture infallible or is there the possibility of error?) are assessed differently by
different scholars. See Rogers and McKim, *Authority,* pp. 109ff.; John D. Woodbridge, *Biblical Authority: A Critique of the Rogers/McKim Proposal* (Grand Rapids:
Zondervan, 1982), pp. 58ff.; and W. Robert Godfrey, "Biblical Authority in the Sixteenth and Seventeenth Centuries: A Question of Transition," in *Scripture and Truth,*
ed. D. A. Carson and John D. Woodbridge (Grand Rapids: Zondervan, 1983), pp. 230ff.
59. On Calvin the exegete see the bibliography in T. H. L. Parker, *Calvin's New
Testament Commentaries* (Grand Rapids: Eerdmans, 1971), pp. 188ff.; idem, "Calvin the Biblical Expositor," in *John Calvin: A Collection of Essays,* ed. Duffield,
pp. 176–86; idem, "Calvin the Exegete: Change and Development," in *Calvinus Ecclesiae Doctor,* ed. Neuser, pp. 33–46; Kraus, "Calvin's Exegetical Principles,"
pp. 8–18; and Benoît Girardin, *Rhétorique et Théologique: Calvin, Le Commentaire
de l'Épitre aux Romains,* Théologie Historique 54 (Paris: Éditions Beauchesne, 1979),
among others. But a comprehensive study still needs undertaking.

available at his time.[60] He turned to such scholars as Guillaume Budé and Erasmus as well as to the theologians of the early church for assistance on philological, textual, and interpretive matters.[61]

Among these early theologians, Calvin relied most heavily on Augustine for theological interpretations and on John Chrysostom for matters of biblical interpretation.[62] Calvin felt that as an exegete Augustine was "oversubtle, with the result that he is less solid and dependable."[63] Calvin also did not agree with Augustine's allegorical interpretations.[64] On the other hand, Calvin appreciated Chrysostom's "supreme concern always not to turn aside even to the slightest degree from the genuine, simple sense of Scripture and to allow himself no liberties by twisting the plain meaning of the words."[65] Chrysostom, as a representative of the Antiochene school of biblical interpretation, kept close to the apparent meaning of a verse and interpreted texts within their own immediate contexts.[66]

Calvin's chief concern in biblical interpretation and exposition was the edification of the church. "In the reading of Scripture we ought ceaselessly to endeavor to seek out and meditate upon those things which make for edification" (1.14.4). In this regard he avoided speculating on matters not directly related to the purpose for which the Scriptures were given, namely, "to direct us aright to the very Creator of the universe" so that He might "become known unto salvation" (1.6.1). Calvin urged that in "all religious doctrine" we "ought to hold to one rule of modesty and sobriety: not to speak, or guess, or even to seek to know, concerning obscure matters anything except what

60. See Parker, *Commentaries, passim,* for details of Calvin's reference sources and methods.

61. See Battles, "Sources," pp. 40ff.; and Parker, *Commentaries, passim.*

62. See John R. Walchenbach, "John Calvin as Biblical Commentator: An Investigation into Calvin's Use of John Chrysostom as an Exegetical Tutor" (Ph.D. dissertation, University of Pittsburgh, 1974).

63. John Calvin, *Praefatio in Chrysostomi Homilias* (*CR* 9.835). See John H. McIndoe, trans., "John Calvin: Preface to the Homilies of Chrysostom," *The Hartford Quarterly* 5 (1965): 19–26.

64. Calvin was quite harsh with the allegorical tradition of biblical interpretation which went back to Origen and continued through Augustine and later. To regard the discovery of allegory as the chief goal of exegesis was, in Calvin's opinion, "the course of many evils." Falling into this trap, "many of the ancients without any restraint played all sorts of games with the sacred Word of God, as if they were tossing a ball to and fro." See *Comm. on 2 Cor.* 3:6 (*CNTC* 10.43).

65. As rendered in Walchenbach, "Investigation," p. 30, from *Praefatio in Chrysostomi Homilias* (*CR* 9.835).

66. On Chrysostom and the Antiochene school see Rogers and McKim, *Authority,* pp. 16ff., and the literature cited there. On Augustine as a biblical interpreter see ibid., pp. 32–33.

has been imparted to us by God's Word" (1.14.4). Thus, if we would be "duly wise, we must leave those empty speculations" (Greek, *mataiōmata*) on such relatively unimportant things as the "nature, orders, and number of angels" (1.14.4), for as Calvin states in the preface to the Geneva Bible,

> the Bible was not given to us to satisfy our foolish curiosity and pride. Yet Paul says it is useful. For what? To instruct us in sound doctrine, to comfort us, to inspire us, and to make us able to perform every good work. If anyone asks us what constructive power we expect to receive from it, the answer can be given in one sentence, that through it we learn to place our trust in God and to walk in fear of him.[67]

There were two guiding principles Calvin sought to follow in his exegetical work. The first was *brevitas*. In his dedicatory letter to Simon Grynaeus in the *Commentary on Romans*, Calvin reminisced that three years before he and Grynaeus both "felt that lucid brevity constituted the particular virtue of an interpreter."[68] Calvin's aim was to discover the "pertinence" or "relevance" of a portion of Scripture and then to relay it in as short and succinct a manner as possible.[69] Lengthy commentaries on texts serve only to exhaust a reader. In this, Calvin had the commentaries of Martin Bucer in mind.[70] Calvin's second principle was *facilitas*. That is, Calvin sought "simplicity" or "what is easily understood." He wanted to get to the natural and obvious meaning of a text as quickly as possible without undue regard for the opinions of other commentators.[71] This primary focus on the mind of the biblical writer is evident in Calvin's comment to Grynaeus that "since it is almost [a commentator's] only task to unfold the mind of the writer whom he has undertaken to expound, he misses his mark, or at least strays outside his limits, by the extent to which he leads his readers away from the meaning of his author."[72] Accordingly, Calvin rejected allegorical exegesis since it violates the real sense of

---

67. Cited in Kraus, "Calvin's Exegetical Principles," p. 11 (*CR* 9.825).
68. See *CNTC* 8.1. On this dedication see also Girardin, *Rhétorique*, pp. 277–86.
69. See Parker, *Commentaries*, pp. 50ff.
70. *CNTC* 8.3.
71. See Parker, *Commentaries*, p. 51. Calvin saw his *Institutes* as a systematic arrangement of theological topics (*loci*). His commentaries he viewed as exegetical and expository material not suitable for the *Institutes*, the theological textbook. See Parker, *Commentaries*, p. 54.
72. *CNTC* 8.1.

Scripture.[73] It is the plain, genuine, natural, or literal sense of Scripture which Calvin sought to expound.[74]

As the Christian humanist scholar turned theologian, Calvin adapted his understanding of how ancient documents should be read to his study of Scripture. To gain insight into the mind or intention of an author, numerous factors must be weighed and considered. For Calvin this meant, with respect to a given passage, a study of the historical and geographical circumstances, the context (see 3.17.14), and the language employed, including special rhetorical forms such as metaphor, synecdoche, metonymy, and anthropomorphism.[75]

Calvin regarded investigation of all of these factors as crucial to an understanding of the meaning of a biblical passage or text. Yet the knowledge gained in this way is not enough. That is to say, Calvin's exegetical work was done with the thorough conviction that all such knowledge must point beyond itself toward Jesus Christ and the salvation found in Him. Jesus Christ is the object of faith and its goal (*scopum fidei* — 3.2.6), and all of Scripture must be interpreted in relation to its purpose of setting Him forth.[76] As Calvin wrote: "The best method of seeking God is to begin at his word"[77] and "the Scrip-

---

73. Calvin permitted only very limited use of allegorical interpretation, warning that it "ought not to go beyond the limits set by the rule of Scripture, let alone suffice as the foundation for any doctrines" (*Inst.* 2.5.19). See the note in the Library of Christian Classics edition, and Rogers and McKim, *Authority,* pp. 143–44, n. 278.

74. See Kraus, "Calvin's Exegetical Principles," p. 14, who identifies Calvin's "real meaning of a statement or a passage" as the original, true, simple, or grammatical meaning (*CR* 59.800; 59.177; *Inst.* 4.17.22). Calvin comments on Galatians 4:22 (*CNTC* 11.85): "Let us know, then, that the true meaning of Scripture is the natural and simple one (*verum sensum scripturae, qui germanus est et simplex*), and let us embrace and hold it resolutely. Let us not merely neglect as doubtful, but boldly set aside as deadly corruptions, those pretended expositions which lead us away from the literal sense (*a literali sensu*)." T. H. L. Parker remarks (*Commentaries,* p. 64): "There is, then, a *verus Scripturae sensus.* Scripture has an objective and constant meaning, and this is the *genuinus sensus,* the *germanus sensus,* the *simplex sensus,* the *literalis sensus.* The adjectives are big with meaning. *Genuinus* and *germanus* echo the objectivity and constancy of *verus*; all three also assert that this is an intended meaning. *Simplex* means more than 'simple.' Taking it as 'onefold,' in distinction to, say, *duplex,* we have an assertion that Scripture bears one sense only. *Literalis* anchors us firmly in the text. The meaning is contained in the words." Calvin also uses the phrase "the true and the natural sense" in his *Comm. on Ps.* 42:4.

75. See Kraus, "Calvin's Exegetical Principles," p. 17. Girardin has listed instances in the *Commentary on Romans* where Calvin makes note of rhetorical figures such as *amplificatio, anastrophe, hyperbole, metaphora, metonymia, periphrasis,* and *synecdoche* (*Rhétorique,* pp. 217–18). Cf. Forstman, *Word and Spirit,* p. 115.

76. See Kraus, "Calvin's Exegetical Principles," p. 17; and Rogers and McKim, *Authority,* pp. 106ff., on "Incarnational Interpretation of Scripture."

77. *Comm. on Gen.* 48:15 (CTS).

tures should be read with the aim of finding Christ in them."[78] The
Holy Spirit works in conjunction with the Word of God to make the
letter of Scripture alive; through the Spirit the text "shows forth Christ"
(1.9.3). Accommodating Himself to us in the incarnation by becoming
human and in Scripture by communicating through human words,
God represents Himself to us "not as he is in himself, but as he seems
to us" (1.17.13). "God is known truly and firmly only in Christ," said
Calvin,[79] and true knowledge of Christ comes when "we receive him
as he is offered by the Father: namely, clothed with his gospel" (3.2.6).
Calvin put it strikingly in a 1543 addition to his preface to Olivétan's
New Testament:

> This is what we should in short seek in the whole of Scripture: truly
> to know Jesus Christ, and the infinite riches that are comprised in
> him and are offered to us by him from God the Father. If one were to
> sift thoroughly the Law and the Prophets, he would not find a single
> word which would not draw and bring us to him. And for a fact, since
> all the treasures of wisdom and understanding are hidden in him,
> there is not the least question of having, or turning toward, another
> goal; not unless we would deliberately turn aside from the light of
> truth, to lose ourselves in the darkness of lies. Therefore, rightly does
> Saint Paul say in another passage that he would know nothing except
> Jesus Christ, and him crucified. And such knowledge although mean
> and contemptible to the mind of the flesh is nevertheless sufficient to
> occupy us all our lives. And we shall not waste our time if we employ
> all our study and apply all our understanding to profit from it. What
> more would we ask for, as spiritual doctrine for our souls, than to
> know God, to be converted (*transformez*) to him, and to have his
> glorious image imprinted in us, so that we may partake of his righ-
> teousness, to become heirs of his Kingdom and to possess it in the
> end in full? But the truth is that from the beginning God has given
> himself, and at present gives himself more fully, that we may contem-
> plate him in the face of his Christ. It is therefore not lawful that we
> turn away and become diverted even in the smallest degree by this or
> that. On the contrary, our minds ought to come to a halt at the point
> where we learn in Scripture to know Jesus Christ and him alone, so
> that we may be directly led by him to the Father who contains in
> himself all perfection.[80]

The living Word, Jesus Christ, is the One through whom the written
Word of Scripture is best interpreted.

---

78. *Comm. on John* 5:39 (*CNTC* 4.139; *CR* 47.125). Cf. Rogers and McKim,
Authority, p. 107.
79. *Comm. on Heb.* 1:3 (*CNTC* 12.8).
80. *Calvin: Commentaries*, ed. Haroutunian, p. 70.

4

Calvin on Universal and Particular Providence

Charles B. Partee

Plato teaches that men are the property (κτήματα) of the gods who are concerned about things both great and small.[1] However, Plato does not develop a doctrine of particular providence in any detail. Cicero seems to accept some kind of particular providence when he writes, "Nor is the care and providence of the immortal gods bestowed only upon the human race in its entirety, but it is also wont to be extended to individuals."[2] Still a few pages later he asserts, "The gods attend to great matters; they neglect small ones."[3] Like the philosophers Calvin affirms a universal providence, but his chief interest is to assert God's particular providence. Calvin's basic insight into God's care of His own and all things finds expression in both his doctrines of providence and predestination. Unlike the philosophers, Calvin's point of view is more concerned with the particularity of God's care rather than its universality, as this chapter seeks to demonstrate.

In the fourteenth chapter of the 1545 treatise, "Contre la secte phantastique et furieuse des Libertines qui se nomment spirituelz," Calvin says that we attribute to God an active power in all creatures. God created, governs, and maintains the world and disposes things as it seems good to Him. To express this view Calvin considers God's work in the government of the world under three aspects. First, there

Reprinted from *Calvin and Classical Philosophy* (Leiden: E. J. Brill, 1977), pp. 126–45. Used by permission.

1. *Laws,* 10.902b, 900c.
2. *De Natura Deorum,* 2.65.164.
3. Ibid., 2.66.167.

is a universal operation by which God conducts all creatures according to the condition and properties which He gives to each of them when they are formed. This direction is called the order of nature. Still unbelievers who view the disposition of the world and the constitution of nature as a goddess who rules over all do not give praise to the will of God who alone rules over all things. When believers see the sun, the moon, and the stars moving in their courses, they know that the command of God is directing them. This universal providence is often mentioned in Scripture to the end that the glory of God may be apprehended in all His works.

The second aspect of God's work in His creatures is that He extends His hand to help His servants and to punish the wicked. The pagans attribute to fortune what Christians assign to the providence of God — not alone to the universal providence — but to a special ordinance by which God directs all things as He sees it to be expedient. Thus prosperity and adversity, rain, wind, sleet, frost, fine weather, abundance, famine, war, and peace are works of the hand of God. The third aspect of the work of God consists in His governance of the faithful, living and reigning in them by His Holy Spirit. In spite of the fact that man's judgment is perverse, his will rebellious, and his nature vicious — God forms new hearts within them and by supernatural grace they are regenerated in a divine life.[4]

In his treatment of the same subject in *De aeterna praedestinatione Dei* Calvin writes, "We mean by providence not an idle observation by God in heaven of what goes on in earth, but his rule of the world which he has made, for he is not the creator of the moment, but the perpetual governor. Thus the providence we ascribe to God belongs not only to his eyes but to his hands." The fact that the sun daily rises, the stars orbit, the seasons recur, and the earth produces is to be ascribed solely to God's directing hand. However the knowledge of God's universal providence, Calvin says, is confused unless it is understood that God cares for individual creatures. In this special providence it is convenient to recognize certain distinct grades. God governs the human race by His providence but with different grades of direction. To make God's providence clear Calvin asserts God's general government of the world, then His care of particular parts so that everything happens by God's will, then His particular care of the human race and finally His protection of the church.[5]

Étienne de Peyer thinks, "General Providence gives to human na-

---

4. *Contre la secte phantastique et furieuse des Libertines qui se nomment spirituelz,* CO 7.186–90.

5. *Concerning Eternal Predestination,* pp. 162–64 (CO 8.348–49).

ture its plenitude and completion. Particular Providence directs the effects of this nature. Saving Providence brings to man the elements of a new nature or of nature restored. . . ."[6] De Peyer believes that particular providence is identical with common grace.[7] Thus he outlines Calvin's doctrine of providence as (1) general providence; (2) particular providence or common grace; and (3) special providence or saving grace.

Calvin does discuss general or universal providence and special or particular providence, also general or common grace and special grace, but Calvin does not work out the implications of the doctrines of providence and grace in the terms which de Peyer suggests. Krusche is correct in saying that Calvin's conceptualization of common grace is not uniform.[8] Calvin's basic distinction however is two-fold rather than tripartite. Thus common grace ought to be associated with universal providence and special grace with particular providence, though it should be noted that Calvin does not refer to common grace in the quotation above.

A great deal of attention has been given to the doctrine of common grace by some Calvin scholars.[9] They expand, schematize, and *distort* Calvin's cautious remarks on the closely related topics of natural or general revelation, universal providence, and common grace. Hermann Bavinck, for example, writes, "[Calvin] found the will of God revealed not merely in Scripture, but also in the world, and he traced the connection and sought to restore the harmony between them."[10] Bav-

6. Étienne de Peyer, "Calvin's Doctrine of Providence," *The Evangelical Quarterly* 10 (1938): 37.

7. Ibid., p. 35.

8. Werner Krusche, *Das Wirken des Heiligen Geistes nach Calvin* (Göttingen: Vandenhoeck and Ruprecht, 1957), p. 100, n. 395. Krusche discusses *gratia generalis,* pp. 95f.

9. Abraham Kuyper, *De Gemeene Gratie,* 3 vols. (Pretoria: Hoveker and Wormser, 1902–1904); Hermann Bavinck, *De Algemeene Genade* (Kampen: G. Ph. Zalsman, 1894); Herman Kuiper, *Calvin on Common Grace* (Grand Rapids: Smitter, 1928); Cornelius Van Til, *Common Grace* (Philadelphia: Presbyterian and Reformed, 1947); H. Henry Meeter, *Calvinism: An Interpretation of Its Basic Ideas* (Grand Rapids: Zondervan, 1939), pp. 69–77. See also William Masselink, *General Revelation and Common Grace* (Grand Rapids: Eerdmans, 1953) — chapter 5 on common grace, chapter 7 on Calvinistic philosophy. See also the essay by A. Lecerf, "Le protestantisme et la philosophie," in *Études Calvinistes* (Paris: Delachaux et Niestle, 1949), pp. 107–13; and J. M. Spier, *What Is Calvinistic Philosophy?* trans. Fred H. Klooster (Grand Rapids: Eerdmans, 1953), and William Young, *Toward a Reformed Philosophy* (Grand Rapids: Piet Hein, 1952).

10. Hermann Bavinck, "Calvin and Common Grace," *Calvin and the Reformation* (New York: Revell, 1909), p. 128. Quirinus Breen, *John Calvin: A Study in French Humanism* (Hamden, Conn.: Archon, 1968), pp. 165ff., adds a new chapter to his

inck also remarks, "Though this gracious and omnipotent will of God is made known in the gospel alone and experienced in faith only, nevertheless it does not stand isolated, but is encompassed, supported and reinforced by the operation of the same will in the world at large. Special grace is encircled by common grace. . . ."[11]

In Bavinck's treatment common grace seems to be the presupposition of special grace. However Calvin does not make special grace depend on common grace nor special providence depend on universal providence. On the contrary, Calvin's main purpose is to insist that God does not sit idly in heaven but governs the world and that the doctrine of universal providence is only a partial understanding of God's providence. Therefore in discussing God's special providence, which he is chiefly concerned to emphasize, Calvin also treats common grace and universal providence. Calvin writes, "The sun discovers to our eyes the most beautiful theater of the earth and heaven and the whole order of nature, but God has visibly displayed the chief glory of his work in his Son."[12] According to Calvin the first of the distinct powers of the Son of God appears in the architecture of the world and in the order of nature and the second in the renewal and restoration of fallen nature. Man lost the light of understanding by the fall, but he still sees and understands because what he naturally possessed from the grace of the Son of God is not entirely destroyed.[13]

The purpose of Calvin's discussion of universal providence is not to define a common ground or territory between the believer and the unbeliever, but to insist that the whole order of nature is the result of the special providence of God. God does not govern by chance or a general operation in nature but by His special providence. It is true that the whole order of nature serves the will of God,[14] but God can do more than nature,[15] and His command changes the order of nature.[16] In the Genesis Commentary, Calvin remarks that Joseph errs

---

second edition defending the doctrine of common grace although his source, Herman Kuiper, *Calvin on Common Grace* (Grand Rapids: Smitter, 1928), pp. 177–78, professes to be able to find the term used by Calvin only four times: *Comm. on Amos* 9:7 (*CO* 43.164); *Comm. on Col.* 1:20 (*CO* 52.89); *Comm. on Heb.* 1:5 (*CO* 55.15); and *Comm. on Rom.* 5:18 (*CO* 49.101). These usages are not uniform nor technical and Calvin's comment in Romans makes the opposite point: "Paul makes grace common to all men, *not because it in fact extends to all*, but because it is offered to all." Emphasis added.

11. Bavinck, "Calvin and Common Grace," p. 126.
12. *Comm. on John* 9:5 (*CO* 47.220).
13. *Comm. on John* 1:5 (*CO* 47.7).
14. *Comm. on 2 Peter* 3:5 (*CO* 55.473–74).
15. As in the birth of John the Baptist, *Comm. on Luke* 1:18 (*CO* 45.18f.).
16. *Comm. on Zech.* 10:11 (*CO* 44.298).

in binding the grace of God to the order of nature as if God does not often purposely change the law of nature in order to teach that what He freely confers upon man is entirely the result of His will.[17] It is God who withholds rain, then pours it down in profusion; He burns the corn with heat, then He tempers the air; now He shows Himself kindly toward men, now angry with them.[18] Thus God deals with His people both in an ordinary and common way and also in a wonderful and miraculous way.[19] It is true that God's daily and common ways are so many miracles, but they seem less wonderful because they are naturally comprehended.[20] When God fed the people, as recorded in Numbers 11, He raised a wind which was a miracle, but God did not cast aside the assistance of nature since He made use of the wind. God also took an herb which ascended to a great height and surpassed the usual course of nature in order to provide a covering for Jonah. The same thing applies to the preparation of the worm which did not happen by chance, but was governed by the hidden providence of God.[21]

Calvin admits that the carnal sense has some noetic value, but faith should not be content with a certain universal motion but understand God's particular providence (*singulari quadam providentia*),[22] and it is upon this particular providence that Calvin chiefly insists. Forstmann is correct in saying that in the section on providence Calvin approaches more nearly the tone of ecstasy than at any other point in the *Institutes*.[23] According to Calvin the knowledge of God's providence is the highest blessedness.[24] Since God's providence is a "rampart of defense,"[25] Calvin objects to the idea of separating creation from providence and understanding providence as the provision of a kind of neutral context for life rather than as God's special care for all that He had created. God's care is experienced by His children and He provides for all things.[26] It is therefore only a partial understanding of providence to attribute to God a general governance of the beginning

17. *Comm. on Gen.* 48:17 (*CO* 23.586).
18. *Comm. on Amos* 4:9 (*CO* 43.62) refers to special providence not a general motion: "Discamus ergo totum naturae ordinem referre ad specialem Dei providentiam."
19. *Comm. on Ps.* 17:7 (*CO* 31.162): God deems only the elect worthy of special grace.
20. *Comm. on Hab.* 3:6 (*CO* 43.572–73).
21. *Comm. on Jonah* 4:6–8 (*CO* 43.275).
22. *Inst.* 1.16.1 (*OS* 3.187.27–28; 188.1–7).
23. H. J. Forstmann, *Word and Spirit* (Stanford: Stanford University, 1962), p. 98.
24. *Inst.* 1.17.11 (*OS* 3.216.27–30).
25. *Comm. on Ps.* 35:22 (*CO* 31.356).
26. *Comm. on Ps.* 25:9 (*CO* 31.255); cf. *Comm. on Ps.* 28:5 (*CO* 31.283–84).

and origin of things without including specific direction of the individual creatures.

Calvin recognizes that in the sense of universal providence many acknowledge that all creatures are governed by God. They consider that man moves by his own free will because God continues the power which He once bestowed. "Their false explanation amounts to this, that the whole machinery of the world is upheld by the hand of God, but that his providence is not interposed to regulate particular movements." What they leave to God is hardly a thousandth part of the government He claims. "Justly, therefore, does Isaiah show that God presides over individual acts, as they call them, so as to move men, like rods, in whatever way he pleases, to guide their plans, to direct their efforts; and, in a word, to regulate their determinations, in order to inform us that everything depends on his providence, and not on the caprice of wicked man."[27]

Calvin could scarcely be more explicit on his view of the place of universal providence. Calvin says that he does not wholly repudiate the doctrine of universal providence provided it is granted that God rules the universe by watching over the order of nature and exercising special care over each of His works.[28] The doctrine of universal providence, Calvin thinks, could leave no place for God's mercy and judgment while the chief thing to believe is that God directs everything to His own end so that all things proceed from His plan and nothing happens by chance.[29] Whatever happens in the universe is governed by God's incomprehensible plans,[30] which the faithful understand from the experience of divine protection.[31]

Calvin believes that God's will is the cause of causes,[32] and that all things are directly governed by God's will which is the source of law and reason and the final appeal of justice.[33] This position is made abundantly clear in the *Institutes*. Calvin rejects

> the opinion of those who imagine a universal providence of God, which does not stoop to the especial care of any particular creature,

27. *Comm. on Isa.* 10:15 (*CO* 36.222).
28. *Inst.* 1.16.4 (*OS* 3.194.9–13).
29. *Inst.* 1.16.4 (*OS* 3.194.27–29). Cf. *Comm. on Joel* 2:11 (*CO* 42.540–41) and *Comm. on Isa.* 7:19 (*CO* 36.161): "nihil temere aut fortuito accidere, sed omnia regi manu Dei."
30. *Inst.* 1.17.2 (*OS* 3.204.9–11).
31. *Comm. on Ps.* 3:6 (*CO* 31.56).
32. *Comm. on Gen.* 25:29 (*CO* 23.354); cf. Plato, *Epinomis,* 983b; also Seneca, *Naturales Quaestiones,* 1.1.13; *Inst.* 3.23.8 (*OS* 4.402.19–20) quoting Augustine.
33. *Comm. on Dan.* 4:34 (*CO* 40.685).

yet first of all it is important that we recognize this special care toward us. Whence Christ, when he declared that not even a tiny sparrow of little worth falls to earth without the Father's will, immediately applies it in this way: that since we are of greater value than sparrows, we ought to realize that God watches over us with all the closer care; and he extends it so far that we may trust the hairs of our head are numbered. What else can we wish for ourselves, if not even one hair can fall from our head without his will? I speak not only concerning mankind; but, because God has chosen the church to be his dwelling place, there is no doubt that he shows by singular proofs his fatherly care in ruling it.[34]

Though Calvin left his major discussion of the church until book four of the *Institutes* he points out even in the first book that the providence of God is concerned to maintain the church. Thus the basic understanding of God's providence is not a neutral common grace, but the conviction that God has power to protect the faithful. This means that every success is to be regarded as God's blessing and every calamity as His curse, so that even the evils visited upon the faithful belong to God.[35] Calvin admits that this position was not without perplexity. To say that Judas was governed by God's providence and was yet guilty was offensive to human reason.[36] However since God is just, men should not debate with Him.[37]

Calvin affirms a universal providence, but he does not seek to find in God's universal providence a common ground between believers and unbelievers. Calvin does not develop a "world view" in which the doctrine of universal providence could be isolated and treated as the presupposition of an anthropology, epistemology, or apologetics. It is true that Calvin thinks that unbelievers are without excuse for not worshiping God and that God's activity is not entirely curtailed by

34. *Inst.* 1.17.6 (*OS* 3.209.34–35; 210.1–13).

35. Calvin makes this point in 1.17.7–8 (*OS* 3.210–12) and often in the Commentaries. For example, *Comm. on Dan.* 9:14 (*CO* 41.151): "In this passage we are taught to recognize God's providence in both prosperity and adversity, for the purpose of stirring us up to be grateful for his benefits, while his punishments ought to produce humility. For when any one explains these things by fortune or chance, he thereby proves his ignorance of the existence of God, or at least the kind of God we worship."

36. *Comm. on Matt.* 26:24 (*CO* 45.702).

37. See sermon on Job 9:1–6 (*CO* 33.406–18). For a contemporary account of the same idea see George Dennis O'Brien, "Prolegomena to a Dissolution to the Problem of Suffering," *Harvard Theological Review* 57 (Oct. 1964): 301–23. O'Brien says, "The monarch cannot consider the formulation of a justification which goes beyond the assertion of his will without suggesting that there is some standard to which he appeals" (pp. 308–09).

unbelief, but he does not use the doctrine of universal providence as a neutral beginning place for all men. God does indeed sustain all men through the power of His Spirit, but Calvin's doctrine of providence is based on God's direct care of the believers.

Calvin not only makes a distinction between general and special providence, he also makes a distinction between general and special election. In commenting on Hosea 12:3 Calvin says that Jacob was *specially* elect and his seed *generally* elect in that God offered His covenant to them. Nonetheless, they were not all regenerated since they were not given the spirit of adoption.[38] The stages of election are more fully expounded in the Commentary on Malachi. In the first place God was pleased to create us men rather than animals. In the second place, although the whole world was under His government, He chose the seed of Abraham. This election was not made on the basis of merit but on the gratuitous love of God. In the third place God selected only a part of the seed of Abraham. Thus God made a distinction between the sons of Abraham, rejecting some and choosing others. The fourth stage is the acceptance of some of the sons of Jacob and the rejection of others. If it is asked why some are faithful and others are reprobate, the only answer is that it pleased God. Abraham was chosen by God in preference to all other nations; Isaac was preferred to Ishmael and Jacob to Esau.

Calvin admits that the scriptural account may seem harsh — that God chooses some and not all, but to object is to attempt to restrain God's will by human judgment. Since the Scripture teaches that after the fall of Adam all are lost and that the election of God is prior to Adam's fall, then all who are saved are chosen in Christ before the creation of the world. God appoints Christ the head of the church so that those who are chosen might be saved in Him.[39] Calvin maintains that it is not entirely unprofitable to be generally elect since this general election is intermediate between the rejection of mankind and the election of the godly.[40] Still, Calvin insists that God's free election is fully explained only when we come to individual persons to whom God not only offers salvation but also the certainty of salvation.[41] This certainty of faith does not result from the acuteness of the human mind but from the illumination of the Spirit. Predestination cannot be examined by the faculties of man, but a certain and clear knowledge is to be gained by the grace of the Holy Spirit.[42]

38. *Comm. on Hos.* 12:3 (*CO* 42.454f.).
39. *Comm. on Mal.* 1:2–6 (*CO* 44.401f.).
40. *Inst.* 3.21.7 (*OS* 4.378.9–10).
41. *Inst.* 3.21.7 (*OS* 4.377.21–22).
42. *Comm. on Rom.* 11:34 (*CO* 49.231).

God's care for believers is the basis of both the doctrines of providence and predestination. However it is not easy to specify the relation between the doctrine of providence and of predestination in Calvin's theology. The problem is whether predestination is an aspect of the doctrine of providence or whether providence is a part of the doctrine of predestination or are they two similar but separate doctrines?

This topic has long been the subject of debate. Alexander Schweizer sees predestination as the central dogma of Reformed Christianity.[43] Against this view Albrecht Ritschl argues that while the doctrine of predestination is a very important appendage (*Anhängsel*) to Calvin's doctrine of redemption, it does not control Calvin's system. "It bears a near analogy to his basic doctrine (*Stammlehre*) of providence through the application to both areas of the causal omnipotence of God."[44] Bohatec observes that the doctrines of providence and predestination stand in closest connection and that most researchers grant that Calvin's doctrine of providence is the theological basis of his doctrine of predestination.[45] According to Doumergue, the three doctrines of providence, bondage of the will, and predestination are characteristic of the theology of the Reformation.[46] Doumergue argues that "the doctrine of predestination is a particular doctrine, inseparable from the general doctrine of providence."[47] Seeberg agrees, "Thus the doctrine of predestination is most closely connected with the concept of omnipotent providence for Calvin. Indeed, it is actually only a special

43. Alexander Schweizer, *Die Protestantischen Centraldogmen in ihrer Entwicklung innerhalb der Reformierten Kirche* (Zurich: Orell, Fuessli, 1854), vol. 1, p. 57. In like manner Otto Ritschl, *Dogmengeschichte des Protestantismus* (Göttingen: Vandenhoeck and Ruprecht, 1926), vol. 3, pp. 156–98, believes that "the thought of predestination has overwhelming significance for the other doctrines of Christian dogmatics." A. M. Hunter, *The Teaching of Calvin* (London: James Clarke, 1950), says that providence is the experiential side of the divine decrees. Predestination is the metaphysical side of the divine decrees (p. 93). That is, providence is the activity of God by which he works out the predestinating decrees (p. 136).

44. Albrecht Ritschl, "Geschichtliche Studien zur Christlichen Lehre von Gott," *Jahrbücher für Deutsche Theologie* (1868): 108.

45. J. Bohatec, "Calvins Vorsehungslehre," *Calvinstudien* (Leipzig: Rudolf Haupt, 1909), p. 394. Paul Jacobs, *Prädestination und Verantwortlichkeit bei Calvin* (Neukirchen Kreis Moers: Buchhandlung des Erziehungsvereins, 1937), p. 69, writes that "Predestination is a type of special providence and would be subordinate to formal providence." Hans Emil Weber, *Reformation, Orthodoxie, und Rationalismus,* 2nd ed. (Darmstadt: Wissenschaftliche Buchgesellschaft, 1966 [1937]), vol. 1, p. 243, says that Calvin and Luther and Melanchthon regard predestination and providence together.

46. Emile Doumergue, *Jean Calvin: Les hommes et les choses de son temps,* 7 vols. (Lausanne: G. Bridel, 1897–1927), vol. 4, p. 155.

47. Ibid., 354. However Doumergue devotes only 7 pages (111–18) to providence and under the doctrine of God and 65 pages in a separate section to predestination (351–416).

case of the latter or its application to the empirical fact that there are sinners who believe and are saved and others who do not believe and are therefore lost."[48] Otten correctly states that "Calvin in his treatment of predestination never starts from the doctrine of God so that he would perhaps construct the gracious election from the idea of sovereignty and sole efficacy of God, but rather predestination is for him a part of soteriology."[49] Likewise, Dowey, in dealing with the two-fold knowledge of God as Creator and Redeemer, rightly insists on the importance of Calvin's location of the doctrine of predestination within his soteriology.[50] In the same direction, Werner Krusche writes:

> The Holy Spirit is the author of providence and (since very special providence [providentia specialissima] equals predestination) the author of the doctrine of predestination. He is the first as the Spirit of the Eternal Son, the second as the Spirit of the Mediator Jesus Christ. The position of the doctrine of providence and predestination in the last edition of the Institutes shows this most clearly. Since it is the Spirit of the Eternal Word which brings the action of divine providence to fruition (Wirkung), the doctrine of providence can be developed in connection with the doctrine of the Trinity. Since it is the Spirit of the Mediator Jesus Christ, who makes the action of God's election efficacious, the doctrine of predestination must form the conclusion of Christology and Pneumatology.[51]

The obvious conclusion to be drawn from this discussion is that Calvin's understanding of God's government of the world and His care of His own are closely related to each other and crucial to his theology. The basic conviction of God's loving concern finds expression in both the doctrine of providence and predestination. However, although Calvin deals with both universal and special providence and general and individual election, his standpoint — unlike the philosophers — is the particularity of God's care. That is to say, Calvin treats the universal aspect of God's work, but his point of view is from God's particular

---

48. Reinhold Seeberg, Lehrbuch der Dogmengeschichte, 5th ed. (Basel: Benno Schwabe, 1960), vol. 4.2, p. 580. Reviews of this discussion are found in Max Scheibe, Calvins Prädestinationslehre (Halle: Max Niemeyer, 1897), pp. 1–5; in Jacobs, Prädestination und Verantwortlichkeit bei Calvin, pp. 15–40; and Heinz Otten, Calvins theologische Anschauung von der Prädestination (Munich: Chr. Kaiser, 1938), pp. 7–15.

49. Ibid., p. 87.

50. Edward A. Dowey, Jr., The Knowledge of God in Calvin's Theology (New York: Columbia University, 1965), p. 222.

51. Krusche, Das Wirken des Heiligen Geistes nach Calvin, p. 14.

work. This fact may be seen in the *development* of the doctrines of predestination and providence.

There are three discernible stages in Calvin's exposition of the doctrines of providence and predestination in the *Institutes*. In the first edition of 1536 providence is treated as part of the belief in God the Father Almighty, Creator of heaven and earth. Calvin writes,

> By this we confess that we have all our trust fixed in God the Father, whom we acknowledge to be Creator of ourselves and of absolutely all things that have been created, which have been established by the Word, his eternal Wisdom (who is the Son), and by his Power (who is the Holy Spirit). And, as he once established, so now he sustains, nourishes, activates, preserves, by his goodness and power, apart from which all things would immediately collapse and fall into nothingness. But when we call him almighty and creator of all things, we must ponder such omnipotence of his whereby he works all things in all, and such providence whereby he regulates all things — not of the sort those Sophists fancy: empty, insensate, idle. By faith are we to be persuaded that whatever happens to us, happy or sad, prosperous or adverse, whether it pertains to the body or to the soul, comes to us from him (sin only being excepted, which is to be imputed to our own wickedness); also by his protection we are kept safe, defended, and preserved from any unfriendly force causing us harm. In short, nothing comes forth from him to us (since we receive all things from his hand) which is not conducive to our welfare, howsoever things may commonly seem at one time prosperous, at another adverse. Indeed all these things are done to us by him, not through any worth of ours, nor by any merit to which he owes this grace, not because we can force his beneficence to make any reciprocal payment. Rather it is through his fatherly kindness and mercy that he has to do with us, the sole cause of which is his goodness. For this reason, we must take care to give thanks for this very great goodness of his, to ponder it with our hearts, proclaim it with our tongue, and to render such praises as we are able. We should so reverence such a Father with grateful piety and burning love, as to devote ourselves wholly to his service, and honor him in all things. We should also so receive all adverse things with calm and peaceful hearts, as if from his hand, thinking that his providence so also looks after us and our salvation while it is afflicting and oppressing us. Therefore whatever may finally happen, we are never to doubt or lose faith that we have in him a propitious and benevolent Father, and no less are to await salvation from him.[52]

52. John Calvin, *Institution of the Christian Religion* (1536), trans. and annotated by Ford Lewis Battles (Atlanta: John Knox, 1975), pp. 66–67 (*OS* 1.75–76).

Calvin teaches here that God does not merely create, but sustains the created order in being by His providence. His omnipotence must therefore be understood not as an empty power, but in such a way that the faithful acknowledge that whatever happens, good or bad, comes from God, who is good and is concerned for their welfare and salvation.

In the first edition, predestination or election is treated in connection with the doctrine of the church. Calvin says that "we believe the holy catholic church — that is, the whole number of the elect, whether angels or men. . . ." They are called "to be one church and society, and one people of God. Of it, Christ our Lord is Leader and Ruler, and as it were Head of the one body; according as through divine goodness, they have been chosen in him before the foundation of the world, in order that all might be gathered into God's Kingdom." Calvin uses election and providence together in his comment that the church is holy "because as many as have been chosen [electus] by God's eternal providence to be adopted as members of the church — all these are made holy by the Lord."[53] However Calvin insists that it is not proper to judge those who are outside the church or to distinguish between the elect and the reprobate since this is the exclusive prerogative of God.[54] This is the first stage.

In his *Loci Communes* (1535) Melanchthon says that the topic of predestination is useless and confusing,[55] but Calvin in his edition of 1539 emphasizes the importance of the doctrines of predestination and providence by devoting a separate chapter to the subject. This is also the order used in the polemical situation which called forth *De aeterna praedestinatione Dei* (1552), and Calvin is still treating providence and predestination together in *Calumniae nebulonis cuiusdam quibus odio et invidia gravare conatus est doctrinam de occulta Dei providentia, et ad easdem responsio* (1558). Calvin defends his doctrine of predestination at greater length than his doctrine of providence, although his conclusions on predestination are already contained in his view of particular providence. In the 1539 edition of the *Institutes* at the beginning of chapter seven on the similarities and differences between the Old and New Testaments, Calvin says that he has expounded the sum of Christian doctrine which consists in the knowledge of God and ourselves. Now he intends to add an article (vice appendix) to establish the truth of the doctrine taught, i.e. that those

53. Ibid., pp. 78–79 (OS 1.86).
54. Ibid., p. 82 (OS 1.88).
55. Philip Melanchthon, Loci Communes, CR 21.452.

whom God called before the foundation of the world into the company of His people attain a certain grace and are united to God.[56]

Calvin begins chapter eight on the predestination and providence of God by remarking that the covenant of life is not equally preached to all and where it is preached it is not equally received. The exterior preaching of the gospel is offered to all, but there is a special interior illumination of the Holy Spirit which the faithful receive. Some men accept the gospel and others reject it. This diversity of response is referred to God's good pleasure. The doctrine of predestination is a mystery of divine wisdom, but those who are predestined are illuminated to salvation. Calvin formally defines predestination as follows:

> Predestination we call the eternal decree of God by which he has determined in himself what he willed to become of each man. For all are not created on equal terms; rather eternal life is foreordained for some and eternal damnation for others. Therefore as any man has been created for one or the other of these ends, we speak of him as predestined to life or to death.[57]

This definition is not changed from 1539 to the final edition; its purpose, according to Calvin, is not to drive men to despair or to curious speculations, but to exalt the grace of God and to deny the saving efficacy of merits. Predestination "builds up faith soundly, trains us to humility, elevates us to admiration of the immense goodness of God towards us, and excites us to praise this goodness."[58] In the *Congrégation sur l'Élection Éternelle de Dieu,* Calvin writes, "God has chosen us — that means not only before we knew him but before the world was created: and that he elected us by his gratuitous goodness, and that he has not sought any other cause; that he deliberated this proposal by itself, and it is necessary that we know that, in order that he be glorified by us as he deserves."[59] Thus the salvation of the faithful is founded on grace and not acquired by works. Jacob and Esau were equal except that God chose one and rejected the other. In the 1539 edition the doctrine of providence *follows* the discussion of predestination. Providence is defined as the order by which God governs the world and guides all things. Providence is not merely a matter of prescience, or a general government, but God's determining what He will do by His wisdom and executing it by His power.

56. *CO* 1.801.
57. *CO* 1.865; *Inst.* 3.21.5 (*OS* 4.374.11–17).
58. *Concerning Eternal Predestination,* p. 56 (*CO* 8.260).
59. *Congrégation sur l'Élection Éternelle de Dieu, CO* 8.103.

The third stage in the development of the doctrines of providence and predestination is reached in the final edition of the *Institutes*. Here the main exposition of providence *precedes* the treatment of predestination though Calvin does not explain why. Providence is placed in book one as part of the doctrine of creation (returning to its location in the 1536 edition) while the doctrine of predestination is placed in book three (before the development of the doctrine of the church) as part of the perception of the grace of Christ.

On this arrangement Wendel comments, "Just as the doctrine of providence placed at the conclusion of the doctrine of God might be said to complete the latter as the keystone finishes an arch, so also does the doctrine of predestination complete and illuminate the whole of the account of redemption."[60] However to be entirely accurate, the main exposition of providence concludes book one of the *Institutes* which deals with the knowledge of God the Creator. Book two deals with the knowledge of God the Redeemer (except for chapters 1–5 which deal with sin), but it is important to recognize that the doctrine of predestination is found at the end of book three (except for the chapter on the resurrection of the body).

This location does not deny the centrality of the doctrine of Christ for the doctrine of election since predestination is now formally and materially part of the understanding of salvation, but it certainly indicates that predestination is not the basic doctrine from which Calvin deduces a theological system. As Victor Monod finely writes, "The Calvinistic predestination certainly did not come from an effort of logical and abstract systematization; it is for Calvin a point of arrival, not a point of departure; a necessary hypothesis, not a principle of explication. The doctrine of election is the imperfect intellectual product of a humble and living faith."[61] The importance of the discussion

60. François Wendel, *Calvin: The Origins and Development of His Religious Thought* (New York: Harper and Row, 1963), p. 268.

61. Victor Monod, "La Prédestination Calviniste," *Foi et Vie* (1909): 645. H. Bois disagrees. In "La prédestination d'après Calvin," *Études sur la Réforme* (Paris: Librairie Armand Colin, 1919), pp. 674f., he argues that predestination is not a doctrine of experience, but a deduction from omnipotence. Providence and predestination are not based on the facts of experience but experience interpreted by certain principles such as (1) the negation of works, (2) the certainty of salvation and most especially (3) the sovereignty of God (p. 678). Predestination is the dogmatic formulation of the idea of the sovereignty of God (p. 679). According to Carla Calvetti, *La filosofia di Giovanni Calvino* (Milan: Società editrice vita e pensiero, 1955), pp. 264–65, predestination is the inevitable logical consequence of the philosophic conception of the absolute sovereignty of God which issues in an essentially irrationalistic pantheism. Maurice Neeser, *Le Dieu de Calvin* (Neuchâtel: Secrétariat de l'Université, 1956), in his highly critical treatment of Calvin's doctrine of providence and predestination

of predestination in book three of the final edition of the *Institutes* should not be minimized, but neither should the close connection between special providence and predestination be forgotten.

In broad terms providence is concerned with God's work and will in creation, while predestination is concerned with God's work and will in redemption. As Otten observes, "The object of providence is accordingly man as creature and his world. The object of predestination is man as sinner and his eternal destination."[62] However, Calvin does not make a sharp distinction between providence and predestination.[63] The same God who elects by His providence also provides for His elect. Thus God, in His special or particular providence, takes care of the believers.[64] If God's particular providence for the believer is not identical with predestination, the doctrines are at least complementary since God is both Creator and Redeemer. Otten makes this point by saying that the unity of providence and predestination is analogous to the unity of God as Creator and Redeemer.[65] Therefore Calvin's doctrine of God's providence in creation cannot be fully expounded apart from God's providence in redemption. The philosophers understood something of the former, but nothing of the latter, as we have seen.

(parts 2 and 3) does not deal with the philosophers and in exalting God as the absolute ignores the fact that Calvin rejected the scholastic notion of *potentia absoluta* (3.23.2 [*OS* 4.396.17]) and considered God's providence and predestination primarily in terms of God's grace rather than His power. Neeser pictures Calvin as logically rigorous rather than trying to struggle to be faithful to the Scriptures. On the *potentia absoluta* see Wendel, *Calvin: The Origins and Development of His Religious Thought*, pp. 127f. Doumergue, *Jean Calvin*, vol. 4, p. 358, agrees with Monod that Calvin's doctrine of predestination is a posteriori and based on experience rather than a priori. Kemper Fullerton, "Calvinism and Capitalism," *Harvard Theological Review* 21 (1928): 172, repeats the ideas that for Calvin God is absolute will which issues in the intellectualized doctrine of the double decrees, in effect denying the roles of experience and emotion. "In other words, Calvinism as a system, though it starts from an irrational conception of God, is worked out in a thoroughly rationalistic way. . . ." A sounder view is found in B. A. Gerrish, " 'To the Unknown God': Luther and Calvin on the Hiddenness of God," *The Journal of Religion* 53.3 (July 1973): 284, who remarks that "although talk about eternal decrees has the sound of rampant speculation, the doctrine of election is in fact woven into the fabric of human experience."

62. Otten, *Calvins theologische Anschauung von der Prädestination*, p. 111. S. Leigh Hunt, "Predestination in the 'Institutes of the Christian Religion,' 1536–1559," *Evangelical Quarterly* 9 (1937): 38–45, makes a distinction between general and particular predestination. Eternal predestination in the sense of government of the world is the same as eternal providence, "the execution of which is actual providence in time" (p. 39).

63. In addition to the 1539 statement (n. 57) see 3.23.3 (*OS* 4.397.4–5); 5 (398.26); 6 (400.8); 8 (402.38); 9 (403.32).

64. 1.17.6 (*OS* 3.209.21–24).

65. Otten, *Calvins theologische Anschauung von der Prädestination*, p. 111.

Although Calvin makes a distinction between universal and particular providence and general and special election, he does not work out a careful view of the relation between God's universal providence for all mankind and His general election of the fathers, or between God's particular providence for Christians and His special election of them. Calvin affirms both a universal providence and a general election, but his chief interest is in particular providence or individual election.

In the final edition of the *Institutes* Calvin deals with providence as part of the understanding of creation, and predestination — not as part of the doctrine of God — but as part of the understanding of the benefits of Christ. However it must be admitted that Calvin does not distinguish between special providence and predestination. His insistence that election (which is a gift of God) precedes faith (which is also a gift of God) leaves the possibility open of relocating the doctrine of predestination in the doctrine of God (as his followers do[66]) rather than in the doctrine of salvation as part of the understanding of the gift of faith (as he himself does). Calvin says, "We see that faith proceeds from the sole election of God, that is to say, that God illumines those whom he had chosen by this gratuitous goodness before the creation of the world."[67] However, "we shall never understand this mystery here and a secret so high and so excellent except by having the meekness to say: Well, if we do not see the reason why God acts thusly, there is so much that it should be sufficient to us that he is just; and on that to profit always in the knowledge of his will."[68]

Calvin believes that his doctrine of predestination is scriptural and Augustinian.[69] Thus he writes against Westphal that he does not begin

66. Weber, *Reformation, Orthodoxie, und Rationalismus,* p. 240, writes, "One may certainly not say that Calvin derived his theology out of his doctrine of predestination as it is done by the Calvinistic scholastics."

67. *Congrégation sur l'Élection Éternelle de Dieu, CO* 8.96.

68. Ibid., 106.

69. Luchesius Smits, *Saint Augustin dans l'oeuvre de Calvin* (Assen: van Gorcum, 1957), vol. 1, p. 109, characterizes the 1559 edition as the *Institutes* of predestination. For Calvin's relation to Augustine see pp. 45f., 61f., and 104f. Reg. Garrigou-Lagrange, *La Prédestination des Saints et la Grâce* (Paris: Declée de Brouwer, 1935), p. 136, believes that Calvin surpasses Luther and Zwingli in drawing logical conclusions and emphasizes the differences between Calvin and Thomas. J. B. Mozley, *A Treatise on the Augustinian Doctrine of Predestination,* 2nd ed. (New York: Dutton, 1878), p. 267 and n. 21, pp. 393f., sees no substantial difference between Augustine, Thomas, and Calvin on the doctrine of predestination. It is true that Calvin thought that he was correcting rather than changing the Christian doc-

with predestination but with the Word,[70] and warns that in investigating predestination one must not go beyond the oracles of God.[71] The Scripture teaches that God chooses Jacob and rejects Esau. Jacob does not differ from Esau in terms of merit, which demonstrates that God chooses on the basis of His mercy alone. Calvin remarks in a sermon on Jacob and Esau that God does not choose on the basis of our beautiful eyes (*quand Dieu élit, ce n'est pas pour nos beaux yeux*).[72] Thus of two men, indistinguishable in merit, God chooses one and rejects the other. God's unmerited grace shows mercy where He wills and God's merited punishment judges where He wills. "The predestination of God is truly a labyrinth from which the mind of man is wholly incapable of extricating itself."[73] This fact does not mean the doctrine should be passed over in silence since it is revealed in Scripture, but Calvin cautions that one should not seek to know more about the subject than the Scripture teaches. The salvation or destruction of men depends on God's free election. In the case of the elect one is invited to contemplate the gracious mercy of God and in the case of the reprobate to acknowledge His righteous judgment. God is not indebted to any man and His kindness is free to bestow where He pleases. Therefore no higher reason than God's will can be suggested to account for election.

---

trine of predestination. It is also true that these thinkers each deny that God is responsible for evil and affirm that man is responsible for sin. However Calvin criticized Thomas on his view of predestination to grace (3.22.9 [*OS* 4.389.31f.]) and went beyond Augustine in the clarity with which he dealt with reprobation. C. Friethoff, "Die Prädestinationslehre bei Thomas von Aquin und Calvin," *Divus Thomas* 3.4 (1926): 71–91, 195–206, 280–302, 445–46, deals carefully with the similarities and differences between Thomas and Calvin. According to Friethoff there is a significant agreement between Thomas and Calvin concerning God's sovereignty that God's foreknowledge of the good works of man is not the cause or occasion of predestination to blessedness, but rather that predestination to blessedness is the cause of good works. However, there is an irreconcilable difference that according to Thomas, God arranged that men receive eternal salvation as the reward of merits which is earned by grace. Calvin denies the meritorious character of works and asserts that man comes into the possession of eternal life only through the stages of good works (p. 206). Calvin insists that reward to good works means that by these stages of His mercy God completes our salvation. That is, works are an order of sequence rather than a cause (3.18.1 [*OS* 4.270.21f.]).

70. "Second Defense against Westphal," *Calvin's Tracts,* 2.343 (*CO* 9.118f.). G. Oorthuys, "La Prédestination dans la Dogmatique Calviniste," in *De l'Élection Éternelle de Dieu* (Genève: Editions Labor, 1936), p. 213, wrote, "Calvin refused to be a philosopher. He wanted to be a theologian, a teacher of the Holy Scripture, purveyor of the Good News, preacher of Christ, witness of the faith, nothing more."

71. *Comm. on Rom.* 11:34 (*CO* 49.231).

72. Sermon on Jacob and Esau, *CO* 58.1–26.

73. *Comm. on Rom.* 9:14 (*CO* 49.180).

Calvin insists that God's will to salvation is revealed in the Scripture and that he has expounded the doctrine with due humility. As an idea in itself, predestination cannot be considered. Men cannot satisfy their curious questions about it; to acknowledge this fact will restrain men from speculative conclusions about election and help them to maintain a proper modesty and humility. The Scripture teaches that God chooses those whom He determined to save and also those whom He devotes to destruction.

Calvin's conception of the relationship of man and God is not based on reason; in fact it is offensive to reason, but it is, for Calvin, consonant with the experience of dealing with God in everything. This notion was already expressed in the 1536 edition of the *Institutes*. Calvin enlarged his treatment of the doctrines of providence and predestination in the 1539 edition, concentrating primarily on defending his view of predestination, although it is difficult, if not impossible, to separate Calvin's doctrine of predestination from his view of special providence. At least it is clear that Calvin's position is not primarily the logical result of a conception of the abstract sovereignty and power of God (though these elements are not entirely absent), but an insistence that everything depends on God. This absolute and direct dependence of man upon God causes problems in the doctrine of man, but the alternative conception of some kind of relative independence of man from God causes problems for a doctrine of God's providence. Calvin could not believe that God, like a bird, anxious and uncertain, awaits the decisions of man.[74] However Calvin recognizes, at least most of the time, that his position is not a conclusion of reason based on God's sovereignty, but a confession of faith. This is made evident in the location of the doctrine of predestination in Calvin's soteriology following faith, regeneration, and justification.

This intent was not followed by others. On Zanchi, Otto Gründler writes, "Thus it appears that for Zanchi the doctrine of predestination, from his first formulation of it until his last works, remained an integral part of the doctrine of God's essence."[75] Gründler concludes, "It is of no small significance that Zanchi should choose to discuss both providence and predestination as part and conclusion of his doc-

74. *Concerning Eternal Predestination*, p. 67 (CO 8.294).
75. Otto Gründler, *Die Gotteslehre Girolami Zanchis und ihre Bedeutung für seine Lehre von der Prädestination* (Neukirchen: Neukirchener Verlag des Erziehungsvereins, 1965), p. 23.

trine of God, thereby following the example of Thomas[76] rather than that of Calvin's final edition of the *Institutes.*"[77]

It must be admitted that Calvin's doctrine of God's particular providence for the believer, and his view that election precedes faith raise the question, which Calvin did not, and perhaps could not, solve, between supra- and infra-lapsarian points of view. H. Bois thinks that Calvin vacillates between a metaphysical point of view which was supralapsarian and an ethical view for which infralapsarianism would be sufficient.[78] The terms infra- and supra-lapsarianism were developed in the Arminian controversy. The infralapsarians hold that the sin of man results in the decree of reprobation. The supralapsarians maintain that the decree of reprobation, through God's permission, results in the sin of man. Calvin is usually claimed as supralapsarian and there is evidence to support this view.[79] However Calvin taught that sin was *positively* decreed (with the supralapsarians) when he was dealing with the doctrine of God; and *permissively* decreed (with the infralapsarians) when he was dealing with the doctrine of man. However neither position solves the problem of sin. The supralapsarian view logically requires that God is the author of sin, but both they, and Calvin, deny this result. The infralapsarian view of a *permissive* decree denies God's sovereignty if the emphasis is placed on permission, while it leads back to the supralapsarian position if the emphasis is placed on decree. Calvin can be claimed in some senses for both sides.

Calvin is not concerned with an abstract defense of the notion of the sovereignty of God and therefore not with a theoretical construction of its extent or its application. Calvin teaches a universal providence, but his exposition is focused on God's intensely loving care of His own. In this context his agreement with the philosophers' view of providence is more apparent than real. Further, Calvin does not move from a theological doctrine of universal providence to develop a view of special providence. Rather he begins with the particularity of God's providence which is clearly seen in his doctrine of eternal election, but also finds expression in his exposition of providence. The doctrine of

76. In the *Summa Theologica* Thomas discusses providence (1ª, qu. 22) and predestination (1ª, qu. 23) in the doctrine of the unity of God, but also deals with predestination in 3ª, qu. 24. See also *Summa Contra Gentiles* 3.64–113.

77. Gründler, *Die Gotteslehre Zanchis,* p. 97. I have cited the German pagination, but used the original English text of Gründler's Princeton Th.D. dissertation.

78. Bois, "La prédestination d'après Calvin," pp. 670ff.

79. Dowey, *The Knowledge of God in Calvin's Theology,* p. 213. Cf. Friethoff, "Die Prädestinationslehre bei Thomas von Aquin und Calvin," pp. 448ff.

predestination is the focus of a good deal of Calvin's attention and debates not because of its logicality but because of its practicality. That is, Calvin is not trying to create a system which a neutral observer would recognize as logical but to expound the Christian faith in God's providential care. The immediacy and singularity of this care lead Calvin to confess, "If our faith is not founded on the eternal election of God, it is certain that our faith would be ravaged by Satan at every moment."[80]

80. Sermon on Eph. 1:3–4 (CO 51.265).

5

Calvin on the Covenant

M. Eugene Osterhaven

Among the many theological contributions that came to the church through the Reformation of the sixteenth century was the doctrine of the covenant. Undeveloped in the preceding centuries, it made an early appearance in the Reformed Church in Zwingli and Bullinger who were driven to the subject by Anabaptists in and around Zurich. From them it passed to Calvin and other Reformers,[1] was further developed by the successors of the latter, and came to play a dominant role in much Reformed theology of the seventeenth and later centuries.[2]

While the doctrine of the covenant does not receive treatment in Calvin's earliest writings,[3] the second edition of the *Institutes of the Christian Religion,* published in 1539, devotes a chapter to the relation of the old and new covenants; the *Commentary on the Epistle to*

A paper prepared for the Theological Committee of the North American and Caribbean Area Council of the World Alliance of Reformed Churches. Reprinted from *Reformed Review* 33 (1979–1980): 136–49. Used by permission.

1. Gottlob Schrenk, *Gottesreich und Bund im älteren Protestantismus* (Darmstadt: Wissenschaftliche Buchgesellschaft, 1967), pp. 36–49; Hans Heinrich Wolf, *Die Einheit des Bundes* (Neukirchen Kreis Moers: Verlag der Buchhandlung des Erziehungsvereins, 1958), pp. 19–24.

2. Schrenk, *Gottesreich und Bund im älteren Protestantismus*; Charles S. McCoy, "Johannes Cocceius: Federal Theologian," *Scottish Journal of Theology* 16 (1963): 352–70; Everett M. Emerson, "Calvin and Covenant Theology," *Church History* 25 (1956): 136–44.

3. The word *covenant,* or *covenants,* appears at least four times in the first edition of the *Institutes,* published in 1536, in the chapter on the sacraments — *Joannis Calvini Opera Selecta,* ed. Petrus Barth (Munich: Chr. Kaiser, 1963), vol. 1, pp. 199, 124, 143, 155.

the Romans, published the same year, makes numerous references to the covenant in the exposition of the ninth chapter; the later commentaries and sermons discuss or refer to the covenant at appropriate times; and the last edition of the *Institutes,* published in 1559, has three chapters on the relation of the Old and the New Testaments of Scripture to each other[4] and makes frequent mention of the covenant in the discussion of the sacraments.[5] It is not a dominant theme in the Reformer's writings, as are salvation by grace through faith in the Lord Jesus Christ, the sovereignty of God, the kingdom of God, the church, the enormity of sin, the reality and power of the Holy Spirit, and Scripture. It is nevertheless an important theme which, one suspects, Calvin had ever in mind so that it is not surprising to come across a reference to the covenant after one has read a long section of a commentary or some sermons in which there is not a single explicit reference to it. Elsewhere, as in the sermons on Deuteronomy, one meets the concept often, and there are numerous places where the discussion centers around the meaning of the covenant for the people of God today. In the third book of the *Institutes,* where the author writes about the Christian life, the covenant is only occasionally mentioned, but the relationship which it denotes is always at hand. Such an instance is the discussion on prayer with its emphasis on the divine promises and the fatherhood of God. Thus explicit allusion to the covenant is easy and natural[6] so that the reader is unaware of the introduction of a new concept when that occurs.[7]

It is incorrect to affirm without qualification then that Calvin was not a covenant theologian, or to set him over against later Reformed theologians on the Continent or in New England as though their theologies of the covenant were utterly different. For while it is true that in Calvin's writings one reads of no covenant of works, covenant of redemption, or certain other refinements developed in a later age, the judgment of Everett Emerson against the opinions of Perry Miller and other recent writers will stand. Emerson writes that Calvin was not

4. *Inst.* 2.9–11.

5. *Inst.* 4.14–17. In the chapter on infant baptism, e.g., the covenant is referred to in paragraphs 7, 9–15, 21, and 24.

6. E.g., *Inst.* 3.20.45.

7. I am somewhat puzzled, therefore, by J. L. Witte's comment about the "few and scattered references," or "infrequent data" (*spaarzame gegevens*), with which one must work in assessing Calvin's covenantal theology. J. L. Witte, *Het Probleem Individu-Gemeenschap in Calvins Geloofsnorm* (Franeker: Wever, 1949), vol. 2, p. 170. In contrast Anthony A. Hoekema writes that "the doctrine of the covenant of grace occupies a very important place in his (Calvin's) thinking" — "Calvin's Doctrine of the Covenant of Grace," *The Reformed Review* 15.4 (May 1962): 3.

a "covenant theologian," as that term is usually understood, "but [that] many of the implications of covenant theology — that man can know beforehand the terms of salvation, that conversion is a process in which man's faculties are gradually transformed — all these are present in Calvin's teaching."[8] Emerson had been comparing "some aspects of covenant theology with the teaching of Calvin in their approaches to the conversion process,"[9] an important area of study for an understanding of Calvin on the covenant, and had questioned the propriety of comparing Calvin's *Institutes* with the sermons of later covenantal theologians, claiming that a more fair comparison would have been that of Calvin's sermons with the sermons of others. He concludes that there is a "near-identity of the approach of Calvin and that of the covenant theologians. . . . Calvin was not so different from the covenant theologians as has been argued."[10] It has been said that Calvin stressed the sovereignty and justice of God and man's inability, while the later covenant theology laid emphasis upon responsibility and action. Thus Perry Miller has written that covenant theologians, after stating the conventional inability of man, "were at liberty to press upon their congregations an obligation to act, as though John Calvin had never lived."[11] As Emerson shows, however, "Calvin likewise pressed on his congregation the obligation to act, and in Calvin's sermons statements of inability are in fact less common than in the sermons of the early New England divines."[12] A facile, comparative handling of the subject will not do therefore, and we propose to limit our inquiry here to a consideration of Calvin's thinking of the covenant as to its (1) foundation, (2) realization in history, and (3) unity.

1. The Foundation of the Covenant

When Calvin uses the expression "covenant"[13] he means by it the divine promise to Abraham and his seed, received in faith, that God will be a God and father to them, His people, and that they, enabled by His freely given grace, will live before Him in loving obedience. The foundation of the covenant is God's "eternal purpose which he

---

8. Emerson, "Calvin and Covenant Theology," p. 141.
9. Ibid., p. 136.
10. Ibid., pp. 141f.
11. Ibid., p. 142.
12. Ibid.
13. The word is usually *foedus* in Latin and *alliance* in French, often with a noun or pronoun added.

has realized in Christ Jesus our Lord" (Eph. 3:11). In his comments on that verse, coming after he had already discussed the teaching of predestination and our eternal election in Christ in the first chapter, Calvin exclaims, "How carefully does he guard against the objection that the purpose of God has been changed! A third time, he repeats that the decree was eternal and unchangeable, but must be carried into effect by Christ Jesus our Lord, because in him it was made." To Calvin whatever happens in history is no happenstance but is the result of the antecedent decree of God. To ascribe to chance the fortunes of history is a "depraved opinion"[14] which Calvin tries to lay to rest. He does so, however, not in the four chapters on predestination in the third book of the *Institutes* but in the three chapters on providence in the first book.

Calvin indeed has much to say on predestination, election, and the eternal decree, prodded as he was by certain of his contemporaries, and his primary reason for doing so is to safeguard belief in the priority of grace in salvation and to enhance faith in the absolute lordship of God. That is why the treatment of predestination and election in the *Institutes* begins with the question why "the covenant of life" which is preached does not gain the same acceptance in the hearts of all people[15] and subsequently makes numerous references to the covenant. Similarly, the discussion of election in the *Commentary on Romans* necessitates constant reference to the covenant, for there the agonizing question for the apostle was the relation of his "brethren," "kinsmen by race," to God's election and covenant. Theirs were "the sonship, the glory, the covenants, the giving of the law, the worship, and the promises . . . the patriarchs, and of their race, according to the flesh, is the Christ" (Rom. 9:3–5). Their unbelief, in the face of God's manifest grace, is beyond Paul's comprehension. Of two things he was sure, that "God's purpose of election" would continue (Rom. 9:11; cf. 11:5, 7) and that His covenant would remain with His ancient people, since the Deliverer would come from Zion to banish ungodliness from Jacob and take away their sins (Rom. 11:26f.). Calvin understood this to mean that God would respect the "old covenant" made with the patriarchs and that, in spite of unbelief, He would always keep for Himself "a certain seed, that the redemption might be effectual in the elect and peculiar nation."[16]

To that nation, Calvin believed, God had added the Gentiles so that together as one people they might serve Him and enjoy His favor.

14. *Inst.* 1.16.2.
15. *Inst.* 3.21.1.
16. *Comm. on Rom.* 11:26.

Much is said about this in the *Commentary on the Book of Genesis.*
Concerning the call of Abraham, for example, it is said that "the
blessing was promised [Abraham] in Christ when he was coming into
the land of Canaan. Therefore, in my judgment," Calvin writes, "God
pronounces that all nations should be blessed in his servant Abraham
because Christ was included in his loins."[17] Earlier, in Noah's blessing
of Japheth whose posterity God would "enlarge," Calvin had marveled
that after thousands of years that progeny which had been "wanderers
and fugitives were received into the same tabernacle" with the covenant people of God. He continues:

> For God, by a new adoption, has formed a people out of those who
> were separated, and has confirmed a fraternal union between alien-
> ated parties. This is done by the sweet and gentle voice of God, which
> he has uttered in the gospel; and this prophecy is still daily receiving
> its fulfillment, since God invites the scattered sheep to join his flock,
> and collects, on every side, those who shall sit down with Abraham,
> Isaac, and Jacob in the kingdom of heaven. It is truly no common
> support of our faith, that the calling of the Gentiles is not only decreed
> in the *eternal counsel of God,* but is openly declared by the mouth of
> the Patriarch; lest we should think it to have happened suddenly, or
> by chance, that the inheritance of eternal life was offered generally to
> all. But the form of the expression, "Japheth shall dwell in the tab-
> ernacle of Shem," commends to us that mutual society which ought
> to exist, and to be cherished among the faithful. For whereas God had
> chosen to himself a church from the progeny of Shem, he afterwards
> chose the Gentiles together with them on this condition: that they
> should join themselves to that people, who were in possession of the
> covenant of life.[18]

In Calvin's treatment of the covenant as grounded in God's eternal
decree of election one notices a remarkable distinction within election.
There is a "general election of the people of Israel," i.e., of the whole
community, and a "second election" for "a part only," the former also
called "external calling" and the latter "the secret election of God."[19]
Calvin felt driven to this distinction within the covenant in commenting on Romans 9:6–8:

> Not all who are descended from Israel belong to Israel, and not all
> are children of Abraham because they are his descendants; but

17. *Comm. on Gen.* 12:3.
18. *Comm. on Gen.* 9:27, emphasis mine.
19. *Comm. on Rom.* 9:6–8.

"Through Isaac shall your descendants be named." This means that
it is not the children of the flesh who are the children of God, but the
children of the promise are reckoned as descendants.

In wrestling with this problem, that not all within the covenant
community receive its spiritual benefits, Calvin concluded that all who
were born into the community "are rightly called heirs and successors
of the covenant made with Abraham . . . sons of promise." For God
had sealed His covenant with Ishmael and Esau as well as with Isaac
and Jacob. One may not call them aliens, therefore, for they had received the sign and seal of the covenant, and the promise of salvation
was offered to them. Their ingratitude and refusal to receive the prof-
ferred grace does not invalidate the covenant, for God remains faithful,
but it does demonstrate their exclusion from the "true election of God."
While this is true, those who are a part of the outer fellowship God
"does not entirely exclude" but "joins" them to His family as "inferior"
members until they cut themselves off. Thus circumcision, or baptism,
is not useless until one repudiates his covenantal birthright, and that
is done by the individual in his own decision.[20]
Calvin saw this same principle at work in his day. God is not "tied"
to the physical progeny of Abraham in His dispensation of grace, but
in His "secret counsel" He effectually draws unto Himself whomsoever
He pleases. "By special privilege some certain persons are chosen out
of the elect people of God in whom the common adoption may be
effectual and firm."[21]
What Calvin had written concerning this two-fold election, of the
whole community and of individuals within it, in his *Commentary on
the Epistle to the Romans* (1539) and his *Commentary on the Book
of Genesis* (1554), he wrote into the final edition of the *Institutes*
(1559) as well. In the first chapter on predestination, after discussing
the election of Abraham and Israel as examples of "a freely given
covenant,"[22] Calvin introduces "a second, more limited degree of election" which touches "individual persons to whom God not only offers
salvation but so assigns it that the certainty of its effect is not in
suspense or doubt." So, while "Ishmael, Esau, and the like" are cut
off from election "by their own defection and guilt" in violating the
"condition [which] had been laid down that they should faithfully keep
God's covenant," He causes His covenant to continue by effectually
wooing others by "special grace." Thus, Calvin writes,

20. *Comm. on Gen.* 17:19.
21. *Comm. on Rom.* 9:7.
22. *Inst.* 3.21.5.

the general election of a people is not always firm and effectual: to those with whom God makes a covenant, he does not at once give the spirit of regeneration that would enable them to persevere in the covenant to the very end. Rather, the outward change, without the working of inner grace, which might have availed to keep them, is intermediate between the rejection of mankind and the election of a meager number of the godly. The whole people of Israel has been called "the inheritance of God" [Deut. 32:9; 1 Kings 8:51; Ps. 28:9; 33:12; etc.], yet many of them were foreigners. But because God has not pointlessly covenanted that he would become their Father and Redeemer, he sees to his freely given favor rather than to the many who treacherously desert him. Even through them his truth was not set aside, for where he preserved some remnant for himself, it appeared that his calling was "without repentance" [Rom. 11:29]. For the fact that God was continually gathering his church from Abraham's children rather than from profane nations had its reason in his covenant, which, when violated by that multitude, he confined to a few that it might not utterly cease. In short, that adoption of Abraham's seed in common was a visible image of the greater benefit that God bestowed on some out of the many. This is why Paul so carefully distinguishes the children of Abraham according to the flesh from the spiritual children who have been called after the example of Isaac [Gal. 4:28]. Not that it was a vain and unprofitable thing simply to be a child of Abraham; God's unchangeable plan, by which he predestined for himself those whom he willed, was in fact intrinsically effectual unto salvation for these spiritual offspring alone. But I advise my readers not to take a prejudiced position on either side until, when the passages of Scripture have been adduced, it shall be clear what opinion ought to be held.[23]

I have quoted at length from Calvin on this point because of its importance to an understanding of his thinking on the covenant. The same is insisted elsewhere in the commentaries and sermons. The intention is to stress covenantal responsibility as well as privilege. To be numbered among the people of God is an inestimable favor indeed; its implication is the expectation of covenantal faith and obedience. Then, according to Calvin, God is honored, the world is offered a witness, and God's people are blessed.

2. The Historical Realization of the Covenant

With the emphasis that one meets in Calvin on the sovereignty of God and the decree from eternity, it might be suspected that history

23. *Inst.* 3.21.7.

and that which happens in it get slight, or at least inadequate, attention. Is not history simply the "execution of the decree," as later dogmaticians wrote? How then can it be decisive or that which happens in it be of lasting consequence?

To questions of that nature Calvin gave a sharp answer insisting that inasmuch as God has declared that our deeds here carry with them an eternal significance it must be so. Along with all the statements in the *Institutes,* the commentaries, and the tracts on predestination which speak about God's absolute sovereignty in disposing of every human being as He pleases, there are as many statements about human responsibility and the importance of proper decisions here and now. And the sermons, we dare say, contain more of the latter than the former! An instance is the following from the heart of the discussion on predestination in the *Institutes:*

> We teach that they act perversely who to seek out the source of their condemnation turn their gaze upon the hidden sanctuary of God's plan, and wink at the corruption of nature from which it really springs. God, to prevent them from charging it against himself, bears testimony to his creation. For even though by God's eternal providence man has been created to undergo that calamity to which he is subject, it still takes its occasion from man himself, not from God, since the only reason for his ruin is that he has degenerated from God's pure creation into vicious and impure perversity.[24]

Thus the reason for condemnation, even of those who have been favored with covenant blessings, is in the despiser of those blessings in history. As sin occurs in history, so does salvation occur within history, the scene of the stupendous activity of God on behalf of mankind.

At the heart of salvation is the covenant of grace which God established with the patriarchs and grounded and consummated in Jesus Christ. Whereas the covenant began formally with Abraham and was reiterated to Isaac and Jacob, there were "other promises which had been given to Adam, Noah, and others [which] referred indiscriminately to all nations."[25] Adam and Eve were given the tree of life and Noah and his posterity a bow in the clouds as signs that God would fulfill His promises. "These Adam and Noah regarded as sacraments." Because they had a certain mark impressed upon them by the Word

24. *Inst.* 3.23.9.
25. *Comm. on Luke* 1:55.

of God, they were constituted "proofs and seals of his covenants."[26] Thus God had dealt with all mankind in the ancient fathers at the beginning. For God had all mankind in mind from the first, and now that Christ has come "the adoption has been extended to all nations, so that those who were not by nature children of Abraham may be his spiritual seed."[27] Thus it is proper to denominate the covenant as "universal" inasmuch as it has been intended for and extended to all nations.[28]

Calvin seems to enjoy reflecting on the divine intention to make Abraham and his posterity a blessing to all the families of the earth so that there would be a spread of the gospel everywhere, for he alludes to it often. The patriarchs, David, Job, Samuel, and the prophets were all a part of God's program in history for the realization of His purpose.

> The Lord held to this orderly plan in administering the covenant of his mercy: as the day of full revelation approached with the passing of time, the more he increased each day the brightness of its manifestation. Accordingly, at the beginning when the first promise of salvation was given to Adam (Gen. 3:15) it glowed like a feeble spark. Then, as it was added to, the light grew in fulness, breaking forth increasingly and shedding its radiance more widely. At last — when all the clouds were dispersed — Christ, the Sun of Righteousness, fully illumined the whole earth (Mal. 4).[29]

With the coming of Christ the full meaning of the covenant was disclosed, for "all the promises of God find their Yes in him" (2 Cor. 1:20). There must be hundreds of places in Calvin's writings where this is alluded to, sometimes by suggestion, frequently by explicit statement. Let one example suffice:

> The law was given to this end, that it might lead us by the hand to another righteousness . . . it always has Christ for its mark. . . . The law in all its parts looks to Christ.[30]

The purpose of the entire Old Testament was to prepare the world for the coming of the Son of God. As a part of the Old Testament the

26. *Inst.* 4.14.18.
27. *Comm. on Luke* 1:55.
28. *Comm. on Luke* 1:50.
29. *Inst.* 2.10.20.
30. *Comm. on Rom.* 10:4.

law was given to cause the people to "despair of their own righteousness [and] flee into the haven of God's goodness, and that is unto
Christ himself. This was the end [i.e., the purpose or goal] of Moses'
ministry."[31] Calvin argues often in the commentaries of the Old Testament what he writes in one sentence in the *Institutes*: "The whole
cultus of the law, taken literally and not as shadows and figures corresponding to the truth, will be ridiculous." Apart from Christ the
ceremonies may be despised and ridiculed "as child's play . . . if the
forms of the law be separated from its end, one must condemn it as
vanity."[32] Now that Christ has come and has brought with Him salvation and the new age, the meaning of history has been made manifest and all creation awaits the time of His return.

3. The Unity of the Covenant

The unity of the covenant that God established with mankind in
Abraham and confirmed in Christ is a major emphasis in Calvin's
teaching. We have already found it necessary to touch on this subject.
Driven to it by persons who disparaged the continuing importance of
the Old Testament after the appearance of Christ,[33] Calvin saw it as
crucial to an understanding of the gospel, and he states this repeatedly
in the exegetical writings. It is also the major theme of the three
chapters in the *Institutes* that treat the relation of the Old and New
Testaments to each other. In the first of these, Calvin defines the
gospel as follows:

> I take the gospel to be the clear manifestation of the mystery of Christ.
> . . . The word "gospel," taken in the broad sense, includes those tes-
> timonies of his mercy and fatherly favor which God gave to the pa-
> triarchs of old. In a higher sense, however, the word refers, I say, to
> the proclamation of the grace manifested in Christ. . . . The gospel

31. *Comm. on Rom.* 10:5.
32. *Inst.* 2.7.1.
33. In the "Argument" of the *Commentary on a Harmony of the Evangelists*
(1555) Calvin says that the gospel writers "had no intention or design to abolish by
their writings *the law and the prophets*; as some fanatics dream that the Old Testament is superfluous, now that the truth of heavenly wisdom has been revealed to
us by Christ and his Apostles." In the *Institutes* (1559) "that wonderful rascal Servetus and certain madmen of the Anabaptist sect" are cited for denigrating the importance of "the Israelites" (2.10.1). Servetus is mentioned for the first time in the
edition of 1559. Willem van den Bergh writes that, while Calvin had long been
disturbed by radical opinion on this subject, "from 1553 on it appears to have been
placed in the foreground in his dogmatics firmly and with emphasis" — *Calvijn over
het Genade Verbond* (The Hague: Beschoot, 1879), p. 71.

did not so supplant the entire law as to bring forward a different way of salvation. Rather, it confirmed and satisfied whatever the law had promised, and gave substance to the shadows.[34]

With that as introductory, Calvin moves into his main argument in the following chapter. The "point" that he wants to make and calls "very important" is "that all men adopted by God into the company of his people since the beginning of the world were covenanted to him [*fuisse ei foederatos*] by this same law and by the bond of the same doctrine as obtains among us."[35] Lest there be any misunderstanding, he goes on to affirm that the patriarchs "participated in the same inheritance and hoped for a common salvation with us by the grace of the same Mediator."[36] A paragraph later, he had progressed to where he can say: "The covenant made with all the patriarchs is so much like ours in substance and reality that the two are actually one and the same."[37] Immediately thereafter he appends a qualification: "Yet they differ in the mode of dispensation." The rest of the chapter is an attempt to substantiate the first proposition, that the covenant is one and the same; the next chapter discusses the varied administration (*administratio tamen variat*) of the two dispensations of the one covenant.

It is interesting to note, as H. H. Wolf remarks, that whereas the captions of chapters 10 and 11, on the "similarity" and "difference" of the Old and New Testaments, suggest two covenants, in Calvin's mind, there are not two covenants at all but, to use his own words, "one and the same." Rather than two covenants, there is "identity between the covenant of the fathers and the covenant established with us."[38] In support of this proposition Calvin argues that in both the old dispensation and the new there was hope in immortality; that in both salvation was by grace alone; and that in both Testaments believers "had and knew Christ as Mediator through whom they were joined to God and were to share in his promises."[39] The difference in mode

34. *Inst.* 2.9.2, 4.
35. *Inst.* 2.10.1.
36. Ibid.
37. *Inst.* 2.10.2.
38. Wolf, *Die Einheit des Bundes,* p. 19. Calvin sees the Davidic covenant (Ps. 89; 2 Sam. 7; 1 Chron. 17; 2 Chron. 7:18) as a high moment in the historic realization of the one covenant of grace. The Davidic covenant derives its significance from the covenant of grace made with Abraham and has no significance apart from it. It finds its true meaning in David's greater Son — *Comm. on Ps.* 89:3f., 35–36.
39. *Inst.* 2.10.2.

of administration consisted of the following: (1) in the Old Testament spiritual blessings were represented by temporal gifts; (2) in the Old Testament truth was conveyed by figures and ceremonies which typified Christ; (3) in the Old Testament truth is of the letter; the New is more spiritual (Jer. 31:31–34; 2 Cor. 3:3–11); (4) there is bondage in the Old Testament, freedom in the New; (5) the Old Testament deals mainly with one nation; the New is concerned with all.

Calvin's position here, in which the unity of the covenant is emphasized, while, in our judgment, correct in fundamental stance, has been widely assailed. One of the most interesting criticisms is from Paul Wernle who wrote,

> It is significant that it was the Reformed Christians precisely who had a specially keen interest in this Christianization of the Old Testament. The Reformed Christians were the practical party in the Reformation movement; the New Testament was not sufficient for their ecclesiastical-political institutions; they were compelled to go back to its Old Testament background and hence needed a unified authoritative Bible. The evangelical national state church and the Christian state as ideally pictured by the Reformed Christians both rest upon the basis of Old Testament theocracy. . . .
>
> In his moral zeal, Calvin utterly denies the difference between the Old and the New Testaments, closes his eyes to all the new values which Jesus brought into the world, and degrades him to the position of an interpreter of the ancient lawgiver Moses. How much more clearly the Baptists saw the truth in this respect. . . .
>
> The New Testament must be fitted in with the authority of the Old Testament; Christ is interpreted according to Moses.[40]

In defending Calvin against charges of this nature Wilhelm Niesel holds that Calvin should not be understood as reading the Old Testament into the New and vice versa. While using each to explain the other, Calvin recognizes that "the Old Testament promises what the New Testament offers to us in Christ. Salvation in both dispensations is in Christ who is the head of the one body, the church; Christ is the foundation of the one covenant to which both Testaments bear wit-

40. Paul Wernle, *Der evangelische Glaube nach den Hauptschriften der Reformatoren* 3 (Calvin) (Tübingen: Mohr [Siebeck], 1919), pp. 268, 13, 30—quoted by Wilhelm Niesel, *The Theology of Calvin,* trans. H. Knight (London: Lutterworth, 1956), pp. 104f.

ness."[41] Whether Niesel is successful in defending Calvin, or whether Calvin is justified in his argumentation, can be debated. Without entering into that, we observe that Calvin's fundamental position has become that of Reformed theology and that it has assumed a most important role in the Reformed understanding of the church and sacraments and the interpretation of the Old Testament.

In stressing the similarity of the Old and New Testaments, Calvin did not in any way wish to depreciate the superiority of the latter. The *Commentary on the Epistle to the Hebrews,* not surprisingly, shows this as clearly as any of Calvin's writings, although one meets the same thought throughout the corpus of his works.

The Father has put forth more fully the power of his Spirit under the Kingdom of Christ and has poured forth more abundantly his mercy on mankind [in him].[42]

Under the old dispensation the promises were "obscure and intricate so that they shone only like the moon and the stars in comparison with the clear light of the gospel which shines brightly on us."[43] Thus Christ is the fulfillment of the Word of God that had gone on before; He gave it its true meaning and showed the glory of the promises of God in a way in which not even the prophets could imagine. Yet we are not to suppose that in Christ we have a wholly new phenomenon. Thus he remarks in commenting on Matthew 5:17:

41. Niesel, *The Theology of Calvin,* p. 105. Doumergue writes, "It is particularly inaccurate, one notices, to repeat that Calvin has confused the Old and the New Testament. And it would not be necessary to deepen these differences between the two covenants very much in order to dig an abyss between them. Calvin has not done that. For him the 'differences' do not destroy 'the unity.' The differences 'refer to the diverse manner which God has used in administering his doctrine rather than the substance' of that doctrine. . . . St. Paul declared that when we read the law of God attentively we prudently look for the spirit which is contained in it which will serve to give us good instruction to lead us to faith, as we also see in experience. For whence have our Lord Jesus Christ and his apostles drawn their teaching except from Moses? And when one shall have carefully sifted through the whole matter, he will find that the gospel is only a simple exposition of that which Moses declared formerly. It is true that there was the obscurity of shadows and figures of the law, that God did not give such grace to the ancient fathers as to us; but nevertheless, if the substance of the gospel is drawn from them, [it is true] that we have a common faith with those who have lived before the coming of our Lord Jesus Christ" — E. Doumergue, *Jean Calvin: Les Hommes et les Choses de son Temps* (Lausanne: George Bridel, 1910), vol. 4, p. 199.

42. *Comm. on Heb.* 8:10.

43. Ibid.

God had, indeed, promised a new covenant at the coming of Christ; but had, at the same time, showed, that it would not be different from the first, but that, on the contrary, its design was, to give a perpetual sanction to the covenant, which he had made, from the beginning, with his own people. "I will write my law (says he) in their hearts, and I will remember their iniquities no more" (Jer. 31:33–34). By these words he is so far from departing from the former covenant, that, on the contrary, he declares, that it will be confirmed and ratified, when it shall be succeeded by the new. This is also the meaning of Christ's words, when he says, that he came to fulfil the law: for he actually fulfilled it, by quickening, with his Spirit, the dead letter, and then exhibited in reality, what had hitherto appeared only in figures.

. . . his doctrine is so far from being at variance with the law, that it agrees perfectly with the law and the prophets, and not only so, but brings the complete fulfilment of them.

According to Calvin, the law and the prophets would have their "complete fulfilment" in Christ because He was their foundation in the first place. We return here to the point made earlier, that Christ is the foundation of the covenant. This is stated nowhere more emphatically than in the commentaries on the prophets. Two examples from Isaiah will suffice:

The covenant which was made with Abraham and his posterity had its foundation in Christ; for the words of the covenant are these: "In thy seed shall all nations be blessed" (Gen. 22:18). And the covenant was ratified in no other manner than in the seed of Abraham, that is, in Christ, by whose coming, though it had been previously made, it was confirmed and actually sanctioned. Hence also Paul says "that the promises of God are yea and amen in Christ" (2 Cor. 1:20) and in another passage calls Christ "the minister of circumcision, to fulfil the promises which were given to the fathers" (Rom. 15:8). Still more clearly does he declare that Christ is "the peace" of all, so that they who were formally separated are united in him, and both they who were far off and they who were near are thus reconciled to God (Eph. 2:17). Hence also it is evident that Christ was promised, not only to the Jews, but to the whole world . . . the doctrine of the gospel came forth out of Zion; because we thence conclude that it is not new, or lately sprung up, but that it is the eternal truth of God, of which a testimony had been given in all ages before it was brought to light.

We also infer that it was necessary that all the ancient ceremonies should be abolished, and that a new form of teaching should be introduced, though the substance of the doctrine continue to be the same; for the law formerly proceeded out of Mount Sinai (Exod. 19:20), but now it proceeded out of Zion, and therefore it assumed a new form. Two things, therefore, must be observed: first, that the doctrine of God is the same, and always agrees with itself; that no one may charge God with changeableness, as if he were inconsistent; and though the law of the Lord be now the same that it ever was, yet it came out of Zion with a new garment; secondly, when ceremonies and shadows had been abolished, Christ was revealed, in whom the reality of them is perceived.[44]

Thus the entire Old Testament was meaningful to Calvin in an unusual manner. Since Christ was the foundation of the covenant and both Testaments found their meaning in Him, that which was said by God to Israel was said to Calvin and us as well. The law was written *to us,* he is fond of saying in his explication of the Old Testament in commentaries and sermons. To cite an instance from the latter, a sermon from the Book of Deuteronomy, Calvin declares:

The law has not only been given as a rule to [help us] live well; but it is based on the covenant which God made with Abraham and with his posterity. By virtue of that covenant we are heirs of a heavenly kingdom, as St. Paul shows. When we seek salvation we have to go to that promise which was given our father Abraham; we must be his spiritual children if we would be servants of the church of God, members of our Lord Jesus Christ. Thus we see that this doctrine has not only served until the coming of the Son of God, but that it is useful to us, and will be until the end of the world. For it is a fortress built on this eternal covenant from which . . . our salvation proceeds, as from its true source.[45]

Inasmuch as God's covenant is essentially one, with Christ its substance in both Testaments, is the New Testament unnecessary? If Christ is revealed in the Old Testament and, in the days of His flesh, was its "faithful expounder,"[46] was more needed? Calvin can write,

44. *Comm. on Isa* 42:6 and 2:3; cf. *Comm. on Rom.* 4:1 where Abraham is eulogized as a "pattern" for the whole church; and on 10:4: "The law was given to this end, that it might lead to another righteousness . . . it always has Christ for its mark. . . . The law in all its parts looks to Christ."

45. Sermon on Deut. 1:1–3 (*CR* 56 [*CO* 25], 611). The sermon on Deut. 5:2f., that "God made a covenant with us in Horeb. Not with our fathers did the Lord make this covenant, but with us, who are all of us here alive this day," gives Calvin the occasion to emphasize the perpetuity of the covenant, and he makes the most of the opportunity (*CR* 56 [*CO* 26], pp. 242–46 particularly). Cf. *Comm. on Jer.* 31:31–34. I. John Hesselink has a splendid treatment of this subject in *Calvin's Concept and Use of the Law,* chap. 7 (unpublished dissertation, Basel, 1961).

46. *Comm. on Matt.* 5:21.

"What is proposed to us in Christ except what God had promised in the law? and therefore Christ is called the end of the law, and elsewhere its spirit: for if the law is separated from Christ, it is like a dead letter: Christ alone gives it life. Since, therefore, God at this day exhibits to us nothing in his only begotten Son but what he had formerly promised in the law, it follows that his covenant is set up again, and so perpetually established."[47] What is the justification for such a statement? Are not Wernle and Calvin's other critics correct?

Not if Calvin is understood. Hesselink has written:

·If Christ is the substance and the soul of the law, the eternal Mediator to whom the law and prophets witness, and apart from whom his ministry is incomprehensible, then Christ's "faithful interpretation" (as well as that of the rest of the New Testament) of the law is nothing other than a self-witness! That is, only through Christ do we understand who Christ is (as witnessed to in "the Scriptures," i.e., the Old Testament).[48]

He then quotes Calvin's pointed comment on Luke 24:27: "In order that Christ may be known to us through the gospel, it is necessary that Moses and the prophets should go before as guides to show us the way. . . . From the law therefore we may properly learn Christ if we consider that the covenant which God made with the fathers was founded on the Mediator." Hesselink remarks:

If the Old Testament is not in some way a "Christian" book, then it can be dropped from the canon. If Christ was not present and active in God's dealings with Israel, then we indeed have an abstract God on the one hand and a shaky "religion of the New Testament" on the other. But if we follow Calvin here, then we will insist that "Christ did not first begin to be manifested in the gospel" (*Comm. on John* 5:39).[49]

In this way Calvin seeks to solve the main hermeneutical problem of the Old and New Testaments. As he sees it, Christ is the key to the understanding of both Testaments. In Him the hermeneutical circle is complete: Christ cannot be understood apart from the Old Testament; the Old Testament cannot be understood, in its true sense, apart from Him.

47. *Comm. on Ezek.* 16:61.
48. Hesselink, *Calvin's Concept and Use of the Law,* chap. 7, p. 13.
49. Ibid., p. 14.

Christ cannot be properly known in any other way than from the Scriptures; and if this is so, it follows that we ought to read the Scriptures with the express design of finding Christ in them. Whoever shall turn aside from this object [*ab hoc scopo*], though he may weary himself throughout his whole life and learning, will never attain the knowledge of the truth. . . . By the Scriptures . . . is here meant the Old Testament; for it was not in the gospel that Christ first began to be manifested, but, having received testimony from the law and the prophets, he was openly exhibited in the gospel.[50]

In the preceding paragraph the "object" of Scripture was cited. This is an important point in Calvin's treatment and it requires some attention. According to him, Christ is the object, the aim, the goal of Scripture in its entirety and, as they find their respective places in relation to the whole, of its several parts. He is its "soul," its "spirit," its "end." As the *unicus scopus totius scripturae,* the single object of all Scripture, the *genuinus sensus scripturae,* the authentic meaning of Scripture, Christ is indeed the *dei loquentis persona* (*Inst.* 1.7.4), God Himself addressing us in it.

Christ is the end of [the law] to which [the law] ought to be referred. It was turned away in another direction when the Jews shut Christ out from it. Hence, as in the law they wander into by-paths, so the law too becomes to them involved like a labyrinth, until it is brought to refer to its end, that is, Christ. If, accordingly, the Jews seek Christ in the law, the truth of God will be distinctly seen by them, but as long as they think they are wise without Christ, they will wander in darkness and never arrive at a right understanding of the law. Now, what is said of the law applies to all Scripture — that where it is not taken as referring to Christ as its one aim, it is mistakenly twisted and perverted.[51]

Having considered Calvin's teaching on the covenant with respect to its foundation in God's eternal purpose in Jesus Christ, its realization in history, and its unity, we have taken up what appear to be the three most important motifs of his thought in this area. There are others with which a comprehensive study would have to deal. The fuller, richer revelation given in the incarnation, death, and resurrection of Christ; the law of the covenant with Calvin's emphasis on duty and obedience; the reality of the Holy Spirit and the motivation that

50. *Comm. on John* 5:39.
51. *Comm. on 2 Cor.* 3:16. Cf. Wolf, *Die Einheit des Bundes,* pp. 140–42; Hesselink, *Calvin's Concept and Use of the Law,* chap. 7, p. 15, and nn. 57 and 58.

comes from Him; the joy that comes in seeking to live as children of the covenant, and prayer; the inclusiveness of the covenant; Calvin's use of both covenant and testament in the interpretation of Hebrews 9:16; covenantal responsibility — these, and undoubtedly others, would surface. All are important and reflect major concerns in the teaching of the Reformer. Inasmuch as it is commonly believed that Calvin's emphases are elsewhere, I close with a typical warning against covenantal irresponsibility. It is taken from the Magnificat of Mary:

> Not all who are descended from Abraham according to the flesh are the true children of Abraham. Mary confines the accomplishment of the promise to the true worshippers of God, *to them that fear him*: as David also does: "The mercy of the Lord is from everlasting to everlasting upon them that fear him, and his righteousness unto children's children; to such as keep his covenant, and to those that remember his commandments to do them" (Ps. 103:17–18). While God promises that he will be merciful to the children of the saints through all generations, this gives no support to the vain confidence of hypocrites: for falsely and groundlessly do they boast of God as their Father, who are the spurious children of the saints, and have departed from their faith and godliness. This exception sets aside the falsehood and arrogance of those who, while they are destitute of faith, are puffed up with false pretenses to the favor of God. A universal covenant of salvation had been made by God with the posterity of Abraham; but, as stones moistened by the rain do not become soft, so the promised righteousness and salvation are prevented from reaching unbelievers through their own hardness of heart. Meanwhile, to maintain the truth and firmness of his promise, God has preserved "a seed" (Rom. 9:29).[52]

---

52. *Comm. on Luke* 1:50. Yet the irresponsibility of His covenant partners does not "disannul" God's covenant faithfulness because the covenant is "founded upon the perfect immutability of his nature," *Comm. on Ps.* 89:34.

6

The Mirror
of God's Goodness
A Key Metaphor in Calvin's View of Man

Brian A. Gerrish

Where there is no zeal to glorify God, the chief part of uprightness is absent.[1]

Whatever the strange figure of the hidden God may have meant for Luther's faith, it is plain that his faith grasped the revealed God as "pure love" (*eitel Liebe*). In his Large Catechism (1529) he writes: "It is God alone, I have often enough repeated, from whom we receive all that is good. . . . He is an eternal fountain which overflows with sheer goodness and pours forth all that is good in name and in fact."[2] Calvin's understanding of man and his place in the world might almost be said to provide a theological exegesis of this matchless confession of Luther's faith.

Reprinted from *The Old Protestantism and the New* (Chicago: University of Chicago, 1982), pp. 150–59, 345–51. © 1982 by The University of Chicago. Originally published in *Concordia Theological Quarterly* 45 (July 1981): 211–22. Used by permission.

1. John Calvin, *Inst.* 2.3.4 (1:294); trans. Ford Lewis Battles. Throughout this chapter, which is intended as a short commentary on two passages from the 1559 *Institutes,* I have adopted Battles's translation (referred to by volume and page in parentheses).

2. Martin Luther, *Deutsch [Grosser] Catechismus* (1529): WA 30¹.135.33ff.; trans. Robert H. Fischer, in *The Book of Concord: The Confessions of the Evangelical Lutheran Church,* ed. Theodore G. Tappert (Philadelphia: Fortress, 1959), p. 368.

In the opening paragraphs of his 1559 *Institutes,* Calvin announces that the knowledge of God and the knowledge of man — the two basic themes of theological wisdom — mutually condition each other. If, then, God is for him, as for Luther, *fons bonorum* (the Fountain of Good), we should expect the being of man to be somehow defined as the correlate of this regulative concept of God. It may be that the systematic coherence of Calvin's anthropology tends to get buried under the sheer mass of dogmatic material; and it has to be remembered that nothing less than the whole of the *Institutes* is required to set out his doctrine of man, just as the work *as a whole* presents his doctrine of God. Nevertheless, it is fair enough to hold that two segments of the *Institutes* are of decisive importance for our theme.

There is, we are told, a twofold knowledge of man. God has made Himself known to us as Creator and Redeemer; correspondingly, we are to know what man was like when first created, and what his condition is since the fall.[3] Human nature as created is the particular theme of book 1, chapter 15; Calvin turns to human nature as fallen in book 2, chapters 1 – 5. That these two segments may not be taken to exhaust his doctrine of man is evident: he subsumes the fall and sin under the knowledge of God the Redeemer, and further discussion on man of course remains, particularly for the sections on Christology and the life of the Christian man.[4] Indeed, there is plainly a sense in which, for Calvin, the restoration of man in Christ has dogmatic precedence even over the doctrine of the original estate, since, so he argues, we know of Adam's original blessedness only by viewing it in Christ, the Second Adam.[5]

If, however, with these reservations, we confine our attention to the two designated segments, we do in fact have enough to uncover a distinctive pattern in Calvin's anthropology. Admittedly, he has a lot of other important things to say even in these two segments, but I think we can fairly sum up the heart of the matter like this: The existence of man in the design of God is defined by thankfulness, the correlate of God's goodness; the existence of man in sin is defined by pride or self-love, the antithesis of God's goodness. To have said this much is, of course, already to recognize that in his understanding of man Calvin was working with ideas inherited from the apostle Paul by way of Augustine.

As with Calvin's doctrine of God, one has to call at the outset for setting aside hoary misconceptions. It is not true that Calvin's was an authoritarian religion, in the sense that man's most fitting posture is

3. *Inst.* 1.2.1 (1:40); 6.1 (1:70–71); 15.1 (1:183); 2.6.1 (1:341).
4. *Inst.* 2.6–17 (1:340–534); 3.6–10 (1:684–725).
5. *Inst.* 1.15.4 (1:178).

one of cringing before the divine despot. (This is what students of psychology may think they have learned from Erich Fromm; but in truth it has more to do with Calvin's notion of idolatry than with his notion of piety.)[6] Neither did Calvin hold that fallen man is in no sense capable of achieving anything beyond his own self-degradation. Here, it must be admitted, his rhetoric sometimes obscures rather than reinforces a theological point. If his description of man as a "five-foot worm" was suggested to him by one of the Psalms (22:6),[7] it is hard not to judge that he was carried away by his own sermonizing when he pronounced man unfit to be ranked with "worms, lice, fleas, and vermin."[8] But *how* does one judge that such language really is, in fact, the obfuscation of a strictly theological point? Only by taking due note of the sober theological distinctions made elsewhere; these enable us to see in the heavy rhetoric Calvin's horror that man in sin has surrendered his very humanity to a life of thanklessness.

Calvin has already introduced man at the end of his chapter on creation. Having fashioned the universe as a magnificent theater of His glory, God placed man in it last of all as the privileged spectator. Even in himself, adorned by God with exceptional gifts, man was the most excellent example of God's works. And he was endowed besides with the capacity to turn his eyes outward and to admire the handiwork of God in others of His creatures.[9]

6. In his widely read Terry Lectures, Fromm takes Calvin as a representative of "authoritarian" (as distinguished from "humanistic") religion, in which a man submits himself in obedience to a transcendent power not because of its moral qualities, but simply because it has control over him and the right to force him to worship it. Armed with one quotation from Calvin (*Inst.* 3.12.6), he thinks it possible to characterize Calvin's religious experience as "that of despising everything in oneself," God being a "symbol of power and force" and "man in juxtaposition . . . utterly powerless" (Erich Fromm, *Psychoanalysis and Religion* [New Haven: Yale University, 1950], pp. 34–36). Similarly, in an earlier work Fromm ascribes to Calvin's God "all the features of a tyrant without any quality of love or even justice" (*Escape from Freedom* [New York: Rinehart, 1941], pp. 87–88). He follows this description with a passage in which Calvin denies the priority of love over faith and hope (*Inst.* 3.2.41), but he substitutes a row of ellipsis points for Calvin's explanation: that it is faith that engenders love. One can only guess how Fromm gathered his scraps from Calvin; had he reached book 3, chapter 2, section 41, by way of sections 1–40, he must have noticed that faith, for Calvin, is directed to the paternal benevolence of God. What he mistakenly identifies as Calvin's religion is closer to the idolatry, hypocrisy, and pagan superstition that Calvin deplores (see, e.g., *Inst.* 1.5.4 [1:50]). Unfortunately, however, such misunderstandings of Calvin are common; otherwise there would be no point in mentioning them.

7. *Inst.* 1.5.4 (1:56).

8. I owe this citation from Calvin's sermons on Job to Cairns (see n. 15), p. 139. It is important to recognize that it is a judgment on man "considered in himself," but for all that it still smacks of hyperbole.

9. *Inst.* 1.14.20–22 (1:179–82).

How great ingratitude would it be now to doubt whether this most gracious Father has us in his care, who we see was concerned for us even before we were born! How impious would it be to tremble for fear that his kindness might at any time fail us in our need, when we see that it was shown, with the greatest abundance of every good thing, when we were yet unborn![10]

There, already, is the heart of Calvin's anthropology. But he turns to man in detail only in chapter 15 of the first book.

It is in this chapter (secs. 3–4) that Calvin writes of the image of God in man. He introduces the subject in a strangely offhanded way, apparently to clinch his argument for the immortality of the soul. But the notion of the divine image has far greater systematic importance than its modest entrance suggests. The way in which Calvin interprets it opens up, better than anything else, the heart of his understanding of man and his place in the world. Further, it constitutes an important link with other parts of the system. It is closely bound up, for instance, with Calvin's teaching on redemption, since Jesus Christ, as the Second Adam, is the one in whom the divine image is restored; being "saved" means being renewed after the image of God in Christ.[11] In addition, Calvin builds his social ethics partly on the endurance of the divine image even in fallen man. The sacredness and dignity of human life are guaranteed by the fact that man was made in the image and likeness of God, and that the remnants of the image persist. It is not only Genesis 1:26 that serves Calvin in this connection, but also Genesis 9:6: "Whoever sheds the blood of man, by man shall his blood be shed; for God made man in his own image." This meant, for him, that the image was not lost but remained regulative of man's social relationships.[12] (The christological connection of the divine image he found in, for example, 2 Corinthians 4:4, which speaks of the "light of the gospel of the glory of Christ, who is the likeness of God.")[13]

Perhaps Calvin's doctrine of the image of God in man did receive a somewhat external interest from the well-known debate between

10. *Inst.* 1.14.22 (1:182).

11. *Inst.* 1.15.4 (1:189); 2.12.6–7 (1:471–72); 3.3.9 (1:601).

12. See, e.g., *Inst.* 3.7.6 (1:696–97); *Comm. on Gen.* 9:6 (*CO* 23.147) (there remains *aliquid residuum*). Translations of all Calvin's commentaries are available in the old edition of the Calvin Translation Society, more than once reprinted; the New Testament commentaries have been revised in the Torrance edition (see n. 34 below).

13. *Inst.* 3.3.9 (1:601).

Barth and Brunner.[14] At least, it is largely to this debate that we owe the careful attention the scholars have paid to this theme in Calvin's theology.[15] But it does not follow that the image was marginal to his own thought. He made extensive use of it, perhaps more than the Scriptures warrant. At any rate, he pulled together under this rubric somewhat diverse biblical topics, linked accidentally by a single word, and gave them a distinctive interpretation. Whether or not the interpretation was strictly original, we do not, for now, need to inquire.[16]

14. The debate was precipitated by Emil Brunner's *Natur und Gnade* and Karl Barth's response *Nein!* Originally published in 1934, both books were translated into English by Peter Fraenkel under the title *Natural Theology* (London: Geoffrey Bles, Centenary, 1946). The exchange continued, especially in Brunner's *Mensch im Widerspruch* (1937) and in the third volume of Barth's *Kirchliche Dogmatik* (pts. 1–2, 1945); and it was Brunner's conviction that over the years the gap between him and Barth narrowed (Brunner, "The New Barth: Observations on Karl Barth's *Doctrine of Man,*" *Scottish Journal of Theology* 4 [1951]: 123–35). The points at issue between Brunner and Barth are perhaps less important for our present theme than one point of fundamental agreement: their common effort to think of the *imago Dei* (and therefore of man's humanity) less in terms of natural endowments and more in terms of personal existence, i.e., of man's dual relationship to God and his fellow men.

15. See especially Wilhelm Niesel, *The Theology of Calvin* [1938], trans. Harold Knight (Philadelphia: Westminster, 1956); T. F. Torrance, *Calvin's Doctrine of Man* (London: Lutterworth, 1949); David Cairns, *The Image of God in Man* (London: SCM, 1953). Torrance's brilliant work is the most detailed and important study of the *imago Dei* in Calvin's theology; it is rich in citations from outside the *Institutes,* especially from the commentaries and the sermons on Job (to which his sixth chapter is almost entirely devoted). But the reader may find its argument more tendentious in the use of primary sources than the innocent methodological remarks in the preface appear willing to acknowledge (pp. 7–8). The author deliberately eschews all reference to the secondary literature on Calvin; but when he notes the relevance of his findings to "the modern theological debate," one cannot help inferring that there has been some "relevance" also in the opposite direction. At points, Torrance admits that he is pressing beyond Calvin's explicit utterances (see, e.g., pp. 44–45); at other points, the mosaic of quotations gives a misleading impression that Calvin says something he is not explicitly saying at all (for an example, taken at random, see the first sentence on p. 70). It should be pointed out that the method of culling citations from all over Calvin's exegetical and homiletical works, important and fruitful though it has proved to be, needs to be used with caution: while it is true that his treatises and the *Institutes* are often determined by polemical considerations, his expositions are even more determined (as one would hope) by his text. There is not much to be gained by quoting Calvin when he offers little more than a paraphrase of his text.

16. Brunner gave a historical excursus on the interpretation of the image in an appendix to his *Man in Revolt: A Christian Anthropology [Mensch im Widerspruch,* 1937], trans. Olive Wyon (London: Lutterworth, 1939), pp. 449–515, and much more briefly in his *Dogmatics,* vol. 2: *The Christian Doctrine of Creation and Redemption* [1950], trans. Olive Wyon (London: Lutterworth, 1952), pp. 75–78. More detailed are the historical chapters in Cairns's *Image of God.* Briefly, we may conclude on the basis of these three studies that there were in fact antecedents for Calvin's distinctive conception of the divine image and likeness. In contrast to the

What does he mean, then, by the "image of God"? His treatment of the term in the *Institutes* is highly characteristic of him. He liked formal definitions. But, being trained in the rhetoric of the Renaissance, he thought it gauche to offer his definition first; it was more elegant to lead up to it. At the risk of appearing gauche, I will begin with it. Calvin writes:

> The integrity with which Adam was endowed is expressed by this word [*imago*], when he had full possession of right understanding, when he had his affections kept within the bounds of reason, all his senses tempered in right order, and he truly referred his excellence to exceptional gifts bestowed upon him by his Maker.[17]

It is apparent that what Calvin seeks in his definition is comprehensiveness. The image is anything and everything that sets man apart from the rest of God's creation;[18] or again, by argument back from the restoration of the image in Christ, it is anything and everything that we receive by redemption.[19] In detail, he seeks to divide the general concept by adopting common psychological categories, according to which, as he goes on to put it in a summary formula, Adam had light of *mind* and uprightness of *heart* (with "soundness of all the parts"). That is to say, Adam's intellect saw with clarity, and the affections were duly subordinated to it.[20]

Surveying the opinions of others (another of his favorite procedures), Calvin appropriates whatever he can, but does not hesitate to tell us where his predecessors went wrong. The distinction of Irenaeus between the "image" and the "likeness" of God he rejects: Irenaeus

---

"image," which he thought of as man's rationality, Irenaeus understood the "likeness" to refer to man's proper relation to God and as such to the goal of redemption. Augustine held that the trinitarian structure of man's psychological faculties is an image of God because it can remember, understand, and love God; and Thomas Aquinas likewise did not identify the image with man's intellectual nature as such, but with the aptitude of his intellectual nature for knowing and loving God. Luther, too, could assert that the image and likeness lie in knowledge and love of God. In short, there was a strong tradition affirming (with variations of detail) that the image or likeness lies in a relationship and not only in man's nature or endowments; and this is the direction that Calvin's thoughts also take.

17. *Inst.* 1.15.3 (1:188).

18. "... a tacit antithesis ... raises man above all other creatures and, as it were, separates him from the common mass" (*Inst.* 1.15.3 [1:188]). See also 2.12.6 (1:471).

19. *Inst.* 1.15.4 (1:189).

20. Ibid. (and the definition quoted above). On the distinction between intellect and will, see *Inst.* 1.15.7 (1:194–95).

did not understand the nature of Hebrew parallelism.[21] Even Augustine went astray by suggesting that the image refers to the psychological "trinity" of man's intellect, will, and memory, which he held to be an image (or analogy) of the Blessed Trinity. This, Calvin decides, is mere speculation.[22] On the other hand, he apparently thinks Chrysostom had a point when he identified the image with man's dominion over nature. At least, this is part of it. But it is not the sole mark by which man resembles God, and the image is to be sought more correctly *within* man as an inner good of the soul.[23] Finally, Calvin does not want to reject out of hand even the exegesis of Osiander, although he was a man "perversely ingenious in futile inventions." Osiander thought the image pertained to the body as well as to the soul, in that Adam's body pointed forward to the incarnation of the Son of God. This, Calvin assures us, is unsound. But he has already admitted that the upright posture of the human body is at least an outward token of the divine image; for, as Ovid says in the *Metamorphoses,* while other living beings are bent over earthwards,

> Man looks aloft and with erected eyes
> Beholds his own hereditary skies.[24]

Perhaps, however, the desire to be comprehensive and to take the opinions of others into account may obscure the distinctive feature of Calvin's interpretation. And one has to look to his commentaries (as well as to other sections of the *Institutes*) to shed further light on his definition. The first point to notice is the exact metaphor Calvin had in mind when he spoke of an "image." He meant the image seen in a mirror — a reflection.[25] This was a metaphor he particularly liked, and he had used it already in earlier chapters of the *Institutes;* the whole

21. *Inst.* 1.15.3 (1:187–88). Calvin does not mention Irenaeus by name, but Cairns shows that the distinction Calvin rejects can in fact be traced back to Irenaeus (*Image of God,* pp. 74–75).

22. *Inst.* 1.15.4 (1:190).

23. Ibid. That it is Chrysostom whom Calvin has in mind, though he does not name him, is clear from *Comm. on Gen.* 1:26, where he admits that Chrysostom has pointed at least to a very small part of the image (*CO* 23.26).

24. *Inst.* 1.15.3 (1:186–87; cf. p. 188). I have borrowed Dryden's version of Ovid's lines from the older (1845) translation of the *Institutes* by Henry Beveridge (London: James Clarke, 1949 reprint), vol. 1, p. 162.

25. "Nondum tamen data esse videtur plena imaginis definitio nisi clarius pateat quibus facultatibus praecellat homo, et quibus speculum censeri debeat gloriae Dei" (*Inst.* 1.15.4; Battles translates *speculum* here as "reflection," 1:189). "Ad imaginem ergo Dei conditus est homo, in quo suam gloriam creator ipse conspici quasi in speculo voluit" (*Inst.* 2.12.6 [1:471]).

of creation had been represented as a mirror in which the glory of God is to be viewed. We are, Calvin says, to "contemplate in all creatures, as in mirrors, those immense riches of his wisdom, justice, goodness, and power."[26] Similarly, in the chapter on man's nature as created Calvin states that "even in the several parts of the world some traces of God's glory shine."[27] If, then, the doctrine of the image of God in man is intended as a "tacit antithesis," to set man apart from the rest of creation, the question must be asked: How, or in what sense, is man peculiarly and particularly a mirror of deity? In what special manner is he the "reflection of God's glory"?

The answer is most clearly read in the last phrase of Calvin's definition: ". . . and he truly referred his excellence to exceptional gifts bestowed upon him by his Maker." While the entire created order reflects God's glory as in a mirror and in this sense "images" God, man is distinguished from the mute creation by his ability to reflect God's glory in a conscious response of thankfulness. It is this, above all, that sets him apart from the brute beasts: they likewise owe their existence to God, but they do not know it.[28] Man is endowed with a soul by which he can consciously acknowledge God as the Fountain of Good; the soul is not itself the image, but rather the mirror in which the image is reflected.[29] Properly, then, we can speak of man as bearing the image of God only when he attributes his excellence to the Maker.[30] Man is the apex of creation in the sense that the entire cre-

26. *Inst.* 1.14.21 (1:180).

27. *Inst.* 1.15.3 (1:188).

28. *Comm. on Heb.* 11:3 (*CO* 55.144 [on man's difference from brute beasts], 145 [on the image of God in the world]). In *Inst.* 1.6.3 (1:72), Calvin speaks of the divine likeness imprinted on the form of the universe; but there the word used is not *imago* but *effigies*.

29. The "seat" (*sedes*) of the divine image is in the soul (*Inst.* 1.15.3 [1:186]). Wilhelm Niesel writes: "Thus man's similitude to God implies something more than his psycho-physical constitution; it signifies his right attitude towards his Creator and thus his right attitude towards all other creatures. . . . The divine similitude consists not in the fact that man is endowed with reason and will, but in the fact that these faculties in original man were directed wholly towards knowledge of and obedience to God" (*Theology of Calvin,* pp. 67–68). This is well said, but it seems to me that the heart of the "right attitude" can be more exactly specified as thankfulness; that is, the attitude that acknowledges man's endowments as gifts. In addition to the last phrase in Calvin's definition of the image, see *Inst.* 2.2.1 (1:256): ". . . Scriptura nihil aliud ei tribuit quam quod creatus esset ad imaginem Dei: quo scilicet insinuat, non propriis bonis sed Dei participatione fuisse beatum."

30. As Torrance rightly puts it: "There is no doubt that Calvin always thinks of the *imago* in terms of a *mirror.* Only while the mirror actually reflects an object does it have the image of that object. There is no such thing in Calvin's thought as an *imago* dissociated from the act of reflecting" (*Calvin's Doctrine of Man,* p. 36). Calvin

ation has its raison d'être in the praise that man alone, of all God's earthly creatures, can return to Him.[31]

To sum up: In Calvin's view, the image of God in man denotes not an endowment only, but also a relationship. That is to say, he does not seek to define the image solely by what man possesses as his "nature," but also by the manner in which he orients himself to God. Man is not made in the image of God simply because he has reason, for instance, whereas the rest of God's earthly creatures do not. Even an individual endowed with a wealth of special "gifts" is not in the image of God, in the fully human sense, unless he *acknowledges* them as gifts of God. The relationship of man to God is thus made constitutive of his humanity; and, as we were led to expect, there is a correlation between the notion that is constitutive of deity and the notion constitutive of humanity. God as Fountain of Good has His counterpart in man as His *thankful* creature. And the disruption of this relationship is, for Calvin, nothing less than dehumanizing.

The distinction implicit here becomes crucial for understanding Calvin's view of sin and the fall. The scholars have found an ambiguity in Calvin's answer to the question: Is the image of God lost in fallen man? But if the image includes both man's rational nature and its proper use toward God, the answer is bound to be two-sided. Insofar as the image culminates in the thought of a "right spiritual attitude" (Niesel),[32] one can hardly speak of it as other than "lost" in fallen

occasionally uses the metaphor of an engraved image, but, so Torrance claims, "never dissociated from the idea of the mirror" (ibid.). I have noted the metaphor of an engraved image in, for example, *Inst.* 1.15.3 (1:188) and 2.12.6 (1:471). Torrance produces a wealth of citations from the commentaries to document his interpretation of Calvin's anthropology; but he provides no specific reference for his statement that in the 1536 *Institutes* "Calvin practically equates the *imago* with the *actio* of gratitude" (p. 71, n. 6).

31. This is a theme suggested to Calvin by, for instance, his exposition of the Psalms. The earth was given to men that they might glorify the Creator; out of sinful humanity the Creator preserves a people for Himself, so that the end (or "final cause") of creation will not be frustrated. "Hic nobis vivendi finis est ut simus in terra praecones gloriae Dei. . . . Nam quum ad pecudes et feras perveniant terrae opes, praecipue tamen in usum hominum creata esse omnia spiritus pronuntiat, ut Deum inde patrem agnoscant. . . . Nisi Deus ecclesiam conservet, inversum iri totum naturae ordinem: quia irrita erit mundi creatio, nisi sit aliquis populus qui Deum invocet" (*Comm. on Ps.* 115:17 [CO 32.192]). Cf.' *Comm. on Ps.* 105:44–45 (CO 32.114–15), where the "glorifying" of God includes keeping His commandments. In his *Commentary on Hebrews* Calvin links the end of creation with the metaphor of the "mirror": "Quare eleganter mundus divinitatis speculum nominatur. . . . Fideles autem, quibus oculos dedit in singulis creaturis, velut emicantes gloriae eius scintillas cernunt. Certe in hunc finem conditus est mundus, ut esset divinae gloriae theatrum" (*Comm. on Heb.* 11:3 [CO 55.146]).

32. *Theology of Calvin,* p. 67.

man, who (by definition) is man fallen out of the right spiritual relationship to God. Redemption, accordingly, is nothing less than restoration of the image. Later, in discussing the effects of the fall, Calvin
will assert that faith and love for God, since they are restored to us
by Christ, must be accounted lost by the fall—taken away. But the
rational nature of man, by which he is *enabled* (in distinction from
mere beasts) to love God, is not simply wiped out.[33] In short, the
image of God in man embraces both a gift and its right use, both
man's rational nature and its orientation to God in thankfulness. For:
"We are no different from brutish beasts if we do not understand that
the world was made by God. Why are men endowed with reason and
intellect except for the purpose of recognizing their Creator?"[34]

With these remarks, the transition is already made from man in
the design of God to man in the state of sin. Once again, the important
point is to grasp the systematic coherence of Calvin's thoughts. Quite
simply, if Adam's original state was one in which he acknowledged
his endowments as the gifts of God, his fallen state was induced by
the pride that claimed something for himself. Not content to be like
God, he wanted to be God's equal; and in seeking his own glory, he
lost the capacity to reflect the glory of God. If one can hold firmly to
this cardinal thought, then much of the nonsense that is commonly
retailed concerning "total depravity" can be quickly disposed of. Cal-

---

33. *Inst.* 2.2.12 (1:270). In this section (1:270–71) Calvin endorses the scholastic distinction between the corruption of man's natural gifts and the loss of the
supernatural gifts. Perhaps the terminology suits his standpoint less well than he
assumes; for if man was created to glorify God with thankful homage, how can it be
said that faith and love for God are "adventitious and beyond nature" (*adventitia
. . . et praeter naturam*)? However, by calling understanding and will "natural gifts"
he intends to stress that, though corrupted, they remain distinguishing characteristics
of man in contrast to brute beasts. Man is, in particular, a "rational being"; this
Calvin infers from the prologue to the Fourth Gospel. But his view of man is incomplete unless one adds the reason *why* man was created a rational being (see the
following note). For some representative statements in the *Institutes* on the question
whether the image is lost, see *Inst.* 1.15.4 (1:189–90); 2.2.17 (1:277); 3.3.9 (1:601);
and the passage cited in n. 12 above. Calvin seems bent on stressing the fearful
deformity of the image in fallen man as far as he can *without* asserting that it is
totally annihilated. But he can also say that the image in Adam was "obliterated"
(*obliterata: Inst.* 2.1.5 [1:246]) or "destroyed" (*deleta: Comm. on Gen.* 1:26 [*CO*
23.26]). Even the statement that the image was "destroyed," however, is immediately
qualified: it means that the traces of the image are vitiated and that no part is free
from the infection of sin (*CO* 23.27).

34. *Comm. on Heb.* 11.3 (*CO* 55.144); English quoted from Calvin, *The Epistle
of Paul the Apostle to the Hebrews and the First and Second Epistles of St. Peter,*
trans. William B. Johnston, Calvin's Commentaries, ed. David W. Torrance and
Thomas F. Torrance (Grand Rapids: Eerdmans, 1963), vol. 12, pp. 158–59.

vin had no interest in belittling the moral and intellectual achievements of man; he was too well schooled in the classics and in Renaissance scholarship to do that. But he had also gone to school with his master Augustine, and what he did wish to show was that all the works of man, even the very best, remain radically defective when the doer no longer receives his life as a gift. And precisely because he knew classical and Renaissance man so well, he could argue his case with penetrating insight.

Now there are several intricate questions in Calvin's discussion of sin that we must risk leaving out. In particular, he wrestled with two problems bequeathed to him by Augustine: the cause of Adam's sin and the mode of its transmission. These are important questions, and Calvin's reflections on them are intriguing.[35] But it is obvious that one could not, in any case, resolve the problems of sin's cause and transmission without determining what sin is. This, then, is the first matter on which I should comment; and the only other matter I wish to take up (because of its pertinence to my central theme) is the extent of the damage wreaked by sin on human nature.

We are not surprised to find that Calvin has his definition of original sin.[36] But what is the nature of the "depravity" and "corruption" to which the definition refers? His analysis of the concept of sin is in fact more clearly given in his interpretation of Genesis 3: it is the "history" of Adam's fall that shows us what sin is.[37] As usual, Calvin

35. On the former question, despite his insistence that Adam was responsible for his fall (*Inst.* 1.15.8 [1:195]), Calvin cannot but argue that Adam fell by divine decree (*Inst.* 3.23.7 [2:955]). He leaves it to the devout reader to affirm two things that carnal reason cannot harmonize: God's decree and Adam's responsibility. See Calvin, *De aeterna Dei praedestinatione,* etc. (1552) (*CO* 8.294–95); English in *Calvin's Calvinism,* pt. 1: *A Treatise on the Eternal Predestination of God,* trans. Henry Cole [1856] (Grand Rapids: Eerdmans, 1956 reprint), pp. 87–88. There is a more recent English version of the treatise on predestination: Calvin, *Concerning the Eternal Predestination of God,* trans. J. K. S. Reid (London: James Clarke, 1961); see pp. 98–99. It is interesting that, despite the fall, Calvin thought Adam belonged to the number of the saved (*Inst.* 2.10.7 [1:434]). On the second question, although Calvin freely uses the traditional language of "hereditary corruption," he expressly denies that the corruption of the whole human race in the person of Adam is to be attributed to procreation; it was the result of "the appointment of God" (*Comm. on John* 3:6 [*CO* 47.57]). One reason for Calvin's conception of sin's transmission was undoubtedly the fact that he did not make the direct connections the Schoolmen made between sin and sensuality.

36. *Inst.* 2.1.8 (1:251).

37. *Inst.* 2.1.4 (1:244–46). All Calvin's quotations in the following three paragraphs are from this section of the *Institutes.* It is instructive to compare Calvin's analysis of the fall with Luther's, who likewise traces the primal sin back to unbelief or doubting the Word. See Luther, *In primum librum Mose enarrationes* (1535–45), *WA* 42.112.20; *Luther's Works* 1.149.

proceeds by telling us what others have said on the subject, especially Augustine.

We read that Adam ate a tempting fruit, "good for food . . . a delight to the eyes" (Gen. 3:6). Was his sin, then, that he indulged his appetite? Calvin answers: "To regard Adam's sin as gluttonous intemperance (a common notion) is childish." The forbidden fruit was a test of obedience, an exercise of faith. In a paradise abounding with delights, abstinence from only one fruit would hardly have made him virtuous. Rather, "the sole purpose of the precept was to keep him content with his lot." So, Calvin moves on to Augustine's interpretation, which states that pride was the beginning of all evils. "For if ambition had not raised man higher than was meet and right, he could have remained in his original state." Is Augustine right? Well, the English translation says that he "speaks rightly." But what Calvin wrote was *non male,* and he seems to have meant it literally: Augustine's answer is not bad, but it is not quite right either.

Calvin wants, in fact, to get behind human pride to the root cause of it. And what is that? He has several words for it; perhaps "unfaithfulness" is the regulative one. But it is crucial to note that, for him, the essence of infidelity is *not listening to God.* That is the way he read the biblical narrative. The serpent's opening gambit, it will be recalled, is to ask the question, "Did God say . . . ?" (v. 1). A little later, somewhat emboldened, he assures Eve: "You will not die" (v. 4). The serpent works by instilling contempt for the Word of God. Here is the theme Calvin wants to pick up, in order to show the root of pride and so to improve on Augustine. Adam, in short, was *verbo incredulus:* he questioned the Word. And this destroyed his reverence for God, whom he pictured as not only deceitful but envious and hostile to His own creature.

Finally, at the end, Calvin seems to return to the theme of carnal desire, and says: "As a result, men, having cast off the fear of God, threw themselves wherever lust carried them." Bondage to carnal desire, in other words, is not the beginning of sin but its final consequence. The heart of the matter, as Calvin saw it, is summed up like this:

> Unfaithfulness, then, was the root of the Fall. But thereafter ambition and pride, together with ungratefulness, arose, because Adam by seeking more than was granted him shamefully spurned God's great bounty, which had been lavished upon him. To have been made in the likeness of God seemed a small matter to a son of earth unless he also attained equality with God — a monstrous wickedness!

It will be noticed, in this passage, how Calvin can equally well make his point with the word "ungratefulness"; or, from the perspective of God, he can state that "Adam carried away by the devil's blasphemies, as far as he was able extinguished the whole glory of God." Plainly, here is the same complex of ideas — with some shifts in terminology — that we have found already in Calvin's thoughts on the image of God in man. But now everything is, so to say, inverted; for whereas man was created to image God's glory in an act of thankful acknowledgment, he has fallen into thankless pride that spurns God's bounty.

Calvin rounds off his anatomy of sin with a remark that points forward to redemption: "The door of salvation is opened to us when we receive the gospel today with our ears, even as death was then admitted by those same windows when they were opened to Satan." (As so often, he is quoting Bernard of Clairvaux.) But his immediate agenda requires him to address himself, next, to original sin and the ravages of sin in the intellect and the will of man. Here we find some of Calvin's gloomiest thoughts; yet they can hardly account for the common opinion that there is a sharp difference between Roman Catholicism and Protestantism on the extent of sin's damage to the soul.

Although he is sharply critical of the Schoolmen at many points, Calvin thinks one cannot improve on their distinction between the natural and the supernatural gifts of God: "The natural gifts in man were corrupted, but the supernatural taken away."[38] The problem is that the Schoolmen did not agree on a satisfactory *explanation* of the formula, and in this respect the earlier Schoolmen are judged better than the "more recent Sophists."[39] Hence a great part of the discussion requires Calvin, as usual, to sort out the sheep from the goats among his predecessors and to arrive at satisfactory definitions of terms. The sole point I want to stress, however, is that he seems explicitly to caution us against "adjudging man's nature wholly corrupted."[40] At

38. *Inst.* 2.2.4 (1:260); cf. n. 33.

39. *Inst.* 2.2.6 (1:263).

40. "Exempla igitur ista monere nos videntur ne hominis naturam in totum vitiosum putemus" (*Inst.* 2.3.3 [1:292]). See T. H. L. Parker, *Calvin's Doctrine of the Knowledge of God,* 2nd ed. (Edinburgh: Oliver and Boyd, 1969), p. 49, n. 2. As Parker's note indicates, there has been some difference of scholarly opinion on the interpretation of this sentence, which he takes to mean: These examples *seem* to warn us against judging man's nature wholly corrupt, but in fact they do not. In other places Calvin does speak expressly of fallen man's powers as "wholly depraved." See, for instance, his *Supplex exhortatio ad Caesarem de restituenda eccle-·sia* (1543), where he accuses his opponents of denying that man's powers are *prorsus depravatas* (*CO* 6.483) — trans. in *Calvin: Theological Treatises,* trans. J. K. S. Reid, Library of Christian Classics, vol. 22 (Philadelphia: Westminster, 1954), p. 198. But against the interpretation Parker represents it has been pointed out that the word

any rate, what he was concerned to establish was, not that man is utterly bad, but that the taint of sin vitiates even his best and leaves no corner of his life unblemished. And he tried to demonstrate this thesis, in turn, with respect to both man's intellectual and his moral achievements.

Writing of the human intellect, Calvin certainly will not allow that it can attain to a sound knowledge of God; for it cannot reach the assurance of God's benevolence (a point that Luther, too, liked to stress).[41] Nevertheless, it is entirely consistent with Calvin's standpoint that he maintained a firmly positive attitude toward the attainments of human culture, since failure to do so would be denial of his fundamental notion of God as *fons bonorum.*

> The mind of man, though fallen and perverted from its wholeness, is nevertheless clothed and ornamented with God's excellent gifts. If we regard the Spirit of God as the sole fountain of truth, we shall neither reject the truth itself, nor despise it wherever it shall appear, unless we wish to dishonor the Spirit of God. For by holding the gifts of the Spirit in light esteem, we contemn and reproach the Spirit himself.[42]

Calvin then parades the cultural achievements of man in law, natural philosophy, logic, medicine, mathematics. And, as a good humanist, he concludes:

> We cannot read the writings of the ancients on these subjects without great admiration. We marvel at them because we are compelled to recognize how preeminent they are. But shall we count anything praiseworthy or noble without recognizing at the same time that it comes from God? Let us be ashamed of such ingratitude, into which

emphasized — "seem" (*videntur*) — does not appear in the Latin editions between 1539 and 1550, nor in the French translation. In any case, it will hardly be denied that if we attribute a doctrine of "total depravity" to Calvin, then we must take it to mean a depravity that extends over the whole man: the totality is extensive rather than intensive. His argument is with theologians who, under the influence of philosophy, tended to equate man's problem with the downward pull of his sensuality, assuming his intellect and even his will to be unimpaired (*Inst.* 2.2.4 [1:258–60]; cf. 2.2.2 [1:257]). In a vivid image, Calvin asserts that the gifts remaining to us since the fall are spoiled like good wine turned sour in a bad vessel (*Comm. on John* 3.6 [CO 47.57]). It was also a concern of Calvin, as of Luther, to deny that sin is merely weakness; in fact, they held, the sinful will is vigorous but vitiated in its motivation. This is Calvin's point in the passage just cited from the *Supplex exhortatio,* and he remembers to add the qualification that of himself man possesses no ability whatever to act aright as far as spiritual righteousness is concerned.

41. *Inst.* 2.2.18 (1:277).
42. *Inst.* 2.2.15 (1:273–74).

not even the pagan poets fell, for they confessed that the gods had invented philosophy, laws, and all useful arts.[43]

Similarly, when Calvin turns to his discussion of the fallen will, he insists that even in sin man cannot be wholly bad; otherwise, we could not say that one man is "better" than another.

> In every age there have been persons who, guided by nature, have striven toward virtue throughout life. I have nothing to say against them even if many lapses can be noted in their moral conduct. . . . Either we must make Camillus equal to Catiline, or we shall have in Camillus an example proving that nature, if carefully cultivated, is not utterly devoid of goodness.[44]

Then, of course, comes the refrain: this "natural goodness," too, must be traced to the special bounty of God. "The endowments resplendent in Camillus were gifts of God." But now the question is this: Did the ancient heroes, such as the patriot Camillus, acknowledge gifts as gifts?

Calvin's answer is that "heroes" are driven by their own ambition. In other words, we may say, the glory they seek is their own. Hence Calvin grants that their virtues will have their praise in the political assembly and in common renown among men, but not that they make for righteousness before the heavenly judgment seat. For "where there is no zeal to glorify God, the chief part of uprightness is absent." While, therefore, in ordinary, day-to-day usage ("common parlance," as Calvin says) we do not hesitate to distinguish one man as "noble" and another as "depraved" in nature, we are still to include both under the theological verdict of human depravity. Plainly, Calvin is making the point that Luther conveyed by his distinction between "Christian" and "civil" righteousness. To say (theologically) that a man is "depraved" is not to say that, morally considered, he is a bad man. All turns on the motivation out of which a man acts: whether or not, that is, his deeds are done in thankfulness to the Fountain of Good. The doctrine of sin is not strictly about a person's moral condition, but about his relationship to God: it pronounces a religious, not an ethical, verdict. Pagan virtues, properly understood, are in truth tokens of

---

43. *Inst.* 2.2.15 (1:274). Calvin's estimate of the capabilities of man's fallen intellect closely parallels Luther's and includes a distinction between "heavenly things" and "earthly things" (*Inst.* 2.2.13 [1:272]).

44. *Inst.* 2.2.3–4 (1:292–93). All quotations in this and the following paragraph are from *Inst.* 2.2.3–4 (1:292–94).

grace; but insofar as they are the virtues of a man who claims them for himself, they differ from the virtues of the justified man because they issue from a quite different orientation of the total self.

While it cannot be claimed that Calvin's language is always perspicuously self-consistent, a consistent thread does run through his thoughts on human nature as created, fallen, and redeemed.[45] Man's being points beyond him to the source of his existence and of the existence of all that is. He was fashioned as the point of creation at which the overflowing goodness of the Creator was to be "mirrored" or reflected back again in thankful piety. This is the condition from which he fell, no longer heeding the voice of God; and it is the condition to which, through hearing the Word of God in Jesus Christ, he is restored. For all Calvin's persuasion that man has a privileged standing in the world, his cosmos is not man-centered: man has his place as spectator and even agent of the manifestation of God's glory, in which alone the cosmos has its final meaning. It may well be that, when demythologized, such an austere view of the dignity and finitude of man takes on a profounder relevance than Calvin ever dreamed of, as Western man moves out of the tight little world of the Middle Ages into the immense, mysterious cosmos of the modern astronomer.[46]

45. Calvin is so anxious to make his point about the radical defect of human good apart from grace (i.e., that such good is vitiated, from the religious point of view, by the absence of thankfulness to God), that he sometimes speaks of it as though it were a mere "show of good" (*Inst.* 2.5.19 [1:340]). But one must surely infer from the passages already cited that fallen man is capable of real good — only in another order than the realm of righteousness before God. Niesel is undoubtedly right in affirming that for Calvin "sin is something other than moral failure" (*Theology of Calvin,* p. 89). But Torrance, with equal justice, concedes that Calvin does not consistently differentiate the moral and the theological points of view (*Calvin's Doctrine of Man,* pp. 19–20); and Cairns thinks that Calvin slips into inconsistency when he "interprets man's perversity in such a sense that the dignity and sacredness of human nature appear to have perished with the Fall" (*Image of God,* p. 138).

46. Calvin frequently speaks of the earth and even the universe as made and furnished for man (see, e.g., *Inst.* 1.14.2 [1:161–62]; 14.22 [1:181–82]; 1.16.6 [1:204]). But this must be understood in relation to his other line of thought according to which man himself was made for God, a thought that receives classic expression in the opening sentences of the Geneva Catechism (1545): ". . . he created us and placed us in this world to be glorified in us" (*CO* 6.10; trans. in *Calvin's Tracts and Treatises,* trans. Henry Beveridge [1844–51] [Grand Rapids: Eerdmans, 1958 reprint], vol. 2, p. 37). See also n. 31 above. This vision of God's glory requires "demythologization," I should think, because the anthropomorphic image of God's glorifying Himself, if taken too literally, presents a narcissistic deity bent on contemplating His own image. But since Calvin does not seem to have felt the problem, there is no need to pursue it here any further.

7

The Incarnation: Christ's Union with Us

Paul van Buren

The Cause of the Incarnation

The Need for a Mediator

Calvin's doctrine of reconciliation is an expansion of his compact statement that, in order to be reconciled to God, it was necessary that man, "who had ruined himself by his disobedience, should remedy his condition by obedience, should satisfy the justice of God, and suffer the punishment for his sin. Our Lord, then, made His appearance as a real man; He put on the character of Adam and assumed his name, to act as his substitute in his obedience to the Father, to lay down our flesh as the price of satisfaction to the justice of God, and to suffer in the same flesh the punishment which we had deserved."[1] The fulcrum of this passage is substitution: Christ in our place. But in order to make clear the substitutionary character of Christ's work it is necessary to review Calvin's doctrine of the incarnation, that it may be evident who is our substitute, how and why He took our place, and the extent to which He took our place.

Calvin begins his treatment of the doctrine of reconciliation with the problem of fallen man.[2] It is not self-evident, however, that this should have been his starting place. Calvin has established in book 1 of his *Institutes* that the knowledge of God must precede the knowl-

Reprinted from *Christ in Our Place* (Edinburgh: Oliver and Boyd, 1957), pp. 3–23. Used by permission.

1. *Inst.* 2.12.3 (*CR* 30.341–42).
2. *Inst.* 2.1–5.

edge of man,[3] and that it is precisely this knowledge of God that has
been lost to man,[4] and which now can be recovered only by means of
God's Word, faithfully heard.[5] *In* Christ, that is, we learn what we
were *out of* Christ. Would it not have been better, therefore, to begin
with the solution rather than with the problem? Would it not have
been more consistent with what he says if Calvin had presented the
event of reconciliation first, and then shown the necessity for reconciliation, a necessity that is to be understood only in the light of the
event itself? It is true that there are many passages in which he does
just that: "If we were firmly persuaded of what, indeed, ought not to
be questioned, that our nature is destitute of all those things which
our heavenly Father confers on His elect through the Spirit of regeneration, there would be no cause for hesitation here."[6] And again: "If
the death of Christ be our redemption, then we were captives; if it be
satisfaction, we were debtors; if it be atonement, we were guilty; if it
be cleansing, we were unclean."[7] Yet in his definitive edition of his
Institutes Calvin chose to present the doctrine of sin first, with Christology following as the solution to this problem. It may be that he saw
the problem of man's fallen condition as a solved problem, speaking
of man-apart-from-Christ from the point of view of man-in-Christ. If
that is true, then it is unfortunate that he did not make this clearer in
the structure of the *Institutes,* a misfortune to which the history of
Protestant theology bears witness.

The starting point, then, is human sin, which Calvin sees essentially as disobedience.[8] Tempted by Satan, man disobeyed God's command, thereby introducing disorder into God's creation.[9] This primal
act of disobedience was Adam's, but we were also involved in it, for
Adam, as the first man, bore a representational character. He was
created as the father of the whole human race, and in dealing with
him God was at the same time dealing with us all. Thus, what Adam
received from God he received for us all: "The Lord deposited with
Adam the gifts He chose to confer on human nature. Therefore, when

3. "Hominem in puram sui notitiam nunquam pervenire constat nisi prius Dei
faciem sit contemplatus" — *Inst.* 1.1.2 (*CR* 30.32).

4. "Porro sive alii evanescant in suis superstitionibus, sive alii data opera mali-
tiose a Deo desciscant, omnes tamen degerant a vera eius notitia" — *Inst.* 1.4.1 (*CR*
30.38).

5. *Inst.* 1.6.2 (*CR* 30.53f.).

6. *Inst.* 2.2.20 (*CR* 30.201).

7. *Comm. on Gal.* 2:21 (*CR* 78.200–01). Cf. *Comm. on Eph.* 1:10 (*CR* 79.151);
Comm. on Isa. 42:1 (*CR* 65.59–60); *Comm. on Acts* 10:43 (*CR* 76.249); *Comm. on
1 John* 4:10 (*CR* 83.354).

8. *Inst.* 2.1.4 (*CR* 30.178).

9. Ibid. Cf. *Comm. on Gen.* 3:1 (*CR* 51.55).

he lost that which he had received, he lost them not only for himself, but also for us."[10] Adam's sin is also ours, not by a biological transmission but because in Adam God was dealing with all men: "for the corruption of all mankind in the person of Adam alone did not proceed from generation, but from the appointment of God, who in one man had adorned us all, and who has in him also deprived us of his gifts."[11] Following Romans 5:12, Calvin points out that we are not innocent creatures who have been loaded with the guilt of another; we have all followed our representative in the path of disobedience. "We derive from him not only the punishment but also a pollution within us which justly deserves the punishment,"[12] and thus all men are made "liable to punishment by their own sinfulness, not by the sinfulness of another."[13]

All men stand as sinners before God, under the curse and the punishment of death. The problem, therefore, arises from this condition of mankind, in which through our own fault we are all in revolt against, and separated from, Him who is Life. "Since our iniquities, intervening between us and Him like a cloud, had alienated us from the Kingdom of Heaven, no one could be a mediator for the restoration of peace except Him who could approach God," an office which could not be undertaken by any of the children of Adam, for "they, with their parent, all dreaded the divine presence."[14] The distance that lies between the holy God and sinful men is far too great for us to find the way across, for not only is there the difference between the Creator and His creatures, but now there is added the barrier of sin. "Although man had remained immaculately innocent, yet his condition would have been too mean for him to approach God without a mediator. What then can he do after having been plunged by his fatal fall into death and Hell, defiled with so many blemishes, putrefied in his own corruption, and in a word overwhelmed with every curse?"[15] Calvin takes man's disobedience and revolt seriously. It is a condition of his being "wholly at variance with God," of being "His enemy."[16] "Since the word *enemies* has a passive as well as an active meaning, it is well suited to us in both respects, so long as we are apart from Christ. For we are both children of wrath from birth, and every thought of

10. *Inst.* 2.1.7 (*CR* 30.181).
11. *Comm. on John* 3:6 (*CR* 75.57).
12. *Inst.* 2.1.8 (*CR* 30.182).
13. *Inst.* 2.1.8 (*CR* 30.183).
14. *Inst.* 2.12.1 (*CR* 30.340).
15. Ibid.
16. *Comm. on Col.* 1:21 (*CR* 80.90).

the flesh is against God."[17] And this condition extends to every man, so that all are in need of reconciliation to God.[18] If we find this judgment too hard, then we are seeing things only by the world's standards rather than according to the truth of God. "But the apostle assumes this as a sure axiom of Scripture (of which these profane sophists are ignorant), that we are born so corrupt and depraved that there is in us as it were an innate hatred of God, so that we desire nothing but what is displeasing to Him, all the passions of our flesh carrying on continual war with His righteousness."[19]

From the side of man, then, the situation is hopeless. All that we had possessed, we had possessed by our "participation in God."[20] This has now been lost, as well as all hope of returning to the source of our life.[21] And that not by anyone's fault but our own, for we have put ourselves in revolt against the source of all our blessings. We have set up our sin as a barrier to keep ourselves away from God. "The whole may be summed up thus: where sin is, there is the wrath of God, and therefore God is not propitious to us without, or before, His blotting out our sins."[22] In need of restoration to God, we have no way of reaching Him, or, in fact, even of wanting restoration.[23] There could be only one source of help in this situation: God Himself would have to come to the aid of His revolting creatures. "Our situation was truly deplorable unless the divine Majesty itself would descend to us, for we could not ascend to it. Thus it was necessary that the Son of God should become Immanuel, that is, God with us."[24]

The Gift of a Mediator

As seriously as Calvin takes the fall of man, he never for a moment regards it as a fall out of the realm of God's love. Although fallen, man remains God's creature and the object of His love. "He loved us gratuitously, even before we were born, and also when, through de-

---

17. Ibid.

18. *Comm. on John* 1:20 (*CR* 75.26).

19. *Comm. on 1 John* 4:10 (*CR* 83.353).

20. *Inst.* 2.2.1 (*CR* 30.186). "In the first place, let us consider that our happiness consists in our cleaving to God, and on the other hand there is nothing more miserable than to be alienated from Him" — *Comm. on Col.* 1:20 (*CR* 80.88).

21. "Christ shows that we are all dead before He quickens us, and hence it is clear what the whole nature of man can accomplish towards procuring salvation" — *Comm. on John* 5:25 (*CR* 75.117).

22. *Comm. on 2 Cor.* 5:19 (*CR* 78.72).

23. "We shun and dread every access to Him unless a mediator comes who can deliver us from fear" — *Comm. on 1 Peter* 1:21 (*CR* 83.226).

24. *Inst.* 2.12.1 (*CR* 30.340).

pravity of nature, we had hearts turned against Him, yielding to no right or godly feelings."[25] Had God not loved fallen man, no possibility would have remained for salvation. Therefore, Calvin insists, "our reconciliation by the death of Christ must not be understood as if the Son reconciled us to (the Father) that He might begin to love those whom He had before hated; but we were reconciled to Him who already loved us, but with whom we were at enmity on account of sin."[26] Reconciliation through Christ is based on God's eternal love, which precedes in time and in order the event of reconciliation: "God did not begin to love us when we were reconciled to Him by the blood of His Son, but He loved us before the creation of the world."[27]

We are the object of reconciliation, not God. He is the activator of the reconciliation of sinful men to Himself, the motivation for this activity on His part being nothing other than the nature of God Himself, for "He will never find in us anything which He ought to love, but He loves us because He is good and merciful."[28] Thus the very first thing to be said about our salvation is that it is all the work of God's eternal love for His sinful creatures: "The love of God precedes our reconciliation in Christ; indeed, because He first loves (1 John 4:19), He afterwards reconciles us to Himself."[29] But this prior and eternal love of God's does not eliminate His wrath against sin, and against man in so far as he is a sinner. Calvin quotes Augustine with approval: God "both hated and loved us at the same time. He hated us being different from what He had made us; but as our iniquity had not destroyed entirely His work in us, He could at the same time in every one of us hate what we had done and love what He had made."[30] In his own words, Calvin puts it this way: "God does not detest in us His own workmanship — that is, that He has made us men — but our uncleanness, which has extinguished the light of His image."[31] In terms of this barrier of sin, therefore, there is a sense in which Calvin is able to speak of God as the object of reconciliation: by the event of our reconciliation to Him, God is able to remove the barrier that stood in the way of the full exercise of His love for us, a barrier that we had erected and which only He could remove. "To remove every obstacle

25. *Comm. on 1 John* 4:10 (*CR* 83.353).
26. *Inst.* 2.16.4 (*CR* 30.370).
27. Ibid.
28. *Comm. on Titus* 3:4 (*CR* 80.429). ". . . a seipso causam petens cur illi benefaciat, quod peccatorum ipsum bonitatis suae sensu afficiat" — *Inst.* 3.11.16 (*CR* 30.547).
29. *Inst.* 2.16.3 (*CR* 30.370).
30. *Inst.* 2.16.4 (*CR* 30.370).
31. *Comm. on Rom.* 3:25 (*CR* 77.62).

in the way of His love for us, God appointed a method of salvation in Christ. . . . For God in a certain inexpressible manner at the same time that He loved us was nevertheless angry with us, until He was reconciled in Christ."[32] This means, then, that for Calvin the gift of reconciliation reveals the true nature of God. In Christ God establishes Himself and reveals to men what He is in all eternity: "It is a common way of speaking in the Scriptures that the world was reconciled to God by the death of Christ, although we know that He was a kind Father in all ages. But because we find no cause for the love of God towards us and no ground for our salvation but in Christ, it is not without good reason that God the Father is said to have shown His goodness to us in Him."[33] The Father is Himself the Reconciler, therefore, for it was He who "appointed this method of salvation for us."[34]

The gift of the Mediator is the realization of God's eternal love[35] and therefore the final revelation of God's eternal will: "It was from God's goodness alone as from a fountain that Christ with all His blessings has come to us. . . . Hence all who inquire apart from Christ what is determined for them in God's secret counsel are mad to their own ruin."[36] It is not our intention to analyze Calvin's doctrine of predestination, that which "is determined for them in God's secret counsel" (which in the *Institutes,* be it noted, follows *after* all that he has to say about Christ, His work, and the Christian life, and is therefore presented as a clarification of what has gone before), but a question may be raised here. Did Calvin really mean that election is to be understood in terms of Christ alone? And if God's decision about every man has been made in Christ, as Calvin seems to say here, why does he speak of a counsel of God that is "secret" and as it were hidden behind or above Christ?

Calvin stresses the priority of God's love by calling it the originating or primary cause (*summa causa*) of our salvation.[37] That is, God's reconciling love is grounded in Himself, in the inner life of the Triune God. The form of this reconciling love is the love of the Father for the Son, and it is by this love that we are to measure the love of God for us. "Surely this is a notable and rich proof of inestimable love, that

32. *Inst.* 2.17.2 (*CR* 30.387).

33. *Comm. on Titus* 3:4 (*CR* 80.428).

34. *Inst.* 2.17.1 (*CR* 30.387). "God of Himself willingly sought out a means by which He might take away our curse"—*Comm. on Rom.* 3:25 (*CR* 77.62).

35. "Christ has now appeared for our salvation, not because this power has been given to Him recently, but because this grace was laid up in Him for us before the creation of the world"—*Comm. on 2 Tim.* 1:10 (*CR* 80.353).

36. *Comm. on 1 John* 4:10 (*CR* 83.353–54).

37. *Inst.* 2.17.2 (*CR* 30.387). Cf. 3.14.17 (*CR* 30.575); 3.14.21 (*CR* 30.578).

the Father has not refused to bestow His Son upon our salvation."[38] . . . God's love for men is none other than the Father's love for the Son. "For if the death of Christ is the pledge of God's love towards us, it follows that *even then we were acceptable* to Him; but now (Paul) says we were enemies. I answer, because God hates sin we are also odious to Him in so far as we are sinners; but as in His secret counsel He elects us *into the body of Christ,* He ceases to hate us."[39] God loves us in Christ with the love that He has for the Son.

In the gift of the Mediator, therefore, we have the revelation of God Himself, giving Himself to men as their Redeemer.[40] In Christ "the love of God is poured out upon us,"[41] for God is the giver of this gift. He is not "a mere spectator, but the author of our salvation."[42] That is, the gift of a mediator is the revelation of God's love in the fullest sense of the word, for the Mediator is none other than God Himself, giving Himself to us in His way of being as the eternal Son: "The most merciful God, when He determined upon our redemption, became Himself our Redeemer in the *persona* of the only-begotten Son."[43] Therefore, in the Mediator we have to do with God Himself. "It is evident that we cannot believe in God except through Christ, in whom God in a manner makes Himself small, that He may accommodate Himself to our comprehension."[44] And the God with whom we have to do here is a God who is *pro nobis.* "We ought not to look at anything else in Christ, therefore, than the fact that God out of His boundless goodness chose to extend His help to save us who were lost."[45] There can be no thought, therefore, of any opposition between the Father and the Son in Calvin's understanding of the atonement. The unity of the Father and the Son is a reciprocal love that finds expression in the perfect obedience of the Son to the Father, and an obedience that is free and voluntary.[46] God as Father and as Son has reconciled the world to Himself, and the saving work ascribed to Christ in the Bible is, Calvin insists, "with equal propriety ascribed in other parts of Scripture to God the Father, for on the one hand the Father decreed this atonement by an eternal purpose and gave this proof of His love to us, that He did not spare His only-begotten Son, but delivered Him

38. *Comm. on Rom.* 8:32 (*CR* 77.163).
39. *Comm. on Rom.* 5:10 (*CR* 77.94).
40. "Dominus . . . in Christi facie redemptor apparet" — *Inst.* 1.2.1 (*CR* 30.34).
41. *Comm. on Eph.* 1:5 (*CR* 79.149). Cf. *Comm. on Eph.* 1:7 (*CR* 79.150).
42. *Inst.* 3.22.6 (*CR* 30.692).
43. *Inst.* 2.12.2 (*CR* 30.341).
44. *Comm. on 1 Peter* 1:21 (*CR* 83.227).
45. *Comm. on John* 3:17 (*CR* 75.66).
46. *Comm. on John* 14:31 (*CR* 75.338). Cf. *Comm. on Phil.* 2:8 (*CR* 80.27).

up for us; and Christ on the other hand offered Himself as a sacrifice in order to reconcile us to God."[47] Reconciliation came by the work of the Son, but it depended first of all on the Father's gift of a mediator. "As the whole matter of our salvation must not be sought anywhere else but in Christ, so we must see whence Christ came to us and why He was offered to be our Savior. Both points are distinctly stated to us: namely, that faith in Christ brings life to all, and that Christ brought life because the Heavenly Father loves the human race and wishes that it should not perish."[48]

The Incarnate

The Divinity of Christ

The Mediator given to us by the Father is God the eternal Son, of one essence with the Father.[49] He is "Himself the eternal and essential Word of the Father,"[50] the same Word who was always the Mediator and through whom God dealt with, and appeared to, the patriarchs before the incarnation.[51] The Son, therefore, is God in His self-revelation: "As all divinely given revelations are rightly called 'the Word of God,' so we ought chiefly to reckon as the source of all revelations Him who is substantially the Word, who is liable to no variation, who remains with God perpetually one and the same, and who is God Himself."[52] The Mediator comes to us from the side of God, not from our side, so that in Him we confront the One to whom we need to be reconciled, in all His divine majesty; "for who of us does not dread the sight of the Son of God, especially when we consider what our condition is and when our sins come to mind?"[53]

But the Son is the incarnate Mediator, not the Father. For men, the Son is one God with the Father, but within the Godhead He is distinct,[54] so that although the Son is "the Lord of life and death, nevertheless He became obedient to His Father, even so far as to endure death."[55] But this work of obedience to which He was sent "was

47. *Comm. on Gal.* 1:4 (*CR* 78.170).
48. *Comm. on John* 3:16 (*CR* 75.63–64).
49. "For where can there be equality with God without robbery excepting only where there is the essence of God?" — *Comm. on Phil.* 2:6 (*CR* 80.25).
50. *Inst.* 1.13.7 (*CR* 30.95).
51. *Inst.* 1.13.10 (*CR* 30.98).
52. *Inst.* 1.13.7 (*CR* 30.95).
53. *Comm. on Heb.* 4:15 (*CR* 83.53).
54. *Inst.* 1.13.19 (*CR* 30.105–06).
55. *Comm. on Phil.* 2:8 (*CR* 80.27).

destined by the eternal decree of God,"[56] so that in this distinction of *personae* we must not try to find any separation or opposition. The incarnation of the Son is the expression of the eternal will of God: "Christ's becoming our Redeemer and His participation in the same nature (with us) have been connected by the eternal decree of God."[57] But it is not enough for Calvin to say that God only as the Son is in Christ. So completely is the work of Christ the work of the Triune God that he goes further, in commenting on the passage "God was in Christ reconciling the world to Himself": "It is also of the Father that this is said, for it would be an improper expression were you to understand it as meaning that the divine nature of Christ was in Him. The Father, therefore, was in the Son in accordance with that statement, 'I am in the Father and the Father in me' (John 10:38). Therefore, he that has the Son has the Father also."[58] The incarnate Son, Jesus Christ, then, is the full and complete revelation of God. "God is wholly found in Him, so that he who is not contented with Christ alone desires something better and more excellent than God. The summary is this: God has manifested Himself to us fully and perfectly in Christ."[59] Again, in Christ, God "communicates Himself to us wholly,"[60] and therefore "they who imagine God in His naked majesty apart from Christ have an idol in place of God."[61]

At this point we must stop and take account of the limitations that Calvin imposes on what he has just said. Do we have in Christ a full gift of God to us and a full revelation of the nature of God? Calvin is willing to let these statements stand only in a limited sense, for, he says, "Christ is not better known to us with respect to His hidden divinity than the Father (!). But He is said to be the clear image of God, because in Him God has fully revealed Himself in so far as God's infinite goodness, wisdom, and power are clearly manifested in Him."[62] Calvin clearly is holding back, reserving, as it were, some other characteristics of God that apparently are not revealed in Christ. We shall find this reservation playing an important part in Calvin's treatment of the work of Christ, where he will speak of the divine nature resting passively during Christ's suffering and not sharing in the work of Christ's human nature. He says, for example, that "the divine nature

56. *Inst.* 2.12.4 (*CR* 30.342).
57. *Inst.* 2.12.5 (*CR* 30.343–44).
58. *Comm. on 2 Cor.* 5:19 (*CR* 78.71).
59. *Comm. on Col.* 2:9 (*CR* 80.104).
60. Ibid.
61. *Comm. on 1 Peter* 1:2 (*CR* 83.210).
62. *Comm. on John* 14:10 (*CR* 75.326).

was *in a state of repose,* and did not exert itself at all whenever it was necessary in discharging the office of Mediator, that the human nature should act separately, according to its peculiar character."[63] Again, Calvin speaks of the "divine glory, which at that time (the earthly life of Christ) shone in the Father only, for in (Christ) it was concealed."[64] This question of the glory of Christ reveals the problem clearly. Calvin refers to the passage where Jesus says that He seeks not His own glory, and says that this must not be referred to Christ as God, but only as man, for as God "He does all things for His own (glory)."[65] On this the question must be put: Is it not to His own glory that God incarnate, precisely as God, seeks not His own glory? Is not this the glory of God, so different from human conceptions of glory, that He can abandon His own glory? What is the source of Calvin's idea of glory, yes, and of his idea of divinity, which permits him to say that they were hidden in God's revelation of Himself in Jesus Christ? Has God truly revealed Himself in Jesus or not? Commenting on the crucial passage in Philippians 2, Calvin says: "Christ, then, before the creation of the world, was in the form of God, because from the beginning He had His glory with the Father, as He says in John 17:5. For in the wisdom of God, prior to assuming our flesh, there was nothing mean or contemptible, but on the contrary a magnificence worthy of God. Being such as He was, He could have shown Himself equal to God without doing wrong to anyone; but *He did not manifest Himself to be what He really was,* nor did He openly assume in the view of men what belonged to Him by right."[66] If that is Calvin's position, then how does he know what Christ "really was"? What other source does he have for the true nature of the Son of God, and therefore of God Himself? If this other source be the resurrection, is it not the resurrection of the crucified, and therefore in no sense a revelation that is in conflict with the cross? And finally, what has become of the Christ who is the same yesterday and today and forever? Clearly there is a serious problem at the very heart of Calvin's theology, a failure to carry through consequentially his statement that "they who imagine God in His naked majesty apart from Christ have an idol in place of God."[67] At one point he comes to the verge of resolving the problem when he says: "The Father of Christ is the only

63. *Comm. on Matt.* 24:36 (*CR* 73.672): "quievit divinitas, seque minime exseruit."
64. *Comm. on Matt.* 25:31 (*CR* 73.686).
65. *Inst.* 2.14.2 (*CR* 30.354).
66. "Sed non prae se tulit quod erat, neque palam sumpsit in oculis hominum quod iure suum erat" — *Comm. on Phil.* 2:6 (*CR* 80.25).
67. *Comm. on 1 Peter* 1:2 (*CR* 83.210).

true God — that is, He is the one God who formerly promised a Redeemer to the world; but the oneness and the truth of Godhead will be found in Christ, *because* Christ was humbled in order that He might raise us on high. When we have understood this, *then* His divine majesty displays itself, *then* we perceive that He is wholly in the Father and that the Father is known wholly in Him. In short, he who separates Christ from the divinity of the Father does not yet acknowledge Him who is the only true God, but rather invents for himself a strange God."[68] Magnificent as this passage is, it stands on the edge and not in the center of Calvin's understanding of the divinity of Christ.

The Humanity of Christ

Without ceasing to be the Son of God, God the Son also became a man in Jesus Christ. "The Son of God began to be a man in such a way that He still continues to be that eternal Word who had no beginning in time."[69] The assumption of real human nature by the Son, the humanity of Christ, plays a most important role in Calvin's doctrine of reconciliation, for as we are to see, it is precisely in His humanity that Christ performs His atoning work. In fact, it is for the sake of this work that the assumption of human nature is necessary: "He put on our nature that He might thus make Himself capable of dying, for as God He was not able to undergo death."[70] We have seen, in the quotation with which this chapter began, that reconciliation required that Christ partake of our nature in order to take our place. Our concern here is to show Calvin's understanding of this human nature of Christ.

In becoming man, the Son of God made Himself the brother of men. "He has adopted us as brothers," Calvin says,[71] and this brotherhood is due to our common nature.[72] Our whole relationship with Christ depends on this common nature. That is why Calvin takes such pains to emphasize the humanity of Christ: "He who is the Son of God by nature has provided Himself with a body from our body, flesh from our flesh, bones from our bones, that He might be the same with us."[73] Thus in Christ we find "a real man composed of body and

68. *Comm. on John* 17:3 (*CR* 75.377).
69. *Comm. on John* 1:14 (*CR* 75.14).
70. *Comm. on Heb.* 2:14 (*CR* 83.32). Cf. *Inst.* 2.12.3 (*CR* 30.342).
71. *Inst.* 2.12.2 (*CR* 30.341).
72. *Comm. on Heb.* 2:16 (*CR* 83.34). "By saying that He came in the flesh, he means that by putting on flesh He became a real man of the same nature with us, that He might become our brother" — *Comm. on 1 John* 4:2 (*CR* 83.349).
73. *Inst.* 2.12.2 (*CR* 341).

soul,"[74] which constitute His human nature, clearly to be distinguished from His divine nature as God the Son.[75] But it should be
noted that Calvin sees the divine assumption of human nature not as
an abstract, metaphysical fact but rather as a personal reality of God's
reaching out to men in Christ. "And indeed, if this were impressed on
the hearts of all, that the Son of God holds out to us the hand of a
brother, and that we are united to Him by the fellowship of our nature
in order that He may raise us to Heaven out of our low condition, who
would not prefer to keep to this straight road, instead of wandering
in rough side roads?"[76]

When Calvin speaks of the human nature of Christ he means human in the full sense of the word: Christ was a man like other men,
and He suffered all the weaknesses to which our nature is subject.
"His goodness, which is never sufficiently celebrated, is conspicuous
in that He was not reluctant to assume our infirmities."[77] "He chose
not only to grow in the body but to make progress in mind," like any
other man, the only difference between Him and ourselves being that
"the weaknesses which press upon us by necessity were undertaken
by Him voluntarily and of His own accord."[78] He was liable to "hunger, thirst, cold, and other infirmities of our nature,"[79] in a body that
was not by nature immune to corruption.[80] But Calvin pushes further
the meaning of the word *infirmities:* "Some understand by it cold and
heat, hunger and other wants of the body, and also contempt, poverty,
and other things of this kind, as in many places in the writings of
Paul, especially in 2 Corinthians 12:10. But their opinion is more
correct who include, together with external evils, the feelings of the
soul, such as fear, sorrow, the dread of death, and similar things."[81]

Thus our Mediator has drawn near to us in all the weakness of our
human condition. "We have not to go far to seek a Mediator, since
Christ of His own accord extends His hand to us; we have no reason
to dread the majesty of Christ, since He is our brother; nor is there
cause to fear lest He, as one unacquainted with evils, should not be
touched by any feeling of humanity so as to bring us help, since He
took upon Him our infirmities in order that He might be more ready

74. *Inst.* 2.13.2 (*CR* 30.349).
75. *Comm. on Rom.* 1:3 (*CR* 77.10).
76. *Comm. on 1 Tim.* 2:5 (*CR* 80.270).
77. *Inst.* 2.16.12 (*CR* 30.378).
78. *Comm. on Luke* 2:40 (*CR* 73.104). Cf. *Comm. on Matt.* 24:36 (*CR* 73.672).
79. *Inst.* 2.13.1 (*CR* 30.348). Cf. *Comm. on Matt.* 21:18 (*CR* 73.584).
80. *Comm. on Acts* 2:23 (*CR* 76.40).
81. *Comm. on Heb.* 4:15 (*CR* 83.54).

to aid us."[82] No matter how miserable our condition, we are always within the realm of existence that God has made His own in Christ.[83] Not that God needed to do this in order to be merciful; rather, the incarnation is the revelation to us of the God who is for us. "The Son of God had no need of experience in order to know the emotions of mercy, but we could not be persuaded that He is merciful and ready to help us had He not been tried by our miseries. But this, as other things, is a gift to us."[84]

There is, however, a difference between the humanity of Christ and ours: the New Testament "expressly distinguishes Him from the common condition of mankind, so that He is a real man, and yet free from all fault and corruption."[85] . . . That is not to say that for Calvin the sinlessness of Christ is primarily a condition of nature. If it is also that, it is in the first place a dynamic relationship of the incarnate Son to the Father. In a word, Calvin understands the sinlessness of Christ primarily as obedience.[86] The difference between Christ and ourselves is that the feelings or passions of the soul that are rebellious in us are in Christ obedient to the will of God. "When God created man, He implanted in him affections, but affections which were obedient and submissive to reason. That those affections are now disorderly and rebellious is an accidental fault. Now, Christ took upon Him human affections, but without disorder; for he who obeys the passions of the flesh is not obedient to God. Christ was indeed troubled and greatly agitated, but in such a way that He kept Himself in subjection to the will of the Father."[87] Calvin emphasizes that Christ assumed voluntarily the weaknesses of our nature in making Himself subject to fear and sorrow and understands them as an essential part of what it meant for the Son of God to take on human nature. "In this way we detract nothing from the glory of Christ when we say that it was a voluntary submission by which He was brought to resemble us in the feelings of the soul. . . . And in this way He proved Himself to be our brother, in order to assure us that we have a Mediator who willingly pardons our infirmities, and who is ready to heal what He has experienced Himself."[88] But this raises a serious problem. Is it because of the infirmities of fear and sorrow and the dread of death that we need

82. *Comm. on Heb.* 4:15 (*CR* 83.54). Cf. *Comm. on Heb.* 5:2 (*CR* 83.58); *Comm. on Col.* 2:18 (*CR* 80.111).

83. *Comm. on Heb.* 4:15 (*CR* 83.55).

84. *Comm. on Heb.* 2:17 (*CR* 83.34).

85. *Inst.* 2.13.4 (*CR* 30.352). Cf. *Comm. on Heb.* 4:15 (*CR* 83.54).

86. *Inst.* 2.16.5 (*CR* 30.370f.).

87. *Comm. on John* 11:33(*CR* 75.266). Cf. *Comm. on Matt.* 26:37 (*CR* 73.720).

88. *Comm. on John* 11:33 (*CR* 75.265).

pardon? Is not pardon required, rather, for precisely those infirmities in which Christ, according to Calvin, had no share? Certainly Christ entered into the situation of natural man, God's good creature, but has He entered into the situation of fallen man, the sinner who needs reconciliation? Is the obedience of Christ the miraculous obedience of one who was made sin, who precisely *from the place of sinful man* was nevertheless obedient to the Father, or does Calvin not see it rather as almost a status or condition that Christ enjoyed?

It is not surprising to see that Calvin understands σάρξ in a special sense in John 1:14, and does so quite consciously. "When Scripture speaks of man contemptuously, it calls him *flesh*. Now, though there is such a great distance between the spiritual glory of the Word of God and the rotten filth of our flesh, nevertheless the Son of God submitted to taking upon Himself that flesh, subject to so many miseries. The word *flesh* is not taken here for corrupt nature, as it is often used by Paul, but for mortal man — though it marks contemptuously his frail and perishing nature, as in these and similar passages: 'for he remembered that we were flesh' (Ps. 78:39); 'all flesh is grass' (Isa. 40:6)."[89] So also where Paul says that Christ came "in the likeness of sinful flesh," Calvin comments: "Although the flesh of Christ was stained with no faults, yet to the sight it seemed sinful, inasmuch as He sustained that punishment which was due to our sins."[90] And where Paul says that Christ was made sin for us, Calvin says: "It is commonly said that *sin* here denotes an expiatory sacrifice for sin."[91] As in Calvin's treatment of the divine nature of Christ, so also here in his understanding of the human nature there is a reservation in the involvement of God in the situation of sinful men. It may be asked whether Calvin has been true to the New Testament witness in seeing the matter in this way. If he would leave something in reserve to God, as it were, would it not have been better to speak of the divine *freedom* in which God has acted and continues to act in Jesus Christ? Would it not have been better to leave God this freedom, rather than to speak of a revelation in which God "does not manifest Himself as He really is," or of a divine nature that is somehow "in repose" and not fully active in every moment of the existence of Jesus Christ? And so also with respect to the humanity of Christ, would it not have been truer to the biblical witness and also to the more consequential development of his theology to have seen the obedience of Christ as an

89. *Comm. on John* 1:14 (*CR* 75.13–14). Cf. *Comm. on Col.* 2:11: "He takes the term *flesh,* as is his custom, to denote corrupt nature" (*CR* 80.105).

90. *Comm. on Rom.* 8:3 (*CR* 77.139).

91. *Comm. on 2 Cor.* 5:21 (*CR* 76.74).

obedience precisely in the condition of fallen man? We do not raise these questions as an attack upon Calvin — he himself has presented us with the problem — but are led to question his solutions on the basis of that very biblical witness that was authoritative for him.

To return to the presentation of Calvin's teaching: we have seen that in assuming human nature, although not fallen human nature, the Son of God has united us to Himself. "When he declares that (Christ) is a man, (Paul) does not deny that the Mediator is God, but wishing to point out the bond that unites us with God he mentions the human nature rather than the divine."[92] Now, since God is dealing with man, as such, in Jesus Christ, He is therefore dealing with all men, and Calvin could say that "the salvation procured by Christ is common to all mankind, since Christ, the author of salvation, is descended from Adam, the common parent of all."[93] All men have this human nature in common with Christ; therefore His work is for all men. "It was by a wonderful purpose of God that Luke presented Christ to us as the son of Adam, whereas Matthew confined Him within the single family of Abraham. For it would be of no advantage to us that Christ was given by the Father as the author of salvation, unless He had been given without discrimination to all in common."[94] But when Calvin says that Christ is given to all, on the basis of a common human nature, he means *all* in a special sense of the word. "The universal term (*all*) ought to be referred always to classes of men and not to individuals, as if (Paul) had said that not only Jews but also Gentiles, not only common people but also princes, were redeemed by the death of Christ."[95] Once more we find Calvin holding back from the consequences of his own exegesis. In fact, the text says "all," with no "as if" or any other reservation, when it occurs in the New Testament,[96] and the logic of what Calvin has said about Christ as the son of Adam calls for a direct exegesis here also. But for Calvin there is a limitation to the union created by God in assuming human nature: "flesh alone does not constitute a fraternal union," for "the children of God are born, not of flesh and blood, but of the Spirit through faith."[97] That is, Calvin refuses to accept a mechanical understanding of reconciliation that might be ours simply on the basis of a biological definition of man. It may well be asked, however, if he

92. *Comm. on 1 Tim.* 2:5 (*CR* 80.270). Cf. *Inst.* 3.2.24 (*CR* 30.418).
93. *Inst.* 2.13.3 (*CR* 30.351).
94. *Comm. on Matt.* 1:1 (*CR* 73.57). Cf. *Comm. on 1 Tim.* 2:5 (*CR* 80.270).
95. *Comm. on 1 Tim.* 2:5 (*CR* 80.270).
96. 1 Cor. 15:22; Rom. 11:32.
97. *Inst.* 2.13.2 (*CR* 30.350).

does not thereby threaten all that he has said about the consequences of the incarnation of the Son of God, as, for example, when he says: "We have confidence that we are sons of God *because* He who is the Son of God by nature has provided Himself with a body from our body . . . that He might be the same as us."[98] His point of course is to establish faith as the *sine qua non* of reconciliation: "The ungodly, by means of their unbelief, break off and dissolve that relationship of flesh by which He has united Himself to us and thus make themselves complete strangers to Him through their own fault."[99] But in doing this Calvin is in danger of raising faith to a higher position than its object — Christ and His work. And he will also be obliged . . . to make Christ only the *possibility* of reconciliation rather than its reality, a high price to pay for the establishment of the necessity of faith. Faith, then, constitutes the boundary within which Calvin maintains that "our common nature is a pledge of our fellowship with the Son of God."[100]

The Person of the Mediator

The Mediator has two distinct natures united in Himself. [It is our task here to examine] Calvin's understanding of the hypostatic union in Christ. The purpose of the incarnation was to provide a Mediator who could "appease God and restore us from death to life."[101] . . . The death of Christ was essential to His work of reconciliation. For this work the two natures were both necessary: the divine, in order to carry out the work that no man could perform; the human, that acting in our place and in our name He might include us with Him in what He accomplished. "It was no mean part which the Mediator had to perform, namely, to restore us to the divine favor so as, of children of men, to make children of God, of heirs of Hell to make heirs of the Kingdom of Heaven. Who could accomplish this, unless the Son of God should become also the Son of Man, and thus receive to Himself what belongs to us and transfer to us that which is His?"[102] Hence the necessity for the two natures: "As it would have been impossible for one who was only God to suffer death, or for one who was only a man to overcome it, He associated the human nature with the divine, that He might submit the weakness of the former to death as an

98. *Inst.* 2.12.2 (*CR* 30.341).
99. *Comm. on Ps.* 22:23 (*CR* 59.231–32).
100. *Inst.* 2.12.3 (*CR* 30.342).
101. *Inst.* 2.12.4 (*CR* 30.343).
102. *Inst.* 2.12.2 (*CR* 30.341).

expiation for sins, and that with the power of the latter He might contend with death and obtain a victory on our behalf."[103]

But in the incarnation of the Son of God the two natures remain distinct: "The unity of person does not hinder the two natures from remaining distinct, so that His divinity retains all that is peculiar to itself, and His humanity holds separately whatever belongs to it."[104] As Calvin understands the matter, there are in Christ "peculiar attributes of divinity" and of humanity that must not be confused.[105] For example, His pre-existence, His glory in common with the Father, and His cooperating work with the Father are "incompatible with humanity" and are attributes of His divinity alone. So also His suffering, His role as Servant, and His death are attributes alone of His humanity.[106] Yet that does not mean that we may separate the two natures. "God certainly has no blood; He does not suffer, nor can He be touched with hands; but since He who was at once the true God and the man Christ was crucified and shed His blood for us, those things which were performed in His human nature are improperly yet not without reason transferred to His divinity."[107] Within the unity, however, there is a distinction of order between Christ's divinity and humanity. For example, He is the heir of the Kingdom of Heaven as God's Son, the human nature that He has in common with us being the means whereby He makes us coheirs with Himself.[108] Christ's divine nature has priority, and from it by way of His humanity we receive His blessings.[109] Christ is our Redeemer in and through His humanity, but only because He is first of all God: "The power of God made the flesh of Christ to be a living and spiritual temple."[110] All that Christ has as man He has not from Himself as man, but from God.[111] "We conclude, therefore, that Christ, as He is God and man, composed of these two natures united but not confounded, is our Lord and the true Son of God even according to His humanity, though not on account of His humanity."[112]

It is in the unity of the two natures that we are to see the Mediator, and Calvin insists that in the Bible, "those things which relate to the

---

103. *Inst.* 2.12.3 (*CR* 30.342).
104. *Comm. on John* 1:14 (*CR* 75.14). Cf. *Inst.* 2.14.1 (*CR* 30.353).
105. *Inst.* 2.14.2 (*CR* 30.354).
106. Ibid.
107. *Inst.* 2.14.2 (*CR* 30.354).
108. *Comm. on Heb.* 1:2 (*CR* 83.11).
109. *Inst.* 4.17.9 (*CR* 30.1009).
110. *Comm. on Heb.* 9:11 (*CR* 83.110). Cf. *Comm. on John* 5:27 (*CR* 75.118).
111. *Comm. on Heb.* 2:11 (*CR* 83.28).
112. *Inst.* 2.14.4 (*CR* 30.356).

office of Mediator do not apply simply to His divinity or simply to His human nature." These include such matters as the power to forgive sins and to bestow salvation.[113] But the way in which Calvin sees this unity is significant. The constantly repeated formula is: He who as man did such and such was at the same time the Son of God. For example, Christ did not suffer "in His divinity, but the Christ who suffered in the flesh as an abject and despised man was also as God the Lord of Glory."[114] Calvin understands the passages in the New Testament in which the properties or attributes of one nature are ascribed to the other as cases of "communication of properties." He feels that, properly speaking, they are not strictly correct, but they serve to stress how close is the unity of the two natures in the one Jesus Christ. The Scriptures "attribute to Him, sometimes those things which are applicable only to His humanity, sometimes those things which belong peculiarly to His divinity, and not infrequently those things which comprehend both His natures but are incompatible with either of them alone. And this union of the two natures in Christ they maintain so carefully that they sometimes attribute to one what belongs to the other, a mode of expression which the ancient writers called *communicatio idiomatum.*"[115]

Although this attribution to one nature of what strictly speaking belongs only to the other is a witness to the unity of the person of Christ, Calvin takes pains to point out that it is only a manner of speaking. This becomes especially clear when it is a question of the work of Christ. "Though God and man are united in one person, it does not follow that the human nature received what was peculiar to the divine nature; but, so far as was necessary for our salvation, the Son of God kept His divine power concealed. What Irenaeus says, that His divine nature was quiescent when He suffered, I understand to refer, not only to bodily death, but also to that amazing distress and agony of soul which drew from Him that complaint, 'My God, why have you forsaken me?' "[116] The reservations that Calvin made in dealing with the divinity of Christ have their consequences in the union of the two natures in Christ. Or rather, those reservations now require that he hold separate the two natures in the very climax of the event of reconciliation on the cross. The distinction of natures has become a distinction in the work of Christ, a division of labor, as it were. Once more we must raise questions. What is the source of

113. *Inst.* 2.14.3 (*CR* 30.355).
114. *Inst.* 4.17.30 (*CR* 30.1031–32). Cf. *Comm. on 1 John* 1:1 (*CR* 83.300).
115. *Inst.* 2.14.1 (*CR* 30.353). Cf. *Comm. on Acts* 20:28 (*CR* 76.469).
116. *Comm. on Luke* 2.40 (*CR* 73.104).

Calvin's knowledge, and of that of Irenaeus before him, of human nature and of divinity that allows him to measure Christ and assign part of His work to this nature and part of it to that? Is not the humiliation of Christ the humiliation of God Himself? And is it not at the same time the glory of God, a glory that is so great that it can afford to make itself small? And is not the humiliation of the Son of God in assuming human nature at the same time the glorification of man, now raised up into obedient union with God in Jesus Christ? Again, let it be said that Calvin himself leads us to ask these questions. He has said that the work of the Mediator is the work of the two natures in one person. But is not this the work of the Mediator: that God humbled Himself to take the place of sinful man and to live the life of obedience in our place, so that in this one man God is dealing with us all, taking upon Himself the judgment pronounced on us, and exalting us in Christ to a new life in fellowship with God? How then can there be any division of labor in this event of reconciliation?

At one point Calvin comes close to maintaining such a unity in the work of Christ, where, commenting on the exaltation of Christ in Philippians 2:10, he says that this "is affirmed with reference to Christ's entire person, seen as God manifested in the flesh. For He did not abase Himself either as to His humanity alone or as to His divinity alone, but inasmuch as clothed in our flesh He concealed Himself under its infirmity. So again, God exalted His own Son in the same flesh in which He had lived in the world abject and despised to the highest rank of honor, that He may sit at His right hand."[117] Yet even here the question may be asked: Is not Jesus Christ the same yesterday and today and forever? Has He not revealed humility to be His glory? And is not man glorified in the very assumption of human nature, prior to the resurrection? We have seen Calvin reaching back as far as Irenaeus in support of his Christology. If Calvin's Christology reveals problems, they are the problems that he has inherited from the history of Christian dogma, whose difficulties are revealed in Calvin's theology because of his efforts to submit his teaching to the biblical witness.

117. *Comm. on Phil.* 2:10 (*CR* 80.29).

8

The Atonement: Sacrifice and Penalty

Robert S. Paul

J ohn Calvin was a more systematic theologian than Luther in the sense that within a single book, *The Institutes of the Christian Religion,* we have his concise but comprehensive exposition of the Christian faith. Undoubtedly a full treatment of his soteriology would ask for a much wider assessment of his writings than the consideration of a single work, but because the *Institutes* became the norm for Calvinistic doctrine, we should be able to find sufficient in it to judge Calvin's central ideas regarding the atonement.

Calvin has been represented as holding the theory of penal substitution "in its harshest form,"[1] and as . . . in the theology of Luther, so with Calvin—the idea and images of the penal theory are undeniably there. Writing of the reasons why the incarnation was necessary he says that "the only end which the Scripture uniformly assigns for the Son of God voluntarily assuming our nature, and even receiving it as a command from the Father, is, that he might propitiate the Father to us by becoming a victim."[2] Anyone who would wish to question too minutely why this was necessary shows, in Calvin's view, that he is dissatisfied with the ordinance of God and even discontented "with that Christ, who has been given us as the price of our redemption."[3] The images that Calvin used here were sacrificial images—propitia-

Reprinted from *The Atonement and the Sacraments* (Nashville: Abingdon, 1960), pp. 98–109. Copyright © 1960 by Abingdon Press. Used by permission.
1. V. J. K. Brook, "The Atonement in Reformation Theology," in *The Atonement in History and in Life,* ed. L. W. Grensted (London: S.P.C.K., 1929), p. 234.
2. *Inst.* 2.12.4 (from the 1845 translation of Henry Beveridge).
3. *Inst.* 2.12.5.

tion, victim — but it is clear that they are often being used with a meaning that is close to penal substitution. In another place within the same chapter he says:

> Another principal part of our reconciliation with God was, that man, who had lost himself by his disobedience, should, by way of remedy, oppose to it obedience, satisfy the justice of God, and pay the penalty of sin. Therefore, our Lord came forth very man, adopted the person of Adam, and assumed his name, that he might in his stead obey the Father; that he might present our flesh as the price of satisfaction to the just judgment of God, and in the same flesh pay the penalty which we had incurred. Finally, since as God only he could not suffer, and as man only could not overcome death, he united the human nature with the divine, that he might subject the weakness of the one to death as an expiation of sin, and by the power of the other, maintaining a struggle with death, might gain us the victory.[4]

These and similar passages could be abstracted from Calvin and woven into a very strict penal theory of the atonement in which our Lord voluntarily (or at the command of the Father?) became the victim of God's wrath against sin, so that the atonement He offered is seen wholly in terms of the satisfaction rendered to divine justice by His substitutionary passion and death.

Yet even in the passage we have just quoted, these are by no means the only concepts that are represented. The penal element is there — very much to the fore — and Calvin puts an accent upon our Lord's human flesh as "the price of satisfaction to the just judgment of God" and tells us that in this same flesh Christ paid "the penalty which we had incurred." But how did our Lord pay the debt within His flesh? If Calvin suggests to some extent that the debt was paid in suffering, it is surely seen at a far deeper level that if the logic of his view is followed, it must have been paid by our Lord's *obedience.* Since Calvin finds the cause of our sinful state in the disobedience of Adam and since he takes up the idea of Christ's "recapitulation" of Adam, it is essential to his thought to set over against each other not Christ's sufferings and Adam's felicity, but the obedience of Christ and Adam's disobedience.

With this in mind let us see how Calvin approaches the subject. What he says about the work of Christ comes in book 2 of the *Institutes* — at the very center of his exposition of the Christian faith. The theme of book 1 is our knowledge of God as Creator and more par-

4. *Inst.* 2.12.3.

ticularly the source of that knowledge through the revelation of God in Holy Scripture. In the first part of book 2 he describes our disobedience and sin in the face of the knowledge of God that is given to us and our need of redemption in view of the fact that we are totally unable to redeem ourselves. Calvin, as Anselm before him, builds up his case to show the absolute necessity of divine intervention if mankind is to be saved, and he shows that the purpose of the Old Testament is *Heilsgeschichte* — the story or panorama of salvation, which in its turn points forward to the divine intervention in the Mediator, Christ. "God," he says, "never showed himself propitious to his ancient people, nor gave them any hope of grace without a Mediator."[5]

We ought to notice from a brief passage quoted previously that Calvin is in line with Anselm in making the atonement the purpose of the incarnation and not simply its fulfillment. Because of this one would insist upon the centrality of the work of God in Christ in the thought of Calvin and therefore the centrality of the atonement in his theology. Although one can find passages which seem to suggest a separation between the Father and the Son, in its totality Christ's work is represented as the intervention of God Himself in history. Calvin cites Irenaeus as saying "that the Father, who is boundless in himself, is bounded in the Son, because he has accommodated himself to our capacity."[6] Having demonstrated on the one hand our complete inability to satisfy the God of righteousness who appears "as the stern avenger of wickedness," Calvin goes on to affirm, "but in Christ his countenance beams forth full of grace and gentleness towards poor unworthy sinners."[7] It is *God* who acted in Jesus Christ, and although in Calvin's view the fulfillment of His purpose involved the satisfaction of a divine justice that He could not repudiate without repudiating Himself, the purpose was the salvation of man. The atonement is central. It was for this reason that he attacked Osiander, who had suggested (because there is no scriptural warrant for showing the contrary) that Christ would probably have become man even if there had been no fall from grace. In reply Calvin quoted from Paul's First Epistle to Timothy, "This is a faithful saying, and worthy of all acceptation, that Christ Jesus came into the world to save sinners,"[8] and he declared that he was determined to adhere to this to the end: in Calvin the purpose of the incarnation is the atonement, that and nothing else.

5. *Inst.* 2.6.2; cf. 2.10.4.
6. *Inst.* 2.6.4.
7. *Inst.* 2.7.8.
8. *Inst.* 2.12.5; cf. 1 Tim. 1:15.

To prove it he shows that the whole Bible points to Christ, and this is the context in which we have to see what Calvin says about the work of Christ. The law was introduced to keep the Israelites "in suspense until his advent; to inflame their desire, and confirm their expectations," and he adds that by the law he understands "not only the Ten Commandments, which contain a complete rule of life, but the whole system of religion delivered by the hand of Moses."[9] In the forefront of this there was the sacrificial system. I suggest that not sufficient attention has been given to the things Calvin said about the Old Testament sacrifices and the significant light they throw upon his idea of the atonement. Why, asks the Reformer, was the sacrificial system instituted? To a sixteenth-century Protestant it did not naturally commend itself as being of the spiritual and ethical quality discovered in the words of the prophets or the witness of Jesus, "for what could be more vain or frivolous than for men to reconcile themselves to God, by offering him the foul odor produced by burning the fat of beasts? or to wipe away their own impurities by besprinkling themselves with water or blood? In short, the whole legal worship (if considered by itself apart from the types and shadows or corresponding truth) is a mere mockery." The Jews would have been as deluded as their pagan neighbors if there had not been a spiritual purpose in this sacrificial worship. To Calvin the meaning was quite clear — it pointed to Jesus Christ, for the Israelites could not attain their true vocation "without a greater and more excellent atonement than the blood of beasts."[10]

Christ and His atoning work are so central to Calvin's exposition of the faith that he holds that "from the beginning of the world Christ was held forth to all the elect as the object of their faith and confidence."[11] As He is the fulfillment of Israel's history and prophecy in His office of prophet and of her messianic hope in His office as king, so in His office as priest He is the fulfillment of her sacrificial worship. The whole passage on the threefold office of our Lord, and particularly that part of it which speaks of His priesthood, puts the work of Christ within its proper setting if we are to understand the central ideas about the atonement in Calvin. Plenty of passages can be taken from the *Institutes* where the theory of penal substitution provides all the metaphors, but that emphasis and its imagery have to be put within the context of what Calvin says about the Bible's plan for salvation, which is the sacrificial context. Look at the following passage:

9. *Inst.* 2.7.1.
10. *Inst.* 2.7.1; cf. Exod. 19:6.
11. *Inst.* 2.6.4.

Because a deserved curse obstructs the entrance, and God in his character of Judge is hostile to us, expiation must necessarily intervene,
that as a priest employed to appease the wrath of God, he may rein-
state us in his favor. Wherefore, in order that Christ might fulfil this
office, it behoved him to appear with a sacrifice. For even under the
law of the priesthood it was forbidden to enter the sanctuary without
blood, to teach the worshipper that however the priest might interpose
to deprecate, God could not be propitiated without the expiation of
sin. . . . The sum comes tp this, that the honor of the priesthood was
competent to none but Christ, because, by the sacrifice of his death,
he wiped away our guilt, and made satisfaction for sin. Of the great
importance of this matter, we are reminded by that solemn oath which
God uttered, and of which he declared he would not repent, "Thou
art a priest for ever, after the order of Melchisedek" (Ps. 110:4). For,
doubtless, his purpose was to ratify that point on which he knew that
our salvation chiefly hinged. . . . Thus we see, that if the benefit and
efficacy of Christ's priesthood is to reach us, the commencement must
be with his death. Whence it follows, that he by whose aid we obtain
favor, must be a perpetual intercessor. . . . But since God under the
Law ordered sacrifices of beasts to be offered to him, there was a
different and new arrangement in regard to Christ, viz., that he should
be at once victim and priest, because no other fit satisfaction for sin
could be found, nor was any one worthy of the honor of offering an
only begotten son to God. Christ now bears the office of priest, not
only that by the eternal law of reconciliation he may render the Father
favorable and propitious to us, but also admit us into this most honorable alliance. For we though in ourselves polluted, in him being
priests (Rev. 1:6), offer ourselves and our all to God, and freely enter
the heavenly sanctuary, so that the sacrifices of prayer and praise
which we present are grateful and of sweet odor before him.[12]

Here two ways of thinking about the atonement are to be found
side by side. The first is judicial — "God in his character as Judge is
hostile to us" — and it developed into the theory of penal substitution,
but the second is the sacrificial concept whereby Christ is thought of
as giving something which is infinitely well-pleasing to God. There
can be little doubt that Calvin reconciled the two ideas often by interpreting the sacrificial element in a punitive and expiatory way rather
than as the offering of a pure gift in love. Nevertheless, it is the
sacrificial aspect of the atonement which provides the context in which
the penal ideas are set, and not the other way around. Calvin was
enough a spiritual son of Anselm to speak of satisfaction and enough

12. *Inst.* 2.15.6.

of a lawyer to speak of satisfaction to the divine justice. But even when he appears to be setting forth the penal theory at its hardest, it is within the setting of sacrifice because this is the setting which is biblical. So although he speaks of Christ appeasing the Father on our account, it is as a sacrifice that He does it, and in describing the priestly function of our Lord as Mediator he declares that "the honor of the priesthood was competent to none but Christ, because by the sacrifice of his death, he wiped away our guilt, and made satisfaction for sin."[13]

On the other hand the legal categories in which Calvin expressed his conception of the work of Christ led directly to the theory of penal substitution. . . . We must consider some of the force of the theory, and then see the other ways — apart from the sacrificial concept — in which the penal theory was modified in the *Institutes.*

Calvin argues, in language reminiscent of Luther, that Christ was numbered with the transgressors so that He might "bear the character of a sinner."[14] He declares that the very form of His death brought Him not under the curse of men but under the curse of the divine law, so that the whole curse that was due to us might be "transferred to him," and that the sacrifice and expiation that He offered were purifications "bearing, by substitution, the curse due to sin."[15] He lays great stress on scriptural passages such as Isaiah 53; 2 Corinthians 5:21; 1 Peter 2:24, which upon any literal interpretation do more than suggest that our sins were laid on Christ in His death by God, and he particularly stresses the descent into hell as our Lord's tasting the meaning of full estrangement from God and the penalty of the spiritual death due to sinners. He maintains that this was introduced into the creed "to teach us that not only was the body of Christ given up as the price of redemption, but that there was a greater and more excellent price — that he bore in his soul the tortures of condemned and ruined man."[16] This is penal substitution.

At the same time, just as we have seen that these ideas occurred within the context of sacrifice, so we discover within Calvin some of the elements of the "classic" theory. The images are not as pronounced as they are in Luther, but they are by no means ignored. There is also a possible difference of emphasis between the two Reformers in that whereas Luther thinks of the work of Christ as a victory over sin, death, hell, the law, and the devil and singles out the law as the main cause of our bondage and the special object of Christ's enmity, Calvin

13. *Inst.* 2.15.6.
14. *Inst.* 2.16.5.
15. *Inst.* 2.16.6.
16. *Inst.* 2.16.10.

often speaks of our Lord's victory as primarily over death. In His descent into the grave our Lord differed from us, for "in permitting himself to be overcome of death, it was not so as to be ingulfed in its abyss, but rather to annihilate it, as it must otherwise have annihilated us; he did not allow himself to be so subdued by it as to be crushed by its power; he rather laid it prostrate, when it was impending over us, and exulting over us as already overcome."[17] Christ's victory over the power of death was consummated by and demonstrated in the resurrection, for "how could he have obtained the victory for us, if he had fallen in the contest?"[18] Earlier in the *Institutes,* when writing of the necessity for our Savior to be both God and man, he declares:

> It was his to swallow up death: who but Life could do so? It was his to conquer sin: who could do so save Righteousness itself? It was his to put to flight the powers of the air and the world: who could do so but the mighty power superior to both? But who possesses life and righteousness, and the dominion and government of heaven, but God alone? Therefore God, in his infinite mercy, having determined to redeem us, became himself our Redeemer in the person of his only begotten Son.[19]

These are the terms and images of the "classic" theory, and although they do not appear in Calvin's thought as regularly or as insistently as in the thought of the great German Reformer, they are present to enrich and to qualify the more usual ideas in which he expounds the work of Christ.

There are, however, other aspects of Calvin's teaching about the work of Christ which modify his presentation of the atonement and which go far beyond the mere use of one image or another in describing the doctrine. These aspects of his teaching are concerned not so much with the picture forms in which Calvin describes the atonement as in the underlying spirit in which the divine initiative was undertaken — the way in which the redemption of man was conceived by God, the principle by which it was made effective in the work of Christ, and the manner by which it brings forth fruit in us by the Holy Spirit.

1. The first is what Calvin says about the love of God. Often in the grip of his forensic logic Calvin seems to let this slip into the background, but a closer reading of the Reformer reveals that it is the

17. *Inst.* 2.16.7.
18. *Inst.* 2.16.13.
19. *Inst.* 2.12.2.

very basis of the view of God's initiative in Christ which he presents. He can speak on one page of Christ expiating with His own blood the sins that make us hateful to God. Yet the whole point of his argument rests upon the fact that it was God the Father's mercy which alone made Christ's action possible, for "had God at the time you were a sinner hated you, and cast you off as you deserved, horrible destruction must have been your doom; but spontaneously and of free indulgence he retained you in his favor, not suffering you to be estranged from him, and in this way rescued you from danger."[20] God does not want to destroy what is His own but tries to find something in us that He can love, "for though it is by our own fault that we are sinners, we are still his creatures. . . . Accordingly, God the Father, by his love, prevents [i.e., "goes before"] and anticipates our reconciliation in Christ. Nay, it is because he first loves us, that he afterwards reconciles us to himself."[21] In a particularly striking passage Calvin reveals his own conception of God's love by paraphrasing the words of Augustine:

> Incomprehensible and immutable is the love of God. For it was not after we were reconciled to him by the blood of his Son that he began to love us, but he loved us before the foundation of the world, that with his only begotten Son we too might be sons of God before we were anything at all. Our being reconciled by the death of Christ must not be understood as if the Son reconciled us, in order that the Father, then hating, might begin to love us, but that we were reconciled to him already, loving, though at enmity with us because of sin. To the truth of both propositions we have the attestation of the Apostle, "God commendeth his love toward us, in that while we were yet sinners, Christ died for us" (Rom. 5:8). Therefore he had this love towards us even when, exercising enmity towards him, we were workers of iniquity. Accordingly, in a manner wondrous and divine, he loved even when he hated us. For he hated us when we were such as he had not made us, and yet because our iniquity had not destroyed his work in every respect, he knew in regard to each one of us, both to hate what we had made, and love what he had made.[22]

"Such," adds Calvin approvingly, "are the words of Augustine," and he then goes on to describe the atonement in terms of our Lord's perfect obedience to the Father throughout life and in the death of the cross. This "incomprehensible and immutable" love of God towards us — which we often wish Calvin had brought more into the fore-

20. *Inst.* 2.16.2.
21. *Inst.* 2.16.3.
22. *Inst.* 2.16.4.

ground of his theology — when it is linked with the very strong sense of unity within the Trinity that he had, with the fact that it was God Himself whose countenance in Christ "beams forth full of grace and gentleness towards unworthy sinners," presents us with a view of the work of Christ in which even the harshest features of the penal theory are to some extent transmuted.

If it is possible to reconcile in this way the apparent incompatibilities and contradictions of the theory of penal substitution, then the strength and attraction of its objectivity become evident. Perhaps it was not primarily the fear of God's wrath, and still less the thought that God is satisfied with the sufferings of His Son, that brought the theory of penal substitution to the center of evangelical religion and kept it there for three hundred years, but rather the belief that God *in His fullness* in the person of Christ took the punishment on "my" behalf that He Himself had decreed against "my" sin.

2. A second feature of Calvin's thought which modifies the penal terms in which he often speaks is the principle of obedience in relation to the sacrifice of our Lord to which we have alluded earlier. It was an insight which if it had been developed might have led to a much stronger emphasis in his theology upon the sacrificial aspect of Christ's atoning work. Calvin says that there is nothing more acceptable to God than obedience.[23] He declares that when it is asked "how Christ, by abolishing sin, removed the enmity between God and us, and purchased a righteousness which made him favorable and kind to us, it may be answered generally, that he accomplished by the whole course of his obedience."[24] Quoting Paul's statement in Romans 5:19 — "as by one man's disobedience many were made sinners, so by the obedience of one many shall be made righteous" — he declares that our Lord even at His baptism fulfilled a part of the righteousness that was required to redeem us by His voluntary obedience to the will of the Father; "in short, from the moment when he assumed the form of a servant, he began, in order to redeem us, to pay the price of deliverance." Calvin firmly maintains that the Bible places the greatest emphasis upon the death of Christ in the work of salvation and points out that in the Apostles' Creed the transition is directly from the birth of Christ to His death upon the cross. But he adds that "there is no exclusion of the other part of obedience which he performed in life," citing Philippians 2:7 in proof of his point.[25]

As we have seen previously, this accent upon the obedience of

23. *Inst.* 2.8.5.
24. *Inst.* 2.16.5.
25. Ibid.

Christ as the central atoning principle actually followed from what Calvin taught about the corporate nature of our disobedience in Adam, for the real "recapitulation" of Adam's defeat and the real "satisfaction" to be given to God must be an ethical and religious victory *in like kind* to the ethical and religious failure in Adam. On Calvin's own estimate of God's nature the Almighty could not be paid simply in terms of physical or spiritual anguish but only in terms of that of which by the disobedience of Adam He had been robbed. Had he held closely to this insight and seen it as the center of what he was trying to say about Christ's work for us, he would not only have avoided overconcentration upon punitive ideas which did not honor the God he wanted to honor, but he would have shown that sacrifice is at the heart of the biblical idea of the atonement, and that the sacrifice offered by Christ was a total sacrifice of the whole life which culminates in His death and is vindicated in His resurrection.

3. The third way in which the penal aspects of Calvin's thought are modified is to be found in his teaching that the love of God calls us to be not merely partakers in the benefits of our Lord's atoning work but sharers in its sacrifice. It is to be found in the passage on the priesthood of Christ that we have quoted previously, where Calvin declares that although we are still sinners, we can be priests in Christ and through Him "offer ourselves and our all to God, and freely enter the heavenly sanctuary."[26] In other words that which our Lord won for us was gained in order that we might be participants not only in His victory but in His sacrifice, not only in His sacrifice but in His glory. He gives us the possibility of becoming sons of God,[27] and relying upon this action of our Lord we have faith that we are the sons of God, "because the natural Son of God assumed to himself a body of our body, flesh of our flesh, bones of our bones, that he might be one with us." Calvin speaks of our "holy brotherhood" with Christ and says that because of this adoption by Christ of us as His brethren, we have a certain inheritance in the heavenly kingdom that He inherits as of right, for if we are brethren, then we are "partners with him in the inheritance."[28] The atonement issues an ethical call to us by which we enter into our Lord's work of salvation: the blood of Christ is indispensable to the work of redemption, but it is available and effective not only as a means of propitiation but also "as a laver to purge our defilements."[29]

26. *Inst.* 2.15.6.
27. *Inst.* 2.12.2.
28. Ibid.
29. *Inst.* 2.16.6.

Although the same cannot always be said for his followers, there was no false opposition in Calvin himself between the love of the Father and the love of the Son toward us. His thought was fully in line with that of the apostle Paul when he said of our Lord that "in him dwelleth all the fulness of the Godhead bodily,"[30] and for Calvin the brotherly concern which Jesus Christ exhibited toward us in the sacrificial giving of Himself was one aspect of the same prevenient grace which made the atonement the very center of God the Father's eternal purpose. To inherit the sacrifice and the victory of our Lord was to achieve what God had intended from the beginning. In the words of a later document, the *Shorter Catechism* of the Westminster Confession, which perfectly reflects Calvin's own thought at this point, "Man's chief end is to glorify God, and to enjoy him for ever." The fact that this was made possible for us was due not only to the suffering and sacrifice of the Son but equally to the continuing work of the Holy Spirit and to the prevenient grace and invincible love of God the Father.

30. Col. 2:9.

9
Justification and Predestination in Calvin

François Wendel

Justification by Faith

"Now," writes Calvin after his discussions of regeneration and of the Christian life, "we must consider at greater length this point of justification by faith, and consider it in such a way as to keep well in mind that this is the principal article of the Christian religion, in order that every one may take great pains and diligence to know the resolution of it."[1] That sentence would be sufficient proof, if proof were needed, that his having placed regeneration before justification in the *Institutes* did not imply any judgment of value on Calvin's part. Elsewhere too, he described justification as "the principle of the whole doctrine of salvation and the foundation of all religion."[2] No more to him than to Luther did regeneration appear to be any sort of infused quality that man could present as a value before God. In fact it is not

Reprinted from *Calvin: The Origins and Development of His Religious Thought*, trans. Philip Mairet (New York: Harper and Row, 1963; London: Collins, 1963), pp. 255–84. Used by permission.

1. *Inst.* 3.11.1. E. Doumergue, *Jean Calvin: Les hommes et les choses de son temps*, Lausanne, 1899–1927, vol. 4, pp. 263–87; P. Wernle, *Der evangelische Glaube nach den Hauptschriften der Reformatoren*, vol. 3, *Johann Calvin*, Tübingen, 1919, pp. 240–66; W. Niesel, *Die Theologie Calvins*, Munich, 1938, pp. 123–32; R. Seeberg, *Lehrbuch der Dogmengeschichte*, Tübingen, 1920, vol. 4.2, pp. 598ff.; W. Luettge, *Die Rechtfertigungslehre Calvins und ihre Bedeutung für seine Frömmigkeit*, Berlin, 1909; A. Lang, *Zwei Calvin Vorträge*, Gütersloh, 1911, pp. 13–20; E. Muelhaupt, *Die Predigt Calvins*, Berlin, 1931, pp. 112–56; E. Emmen, *De christologie van Calvijn*, Amsterdam, 1935, pp. 110–23; W. A. Hauck, *Calvin und die Rechtfertigung*, Gütersloh, 1938.

2. Sermon on Luke 1:5–10 (*CR* 46.23).

by regeneration at all, but by the forgiveness of sins in Jesus Christ, that God justifies men.

However, we must bear in mind that "justifying grace is not separate from regeneration although these are distinct things."[3] Calvin was not content with the mere juxtaposition of justification and regeneration. Not that he placed them in a chronological relation, as one might be led to think by a certain passage in the *Consensus Tigurinus*.[4] Nor was there any causal relation between them. One must also avoid making one the final aim of the other. Sanctification is not the purpose of justification. It proceeds from the same source but remains independent, or, more correctly, is logically distinct from justification. Calvin insisted again and again upon the existence and the nature of the bond that unites these two benefits proceeding from union with Christ. Notably, he showed that this bond consists precisely in the *insitio in Christum,* in the union or the communion with Christ. "When it is said (1 Cor. 1:30)," we read in the *Institutes,* "that Christ is made unto us redemption, wisdom and righteousness, it is also added that he is made our sanctification. From this it follows that Christ justifies no one whom he does not sanctify at the same time. For his benefits are joined together as by a perpetual bond, so that when he enlightens us with his wisdom he redeems us; when he redeems us, he justifies us; when he justifies us, he sanctifies us. . . . Since thus it is, that the Lord Jesus never gives anyone the enjoyment of his benefits save in giving himself, he bestows both together and never the one without the other."[5] All the benefits of Christ, all the graces that He has acquired for us, are therefore closely locked together by the foundation of them all, which is Jesus Christ.[6] Nevertheless it is important not to confuse them together, "in order that the variety of the graces of God may so much the better appear to us. . . . [Paul] shows clearly enough that it is one thing to be justified and another to be made new creatures."[7] Indeed, sanctification can be no more than begun during this life, where, whatever progress the faithful may make, they remain

3. *Inst.* 3.11.11. Cf. A. Goehler, *Calvins Lehre von der Heiligung,* Munich, 1934, pp. 83–88; Emmen, *De christologie van Calvijn,* pp. 123f.

4. *CR* 7.735: "Dum fide inserti in Christi corpus, idque spiritus sancti virtute, primum iusti censemur gratuitae iustitiae imputatione, de inde regeneramur in novam vitam." W. Kolfhaus, *Christusgemeinschaft bei Calvin,* Neukirchen, 1939, p. 66, has shown that what is intended here is a logical, but not a temporal, sequence.

5. *Inst.* 3.16.1.

6. *Inst.* 3.11.6: "Even as one certainly cannot tear Jesus Christ into pieces, so also these two things are inseparable, since we receive them together, and conjointly in him: namely, righteousness and sanctification."

7. Ibid.

sinners to their deaths. Justification, on the contrary, is perfect from its first reception, as perfect as the righteousness of the Christ with which it clothes us.[8] For the rest, and from the point of view of the history of theology, it is not this distinction that presents the most interest but the fact that, for Calvin, justification and sanctification are two graces of equal value. The author of the *Institutes* finds himself here in reaction against the unilateral accentuation of justification that one meets with in Luther and his disciples.[9] We may even wonder whether, on this particular point, he had not felt the influence of Erasmus.

In 1536 Calvin did not think it necessary to give an explicit definition of justification, nor to devote a special discussion to it. But it was nonetheless taken as read throughout the book. In the second edition, on the other hand, we find the following definition: "He will be said to be justified by faith who, being excluded from the righteousness of works, appropriates by faith the righteousness of Christ, being clothed wherewith he appears before the face of God not as a sinner, but as righteous."[10] In 1543 he completed this explanation with the following particulars: "Thus we say, in short, that our righteousness before God is an acceptance, whereby, receiving us into his grace, he regards us as righteous. And we say that this same consists in the remission of sins, and in this: that the righteousness of Jesus Christ is imputed to us."[11] But this imputation is made possible only by our union with the Christ and because we become at that same moment members of His body, although the union with Christ cannot be regarded as the cause of the imputation of righteousness. Imputation and union with Christ are, rather, two inseparable aspects of one and the same divine grace: the one is not possible without the other.

The notion of justification does therefore include (as with Luther and Melanchthon) the idea of a righteousness which is extrinsic and is only imputed to us, without any prejudgment of the real state in

8. *Inst.* 3.11.11: "God commences so to reform his elect in the present life, that he proceeds with this work little by little and does not fully achieve it until death, so that they are still guilty before his judgment. But he does not justify in part, but so that the faithful, being clothed in the purity of Christ, may dare frankly to appear before heaven."

9. Goehler, *Calvins Lehre von der Heiligung,* p. 85.

10. *Inst.* 3.11.2.

11. On justification considered as imputation of righteousness and the remission of sins, see Leuttge, *Die Rechtfertigungslehre Calvins,* pp. 75–79; Niesel, "Calvin wider Osianders Rechtfertigungslehre," *Zeitschrift für Kirchengeschichte* 46 (1928): 425f. On the relations between imputation and union with Christ, see Kolfhaus, *Christusgemeinschaft,* pp. 60f.

which we happen to be. Since 1536 Calvin had affirmed that "the righteousness of faith is Christ's righteousness, not our own, that it is in him and not in us, but that it becomes ours by imputation. . . . Thus we are not really righteous, except by imputation; and we are unrighteous but held to be righteous by imputation, in so far as we possess the righteousness of Christ by faith."[12] The same conception is taken up and developed in the successive editions of the *Institutes*: it is reemphasized after the publication of the writings of Osiander, who supposed that the aim of justification was to render believers really righteous, and who saw the remission of sins as no more than a side-issue; whereas, for Calvin, the remission of sins constituted the very basis of justification. But before this he had already imparted a profound resonance to this doctrine of a righteousness imputed to the sinner, by making it the counterpart of the sin assumed by Christ: "How are we righteous before God?" he asks, in the *Commentary on 2 Corinthians* 5:21 (of 1547–1548). "Certainly in just the same way as Christ was a sinner. For he took on our person to the end that he might be guilty in our name and be judged as a sinner: not for his sins but for the sins of others. . . . Certainly in just the same manner we are now righteous in him, not that we satisfy the judgment of God by our works, but because we are considered according to the righteousness of Christ which we have put on by faith, in order that it might be made ours."[13] The logical consequence of that doctrine of the imputation of the righteousness of Christ is that never, not even after the remission of our sins, are we really righteous. On the contrary, we have noted that the sanctification which accompanies justification, or at least begins with it, enables us to become more and more precisely aware of our sin.

Calvin's fear of anything that might have led to the admission of any deification of man, even by way of Jesus Christ and even in His person, led him here again, in regard to the righteousness of Christ that is imputed to us, to underline the radical distinction between the two natures of the Christ. Against Osiander, who maintained that it was only the divine nature in Christ that could accomplish the work of our justification, Calvin affirmed:

Jesus Christ was made our righteousness, taking the form of a servant: . . . he justifies us because he obeyed God his Father. Thus he does not communicate so great a benefit according to his divine na-

12. *CR* 1.60 (*OS* 1.73).
13. *CR* 50.74.

ture, but according to the dispensation entrusted to him.[14] . . . If Osiander answers that to justify us is a work of such dignity that there is no faculty in men that would be equal to it, I grant him that. If he argues from this that no nature except the divine could have had such an effect, I say that he is too grossly mistaken. For although Jesus Christ would not have been able to cleanse our souls by his blood, nor to appease the Father towards us by his sacrifice, nor to absolve us from the condemnation under which we stood, nor, in short, to perform the sacrificial office at all, had he not been truly God (since all the abilities of the flesh were quite unequal to so heavy a burden), yet nevertheless he did accomplish all those things according to his human nature.[15]

Calvin goes on to point out that it is by the obedience of the Christ that we are justified, but that He could not have manifested that obedience except in His quality as a servant; that is, according to His human nature. He finds another argument in favor of this thesis in the fact that "God had prepared as a sacrifice for sin him who knew not sin." It would be repellent to the very notion of divinity if the divine nature of Christ had been the offering presented for our sins. And since, on the other hand, it was for humanity that the sacrifice had to be offered, in order to answer to the notion of satisfaction, it was according to His human nature only that the Christ could offer Himself for us.

We cannot of ourselves, then, acquire the righteousness that would justify us before God. If nevertheless we are justified, that is because we have been grafted into Him and, in that sense, have received His righteousness. In short, Christ puts Himself in our place and accomplishes what we ought to have done. And this is not a single act, a beneficence that comes to an end at our justification. If it were, the deeds that we did after that justification would have to be taken into account in the judgment that God pronounces upon us. That judgment, in other words, would have to be based on the new life that we had acquired. But to be able to pass that test we should have to be effectually saintly and definitely freed from all present sin; whereas we know that the Christian, right up to his death, is battling against sin, which never ceases to assail him and to which he often happens to yield. Even after we have received the faith, our works are still contaminated by sin: nevertheless God does not impute them to us as

14. That is to say, because God willed it so. and gave the Christ the power to do it.

15. *Inst.* 3.11.8–9.

sins but holds them acceptable. Calvin is thus led to formulate the doctrine of double justification; first, the justification of the sinner, and then the justification of the justified, or more correctly of their works.

> When God, after having taken man out of such a pit of perdition, has sanctified him by the grace of adoption, because he has regenerated and reformed him in a new life, he also receives and embraces him as a new creature with the gifts of the Spirit. . . . The faithful, after their calling, are acceptable to God even in regard to their works, for it cannot but be that God loves the good things he has conferred upon them by his Spirit. Nevertheless we must always remember this: that they are not otherwise acceptable to God by reason of their works, except inasmuch as God, for the love he freely bears them and by ever increasing his liberality, accepts those works. . . . But because the faithful, so long as they are encased in their mortal flesh, are still sinners, and their good works are only just begun and there is much that is vicious, God cannot be gracious either to his children or to their works unless he is receiving them in Christ rather than in themselves.[16]

The righteousness of the works of the justified therefore depends, like the justification of the sinner, upon the grace of Christ. In his *Sermon on the Double Righteousness* of 1519, Luther also had made the justification of the works of the justified dependent upon the justification of the sinner: "The second righteousness is proper to ourselves, not that we are the sole authors of it, but because we are cooperating with that first righteousness which is extraneous . . . this righteousness is the work of the former righteousness, and its consequence."[17] But Calvin places more emphasis upon the parallelism between the two justifications, notably in a passage inserted into the *Institutes* of 1543: "Just as, then, we appear righteous before God after we have been made members of Christ, inasmuch as our faults are hidden under

16. *Inst.* 3.17.5. See Goehler, *Calvins Lehre von der Heiligung,* pp. 93ff.; W. A. Hauck, *Calvin und die Rechtfertigung,* pp. 52–68.

17. M. Luther, *Sermo de duplici iustitia, WA* 2.146f. Melanchthon, *Loci communes,* 1543 (*CR* 21.771f.): "Opportere inchoari obedientiam et iustitiam bonae conscientiae, et hanc quanquam procul abest a perfectione legis, tamen in reconciliatis placere Deo propter filium Mediatorem, qui nostram invocationem in nostros cultus perfert ad Patrem, et condonat infirmitatem. Ita propter Christum primum reconciliatur persona, postea et opera recipiuntur, et fides, in utroque luceat." Cf. Seeberg, *Dogmengeschichte,* vol. 4.2, p. 472. Upon Bucer's attitude and the Erasmian influence it reveals, see R. Stupperich, *Der Humanismus und die Wiedervereinigung der Konfessionen,* Leipzig, 1936, pp. 22–26, 81.

his innocence, so are our works held to be righteous, inasmuch as the evil that they contain, being covered by the purity of Christ, is not imputed to us. Wherefore we have a good right to say that by faith alone not only the man is justified, but also his works. But though this righteousness of the works, such as it is, proceeds from faith and gratuitous justification, it must not be supposed to destroy or obscure the grace upon which it depends; but must rather be included in it, and referred back to it, as the fruit to the tree."[18] That last remark places the whole of the exposition in its true light, by giving prominence to the fact that it is not a question of an objective righteousness of the works nor, consequently, of a return to Roman doctrine. The works of the justified are simply reputed righteous, by virtue of the faith of him who does them, and because they are in some sort covered by the grace of Christ. Imperfect though they are, God can accept them as righteous in the same way that He imputes the righteousness of Christ to sinful man.

It must be noted, on the other hand, that while he affirms that it is by the mediation of faith that we are justified, Calvin does not insist upon this part played by faith. In his view, as we have said, faith is nothing in itself. It acquires its value only by its content; that is, by Jesus Christ. "We say that faith justifies, not that it is accounted as righteousness to us for its own worth, but because it is an instrument by which we freely obtain the righteousness of Christ."[19] What matters to Calvin is evidently not that instrument, but the Christ and His work. Furthermore, if we are to believe the *Institutes,* there would be a real danger in overemphasizing the function of faith, for "if faith in itself justified one by its own virtue, then, seeing that it is always weakly and imperfect, it would be only partly effectual and give us only a part of salvation."[20] Besides the polemic against Roman teaching upon justification by works, which dominates Calvin's whole development of this idea, there is a point here that is very clearly aimed against the Zwinglian conception of the perfection of faith, no less than against the consequences that Osiander had thought himself entitled to draw from "the fantasy" in which he affirmed "that man is justified by faith inasmuch as by this same he receives the Spirit

18. *Inst.* 3.17.10. It is in this sense that Calvin could write in *Inst.* 3.16.1: "We are not justified at all without the works, although not at all by the works, forasmuch as, in the participation in Christ in which our justification resides, sanctification is no less included." One may observe here again, the tendency to rehabilitate sanctification along with justification.

19. *Inst.* 3.18.8.

20. *Inst.* 3.11.7.

of God by which he is made righteous."[21] Meanwhile Calvin himself has no hesitation, as we have seen, in repeating that faith justifies, but upon condition that we see it as no more than a means by which we are brought into relation with Christ. For definitely, "it is solely by means of the righteousness of Christ that we are justified before God." We must, no doubt, attribute all these precautions to Calvin's constant preoccupation not to grant too much to man. Faith may indeed be an absolutely free gift of God; it is no less surely ours, once we have received it; but by too much insistence upon the part it is called upon to play in justification, we might presume upon it and to that extent diminish the work of the Christ and the glory of God.

Predestination

After Alexander Schweizer in 1844 and Ferdinand Christian Baur in 1847[22] had claimed that predestination was the central doctrine of Calvin's theology and that all the originality of his teaching proceeded from it, historians and dogmaticians went on for three-quarters of a century repeating that affirmation like an article of faith which did not even need to be verified.[23] It is true enough that Calvin attributed

21. *Inst.* 3.11.23.

22. Alexander Schweizer, *Die Glaubenslehre der evangelisch-reformierten Kirche,* Zurich, 1844–45; F. C. Baur, *Lehrbuch der christlichen Dogmengeschichte,* 3rd ed., Stuttgart, 1867.

23. There were, however, a few notable exceptions. Thus A. Ritschl, from 1868, contested the unique importance of predestination in Calvinist theology ("Geschichtliche Studien zur Christlichen Lehre von Gott," *Jahrbuch für deutsche Theologie,* p. 108); so did A. Kuyper, "Calvinism and Confessional Revision," in the *Presbyterian and Reformed Review,* 1891, pp. 379ff., quoted and in part followed by Doumergue, *Jean Calvin,* vol. 4, pp. 361f. The last considerable exposition that gives a central place to predestination is that of O. Ritschl, *Dogmengeschichte des Protestantismus,* vol. 3, Göttingen, 1926. The author even goes so far as to reproach Calvin for not having given predestination the place to which it was logically entitled in his system. There is a critical review of the principal works devoted to predestination according to Calvin since the middle of the nineteenth century in the important treatise of P. Jacobs, *Prädestination und Verantwortlichkeit bei Calvin,* Neukirchen, 1927, pp. 20–40. Here let it suffice to mention the following works: Doumergue, *Jean Calvin,* vol. 4, pp. 351–416; L. Goumaz, *La Doctrine du salut d'après les commentaires de Jean Calvin sur le Nouveau Testament,* Nyon, 1917, pp. 261–72; Wernle, *Der evangelische Glaube,* pp. 276–305; Seeberg, *Dogmengeschichte,* vol. 4.2, pp. 578ff.; O. Ritschl, *Dogmengeschichte,* pp. 167–85; A. Lecerf, *Le Déterminisme et la responsabilité dans le système de Calvin,* Paris, 1895, pp. 49ff., 108ff.; M. Scheibe, *Calvins Praedestinationslehre,* Halle, 1897; Emmen, *De Christologie van Calvijn,* pp. 67–83; A. D. R. Polman, *De Praedestinatieleer van Augustinus, Thomas van Aquino en Calvijn,* Franeker, 1936, pp. 307–92; "De l'élection éternelle de Dieu" in the *Actes du Congrès internationale de Théologie Calviniste,* Geneva, 1936; H. Otten, *Calvins theologisch Anschauung von der Prädestination,* Munich, 1938; G. Deluz, *Prédestination et liberté,* Neuchâtel, 1942, pp. 49–61.

great importance to predestination in both its forms — election and reprobation — and that he never shared the point of view of Melanchthon, who thought it a subject hardly suitable for discussion.[24] In the different editions of the *Institutes* Calvin gave it more and more space and, in consequence of attacks that were made upon the doctrine, he was moved to defend it in several special writings, notably in the *Congrégation sur l'élection éternelle* of 1551 (published in 1562) against Jérôme Bolsec, and in the second work against Pighius which appeared in 1552 as the treatise *Upon the Eternal Predestination of God.*[25] But to recognize that Calvin taught double predestination, and underlined its dogmatic and practical interest, is not to say that this must be taken to be the very center of his teaching. His earliest writings do not contain any systematic statement of the problem, and although, later on and under the influence of Augustine and of Bucer,[26] he accorded a growing importance to it, he did so under the sway of ecclesiological and pastoral preoccupations rather than in order to make it a main foundation of his theology. While he never ceases, in discussions of the most various questions, to repeat the great themes of the freedom of God and His glory and of the divinity of Christ, he only very rarely speaks of predestination except in the four chapters that are devoted to it in the edition of 1559. As Wernle has said, "It cannot be over-emphasized: faith in predestination is a long way from being the center of Calvinism; much rather is it the last consequence of faith in the grace of Christ in the presence of the enigmas of experience."[27]

In the *Institutes* of 1536, predestination did not yet appear as an independent doctrine. Calvin mentioned it only in two places; in the explanation of the second article of the Creed, and in regard to the definition of the church. He indicated, without, however, dwelling upon the point, that the descent into hell being inadmissible in the literal sense of the text of 1 Peter 3:18–19, it must be interpreted as the manifestation of the power of the redemption to those who had died before the time of Christ. "The faithful who had always looked to him for their salvation then had clear sight of his presence. The reprobate, on the other hand, realizing too late that he was the one

24. Cf. Herrlinger, *Die Theologie Melanchthons,* Gotha, 1879, pp. 70f., 84f. A very moderate criticism of Melanchthon's point of view is to be found in the preface by Calvin to the translation of the *Loci communes, CR* 9.848f.

25. *CR* 8.85–138, 249–366.

26. Doumergue, *Jean Calvin,* vol. 4, pp. 406f., concerning Bucer's influence on Calvin in this domain, generalizes too much. The comparisons with Augustine, on the other hand, claim our attention almost constantly.

27. Wernle, *Der evangelische Glaube,* p. 403.

and only salvation from which they would be shut out, now knew perfectly that they had no hope."[28] Did the opposition here between the faithful and the reprobate already imply the doctrine of predestination that Calvin was afterwards to elaborate? That is debatable. But be that as it may, no further doubt seems permissible when we come to the passage about the church. Here Calvin mentions, one after another and each in a brief sentence, the union of the faithful in Christ, the community of the elect, the consequences of election — namely the calling, justification and glorification — then the perseverance of the elect and their separation from among the reprobate. He points out the close relation between vocation and justification on the one hand and election on the other: "No one can enter into the glory of the heavenly kingdom unless he has been in this manner called and justified; seeing that without any exception the Lord promotes and manifests his election in this way in all the men he has elected."[29] As he was to do later, he insists most particularly upon the "unloseableness" of the salvation that is founded upon election, and upon the fact that the elect are entrusted to the keeping of Christ. He observes that the separation of the elect from the reprobate is effected by God, but that as far as we are concerned, we cannot clearly distinguish the elect from the reprobate in spite of some "sure signs" to that effect given us in the Scriptures.[30] We must therefore be content to exercise a "judgment of charity," and count as elect and as members of the church all those who by their words and conduct "profess one and the same God and Christ with us." From that moment, then, Calvin had adopted as his own the doctrine upon election which was common to the Reformers. Had he also adopted the doctrine of reprobation, considered as the result of a special decree of God? That is not certain.[31]

The French *Catechism* that Calvin wrote in Geneva in 1537 marks, in this respect, an important and decisive stage. In this the question of predestination is raised, after the exposition of the law and before

28. *CR* 1.70 (*OS* 1.83).

29. *CR* 1.73 (*OS* 1.86f.). Cf. Augustine, *De praedestinatione sanctorum* 17.34 (*ML* 44.986); Bucer, *Metaphrases epistolarum Pauli,* 1536, p. 359.

30. *CR* 1.75 (*OS* 1.89): "Quanquam autem fidei certitudine agnosci a nobis electi non possunt, quando tamen scriptura certas quasdam notas nobis describit, ut antea dictum est, quibus electos et filios Dei a reprobis et extraneis distinguamus, quatenus a nobis vult agnosci, debent quodam caritatis iudicio pro electis ac ecclesiae membris haberi omnes, qui et fidei confessione et vitae exemplo et sacramentorum participatione eundem nobiscum Deum ac Christum profitentur."

31. We may wonder, too, whether Calvin did not begin by sharing the opinion of Luther and Bucer, who made no separation between predestination and foreknowledge. A sentence like this: "Solius Dei oculi vident, qui in finem usque sint perseveraturi" (*CR* 1.75), might lead one to think so.

the articles that deal with the redemption. Calvin introduces his material with the following statement: "The seed of the word of God takes root and grows fruitful only in those whom the Lord, by his eternal election, has predestined to be his children and heirs of the heavenly kingdom. To all the others who, by the same counsel of God before the constitution of the world, are reprobate, the clear and evident preaching of the truth can be nothing else but an odor of death in death."[32] The point of departure, as in the *Institutes,* is the fact that the preaching of the Word does not equally move all those that hear it, but bears its fruits only in the elect, whereas to the reprobate it brings only death. The practical and ecclesiological point of view is evident and clear, as it is also in Augustine and in Bucer. And this, in spite of the theoretical developments, is what dominates the exposition of predestination to the end. Similarly, we find in this text of 1537 that reprobation is affirmed by the same warrant as election, and this again is both Augustinian and Bucerian, but not Lutheran. Lastly, Calvin tells us (still in his *Catechism*) that the elect and the reprobate have to serve "as argument and matter to exalt the glory of God," which is also one of the constant themes of the Reformer when he is speaking of predestination.[33]

In 1539, predestination became still more closely involved with ecclesiology, and its outward manifestation with the results of preaching. But Calvin placed this further development after the work of salvation and in a chapter also containing an exposition upon providence; and thus it remained up to and in the edition of 1554. But in 1559 Calvin once more revised his plan, by placing the discussion of providence at the end of the doctrine of God, and predestination after the developments upon sanctification and justification. The comparison established between predestination and providence in 1559 may have been based upon the conviction that predestination and providence both proceeded from one decision of the divine will, an eternal decision situated outside time. But it must not be forgotten that Augustine too, whose influence on Calvin's thought is so strongly apparent at that period, had brought these two concepts into close relation, and that the author of the *Institutes* may have allowed himself to be led by this precedent. In correlation with Augustine, predestination had been considered by a good many theologians, such as Thomas Aquinas, as a special application of the divine providence,[34] of which

32. *CR* 22.46. Cf. Jacobs, *Prädestination,* pp. 62–71.
33. *CR* 22.47.
34. Thomas Aquinas, *Summa Theologica* 1, q. 23, a. 1 and 3: "Praedestinatio quantum ad obiecta, est quaedam pars providentiae."

it was a particular case, concerned with each person taken individually. That notion was not unknown to Calvin. However, bearing in mind that for Calvin man was the immediate end of the creation, we can also affirm, conversely, that predestination in a certain sense conditions providence, which is then limited to a preparation of ways and means. That is very likely what Calvin intended to convey when he said, in a sermon on Job: "Let us note that God has decreed for us what he means to make of us in regard to the eternal salvation of our souls, and then he has decreed it also in respect of this present life."[35] One might therefore have expected him to put predestination immediately after the exposition on providence — even, indeed, before the chapters on the creation; and that is in fact what was done by several theologians who claimed Calvin as their authority, beginning with Théodore de Bèze.[36] But in 1559 Calvin said that the question of predestination which might be raised in relation to the doctrine of God was inopportune.[37] On the other hand, he connected predestination with the Christ and His work, in order to show more clearly that it is in Christ that election takes place.[38] Just as the doctrine of providence, placed at the conclusion of the doctrine of God, might be said to complete the latter as the keystone finishes an arch, so also does the doctrine of predestination complete and illuminate the whole of the account of the redemption. The link between predestination and providence subsists, then, in the last edition of the *Institutes,* in their two parallel functions.

These questions about the position allotted to predestination in the dogmatic exposition as a whole do not arise, as one can see, from mere erudition: they enable one to see more clearly what importance Calvin meant to give to the problem, and his reasons for doing so. So far as the basis of his teaching was concerned there was, however,

35. *CR* 34.363.
36. See, in this sense, O. Ritschl, *Dogmengeschichte,* vol. 3, p. 163: "He could, in the edition of 1559, have dealt with the doctrine of predestination in relation with that of the divine providence, among the primary aspects of the doctrine of God; and some of the later Reformed theologians did so." Cf. A. Ritschl, *Geschichtliche Studien" in the Jahrbuch für deutsche Theologie,* pp. 95ff.; K. F. Noesgen, "Calvins Lehre von Gott und ihr Verhältnis zur Gotteslehre anderer Reformatoren," *Neue kirchliche Zeitschrift* 23 (1912): 709ff.
37. *Inst.* 1.15:8.
38. It is the merit of Jacobs, *Prädestination,* p. 92, to have given prominence to the theological motive which determined Calvin's final choice of his plan: "That the doctrine of predestination does not appear (in conformity with the place of election in the economy of salvation) before the doctrine of creation follows from the fact that it cannot be properly considered except from a Christocentric point of view." Cf. ibid., p. 147.

hardly any change. As early as the edition of 1539 he had expounded it in all essentials, including those that touch upon reprobation. Calvin had then just completed his *Commentary on the Epistle to the Romans,* and he had also thoroughly read the work published by Bucer three years earlier upon this same epistle. The concentration of his reflection upon the various aspects of the problem of predestination must have led him very quickly to definitive results. In effect, the additions that were made to the subsequent editions of the *Institutes* — additions in which some have tried to see signs of a modification of Calvin's attitude and a hardening of his doctrine — are in reality reducible to some new definitions and some more extended biblical quotations. As for the passages relating to reprobation, no doubt they appear in more amplified form, notably so in 1559, as one might have expected in view of the attacks that had been made upon this point of his teaching, but they contain no element of doctrine that is really new.

Not enough is ever said about the preoccupations of a practical kind which were predominant with Calvin, as they had been with Augustine and with Bucer, whenever he applied his mind to the problem of predestination. In his view, this was never to be discussed as an indulgence in metaphysical speculations, but to throw a fuller light upon the doctrine of justification by grace alone and give a theological basis for ecclesiology. That is apparent from the opening of the first chapter upon predestination. "Now, that the covenant of life is not preached equally to everyone, and even where it is preached is not equally received by all — in this diversity there appears a wonderful secret of the judgment of God. For there is no doubt that this variety serves to his good pleasure. But, if it is evident that this takes place by the will of God, that salvation should be offered to some and the rest be excluded from it, from this there arise great and high questions which cannot be resolved otherwise than by instructing the faithful as to what they should hold concerning election and predestination by God."[39] Here, Calvin is dissenting from those who, like Melanchthon, feared that to meditate upon predestination might lead Christians into despair. The questions raised by divine predestination were inescapable; it was necessary, then, to show the faithful what they ought to think about them. Only upon that condition would they be persuaded that they held all grace from the goodness of God, and thus the glory

39. *Inst.* 3.21.1. Cf. Augustine, *De dono perseverantiae* 15–17 (*ML* 45.1016–20 — quoted by Calvin, *CR* 8.326, and frequently); Bucer, *Enarrationes in Evangelia,* 1536, p. 672: "Satis constat illos nescire quid dicant, qui negant ista palam praedicanda."

of God would be fulfilled. "Everyone confesses how much the ignorance of this principle diminishes the glory of God and also how much it takes away from true humility: it is not placing the entire cause of our salvation in God alone." However, we must also avoid the contrary excess of wishing to enter into the secrets of God, which would anyhow be impossible for us. It would also be an act of impiety, for we should be presuming to do without the means that God puts at our disposal to assure ourselves of our salvation. "The election of God is hidden and secret in itself, but the Lord manifests it by the calling; that is, when he does this good to us by calling us. Wherefore men are being fantastic or fanatical if they look for their salvation or for the salvation of others in the labyrinth of predestination instead of keeping to the way of faith which is offered them. . . . To each one, his faith is a sufficient witness of the eternal predestination of God, so that it would be a horrible sacrilege to seek higher assurance; for whoever makes difficulties about subscribing to the simple testimony of the Holy Spirit does him great dishonor."[40] Under these conditions, one must draw the line between speculations arising from an impious curiosity and legitimate knowledge of the doctrine of predestination. The limit between these two domains is indicated by the Scriptures, which give us knowledge of what is useful and salutary for us. So Calvin, for his own explanations, intends to keep to the data of revelation alone. "Let us, then, keep this in view above all other things, that it is no less insane to crave for other knowledge of predestination besides that which is given us in the word of God, than if one wanted to walk over inaccessible rocks or to see in darkness."[41]

Seeing that predestination is taught by the Scriptures, it must be admitted, and not only admitted but preached in public. Is it really as scandalous as its adversaries pretend? Or does it not, on the contrary,

40. *Comm. on John* 6:40 (*CR* 47.147); cf. *Inst.* 3.21.1, and sermon on Eph. 1:3–4: "Paul is speaking there of what we know by experience. . . . We could not understand all that if we were not enlightened by the Holy Spirit. How, then, should we understand a thing which is far higher; that is, know whether God, before the creation of the world, elected us?" Augustine, *De dono perseverantiae* 11 (*ML* 45.1007); *Contra duas epistolas Pelagianorum* 4.6.16 (*ML* 44.621).

41. *Inst.* 3.21.2. The assertion that the Scripture reveals to us all that we ought to know about predestination was often repeated by Calvin. He defines his attitude in his letter to L. Socin of January 1552: "Ego certe, si quis alius, semper a paradoxis abhorrui et argutiis minime delector. Sed nihil me unquam impediet, quin profitear ingenue quod ex Dei verbo didici" (*CR* 14.230). Bucer says the same, on the subject of predestination: "Ubique sane induit se Deus homine, agens nobiscum hominibus, proponit nobis sua de nobis consilia ea ratione, qua nos illa ad salutem nostram maxime percipere possumus. Proinde quae praecipit nobis atque consulit, ea debemus simpliciter amplecti, nusquam inquirere vel causam eorum quae iubemur, ultra eas quas Deus ipse verbo suo explicat, vel etiam congruentiam eorum cum aliis eius factis et dictis" (*Metaphrases epistolarum Pauli*, 1536, p. 399).

share with the principal articles of the Christian faith, such as the Trinity, the creation and the divinity of Christ, the privilege of provoking mockery from "rebellious minds"? To reject the explanations of predestination on the pretext that they may trouble "weaker souls" is openly to contradict God "as though he had happened by inadvertence to publish something that could not but be harmful to the Church."[42] Certain opponents of predestination have taken account of this; they do not deny it, but strive at least to diminish its scope. "A good many cover it up with diverse cavilings, above all those that seek to base it upon his foreknowledge." This was no doubt aimed at Pighius and his *Treatise upon Free Will*; but Pighius was no more than the inheritor of a long tradition which had endeavored to make predestination dependent upon foreknowledge of merits. Others, however, following in this the opinion of Augustine in his latest writings, affirmed that the eternal decree of God could not be determined by an external cause such as the future behavior of each individual, but that since God knew in advance what He would bring about in them, predestination and foreknowledge coincided in fact.[43] That indeed was the solution at which both Luther and Bucer had arrived.[44] But Calvin gave forcible emphasis to the distinction between predestination and foreknowledge. "We say rightly that [God] foresees all things, even as he disposes of them; but it is confusing everything to say that God elects and rejects according to his foresight of this or that. When we attribute foreknowledge to God, we mean that all things have always been and eternally remain under his observation, so that nothing is either future or past to his knowledge: he sees and regards them in the truth, as though they were before his face. We say that this foreknowledge extends throughout the circuit of the world and over all his creatures. We call predestination the eternal decree of God by which he decided what he would do with each man. For he does not create them all in like condition, but ordains some to eternal life, the

42. *Inst.* 3.21.4.

43. Augustine, *De dono perseverantiae* 14: "Haec est praedestinatio sanctorum, nihil aliud: praescientia scilicet, et praeparatio beneficiorum Dei, quibus certissime liberantur, quicunque liberantur"; 18: "Sine dubio enim praescivit si praedestinavit, sed praedestinasse est hoc praescisse, quod fuerat ipse facturus" (*ML* 45.1014, 1023). Cf. Thomas Aquinas, *Summa Theologica* 1, q. 23, a. 5.

44. Luther, *De servo arbitrio, WA* 18.615ff.; *Comm. on Gen.* 26:9 (*WA* 43.457); Bucer, *Metaphrases epistolarum Pauli,* 1536, p. 355: "Praescire et praenosse . . . nihil aliud est, quam Deum suos iam antequam sint, animo praesumere, et iam tum tanquam essent, inter suos computare. Nam ut si quis ex turba aliqua hominum quosdam animo notet et designet, quos velit sibi ad rem aliquam peculiariter adhibere, ita Deus ex perdita hominum colluvie praevidet ac praenoscit quos vult, eosque iam tum ab aliis apud se seiungit et in sortem sanctorum cooptat, id est, praedestinat"; on p. 360, he expressly approves of the attitude of Thomas Aquinas.

others to eternal damnation."[45] The distinction was vital to him, for we find him frequently returning to it even in his sermons, in order to throw into relief the absolutely gratuitous nature of election. Election, like reprobation, is an entirely free act of the divine will. "If we ask why God takes pity on some, and why he lets go of the others and leaves them, there is no other answer but that it pleased him to do so."[46] To set up a causal relation between foreknowledge and predestination, whether this foreknowledge was of the merits of man or of the graces that God will grant him — this is only another way of placing the will of God in dependence upon a cause external to the act of the will itself, and therefore of limiting it; whereas by definition it allows of no diminution whatever. And this, Calvin thought, would lead one sooner or later to readmit human freedom in some roundabout way, and so ruin predestination. It is noteworthy that a similar argument is to be found in Duns Scotus, who had strongly affirmed the absolute independence of the divine will and its priority in relation to faith and to human works, and had concluded that whatever foreknowledge God might have of this faith or of those works, it could in no way determine the entirely free and sovereign decree of election.[47]

It is advisable here to recall that this will of God manifested in the calling addressed to the elect can encounter no obstacle on their part, which is to say that grace is irresistible. Just as sinful man necessarily willed and did evil, by reason of the internal necessity of his condition, so does justified man conform himself to the necessity of his new condition by obeying the divine will and necessarily doing what it orders him to do. "The Apostle teaches not only that grace to will the good is offered us if we will accept it, but that God makes and forms that will within us, which is to say no other thing than that God by his spirit trains, inclines, moderates our heart, and that he rules it as his own possession."[48] Following Augustine, Calvin affirms more ex-

45. *Inst.* 3.21.5. When Calvin writes, quoting from Laurent Valla, *Inst.* 3.23.6, *in fine*: "But since [God] sees things to come for no other reason than that he has determined that they should come, it is folly to dispute and debate what his prescience is doing, when it is apparent that everything occurs by his ordinance and disposition," he is not denying that distinction, but on the contrary maintaining the difference of nature between foreknowledge and predestination. Foreknowledge has for its object the decisions of the divine will; predestination is identical with that will.

46. Sermon on Eph. 1:3–4 (*CR* 51.259); cf. *CR* 26.520; 47.297; 51.149; 55.353, etc.

47. Comm. on the *Sentences* 1.41.10–11; cf. Seeberg, *Dogmengeschichte,* vol. 3, p. 655, n. 1.

48. *Inst.* 2.3.10. This is what Bucer said when he claimed that: "nos tum demum plenam libertatem habebimus quando . . . necessario volumus, quae bonae sunt" (*Metaphrases epistolarum Pauli,* p. 360).

plicitly: "Grace is by no means offered by God only to be rejected or accepted as it may seem good to one; it is that same grace alone which inclines our heart to follow its movement, and produces in it the choice as much as the will; so that all the good works that follow after are fruits of the same."[49] Assuredly, this is so only to the measure of our sanctification, but the elect soul is nonetheless incapable of resisting God. He is an instrument of the divine will, although this is not to say that his will is annihilated. On the contrary, regeneration liberates his will, but by making him will what God expects of him.[50]

As we have already noted with regard to the relations between redemption and predestination, for Calvin the latter was founded upon Jesus Christ. As it is in Him that the promises of salvation find their guarantee, so it is in Him that election is sealed. Doubly so, seeing that the Christ took part in the decree of election in His capacity as second person of the Holy Trinity, and that He is also the artisan of this election in His capacity as Mediator. Whether we place the accent upon predestination itself, logically conceived as the prior condition of salvation, or — where Calvin usually places it — upon the offer of salvation in Christ, we are brought back to Jesus Christ in either case. That Calvin insists so much upon predestination is precisely for this reason. It is in the fact that election is founded upon Christ that he finds assurance of the certitude of salvation. Communion with Christ ought to relieve us of all doubt on that point: it is the proof of our election. "Whoever finds himself in Jesus Christ and is a member of his body by faith, he is assured of his salvation; and when we want to know this, we do not need to go up on high to inquire about something that must now be hidden from us. For behold! God himself comes down to us; he shows us enough in his Son; it is as though he were saying: Here I am, contemplate me, and know that I have adopted you as my children. When we receive this message of salvation which is brought to us by the Gospel, from that we know, and are assured, that God has chosen us."[51] Thus, then, the believer who is united with Christ has no longer any reason for lengthy speculations about his election; it is certified to him. And here, by the way, we can grasp one of the reasons why Calvin gave so much importance to the union

49. *Inst.* 2.3.13; Augustine, *De correptione et gratia* 11 (*ML* 44.917f.); Bucer, *Metaphrases epistolarum Pauli,* p. 358: "[Praedestinationem] certam esse et immotam hanc Dei voluntatem de nostra salute, quam avertere nulla creatura potest."

50. See Jacobs, *Prädestination,* p. 136.

51. *Congrégation sur l'élection éternelle, CR* 8.114. Cf. Bucer, *Metaphrases epistolarum Pauli,* p. 359: "Altera pars huius quaestionis erat, ad quid sit praedestinatio consideranda. . . . Ad nihil sane aliud, quam ut de salute tua certior sis et firmior inhaereas promissionibus Dei."

with Christ and the function it fulfils in piety. The practical interest he took in the problem of predestination must have brought him back a good many times to this relation between election and union with Christ; and in the *Institutes* he defines something of his thought upon it:

> Of those whom God has chosen as his children it is not said that he elected them in themselves, but in his Christ, because he could not love them except in him, and could not honor them with his heritage without having first made them participants in him. But if we are elected in Christ we shall find no certitude at all of our election in ourselves; nor even in God the Father if we imagine him alone without his Son. Christ, then, is like a mirror in which we have to contemplate our election. . . . For, since it is he in whom the heavenly Father has proposed to incorporate those whom he has willed from all eternity to be his own, to acknowledge as his children all those whom he recognizes as members of the same, we have testimony strong and evident enough that we are written in the book of life if we communicate with Christ.[52]

But there is something more. Election manifests itself, indeed, by clear and positive signs in the lives of the elect, and more particularly by the calling, and the righteousness which expresses it in concrete reality. "We teach that the calling of the elect is as a sign and testimony of their election. Similarly, that their justification is another mark and evidence of it, until they come into the glory wherein lies its fulfilment."[53] The preaching of the gospel is in itself alone a sign that God has taken pity on us; but the sure sign of our adoption is that "we take to heart, and with affection, the doctrine that is preached to us."[54] The signs never deceive, but faith alone is able to recognize them and draw the conclusions that follow, and notably to ascend from the

52. *Inst.* 3.25.5. Cf. *Comm. on Matt.* 11:27 (*CR* 45.319): "Although our salvation has always been hidden in God, Jesus Christ is nevertheless the channel through whom this salvation flows down to us; and we receive it by faith so that it may be firm and well ratified in our hearts." Add also *CR* 8.321.

53. *Inst.* 3.21.7; cf. 3.24.4.

54. Sermon on Eph. 1:3–4 (*CR* 51.260); Bucer, *Enarrationes in Evangelia,* 1536, p. 579: "Hanc autem gratuitam adoptionem tum demum sentiunt electi, cum Christum fide agnoverint, spiritu sancto, in quo Deum patrem per Christum invocent, donati." However, Bucer's view was that each of the elect had hidden within him a "seed of election" even before he had received the faith. "Semper tamen sentias quoddam in electis semen Dei et veritatis studium, etiam tum, cum veritatem oppugnant, aut certe pugnantem cum illa vitam degunt" (pp. 308f.). And he invokes in support the example of Paul before his conversion. Calvin reacted against this notion with some vehemence — *Inst.* 3.24.10–11.

calling to election. However, in the chapter of the *Institutes* where he is counting the blessings of justification, Calvin seems to be speaking another language, and trying to discern the proof of election in the works that proceed from faith. "If all the gifts that God has bestowed upon us, when we recall them in memory, are as rays of the light of his countenance, to illuminate our contemplation of the sovereign light of his goodness, all the more surely should the good works he has given us serve thereto, which demonstrate that the Spirit of adoption has been given to us."[55] This passage is indeed a surprising one. May it not confirm the opinion of those who think they can see in Calvin the germs of the future puritanism? In reality, the author of the *Institutes* admits the testimony of works only under the restrictions required by his theology as a whole, and as signs of a very inferior kind. "The saints," he writes, "well understand that their integrity is not complete but is mixed with many imperfections and relics of the flesh." So it is necessary to begin with an apprehension of the "goodness of God, assuring oneself of this by the promises of the Gospel alone. For if they once begin to repute it according to works, nothing could be more uncertain and infirm; since, if works are valued in themselves, they will no less put the man in danger of the wrath of God by their imperfection than bear him witness of man's benevolence by their indifferent purity of intention."[56] What assures us of our election, then, is first, our faith in Christ and our union with Him, and secondly, the gifts that God grants in sanctifying us. We know that some disciples of Calvin took a much more affirmative position with regard to the testimony of works, and that for a number of his spiritual successors the abundance and the success of our works provided the manifest proof of our election and our salvation. But this tendency, it must be repeated, is contrary to authentic Calvinist thought.

It was again upon the union with Christ that Calvin relied for the definitive and unloseable character of the salvation conferred by election. He rejected the opinions of those "who taught that the virtue and firmness of an election depended upon the faith"; the latter could only make the election manifest, but not give it efficacy.[57] "To have the full firmness and efficacy of election, one must appeal to the Head, by whom the heavenly Father has joined his elect to himself, and has also bound them together in an indissoluble bond. Thus, by the adop-

55. *Inst.* 3.14.18.
56. *Inst.* 3.14.19. On this "practical syllogism," which refers works back to election, see Niesel, *Die Theologie Calvins*, pp. 164–73.
57. *Inst.* 3.24.3–4.

tion of the posterity of Abraham, God's liberal favor, which he withheld from all others, did indeed appear; but the grace extended to the
members of Jesus Christ has quite another pre-eminence of dignity,
for, being united with their Head, they are never cut off from their
salvation."[58] Whether he is speaking of union with Christ, or of the
immutability of the divine will, or of the church and the promises
made to her, Calvin always comes back to this idea that the elect
cannot lose salvation whatever they do. Besides, their election includes
the gift of perseverance, a free gift, independent of our will or our
merits, since the grace of election is irresistible. "The Spirit of God,
being consistent with itself, nourishes and confirms the love of obedience in us."[59] Calvin was trying to group all these things together
when he defined as follows the foundations upon which our salvation
rests: "Firstly, it is founded upon the election of God, and could never
fail unless his eternal providence were dispelled. Further, it is confirmed inasmuch as Christ must remain in his wholeness, and will no
more suffer his faithful to be taken away from him than allow his
members to be torn in pieces. In addition, we are certain that inasmuch as we dwell within the bosom of the Church, the truth dwells
in us. Finally, we understand that those promises belong to us, in
which it is said that there will be salvation in Sion: God will dwell
for ever in Jerusalem and never depart out of the midst of it."[60] In
fact, if we ascribe any reality to predestination, it must indeed be
admitted that the decree of election must be able to triumph not only
over our initial resistances, but our permanent weaknesses and our
liability to fall back into sin and disobedience. God must have the will
and the power to apply it, otherwise we should be going back to the
idea that the divine will was dependent upon the good will of man.
Election has been decided once for all; it can no more be rendered out
of date than the divine will can be changed. This had already been

58. *Inst.* 3.21.7. Cf. Sermon on Eph. 1:4–6 (*CR* 51.282): "If we are his members
and we hold that he is our head, as he allied himself with us, and that there is this
holy union which can never be broken while we believe in his Gospel, it is there that
we must go in order to be assured of our salvation."

59. *Inst.* 2.3.11; cf. 2.5.3; 3.24.6–7; *Comm. on 1 Cor.* 1:9 *in fine* (*CR* 49.313):
"When the Christian looks at himself, he sees only matter for trembling, or rather
for despairing; but because he is called into the communion of Christ, he ought to
have no thought of self when it is a question of his assurance of salvation, except as
a member of Jesus Christ, in such sort that he ought to hold all [the Lord's] goods
as his own. Thus he will conceive, beyond all doubt, a certain hope of final perseverance, as they say, holding himself to be a member of him who is in no peril of
falling."

60. *Inst.* 4.1.3.

laid down by Augustine in many passages of his anti-Pelagian writings and Bucer, following his lead, was never tired of repeating it.[61] Calvin, as early as the *Institutes* of 1536, was already taking some account of this idea which was afterwards to assume such great importance in his thinking: "It cannot be," he then wrote, "that the true members of the elect people of God should in the end perish or be lost. Their salvation has such sure and firm supports that even if the whole machine of the world broke down, this could not fall. It rests upon the election of God, and could change or disappear only with the eternal wisdom."[62]

And yet the permanence of election is not strictly certain except in so far as the predestination of individuals is concerned. In order to take account of this fact, Calvin was led, especially in the last edition of his work, to distinguish two, or even three, sorts of election. Here he established a very clear difference between the election of the people of Israel in the person of Abraham, the election throughout Abraham's posterity of the truly faithful descendants of Jacob, and finally the election by Christ of "those single persons to whom God not only offers salvation but also assigns such a certitude of it that its effect cannot be in suspense or doubt."[63] The election of Israel in Abraham, whether this concerned the entire people or only the descendants of Jacob, is general; the election of the Christian is special. Four years earlier Calvin had already given expression to that idea in a sermon on Deuteronomy 7:7:

> What is spoken of here is the general election of all the people, inasmuch as they were adopted by God. And this is indeed noteworthy. For in calling Abraham, God extended the promise of salvation to all his posterity. He said to Abraham: I will be the God of your descendants after you. That is an election that we call general, of all the people, in so far as God has separated it from the rest of the world, and said that he was retaining it for his heritage and his Church. ... But there is another, a second election which is stricter, so to speak; which is, namely, that God chooses out of that posterity those whom it pleases him ... there is nothing contradictory in that. ... But now, it is a gratuitous election by God, that we have his word purely preached to us, that we have the Gospel and the sacraments.

61. See, for example, Augustine, *Contra Julianum* 5.4.14 (*ML* 44.792); *De correptione et gratia* 9.23, 13.40 (*ML* 44.930, 941); Bucer, *Enarrationes in Evangelia,* 1536, p. 716: "Docet, omnia a divina electione pendere, eosque quibus semel datum fuerit oves esse, perire nunquam posse."
62. *CR* 1.73 (*OS* 1.87).
63. *Inst.* 3.21.5–7.

... But nevertheless, he still keeps for himself such as he thinks fit, so that people should not put their trust in those outward signs, without faith and without obedience. But above all, when it pleases God to imprint the certitude of his promises in our hearts by his Holy Spirit, now that indeed is a more special adoption, when he assures us that we are of that little number whom he has reserved for himself.[64]

Thanks to this distinction between general election and particular election, Calvin thought he could explain how the people of Israel had been the object of an election in the proper meaning of the word, but had lost the benefit of that grace, while the believer who is the object of a special election cannot be deprived of it. It must be confessed that this is a purely verbal explanation; otherwise Calvin would have had to develop the idea that he no more than touched upon when he said, in the *Institutes,* that "not all are effectually elected with an equal grace,"[65] and insist upon the fact that the election of Israel is something very different from election to salvation in Jesus Christ.

The logical counterpart of election is presented by reprobation. Calvin was never content with the statement that God, in His goodness, elected to salvation a certain number of men taken from the mass of sinners; he thought that those who had not been chosen had also been the object of a special decree, that of reprobation. "Election would be inconsistent," he wrote, "if it were not placed in opposition to reprobation. We are told that God separates those he adopts to salvation; it would be too crass a stupidity, then, to say that those who are not elected obtain by mere chance, or acquire by their industry, that which is given from on high to only a few people. Thus, those whom God leaves out of his election he is also reproving, and this for no other reason than that he wills to exclude them from the heritage that he has predestined to his children."[66] On this particular point Calvin diverges from Augustine, for whom the elect alone are the object of a special decision which withdraws them from the *massa perditionis,* while the reprobate are simply abandoned by God to the ruin that they have incurred by their sins.[67] The author of the *Institutes,* on the

64. *CR* 26.521–24.

65. *Inst.* 3.21.7.

66. *Inst.* 3.23.1; cf. 3.21.7; Bucer, *Metaphrases epistolarum Pauli,* 1536, p 358: "Atqui scriptura non veretur dicere, Deum tradere quosdam homines in sensum reprobum et agere in perniciem, quid igitur indignum Deo, dicere, etiam statuisse antea ut illos in sensum reprobum traderet et ageret in perniciem?" Luther, *De servo arbitrio, WA* 18.712f.

67. Augustine, *De correptione et gratia* 7.12 (*ML* 44.923).

other hand, cannot admit that Christ would be unable to attract the recalcitrant souls to Himself and so save them in spite of themselves. Neither could he admit that it was by an effect of natural laws that man was subject to death: "The Scripture says loudly and clearly that all mortal creatures have been made subject to death in the person of one man. Since that cannot be attributed to nature, it must clearly have proceeded from the wonderful counsel of God."[68] Here we have to do with an inscrutable secret of the divine judgment. Reduced to his own resources, man is incapable of either accepting or refusing the message of Christ. The reason why some accept and others reject it is to be sought only in God, in a decision of His will which is incomprehensible to us and which we must not even seek to penetrate. Calvin finds no difficulty in declaring: "I confess that this decree ought to appall us." At least, that is how it is when we think of it according to human reason.[69] But in reality that judgment cannot be unjust, because by definition every manifestation of the will of God is the expression of righteousness itself. And thus, while fully maintaining the incomprehensibility of the decree of reprobation, Calvin is led to affirm that the reprobate are condemned justly and by their fault. "Since it is certain that they were not unworthy of being predestined to such an end, it is also certain that the ruin into which they fall by the predestination of God is just and equitable. Furthermore, their perdition proceeds from God's predestination in such a manner that the cause and matter of it will be found in them. The first man fell because God had judged that to be expedient. But of why he had so judged, we know nothing. Yet it is nevertheless certain that he had not done so had he not seen that this would redound to the glory of his Name. But when mention is made of the glory of God, let us think also of his righteousness, for that which deserves praise must necessarily be equitable. Man stumbles, then, even as God ordained that he should, but he stumbles on account of his depravity. . . ."[70] Attempts have sometimes been made to see this reasoning as an originality on Calvin's part. It is no such thing, and one need only recall the parallel passages in Luther and in Bucer to find that here again,

68. *Inst.* 3.23.7.

69. Bucer writes the same, *Metaphrases epistolarum Pauli,* p. 359: "Tum non potest non inhumanum iudicare, Deum vel permittere labi, quos solus a lapsu servare potest, et crudele, poenas sumere de lapsis, qui ope eius destituti non potuerunt non labi. Proinde iudicium rationis hic penitus reiciendum est, et fatendum iudicia Dei esse abyssum multam, esse imperscrutabilia."

70. *Inst.* 3.23.8.

the *Institutes* move along lines that had been traditional since Augustine.[71]

Reprobation is required to be just, so that, by the same right as election, it may manifest the glory of God in the sight of the faithful precisely by the mystery in which it is veiled; which also serves to emphasize the omnipotence of the divine will, and not only its omnipotence but also its mercy. "The wicked are created on the day of their perdition. For that does not come to pass except in so far as God wills to heighten his glory. . . . We have therefore to be resolved of this, that God had such a care for our salvation that he did not meanwhile forget himself, but willed that the world should be as a theater for his glory."[72]

Calvin was again drawing inspiration from the author of the *City of God* when he explained how the reprobate, right up to the day of judgment, lived side by side with the elect upon earth and even within the church. No sure means are at our disposal which would enable us to discern the reprobate. At the most, reprobation manifests itself by signs which may authorize us, in a certain measure, to assume the presence of that eternal decree of God. Even then, such an inference is possible only in the eyes of faith, and therefore is not within the power of the reprobate themselves. Non-success in the preaching of the gospel or the fact that it does not touch all men are signs of this sort; others can be found in the absence of sanctification: "All those who are of the number of the reprobate, as they are instruments made for opprobrium, never cease to provoke the wrath of God by endless crimes, and to confirm by obvious signs the judgment of God that is decreed against them."[73] Nevertheless, the reprobate sometimes show

71. Augustine, *Enchiridion ad Laurentium* 25.99 (*ML* 40.278): "Videt enim . . . universum genus humanum tam iusto iudicio divino . . . damnatum, ut etiam si nullus inde liberaretur, nemo recte posset Dei vituperare iustitiam"; *De anima* 4.11.16 (*ML* 44.533); *De dono perseverantiae* 8.16 (*ML* 45.1002). Luther, *De servo arbitrio*, *WA* 18.785: "Hic tam lumen naturae quam lumen gratiae dictant culpam esse non miseri hominis sed iniqui Dei, nec enim aliud iudicare possunt de Deo, qui hominem impium gratis sine meritis coronat et alium non coronat, sed damnat forte minus vel saltem non magis impium. At lumen gloriae aliud dictat, et Deum, cuius modo est iudicium incomprehensibilis iustitiae, tunc ostendet esse iustissimae et manifestissimae iustitiae." Bucer, *Metaphrases epistolarum Pauli*, 1536, p. 359: "Fatendum itaque nobis est, Deum iuste exigere a nobis vitam sanctam et virtutibus omnibus ornatum: iuste etiam quos vult indurare, excaecare et tradere in sensum reprobum: iuste denique hos damnare et punire: nobis autem omnem culpam nostrae perditionis adscribendam esse."

72. *CR* 8.293f. Cf. Bucer, *Metaphrases epistolarum Pauli*, p. 359: "Propter se enim Deus, et in gloriam suam fecit omnia etiam impium ad diem malum. . . . Et ubique in Scripturis gloria domini finis esse ultionis malorum praedicatur."

73. *Inst.* 3.23.12; cf. 3.21.7, *in fine.*

signs analogous to those of vocation.[74] "Experience shows that the reprobate are occasionally touched almost by a like sentiment as the elect, so that in their opinion they ought to be included in the ranks of the faithful. . . . Not that they understand what the virtue of the Spirit is, nor that they knowingly and vividly receive it, nor that they have the true light of faith; but because God, in order to keep them convinced and render them so much the more inexcusable, insinuates himself into their understanding."[75] Will not these, only apparently elect, sow confusion in the minds of true believers, who might be shaken in the certitude of their salvation by seeing that some of the reprobate share the signs of election with them? To this Calvin replies somewhat briefly: "Although there may be great similarity and affinity between the elect and those of a lapsed and transitory faith, nevertheless the trust of which Paul speaks, namely, that dares to invoke God heartily as Father, is in full vigor only among the elect. Wherefore, since God regenerates the elect alone in perpetuity by the incorruptible seed, and never permits the seed he has planted in their hearts to perish, so there is no doubt that he seals in their hearts, in a special fashion, the certitude of his grace."[76] Still, it is true that we may have beside us, in the church itself, reprobates whose real condition is unknown to themselves, and all the more surely unknown to us. But there are cases where no doubt at all seems possible; for example, when we find ourselves in the presence of obstinate heretics, or again, of individuals whose conduct arouses scandal in the church. We have to believe, in these cases, that the signs of reprobation present unchallengeable evidence; and in fact, the church must separate itself from these rotten members by excommunicating them. But even then, the disciplinary sentence of the church in no way forestalls the definitive judgment of God. "We ought never to expunge the excommunicated from the number of the elect or to despair of them as if they were already lost . . . and the more we perceive pride and obstinacy in them instead of humility, the more we ought to commit them to the hand of God and commend them to his goodness, hoping better for the future than we can see for the present."[77] This is no more than an application of the principle that the judgments of God are incomprehensible and unfathomable to us, and that it is therefore impossible,

74. *Inst.* 3.24.7.
75. *Inst.* 3.2.11. Cf. Augustine, *De correptione et gratia* 9.20, 13.42 (*ML* 44.928, 942).
76. *Inst.* 3.2.11.
77. *Inst.* 4.12.9; cf. *Comm. on Ps.* 119:16 (*CR* 32.153) and *Comm. on 1 John* 5:16 (*CR* 55.371ff.).

in spite of all the "signs" that may be given, for us at this present time to distinguish the elect from the reprobate. Although Calvin drew the practical consequences from his doctrine of predestination in what concerned the elect, he did not do the same with regard to reprobation. Undoubtedly, the knowledge we have of the latter is not merely theoretical, and striking examples may brutally convince us of its reality. But we have no right to inquire into its effects upon the plane of the church or in our relations with other men. We have not to make ourselves the executors of the judgments that we may attribute with more or less probability to God. Predestination will be fully revealed to us only in the life beyond.

10

Christ, the Law, and the Christian

An Unexplored Aspect of the Third Use of the Law in Calvin's Theology

I. John Hesselink

The Question of the Third Use of the Law

It is well known that the law of God plays a prominent role in Calvin's theology. He, more than any other Reformer, stressed in particular the continuing need of the law as a norm and guide in the Christian life. This, the so-called third use of the law (*usus tertius legis*), was for Calvin the "principal use."[1] This third and positive use

Reprinted from *Reformatio Perennis: Essays on Calvin and the Reformation in Honor of Ford Lewis Battles,* ed. Brian A. Gerrish (Pittsburgh: Pickwick, 1981), pp. 11–26. Used by permission.

1. *Inst.* 2.7.12. In general I am using the translation of Ford Lewis Battles (ed. John T. McNeill) in the Library of Christian Classics series (Philadelphia: Westminster, 1960). For Melanchthon and Luther the second use of the law, the *usus elenchticus* or *theologicus,* is the "proper and principal use" ("*Secundum officium ac proprium legis divinae et praecipuum est . . .*") (Melanchthon, *CR* 21.405). Luther uses the same terminology to describe the *third* use of the law Calvin was engaging in a polemic against Luther although Werner Elert, the late Lutheran theologian from Erlangen, was convinced that this was indeed Calvin's purpose. See his *Law and Gospel* (Philadelphia: Fortress, 1967), p. 44. This is a translation of an

or function of the law is not unique to Calvin; it was also propounded by Melanchthon[2] and appears in the Lutheran Formula of Concord (1577).[3] Nevertheless, this positive function of the law as a norm and guide has come to be associated primarily with Calvin and is considered a special characteristic of Reformed ethics and piety. Many Lutherans, in fact, regard this as a fundamental difference between Luther and Calvin, although others, such as the Danish ethicist, N. H. Søe, conclude that there "was no essential difference between the two Reformers on this question."[4]

The notion of a continuing, positive function of the law for Christians continues to be rejected by certain types of Lutherans, liberals, and fundamentalists (especially dispensationalists), who are convinced that "the ethic of Jesus" or the principle of Christian freedom as propounded by the apostle Paul does away with any such use of law. Others, who would not fit any of the above classifications, are equally adamant that "the New Testament knows nothing of a third use of the law."[5]

The Recent Rejection of Laws and Principles by Ethical Situationalists

This animus toward the third use of the law was trumpeted with particular boldness in the 1960s when situation ethics and a general reaction against tradition and authority dominated the theological scene. It may be only a coincidence that the three most outspoken

---

essay which originally appeared in a larger work of Elert's: *Zwischen Gnade und Ungnade: Abhandlungen des Themas Gesetz und Evangelium* (Munich, 1948).

For other parallels in Melanchthon and Zwingli see the long, valuable note on pages 334–35 in Ford Lewis Battles's English edition of the *Institution of the Christian Religion* (1536) (Atlanta: John Knox, 1975).

2. In his *Loci Communes*, both the second and third editions (*CR* 21 406). Cf. the English translation of the 1555 edition of the *Loci Communes* entitled *Melanchthon on Christian Doctrine*, ed. Clyde L. Manschreck, Library of Protestant Thought (New York: Oxford University, 1965), pp. 122–28.

3. Section 6 is entitled "The Third Function of the Law." See *The Book of Concord*, ed. Theodore G. Tappert (Philadelphia: Fortress, 1959), pp. 479f.

4. N. H. Søe, "The Three 'Uses' of the Law," in *Norm and Content in Christian Ethics*, ed. Gene H. Outka and Paul Ramsey (New York: Scribner's, 1968), p. 310.

5. Emil Brunner, *Dogmatics*, vol. 3, *The Christian Doctrine of the Church, Faith, and Consummation* (Philadelphia: Westminster, 1962), p. 301. Brunner here reverses a position taken earlier in his ethics, *The Divine Imperative (Das Gebot und die Ordnungen)* (Philadelphia: Westminster, 1937), p. 149. See my discussion of this question in relation to the treatment of the law in part 3 of the Heidelberg Catechism in *Guilt, Grace, and Gratitude*, ed. Donald J. Bruggink (New York: Half Moon, 1963), pp. 149ff.

situationalists were Anglicans: Professor Joseph Fletcher,[6] Bishop John
A. T. Robinson,[7] and Canon Douglas A. Rhymes,[8] the former two
also proclaiming a "new morality" and the last named being even more
radical. Their fans and followers, however — and they were and are
legion — on both sides of the Atlantic represented most denominational
backgrounds.

Fletcher, Robinson, and Rhymes do not appear to know about Calvin; at least, they don't bother referring to him. But their attacks
against laws, rules, and general principles, as well as traditional morality, if valid, would be devastating for Calvin's concept and use of
the law. For in the Ten Commandments Calvin found principles which
are valid forever. These commandments, he repeatedly affirms, are
the rule of life (*regula vivendi*) which God has given to the universal
church.[9] For Calvin there is nothing worse than trying to live the
Christian life without definite, revealed norms or rules. This is why
God's law, as revealed in the Scriptures, is indispensable and crucial
for living the Christian life. "For unless he prescribes to us what his
will is and regulates all the actions of our life according to a certain
rule (*certam regulam*), we would be perpetually going astray."[10]

Other ethicists, writing in the 1960s, were more aware and appre-
ciative of Calvin's viewpoint, but sought to move beyond it. Paul Lehmann's *Ethics in a Christian Context*[11] appeared the same year as
Robinson's *Honest to God* (1963). His contextual, *koinonia* ethic is
more moderate and more carefully reasoned than Fletcher's situational
approach. He quotes Calvin frequently and usually with favor, but it
is significant that at one crucial point he criticizes the Reformers for
slipping "back to a preceptual reading of the law."[12] This is not incidental, for there are several aspects of his position, particularly his
eschewing of moral principles in general, which are inimical to Calvin's understanding of the law. The same can be said of the Princeton

6. Joseph Fletcher, *Situation Ethics: The New Morality* (Philadelphia: Westminster, 1966). Fletcher is the best known and most widely read and discussed representative of this movement.

7. One of the most controversial chapters in John A. T. Robinson's best seller
Honest to God (London: SCM, 1963), "The New Morality," is indebted to an earlier,
programmatic essay by Joseph Fletcher. See also Robinson's later work, *Christian
Morals Today* (Philadelphia: Westminster, 1964).

8. Douglas A. Rhymes, *No New Morality* (London: Constable, 1964).

9. *Inst.* 4.13.12.

10. *Comm. on Jer.* 32:33 (*CO* 39.20); cf. Preface, *Comm. on Isa.* (*CO* 36.19);
Comm. on Acts 2:23 (*CO* 48.40).

11. Paul Lehmann, *Ethics in a Christian Context* (New York: Harper and Row,
1963).

12. Ibid., p. 78, n. 2.

ethicist, Paul Ramsey, a sharp critic of situationalist ethics. In his *Deeds and Rules in Christian Ethics* (1965)[13] he in effect defends the third use of the law, but not in Calvin's terms.

Of all the criticisms of situational and contextual ethics,[14] one of the most balanced and perceptive was that of Professor James M. Gustafson, then at Yale University and now at the University of Chicago. In 1965, in the midst of all the furor about the new approach to ethics, he wrote an essay which has been reprinted elsewhere and cited frequently: "Context versus Principles: A Misplaced Debate in Christian Ethics."[15] The debate between situationalists and those who stress objective moral principles is "no longer a fruitful one," maintains Gustafson, both because it is difficult, if not impossible, to know who belongs to which camp, and, more importantly, because in responsible decision making no one is simply a situationalist or traditional moralist.[16] Gustafson concludes his essay with a question which brings us back to the key issue being dealt with here in regard to what are the ultimate norms for Calvin in living the Christian life, namely, "Is there one normative starting point, or base point, for work in Christian ethics around which other discussion ought to cohere?"[17]

The Issue at Stake

This debate about context versus principles, and rules versus a "love monism," confused certain basic issues in Christian ethics, but sharpened others. Above all, the debate forced ethicists to clarify how

13. The first edition of this work was published in Edinburgh in 1965; an enlarged version, which included a response to Fletcher, was published in 1967 by Charles Scribner's Sons. This work represents a considerable shift in thinking — and a marked improvement — vis-à-vis his earlier *Basic Christian Ethics* (New York: Scribner's, 1950).

14. See three valuable symposia: *The Situation Ethics Debate,* ed. Harvey Cox (Philadelphia: Westminster, 1968); *Storm over Ethics,* ed. John C. Bennett, James M. Gustafson, E. Clinton Gardner, et al. (Philadelphia: United Church, 1967); *Norm and Context in Christian Ethics,* ed. Gene H. Outka and Paul Ramsey (New York: Scribner's, 1968).

15. This essay first appeared in the April 1965 *Harvard Theological Review* and was reprinted in *New Theology No. 3,* ed. Martin E. Marty and Dean G. Peerman (New York: Macmillan, 1966).

16. Ibid., pp. 70ff.

17. Ibid., p. 99. Gustafson deals with this in his outstanding book *Christ and the Moral Life* (New York: Harper and Row, 1968). Calvin is treated here in a perceptive and sympathetic manner, but Gustafson does not deal explicitly with the question I pose.

responsible and meaningful moral or ethical decisions could be made in an exceedingly complex age. Calvin, of course, could not have anticipated some of the issues which defy neat and simple answers, such as abortion and euthanasia. However, my thesis is that Calvin is surprisingly evangelical and flexible in his treatment of this fundamental issue of norms.

Many of the critics of Fletcher and Robinson have pointed out the inadequacy of affirming that love is the only binding obligation and that love must not be regarded as a principle. When Fletcher insists that "the ruling norm of Christian decision is love: nothing else,"[18] the question inevitably arises, "And how do we know what love is?" According to the New Testament, "love is the fulfilling of the law" (Rom. 13:10), but Fletcher and Robinson — and many others — assume this means that love abrogates the law. The appeal is often to the teachings of Jesus or the example of Jesus Himself. But in the former case we are back to principles of some sort, and in the latter case one must ask, "Which Jesus?" In either case, the result is a modern version of an old-fashioned antinomianism not too different from that taught by Luther's critic, Agricola. Love and love alone, or love plus the situation (Fletcher's solution), do not provide us with a solution, for " 'love,' like 'situation,' is a word that runs through Fletcher's book like a greased pig."[19]

Love without law is a vacuous thing. Moreover, as Elton Eenigenburg, among others, reminds us, "Love is not everything!" There are also justice and righteousness and the obedience of faith. Jesus Himself said that He did not come to destroy the law and the prophets but to fulfill them (Matt. 5:17). "He did so with a love unsurpassable in its depth and embrace. Love as instrument is secondary and functional to that primary thing, God's revealed will."[20]

This is precisely where one must begin with Calvin in seeking to determine what is the ultimate norm for the Christian, or what we today would call responsible decision making. The answer, for

18. Fletcher, *Situation Ethics,* p. 69.
19. James M. Gustafson, from "How Does Love Reign?" originally a review in the *Christian Century,* May 12, 1966, and reprinted in *The Situation Ethics Debate,* p. 81. See also his essay "Love Monism" in *Storm over Ethics.* Here he compares the "love monism" of Fletcher and Ramsey and concludes: "For both writers love is king; how he reigns, however, makes a lot of difference" (p. 37).
20. Elton Eenigenburg, "How New Is the New Morality?" in *The Situation Ethics Debate,* pp. 220–21. This appeared originally in the *Reformed Review* 20.3 (March 1967).

Calvin, is surprisingly subtle, one which even Calvin scholars have overlooked.[21]

The Law as an Expression of the Will of God

Calvin in various connections either speaks of the law as an expression of the will of God or simply directs all of our activity to the will of God as the ultimate and most comprehensive norm of the Christian life. To illustrate this, we could point to such statements as "he alone has truly denied himself who has so totally resigned himself to the Lord that he permits every part of his life to be governed by God's will."[22] In short, Christians "are taught to live not according to their own whim but according to God's will."[23]

This much is almost self-evident and would hardly be a point of controversy. For it is generally agreed that the Christian life is to be lived, insofar as possible, in accordance with God's will. The matter becomes more complicated and more problematic, however, when we try to determine how and where God's will is to be known — especially when facing difficult and often ambiguous ethical decisions. Yet for Calvin it would seem as if the answer were relatively easy; for he simply affirms that "the precepts of the law . . . comprehend the will of God."[24] "God has revealed his will in the law."[25] In the law He has delineated His own character;[26] here His will, so to speak, is placed before our eyes.[27] Moreover, not only does God reveal in the law what kind of God He is, but there He also "lays down what he demands from us, and, in short, everything necessary to be known."[28]

In some of the above references the word *law* may refer to the Mosaic revelation or the Pentateuch. Nevertheless, Calvin does not hesitate to speak in the same way about the moral law as compre-

---

21. In contrast to ethicists (and historians) who simply label Calvin a legalist and find in him "a streak of ethical fundamentalism" (so N. H. G. Robinson, *The Groundwork of Christian Ethics* [Grand Rapids: Eerdmans, 1971], p. 20), it is refreshing to find one of America's foremost ethicists recognizing that in his understanding of the moral life "Calvin is more complex" than either Luther's or the Catholic approach (James M. Gustafson, *Theology and Christian Ethics* [Philadelphia: United Church, 1974], p. 173).

22. *Inst.* 3.7.10.

23. *Inst.* 3.8.4.

24. *Inst.* 1.17.2.

25. *Inst.* 2.8.59.

26. *Inst.* 2.8.51.

27. *Comm. on Jer.* 9:15 (*CO* 38.41).

28. *Comm. on Isa.* 8:20 (*CO* 36.184).

hended in the Decalogue.[29] Since it contains "a perfect pattern of righteousness," it is the "one everlasting and unchangeable rule to live by."[30]

It is at this point that Calvin and the other Reformers are often criticized; for in their catechisms in particular they give the impression that the only norm for the Christian life is the Decalogue. The "reduction" of the will of God to the Decalogue without any consideration of the Sermon on the Mount, the apostolic exhortations and injunctions, etc., is held to be an unfortunate hangover from the earlier Catholic tradition. Moreover, it is pointed out that this approach is also unbiblical since the Old Testament law rather than Jesus Christ is declared to be the sole source and norm of the Christian life. These criticisms can be found in a published doctoral dissertation by a Swiss scholar which is critical of the whole tradition of giving a central place to an exposition of the Decalogue in catechetical instruction.[31] In regard to Calvin, however, this critic, Hugo Röthlisberger, finds a different approach in the *Institutes* from that in his Catechisms. In the former he finds *two* norms for the Christian life, viz., the law and Christ, whereas in the latter he maintains that only the law is the norm.[32] That this is not an adequate understanding of Calvin's approach will be shown below. Emil Brunner also chides the Reformers for having overlooked the fact that in the New Testament the Decalogue scarcely appears to be the norm for the Christian church.[33]

The question then is whether Calvin limits the knowledge of the will of God to the law and, further, whether he unconsciously operates with two norms (the law and Christ). A related question is whether Calvin in practice overlooks Christ and the new insights of the gospel in his treatment of the third use of the law. In sum, what is the concrete content of the will of God? There is no simple answer to these questions, but a perusal of Calvin's interpretation of the Decalogue, together with an examination of what is normative in his exposition of the Christian life in book 3 of the *Institutes,* will shed light on these questions.

29. See *Inst.* 2.8.5; 4.13.12; Genevan Catechism, questions 130–32 (*OS* 2.96).
30. *Inst.* 2.7.13.
31. Hugo Röthlisberger, *Kirche am Sinai — Die Zehn Gebote in der christlichen Unterweisung* (Zurich: Zwingli, 1965). See especially pp. 130f., 143f.
32. Ibid., p. 101.
33. Emil Brunner, *Dogmatics,* vol. 2, *The Christian Doctrine of Creation and Redemption* (Philadelphia: Westminster, 1952), p. 219.

Christ the Best Interpreter of the Law

Calvin's high estimate of the Decalogue and praise of the law in general can be grossly misunderstood if his three principles for interpreting the Ten Commandments are overlooked. The first and crucial principle is that in interpreting and applying the law we must follow "Christ, its best interpreter."[34] The implications and consequences of this affirmation are extremely significant. For what Calvin proceeds to do is to interpret the various commandments in the light of the New Testament. He eschews a literalistic interpretation of the commandments — "he who would confine his understanding of the law within the narrowness of the words deserves to be laughed at";[35] he seeks behind the negative commands their positive implications;[36] and he stresses the significance of the division of the law into two tables[37] and accordingly concentrates on the sum of the law or great commandment where we are commanded to love God and our neighbor. Not only does he conclude his exposition of the Decalogue with a discussion of the principles of the law in the light of Christ's teaching,[38] but his whole treatment of the Decalogue is suffused with the spirit of the New Testament.

Hence, although there is no separate treatment of the Sermon on the Mount (nor is there in most contemporary dogmatics), chapter 8 of book 2 (the exposition of the Ten Commandments) is in effect a treatment of many of the themes in the Sermon on the Mount.[39] Thus it is quite unjust to declare that "unlike Jesus, he (Calvin) conceived of the will of God in terms of biblical literalism and set up a legalistic moral code."[40] And it is equally far off the mark to assert that his "whole outlook on life is tinctured with the spirit of Moses rather than Christ. . . ."[41] It would be closer to the mark to make the opposite

34. *Inst.* 2.8.7.

35. *Inst.* 2.8.8. Here Calvin is employing the principle of *synecdoche,* a figure of speech in which a part is used for the whole. For example, a commandment such as "Thou shalt not kill" is by *synecdoche* only a partial statement of what God fully intends by this commandment.

36. Ibid.

37. *Inst.* 2.8.11.

38. He does this both in his *Comm. on the Last Four Books of Moses* (CO 24.721–28) and in *Inst.* 2.8.51–59.

39. Actually, there are numerous references to Matthew 5 in this chapter of the *Institutes.* See especially 2.8.7, 26, 57, 59.

40. Georgia Harkness, *John Calvin: The Man and His Ethics* (Nashville: Abingdon, 1958 reprint), p. 63.

41. Ibid., p. 113.

complaint, namely, that Calvin has so christianized the law[42] that the norm of the Christian life is not so much the Ten Commandments as the teaching of Jesus! Calvin, in any case, would acknowledge no such polarization as law over against Christ, the Ten Commandments over against the Sermon on the Mount. As Paul Lehmann observes, "Indeed, on the basis of an inner meaning of the law, the reformers were right in seeing an intrinsic parallelism between the Sermon on the Mount and the decalogue."[43]

A More Precise Principle

The three uses of the law are discussed briefly in book 2 of the *Institutes*; but whereas the civil or political use is taken up again in chapter 20 of book 4 ("Civil Government"), at first glance it appears that the third and "principal use" is dropped after the brief treatment in sections 12 and 13. (There is also an allusion to this function of the law in 3.19.2.) This, however, is not actually the case, for Calvin takes up the third use of the law again in his discussion of the Christian life in book 3, particularly chapters 6 and 7. There is no explicit reference to the third use of the law in either of these chapters, but rather incidental references to the law at the beginning of both chapters indicate that Calvin is presupposing the discussion of the law in book 2, chapter 7. As Paul Jacobs has pointed out, "The treatment of the doctrine of sanctification, the so-called ethic of Calvin's, is an unfolding of the doctrine of the *tertius usus legis.*"[44]

In chapter 6, where Calvin collects various scriptural data relevant to the Christian life, after noting the object of regeneration he states: "The law of God contains in itself that newness by which his image can be restored in us."[45] But that is the last reference to the law in this chapter! He continues: "But because our slowness needs many goads and helps, it will be profitable to assemble from various passages of Scripture a plan for the regulation of our life (*rationem vitae formandae*) in order that those who heartily repent may not err in their zeal."[46]

---

42. So Paul Wernle, *Der evangelische Glaube nach den Hauptschriften der Reformatoren* (Tübingen: Mohr, 1919), vol. 3, p. 397. His actual words are "das verchristliche Gesetz."

43. Paul Lehmann, *Ethics in a Christian Context* (New York: Harper and Row, 1963), p. 78.

44. Paul Jacobs, *Prädestination und Verantwortlichkeit bei Calvin* (Darmstadt: Wissenschaftliche Buchgesellschaft, 1968 reprint), p. 103.

45. *Inst.* 3.6.1.

46. Ibid.

Calvin concedes the impossibility of doing justice to this subject in one short chapter, so he tries to find some "universal rule" (*regulam*) which aids the believer in living a "rightly ordered life."[47] Since we have been adopted as sons by God in order to live in harmony with Him, the first principle must be a love of righteousness or holiness on our part. The goal of our calling is that we should be holy because our God is holy (Lev. 19:2; 1 Peter 1:15–16).[48] "The beginning of living rightly is spiritual, where the inner feeling of the mind is unfeignedly dedicated to God for the cultivation of holiness and righteousness."[49]

But Calvin proceeds to make another significant qualification in this chapter. He acknowledges that in many places in Scripture we are exhorted to live righteously, but he finds a stronger motive for holy living in the redemptive work of Christ. Consequently, "to wake us more effectively, Scripture shows that God the Father, as he has reconciled us to himself in his Christ, has in him stamped for us the likeness (*imaginem*) to which he would have us conform."[50] Later, in refuting the charge that the doctrine of justification by faith stifles the zeal for good works, Calvin lists more than ten scriptural motives (or "spurs") arousing us to fulfill our calling. The first is one of gratitude to "reciprocate the love of him 'who first loved us' " (1 John 4:19).[51] For no one will truly pursue holiness unless he has first "imbibed" the doctrine that we are justified by Christ's merit alone.[52]

The prime motive for the Christian life is thus the grace and forgiveness we have received in Jesus Christ. He is also the model of the Christian life. For Christ "has been set before us as an example (*exemplar*) whose image (*formam*; French, *l'image*) we ought to express in our life."[53] Does Calvin then operate with two norms, the law and

47. Ibid.
48. *Inst.* 3.6.2.
49. *Inst.* 3.6.5.
50. *Inst.* 3.6.3. "The apostle teaches that God has destined all his children to the end that they be conformed to Christ (Rom. 8:29)" (*Inst.* 3.8.1). The context here is the key to the Christian life, viz., bearing the cross and sharing Christ's sufferings.
51. *Inst.* 3.16.2.
52. *Inst.* 3.16.3.
53. *Inst.* 3.6.3. Beveridge translates *exemplar* as "model"; cf. *Comm. on Phil.* 3:17 (*CO* 52.54). I have concentrated on the commentaries, but Ronald Wallace notes that "throughout his *Sermons* he frequently refers to Christ as the '*patron*' (i.e., 'pattern') after which the children of God must be modeled (*configurez*) or to which they must be conformed (*conformez*)" (*Calvin's Doctrine of the Christian Life* [Edinburgh: Oliver and Boyd, 1957], p. 41). A good example is found in a sermon on Eph. 4:23–24 (but not cited by Wallace): "Let us know that our Lord Jesus Christ is given us for an example (*example*) and pattern (*patron*), and moreover, that it is his office so to reform us by the Spirit of God his Father, that we may walk in newness of life . . ." (*CO* 51.623; cf. *CO* 51.619).

Christ, as Röthlisberger maintains? Hardly. Granted, in 3.6.1 Calvin says that we have been adopted as sons so that His image may be restored in us through the *law*; and in 3.6.3 he says that we have been adopted as sons (note the identical language) on the condition "that our life express (*repraesentet*) *Christ,* the bond of our adoption." But there is no contradiction here. Since Christ is the "very soul" (*vere anima*),[54] the life,[55] the goal and end (fulfillment) of the law,[56] "the law in all its parts has reference to him . . . indeed, every doctrine of the law, every command, every promise always points to Christ."[57] Christ is thus not only the best interpreter of the law; He is also its substance and fulfillment.[58] Hence, for Calvin there is no inconsistency in referring sometimes to the law and other times to Christ as the norm or rule of godly living and as the expression of the will of God. Nevertheless, it is not without significance that in his discussion of the Christian life, he prefers to refer to Christ, rather than the law, as the model and image to which God would have us conform and whose life we are to emulate.

We find much the same approach in chapter 7 of book 3: "The Sum of the Christian Life: The Denial of Ourselves." Again Calvin begins with a reference to the law (its third use), and again he quickly passes on to "an even more exact plan" (*accuratiore etiamnum ratione*). "Even though the law of the Lord provides the finest and best-disposed method of ordering a man's life (*constituendae vitae*), it seemed good to the Heavenly Teacher to shape his people by an even more exact plan (or precise principle) to that rule (*regulam*) which he had set forth in his law."[59] Note that as in the beginning of chapter 6 the law is spoken of in the highest terms. Calvin has not forgotten the law, nor is he about to reject it in favor of some alleged antithetical New Testament insight or principle. He knows no either/or, i.e., either the Old Testament or the New Testament, either the law or Christ. At the same time, however, he tacitly acknowledges that in the law we have

54. *Comm. on Acts* 7:30 (*CO* 48.144); cf. *Comm. on John* 1:17 (*CO* 47.18) and 5:38 (*CO* 47.124).

55. *Comm. on 2 Cor.* 3:16 (*CO* 50.45).

56. *Comm. on Rom.* 10:4 (*CO* 49.196); *Inst.* 2.7.2.

57. *Comm. on Rom.* 10:4 (*CO* 49.196).

58. James Gustafson, in his book *Christ and the Moral Life,* designates five ways in which Jesus Christ influences or determines the moral life: as the Lord who is creator and redeemer, as the sanctifier, the justifier, the pattern, and the teacher. He refers to Calvin in the discussion of all five categories, but finds him particularly illuminating on the last two. This corresponds to my own findings except that, if space permitted, it could be shown that Calvin stressed growth and progress in the Christian life much more than did Luther and therefore Calvin should receive more attention in the chapter "Jesus Christ, the Sanctifier."

59. *Inst.* 3.7.1.

not exhausted the meaning and purpose of God's will for our lives.[60] Hence, in both chapters the praise of the law is followed by a crucial qualification. In chapter 6 he spoke of a means by which God awakens us "more effectively,"[61] and in chapter 7 he speaks of a "more exact plan."[62]

The "beginning of this plan" (*principium rationis*) in chapter 7 is found in Romans 12:1–2. For Calvin this is a programmatic text of special significance: "I appeal to you therefore brethren, by the mercies of God, to present your bodies as a living sacrifice, holy and acceptable unto God, which is your spiritual worship. Do not be conformed to this world but be transformed by the renewal of your mind, that you may prove what is the will of God. . . ."[63] After citing this passage Calvin proceeds to elaborate the nature of the Christian life in terms of a repeated contrast: "We are not our own . . . we are the Lord's" (see Rom. 14:8; 1 Cor. 6:19). This is Calvin's "Christian philosophy" (*Christiana philosophia*) which "bids reason give way to, submit and subject itself to the Holy Spirit so that man himself may no longer live but hear Christ living and reigning within him" (Gal. 2:20).[64]

In this section Calvin also refers to Ephesians 4:23, another key text in his understanding of the Christian life. For in Ephesians 4:22–24 he finds the two basic principles of Christian living, namely, putting off the old nature and putting on the new nature. (These are also the two elements of repentance, i.e., mortification and vivification.)[65] In reference to this passage Calvin refers to two rules for a godly and holy life. The first is "the denial of ourselves and the re-generation of the Holy Spirit." The second—and here again we have an echo of 3.7.1—is "to live, not by our own spirit, but by the Spirit of Christ."[66]

These are not the only texts which Calvin considers important for a "well-ordered life" (*vitae bene compositae*). In the *Institutes* he also points to Titus 2:11–17[67] and "the rule of love" as found in

---

60. Even though in another context he affirms, "Now it is certain that God's law has not taught us by halves (*a point enseignez à demi*) what we have to do, but God has shown us in it a right rule (*choite reigle*) to which nothing can be added, nor anything taken from it. For in these two points [love of God and neighbor] all our righteousness is contained . . ." (Sermon on Eph. 4:23–24 [CO 51.622]).
61. *Inst.* 3.6.1.
62. *Inst.* 3.7.1.
63. Ibid.
64. Ibid.
65. See *Inst.* 3.3.5–9.
66. *Comm. on Eph.* 4:22–23 (CO 51.208); cf. *Inst.* 3.7.10.
67. *Inst.* 3.7.3.

1 Corinthians 13:4–5.[68] But the important thing to keep in mind is that this is what Calvin means by the third use of the law![69] It does not mean that we live according to the spirit of Moses and the Old Testament, but rather that with the law and the prophets as our foundation we live in Christ, for Christ, and by His Spirit. This is the will of God and the ultimate end of the rule of the law, which is the rule of love.[70]

---

68. *Inst.* 3.7.5–7.

69. This is by no means an exhaustive answer to the question of norms and decision making in regard to Calvin's treatment of the third use of the law. Two other facets of Calvin's approach which are significant are the role of the Christian community, the church, and the Holy Spirit. In the case of the former, Calvin comes close to Paul Lehmann's *koinonia* ethic. In fact, many years ago Paul Jacobs described Calvin's ethics as a *Gemeinschaftsethik* (*Prädestination und Verantwortlichkeit bei Calvin,* p. 91). The role of the Holy Spirit in decision making is immediately apparent in Calvin's frequent use (especially in the commentaries and sermons) of phrases like "the leading or guidance of the Spirit." See *Inst.* 3.14.9 ("sancti Spiritus ductu"); 4.19.6 ("ductor et director"); *Comm. on Acts* 17:11 (*CO* 48.401); *Comm. on Rom.* 11:34 (*CO* 49.231); *Comm. on 1 John* 4:1 (*CO* 55.347); sermons on Eph. 2:16–19 (*CO* 51.418); 4:23 (*CO* 51.617); 4:29–30 ("nous conduise et gouverne" [*CO* 51.654]).

70. See *Inst.* 2.8.49, 57; 3.7.5.

11
True Piety According to Calvin

Ford Lewis Battles

Piety Defined in Word and Act

Piety Defined by Calvin

In his first *Catechism* (published in French in 1537 and in Latin in 1538), John Calvin defined the untranslatable word *pietas,* which for him was the shorthand symbol for his whole understanding and practice of Christian faith and life:

> True piety does not consist in a fear which willingly indeed flees God's judgment, but since it cannot escape is terrified. True piety consists rather in a sincere feeling which loves God as Father as much as it fears and reverences Him as Lord, embraces His righteousness, and dreads offending Him worse than death. And whoever have been endowed with this piety dare not fashion out of their own rashness any God for themselves. Rather, they seek from Him the knowledge of the true God, and conceive Him just as He shows and declares Himself to be.[1]

Calvin more succinctly defined *pietas* in the *Institutes* as "that reverence joined with love of God which the knowledge of his benefits induces."[2] Beside *pietas* he set *religio*: ". . . faith so joined with an

Reprinted from *The Piety of John Calvin* (Grand Rapids: Baker, 1978), pp. 13–26. Used by permission.

1. John Calvin, *Catechism* (1537), ed. and trans. Ford Lewis Battles (Pittsburgh: Pittsburgh Theological Seminary, 1972), p. 2.
2. *Inst.* 1.2.1.

earnest fear of God that this fear also embraces willing reverence, and carries with it such legitimate worship as is prescribed in the law."[3] Note that in these definitions of *pietas* and *religio,* a number of other basic terms are interlaced: *faith, fear, reverence, love, knowledge.* The interrelationship among these terms is diagramed in Figure 11.1.

Figure 11.1

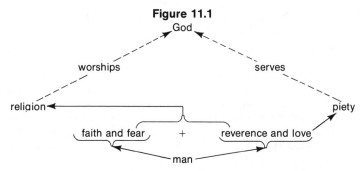

To grasp the full amplitude of *pietas,* let us examine a few of the many references to the word scattered through his commentaries and other writings. In the *Commentary on the Psalms* (119:78f.) he taught that the true nature of *pietas* is seen in the two marks of believers: (1) honor, the obedience rendered to Him as Father; (2) fear, the service done Him as Lord.[4] Distinct from this is the unbeliever's fear which rests not upon faith (*fides*) but upon unfaith (*diffidentia*).[5] Knowledge also enters largely into the concept of *pietas.* In the *Commentary on Jeremiah* (10:25), Calvin spoke of knowledge of God (*cognitio Dei*) as the beginning of *pietas.* Calling upon God's name (*invocatio*) is the fruit of the knowledge of God and is evidence of *pietas.*[6] In the *Institutes* Calvin spoke of the first step toward *pietas* as "to know that God is a father to us."[7] Elsewhere he asserted that there is no *pietas* without true instruction, as the name *disciples* indicates.[8] "True religion and worship of God," he said, "arise out of faith, so that no one duly serves God save him who has been educated in His school."[9]

Calvin also related piety and love (*caritas*). In *Praelectiones in*

3. *Inst.* 1.2.2.
4. *CO* 32.249; cf. *Inst.* 3.2.26.
5. *Inst.* 3.2.27.
6. *CO* 38.96.
7. *Inst.* 2.6.4.
8. *Comm. on Acts* 18:22 (*CO* 48.435).
9. *Comm. on Psalms* 119:78f. (*CO* 32.249).

Ezekiel (18:5) he spoke of *pietas* as the root of *caritas.*[10] *Pietas* means the fear or reverence of God, but we also fear God when we live justly among our brethren.[11] This relationship between our reverential attitude toward God and our attitude toward neighbor is further developed in a sermon on Deuteronomy 5:16:

> And this is why the heathen have applied this word *pietas* to the honor we render to father, mother, and all those in authority over us. *Pietas,* properly speaking, is the reverence we owe to God: but the pagans, although they were poor blind folk, recognized that God not only wills to be served in His majesty, but when we obey the persons who rule over us, in sum, He wills to prove our obedience at this point. And thus, inasmuch as fathers and mothers, magistrates, and all those who have authority, are lieutenants of God and represent His person, it is certain that if one show them contempt and reject them, it is like declaring that one does not want to obey God at all.[12]

Yet Calvin places *pietas* higher than *caritas,* for God towers over man; still, "believers seriously testify, by honoring mutual righteousness among themselves, that they honor God."[13]

The connection between the pagan and Christian notions of *pietas* is pursued further in the *Commentary on John.* Here Calvin admitted "that some grains of *pietas* were ever scattered throughout the world" but "that by God, through the hand of philosophers and profane writers, were sowed the excellent sentiments to be found in their writings."[14] Aratus's couplet quoted by Paul (who spoke to infidels and men ignorant of true *pietas*) is "the testimony of a poet who confessed a knowledge engraved by nature upon men's minds."[15]

That Calvin's youthful classical studies had laid the groundwork for this classical as well as Christian understanding of the word *pietas* is clear from his *Commentary on Seneca's "De Clementia,"* published in 1532 when Calvin was twenty-two years of age. In explaining the Senecan phrase "nor the piety of his children," Calvin drew together what we may assume were the chief classical texts that were mingled, after his conversion, with scriptural and patristic uses to shape the

10. *CO* 40.426.
11. See renderings of *ḥāsîd, mansuetus,* etc., where piety is related to the kindness of man (Ps. 16:10, etc.).
12. *CO* 26.312.
13. Ibid. This is the habitual twofold division (God and man) that Calvin applied to the Decalogue (*Inst.* 2.8.11) and the Lord's Prayer (3.20.35).
14. *Comm. on John* 4:36 (*CO* 47.96).
15. *Comm. on Acts* 17:28 (*CO* 48.417).

word in his thought. Note that among the pagan classical writers is to be found a quotation from Augustine's *City of God*. Here are Calvin's words:

> Cicero, *Pro Plancia* (33.80): *What is piety, if not a benevolent gratitude to one's parents?* Quintilian (5.10.12): *Just as those things that are admitted by the general consent of mankind, such as that there are gods, and that piety is to be shown to parents.* Yet in order that my readers may understand what piety really is, I shall append Cicero's words from the *Topics* (23.90): *Equity is also said to have three parts: one pertains to the gods in heaven, the second to the spirits of the departed, the third to men. The first is called "piety," the second "sanctity," the third "justice" or "equity."* Thus far Cicero. But since parents are for us so to speak in the place of the gods, to them is diverted what Augustine hints at (*DCD*, 10.1.3): *Piety, properly speaking, is commonly understood as worship of God, which the Greeks call eusebeia. Yet this eusebeia is said to be exercised by way of obligation toward parents also.* But we also use the term when we wish to express a particularly forceful love. Cicero (*Ep. Fam.*, 1.9.1): *I was very much pleased with your letter, which made me realize that you fully appreciate my piety toward you; for why should I say "my good will" whenever the term "piety" itself, most solemn and sacred as it is, does not seem to me impressive enough to describe my obligation to you?*[16]

As this collection of classical passages indicates, the words *pius* and *pietas* in classical Latin referred first to the relationship of children to their parents.[17] In the Roman family of the *paterfamilias* and the *materfamilias*, children were expected to fear, honor, obey, and love their parents. *Pietas* bespoke the mutual love and care between parents and their offspring.

The state was, after all (as Aristotle described it in his *Politics*),[18] but the extension of the family. The king or emperor was the *pater patriae*, the father of his country.[19] Parricide, in Roman eyes the most horrendous crime of which man is capable, and subject to the cruelest and most unusual punishment of all, was extended to assassination

16. John Calvin, *Commentary on Seneca's "De Clementia,"* ed. and trans. Ford Lewis Battles and André Malan Hugo (Leiden: Brill, 1969), pp. 226–29.

17. Compare Justinian's comment: "For the power of the father ought to consist in piety, not cruelty"—*Digest* 48.9.5, cited by Calvin in *Commentary on Seneca's "De Clementia,"* pp. 254–57.

18. 1.3–13 (1253 bl–1260 b25); cf. *Nicomachean Ethics* 8.11 (1160 cl). Calvin cites Aristotle in *Commentary on Seneca's "De Clementia,"* pp. 170f.

19. Calvin, *Commentary on Seneca's "De Clementia,"* pp. 236–39.

of the ruler, as the parent of all.[20] *Pietas,* then, in the larger sense summarized all the feelings of loyalty, love of country, and self-sacrifice for the common good which marked Roman citizenship.

The early Christians, whose supreme Ruler and Father was God, without divesting the word *pietas* of its familial and national meaning, carried the word to a higher use. For them the whole complex of relationships between God the Father and His earthly children was summed up in this one word. For Calvin, then, there is in the word the classical overshine of filial obedience. *Pietas* bespeaks the walk of us adopted children of God the Father, adopted brothers and sisters of Christ the Son.

So far we have dealt mainly with the "inner" meaning of *pietas.* It also had an external meaning for Calvin. In *On the Harmony of the Gospels* (Matt. 12:7 and parallels) he argued, with our Lord, that certain types of manual labor were permitted on the Sabbath — those connected with the worship of God — and spoke of the *officia pietatis,* which we might render "religious duties." In the same passage Calvin suggested the modern hypocritical connotation of *piety,* speaking of the "hypocrites who pretend *pietas* by outward signs and grievously pervert it by sticking in carnal worship alone."[21]

Calvin's meaning will emerge more clearly as we seek out the scriptural basis of his concept of *pietas.* The New Testament word uniformly rendered by the Latin *pietas* is εὐσέβεια. It is found almost exclusively in the pastoral and general Epistles, appearing elsewhere in the New Testament only at Acts 3:12. Of the fifteen references in the former, the RSV translates all but three as "godliness." The word is used in the Septuagint to denote "the duty which man owes to God — piety, godliness, religion."[22] In the Septuagint the word is chiefly found in the Apocrypha.

Piety Mirrored in Calvin's Life

If this then is what piety meant for Calvin, we will certainly find in the accounts of his conversion, however meager, help in understanding how this concept was shaped in his own life.

Much ink has been spilled in discussion and speculation on the date, circumstances, and character of Calvin's decision to accept the Reformation faith. I have dealt with the shape of his conversion in my

20. Ibid., pp. 252–55; cf. pp. 308f.

21. *CO* 45.324f.; cf. *Inst.* 1.4.4, where Calvin contrasted true and false *pietas.*

22. Walter Bauer, *A Greek-English Lexicon of the New Testament,* ed. and trans. William F. Arndt and F. Wilbur Gingrich, 4th ed. (Chicago: University of Chicago, 1952), p. 326.

translation of the *Institution* of 1536.[23] Classic accounts of conversion usually cite some verse of Scripture as triggering the change. Augustine's experience of *"Tolle, lege!"* ("Take up and read!") in the garden near Milan led him through Romans 13:13f. to Bishop Ambrose and Christian baptism. Luther was captivated by Romans 1:17. We have no such definite information on the specific Scripture that brought Calvin's change of heart. A close study of the evidence has, however, led me to suggest that it very probably was Romans 1:18–25. More specifically the text may well have been Romans 1:21 (". . . for although they knew God they did not honor him as God or give thanks to him, but they became futile in their thinking and their senseless minds were darkened" — RSV).[24]

The central themes of Calvin's piety are the honoring of God and being thankful to Him; they are interwoven in the recital of his conversion in the preface to the *Commentary on the Psalms* and in the account of the Reformed Christian's confession before God's judgment seat in Calvin's *Reply to Cardinal Sadolet.*[25]

Calvin's new-found faith is early expressed in his preface to the French translation of the New Testament made by his cousin Pierre Robert (Olivétan).[26] Almost contemporaneous with this are the early pages of chapter 1, "On the Law," of the 1536 *Institution* [I call these pages the kernel of Calvin's faith].

It is the intolerable contrast between God's absolute perfection and man's fallenness that initiated Calvin's religious quest. Like Augustine, he saw no instant perfection succeeding the event of conversion however *"subita"* it seemed; there is rather a growth into the Christian life to a perfection beyond death — all the gracious gift of God in Christ. So he begins this "kernel" account of faith with the two knowledges: of God's glory, justice, mercy, and gentleness; and of fallen man's ignorance, iniquity, impotence, death, judgment. In the third place, we are shown the law, the written law of the Old Testament and the inwardly written law of the conscience, as God's first effort to bridge the gulf between Creator and created. The law is for us a mirror in which to discern and contemplate our sin and curse. It leads us to the impasse of being called to glorify, honor, and love our Lord

23. In my introduction to *Institution of the Christian Religion . . . 1536,* trans. and an. Ford Lewis Battles (Atlanta: John Knox, 1975), pp. xvi ff.

24. Ibid., pp. xvii f.

25. See my introduction to *Institution,* pp. xxiii ff. T. H. L. Parker rejected the passage from Calvin's *Reply to Cardinal Sadolet* as a "source" — *John Calvin: A Biography* (Philadelphia: Westminster, 1975), p. 162.

26. Battles, "Introduction," *Institution,* pp. xxiv f.

and Father, but unable to perform these duties. Therefore we deserve the curse, judgment — eternal death. This was indeed the sequence of Calvin's experience, or more accurately, it was the shape which in retrospect he gave his experience in the light of the Pauline-Augustinian tradition and which he generalized in his teaching.

But the impasse, through God's mercy, is breached; another way is opened to us. It is forgiveness of sins through Christ. Calvin's "kernel," in its fourth and final section, comes back once more to the knowledge of ourselves, of our poverty and ruin. The lesson of this knowledge is that we learn to humble ourselves, cast ourselves before God, seek His mercy. Thus will Christ, our leader, the only Way to reach the Father, bring us into eternal blessedness. Our piety then is our pathway, in grace, from estrangement to reunion with our Creator. It is the way of suffering, but also of joy.

Thus Calvin's conversion took a lifetime to be worked out. We cannot here summarize that brief but crowded life. But we can look at several episodes in it that will explain why he believed in the third use of the law — its pedagogical use as tutor to converted Christians — and denominated it the law's chief use.[27] His life will also exemplify his teaching on calling, that the Christian must, like a sentry, stand guard at his post while he lives.[28]

First, look at how Calvin was called to his initial ministry in Geneva. His initial vision of the Christian life (like Augustine's) was that of a retired, contemplative, intellectual study of the faith. William Farel, that hotheaded pioneer of the French-language Reformation who was spurned in his invitation to Calvin to work with him in Geneva, a city that had just chosen the Reformed faith, had recourse to imprecation and threat: "You are following," he thundered at Calvin, "your own wishes and I declare, in the name of God Almighty, that if you do not assist us in this work of the Lord, the Lord will punish you for seeking your own interest rather than his."[29]

And so, against his will, Calvin took up the task at Geneva as at the invitation of God Himself. After Calvin's banishment in 1538 from Geneva, Bucer used the same threat to persuade him to assume pastoral and teaching duties at Strasbourg.

Calvin was subsequently importuned from his happy pastoral re-

27. Calvin called the law the perfect guide to all duties of piety and love — *Inst.* 2.8.51.

28. *Inst.* 3.9.4; 3.10.6.

29. Beza, *Vita Calvini,* in *CO* 21.125.41ff. — English translation by Henry Beveridge in John Calvin, *Tracts and Treatises in Defense of the Reformed Faith,* 3 vols. (Grand Rapids: Eerdmans, 1958), vol. 1, p. xxix.

lationship with a tiny French congregation in Strasbourg to return to
Geneva. It must be said that the Strasbourg sojourn was crucial in
working out pastorally and practically and liturgically the full meaning
of *pietas.* In his study of the sufferings of the patriarchs, Calvin mirrored his own *tolerantia crucis:* Abraham, Isaac, Jacob, and the rest,
David included, withstood terrible hardships, pain, suffering, because
they were on pilgrimage. The hope that was to come fed them on their
journey.[30] This too was the secret of Calvin's triumphant struggle
against the overwhelming odds that faced him and his world. This
too kept alive his feeble body, taxed as it constantly was beyond its
strength. This too enabled him to maintain a ceaseless literary output
of the highest order and one so decisive for posterity.

Piety in Calvin's View of the Christian Life

We have endeavored to define *pietas* in Calvin's own words and
his own acts. Let us now turn to the principles of *pietas* as he worked
them out in his *Institutes of the Christian Religion.* In doing this, it
will be necessary to examine more fully the transition years 1538 – 1541
of the Strasbourg exile, which we have just now lightly sketched.

The portion of Calvin's *Institutes* on which we would like to con-
centrate our attention at this time comprises, in the final Latin edition
of that work printed in the author's lifetime (1559), chapters 6 – 10 of
book 3. One may search in vain the pages of the first edition of that
work (1536) for any section corresponding to this one on the Christian
life.[31] Actually (with some subsequent additions) it dates from 1539,
the year of the second Latin edition, and remained in all editions from
1539 to 1554 the final chapter of the *Institutes.* Why was such an
important subject so belatedly treated by Calvin?

The clue to the answer lies, I believe, in a comparison of what
Calvin wrote before he went to Strasbourg in 1538 and what he wrote
after that date. On the one hand, examine the *Institution* of 1536, the
Articles Concerning the Organization of the Church and Worship of
January 1537,[32] and the *Confession and Catechism of the Church of
Geneva* of 1537 – 1538.[33] On the other hand, examine the *Institutes*
of 1539 (in which he placed the treatise "On the Christian Life"), his
Several Psalms and Songs Set for Singing, also of 1539, and his 1540

30. *Inst.* 2.10f.
31. Section 3.8.1ff. of the 1559 edition of the *Institutes* is hinted at in the 1536
edition — *Institution,* p. 55.
32. See John Calvin, *Theological Treatises,* ed. and trans. J. K. S. Reid, Library
of Christian Classics, vol. 22 (Philadelphia: Westminster, 1954), pp. 47 – 55.
33. See "Letter" in *Catechism,* pp. vii ff.

Commentary on Romans. Add to these the literary output immediately
following his return to Geneva from Strasbourg in 1541 — that is, the
Draft Ecclesiastical Ordinances of 1541, *The Form of Prayers* of
1542, and the third Latin edition of the *Institutes* (1543). What does
a comparison show?[34] We see a real growth in Calvin the churchman,
in his grasp of the practical problems both of individual Christians
and of the church as the society of Christians. All of these words are
directed to the perfecting either of the Christian life or of the liturgical
and disciplinary functioning of the church. Together they mark the
significant changes that were later to be incorporated into books 3
and 4 of the 1559 *Institutes.* Both the *Institution* of 1536 and the
Catechism of 1537–1538 were cast in the traditional catechetical
mold: Decalogue, Apostles' Creed, Lord's Prayer, sacraments. In Geneva the efforts to enforce acceptance of the *Confession and Catechism* of 1537–1538, household by household, and oversight of morals,
district by district, ended in failure and banishment from the city for
both Farel and Calvin, as we have seen, in April 1538. What had
gone wrong? Let us quickly review the facts.

On Sunday, May 21, 1536, the General Council of Geneva had
unanimously voted by a show of hands to abolish the mass and other
papal ceremonies and abuses, images, and idols, and had sworn with
God's help to live in the Word of God. The duly appointed Reforming
pastors, William Farel and John Calvin, had taken their city fathers
at their word and had planned literally to transform the city into a
gospel community which had its true center in the Lord's table. This
was not to be, however. The public documents of 1536–1537, as a
consequence, underwent (after Calvin's Strasbourg sojourn) a clarification of disciplinary procedures and a development of church polity
in the documents of 1541–1543. The *Institutes* of 1539 shows a
greater maturity and fullness in its understanding of the formation of
the individual Christian than does the *Institution* of 1536. Similarly,
the next edition, that of 1543, quite surpasses both the first and the
second editions in its grasp of ecclesiology. Calvin indeed learned from
experience, both in the first two years in Geneva and in the three-year
interim in Strasbourg under Martin Bucer's tutelage.

We may infer that the short treatise "On the Christian Life" is in
a sense the first fruits of Calvin's reflection on his 1536–1538 failure.
He realized, it would seem, that catechetical statements on such topics
as faith, repentance, justification, regeneration, election, and related

34. See Ford Lewis Battles, "Against Luxury and License in Geneva," *Interpretation* 19 (1965): 186ff.

heads of doctrine — however clearly stated — would not suffice to transform men's hearts, even though their minds might give intellectual assent to the new faith. A deeper reflection on the christological foundations of the Christian life, particularly as they had been set forth by the apostle Paul, was called for. This short treatise supplied the lack we have noted in the 1536 *Institution* and the *Catechism* of 1537–1538.

We must, however, slightly qualify this judgment. The 1536 *Institution* contains certain short blank spaces in the text as printed, called *alinea,* at which points — in later editions — expansions of materials were made. This fact seems to bear out what Calvin himself says of his progress through the various editions of the *Institutes,* as he speaks to the reader in 1559: "I was never satisfied until the work had been arranged in the order now set forth." Also, the *Catechism* of 1537–1538, while largely an epitome of the prior edition of the *Institution,* does presage important changes to come in the *Institutes* of 1539.[35]

What then does the short treatise "On the Christian Life" tell us about Calvin's continuing pilgrimage of faith?

First, we see further reflection on the contrast between the philosophers and Scripture.[36] He had, in his conversion, already rejected the Greek and Latin authors as moral guides. Here the contrast between them becomes sharper and more detailed. But some vestiges of their influence still remain. This can be illustrated by his attitude here expressed toward Stoicism. Rejected are Stoic notions of fate and of the passionless wise man and Stoic strictures against pity. We might here note in passing that even before his conversion Calvin had begun to show such an attitude, as his *Commentary on Seneca's "De Clementia,"* which we previously quoted, reveals. But the Stoics' call to follow God, their insistence that we are born to help one another, and their preaching of moderation and frugality[37] are sufficiently close to Calvin's Christian piety to remain a part of his moral teaching.

Second, since penning his first great theological essay of 1536, Calvin had come to know the early church fathers, both Greek and Latin, far better. The homilies of a Basil or of a Chrysostom or the

35. See my preface to *Catechism* (p. x) and the comparative table at the end of that volume.

36. See *Inst.* 1.15.8. The crucial place of man's fall, not understood by the philosophers, was recognized by Calvin in his understanding of the soul in its present state (1.15.6–8; this is apparent mainly in the 1559 edition but to some extent in the 1539 edition), a reflection of Calvin's conversion insight.

37. On Calvin's teaching on frugality and its relation to the "blue laws" of Geneva, see Battles, "Against Luxury," pp. 182ff.

writings of a Cyprian or an Ambrose filled in gaps in his pastoral knowledge. Most important of all, Augustine brought him to a deeper understanding of Paul.[38] He was therefore in a position in the spring of 1539, after five months as pastor of the French congregation in Strasbourg and a brief visit with Bucer to Frankfurt, to write this portion of his forthcoming second Latin edition of the *Institutes.* On May 12 Calvin began to lecture on the Epistles of Paul to the Corinthians. On October 16 he dedicated his shortly-to-be-published *Commentary on Romans* to the Basel savant Simon Grynaeus. This concentration on Pauline studies is reflected in the treatise "On the Christian Life." Not only is it steeped in Paul's thought; Calvin's very purpose smacks of Paul's way of working in the churches: ". . . to show some order whereby the Christian man may be led and directed to order his life aright." This is Calvin's announced intention.

The treatise "On the Christian Life" is a marvel of brevity. After a call to the holiness that God demands of His children, a holiness deep within the heart, Calvin began to describe the lifelong process of growth into Christian perfection in and through Christ. Here Calvin was consciously standing on a middle ground between the two-tiered Roman Catholic notion of the Christian life[39] and the instant perfection he rightly or wrongly inferred from the teaching of the Anabaptists.[40]

He then moved on to describe the christological pattern as it unfolds inwardly in the heart — "Denial of Self." The same following of Christ is then traced in the outward life as the "Bearing of the Cross."

He next turned to an examination first of the present, then of the future life. I have sometimes asked my students reading book 3 in the *Institutes* to stop after reading chapter 9 and write down their impressions, then go on to chapter 10 and do the same once more. At the end of chapter 9 Calvin sounds like a medieval monk, reflecting on the vanities of the world; at the end of chapter 10, he is clearly free of medievalism! The secret? *It is the hope of the life to come that gives meaning and purpose to the life in which we presently are.*

As one reads these pages, one feels he is in a field of magnetic force set between poles. Calvin's deep religious insight was born in contro-

38. Referring to the tenth commandment, Calvin said, "It was Augustine who first opened the way for me to understand this commandment" — *Inst.* 2.8.50.

39. In his *Reply to Cardinal Sadolet* (1539) Calvin confessed that his own Christian nurture (under the Romanism into which he had been born) was quite inadequate for right worship, hope of salvation, or duties of the Christian life. See *Institution,* pp. xix f. But see note 25.

40. See *Institution,* pp. 375f. (note on line 34, p. 152).

versy. Constantly he strove to find a middle, scripturally informed ground between extremes: here it lies between Roman Catholic and Anabaptist. When we study Calvin, we can never flatten out his thought, excerpt it, generalize from it. We must read it in its totality, and within the historical, biblical, and theological context out of which it came. Our own view and practice of the Christian life, in like manner, must issue from pondering on the deep antinomies of the faith in our own time. Yet there is a great deal that Calvin can say to us about the conduct of the Christian life in this last quarter of the twentieth century. Right in this section, for example, he enunciated a principle of Christian stewardship of nature and of style of living that speaks to our present ecological crisis. Before the great technological advances of recent centuries, before the present age of extraterrestrial exploration, Calvin knew the planet Earth was what we today call a "closed eco-system." Here and elsewhere in his writings he tells us how the creation is to be used by man.

Moses now adds, that the earth was given to man, with this condition, that he should occupy himself in its cultivation. Whence it follows, that men were created to employ themselves in some work, and not to lie down in inactivity and idleness. This labor, truly, was pleasant, and full of delight, entirely exempt from all trouble and weariness; since, however, God ordained that man should be exercised in the culture of the ground, he condemned, in his person, all indolent repose. Wherefore, nothing is more contrary to the order of nature, than to consume life in eating, drinking, and sleeping, while in the meantime we propose nothing to ourselves to do. Moses adds, that the custody of the garden was given in charge to Adam, to show that we possess the things which God has committed to our hands, on the condition, that being content with a frugal and moderate use of them, we should take care of what shall remain. Let him who possesses a field, so partake of its yearly fruits, that he may not suffer the ground to be injured by his negligence; but let him endeavor to hand it down to posterity as he received it, or even better cultivated. Let him so feed on its fruits, that he neither dissipates it by luxury, nor permits [it] to be marred or ruined by neglect. Moreover, that this economy, and this diligence, with respect to those good things which God has given us to enjoy, may flourish among us; let every one regard himself as the steward of God in all things which he possesses. Then he will neither conduct himself dissolutely, nor corrupt by abuse those things which God requires to be preserved.[41]

41. *Comm. on Gen.* 2:15, trans. John King, 2 vols. (Edinburgh: Calvin Translation Society, 1847–1850), vol. 1, p. 125.

Calvin believed, too, as we have said, in gradual growth in the Christian life.[42] Does not the very writing of this section illustrate his own growth, not to be complete until his death in 1564?

How may we sum up, for our own use, Calvin's teaching on *pietas,* on Christian discipleship? From Calvin's experience, as we have just reviewed it, and from our own experience of trying to live the Christian life in these times, we may infer a few general principles that may assist us in our search for a style of living commensurate with the gospel.

1. One cannot really understand a particular Christian's view of discipleship apart from his times and apart from his own distinctive experience of Christ.

2. Also, certain tacit assumptions which we make in our daily living must be identified, and at least momentarily set aside, if we are to understand a classic theologian's teaching: for example, (1) the myth of human self-sufficiency and of scientific-technological supremacy; (2) the treatment of God as a shadowy concept, not very important for daily life; (3) the notion of the Scriptures as a human book, rather like other books; (4) the rejection of an afterlife and the concentration of all human attention and effort on the present life; (5) the emphasis on the production of goods and the notion of man as a consuming animal; and (6) the view of man as a creature whose wants are to be satisfied.

3. Conversely, to understand Calvin's view of Christian discipleship, we must for the moment open our minds to certain basic assumptions that he makes: (1) man's total dependence upon God; (2) nature's being ours to use and enjoy, but with moderation and accountability; (3) God's providential care; (4) the contrast between philosophers and Scripture; (5) the afterlife's being not only the goal of the present life, but its nourishment in hope; (6) all goods as the gifts of God's kindness to us; and (7) the account we will at the end render to God of their use.

Obstacles to Piety According to the Polemical Tracts

One thing that has marked all great theologians, from Paul the apostle onward, is that their finest theology has been called forth by specific requests for help. At bottom, then, true theology and true exegesis are an exercise of the pastoral office. Calvin claimed a double pastoral intent for the *Institutes:* (1) to introduce neophytes to the

42. See note 39.

study of the Scriptures; (2) to justify the French evangelicals before a hostile government and (if we may add its corollary) to hearten these evangelicals in their effort to lead a Christian life under harsh circumstances.

Also for the heartening of beleaguered Christians, but even more pointed than Calvin's theological and exegetical works, are selected polemical works from his pen, most of them undertaken in response to anguished cries for help from evangelical Christians. This class of writings is virtually unknown except to specialists, yet they carry the teaching of *pietas* that necessary further step: to overcome the obstacles that commonly stand in the way of leading the Christian life for members of churches in the Reformed tradition. From this rich store of pastoral instruction, we have selected three tracts for a brief perusal: *On Scandals* (1550),[43] *Excuse to the Nicodemites* (1544),[44] and *What a Faithful Man . . . Ought to Do Dwelling Amongst the Papists* (1543).[45]

On Scandals (1550)

Reformed Christians, especially Frenchmen, underwent great vexations on account of the faith. Calvin for a long time pondered writing a tract to amplify the spiritual advice he had already given in the *Institutes.* Many persecuted evangelicals sought refuge in Geneva; extensive correspondence also kept Calvin informed of the plight of his countrymen who remained at home. In September 1546 Calvin wrote to Farel that he was suspending work on such a tract because of labors on the *Commentary on Galatians;* the tract was completed in August 1550. The occasion for it was the misfortune of his friend, Laurence de Normandie, who after accepting the Reformed faith gave up his country and social position in favor of the gospel, and in the space of a year lost his father, wife, and little daughter. It is understandable that Laurence was tempted to read in these events the curse of God attendant upon his change of religion. Calvin took up his pen both to console Laurence in his great loss and to strengthen him in the faith.

The gospel teaches that Christ Himself is a scandal, and we cannot follow the gospel apart from scandal. The danger of this rock of offense has turned four classes of men away from the gospel: those who are so naturally modest as to be horror-struck at the scandal, and dare not even taste the gospel; those who are too lazy or sluggish or unteachable to bother with the gospel; those who reject the gospel because they are arrogant and perversely convinced of their own wisdom; and finally those who maliciously and deliberately collect all sorts of scandal and even invent many to deform the gospel out of hatred for it.

Calvin saw three sorts of scandals on which men stumble: those intrinsic to gospel-teaching itself; those "annexed" scandals that arise out of the preaching of the gospel; finally those "adventitious" scandals that spring from moral depravity, hypocrisy, the ingratitude and vanity of worldly professors of the faith.

"Intrinsic" scandals characterize those who take offense at the gospel because of the simplicity of its language. The Christian doctrines, in Calvin's view, that commonly stir disgust in men's minds include: the two natures of Christ, salvation obtained from Christ's sufferings alone, His becoming a curse for us and thus blessing us, our righteousness being in God only and not in ourselves, Christ's cross, our self-denial, and constancy in time of persecution. Here Calvin eloquently summarized the long chronicle of the church's sufferings. Finally he noted the scandals of those who ascribe their sins to God or stumble at the doctrine of predestination.

The "annexed" scandals that arise when the gospel is preached lead to sects and controversies among Christian teachers. Some men are offended because the gospel often gives rise to strife and war. Calvin replied that war is justified if it is for souls; Christ foretold wars. The "cultured despisers" of the gospel (such as the circle of Rabelais) raise a scandal by converting Christian freedom into licentiousness.

Wicked ministers of the gospel living among the good are the cause of scandal; the gospel is not chargeable with their guilt; throughout its history offenses appear; the commingling of the wicked with the good is intended to prove the faith of the latter. Another source of offense is the easy enticement of some people from the profession of the truth. Over against this, Calvin set the courage of the women of Artois and the Netherlands.

"Adventitious" scandals spring from moral depravity, hypocrisy, and the ingratitude and vanity of worldly professors of the faith. Among the calumnies hurled at Reformed Christians by opposing preachers were the charges that the Reformed had abrogated auricular confession, condemned fasting, abandoned celibacy, and opened marriage to all.

Calvin closed the treatise with an eloquent admonition, translated here in the colorful language of the Elizabethan Age, to unity under Christ, the sole foundation. Christians

> ... being armed with the remedies by me showed, they rather keep Christ still for their foundation, than by their rash and ignorant running against Him, make Him to themselves a stone to stumble at, and a rock to dash against. It cannot otherwise be but that in this world, many occasions of offense must from time to time be fathered upon the faithful. From these not even Christ himself was free. Rather, it is scarcely to be hoped for, that they should step one pace, but that the devil cast some stumbling block in their way. So must they walk through innumerable offenses. But albeit the variety of them be manifold, and the heap thick packed, yet shall none be a Christian, but he that wadeth through them with victory.

Excuse to the Nicodemites (1544)

Laodicean lukewarmness, ever a problem in the Christian church, seems today one of the chief plagues of the old-line denominations in affluent America. Calvin had a name for the general class of such persons, "Messrs. the Nicodemites." They received their sobriquet from the well-known inquirer in John's Gospel. Calvin first encountered such people at the court of Marguerite at Ferrara, which he visited in 1536 on the eve of his detention by Farel in Geneva. Calvin directed several tracts against these siren prophets of religious compromise and sweet reasonableness. We shall look only at the *Excuse.*

Calvin's basic argument was that God is the Lord of the body no less than of the soul of the elect. Therefore the believer must honor God by public worship, upright life, and abstention from idolatrous conformity to the papal church. He directed his critique of religious lukewarmness against four kinds of "Nicodemites." There are evangelical priests and bishops who preach from Catholic pulpits the evangelical message but give their congregations the impression that they have thereby made acceptable the whole superstition-encrusted ecclesiastical shell in which the unreformed church hobbles. The second Nicodemite sect he found in the "delicate prothonotaries" who play religion with the ladies of the court and beguile them with sweet theological niceties, all of them condemning with one voice the too great austerity of Geneva. This is the religion of the theological salon. A third group is comprised of the men of letters, given to philosophy and the tolerance of the foolish superstitions of the papacy. For them it is enough to know God by books and contemplation in their ivory towers, without becoming strained or sullied by involvement in the organization of the community of faith, worship, and Christian action. These men half-convert Christianity into philosophy. In a rather extremely worded condemnation of them, Calvin said: "I would prefer that all human sciences were exterminated from the earth, than for them to be the cause of freezing the zeal of Christians and turning them from God."[46] The last group will raise a respondent chord in American hearts. This includes the merchants and common people, who would prefer that their pastors or priests not become so much involved in the fine points of doctrine and thereby disturb commerce and the workaday tasks and satisfactions.

What a Faithful Man . . . Ought to Do Dwelling Amongst the Papists (1543)

A basic issue in the two works already examined is what a Reformed Christian is to do when pressed to conform to the religious practices and beliefs of the unreformed church that dominates his native place. Calvin was indeed aware of the bitter prospect of losing body and goods, of stirring the world to opprobrium against oneself, and of forsaking the ease of life in one's own country for harsh exile in a foreign land. (Here one is reminded of the impassioned lines at the close of the dedicatory letter to Francis I of France that introduces the *Institutes of the Christian Religion*.)[47] This is the very route Calvin himself had taken. Many had been asking him how they should live and worship in accord with their own conscience when law and custom work against this. The tract was a detailed answer to them; it is also an extended application of *pietas*.

What shall men do? Calvin replied: We must not measure our duty to God according to our own advantage or physical convenience. We are not to rely on our own brain but rather to trust God's own providence, that He will keep us even in the midst of a thousand deaths.

What should be the general principles of Christian behavior? If God declares His will to us through His Word, we should follow it and not debate with God. The first lesson in Christ's school is that if we are ashamed of Him or His Word, He will be ashamed of us when He comes in judgment. God is not satisfied that we acknowledge Him secretly in our hearts; we are to profess outwardly that we are His. Or to put it in the language of the treatise "On the Christian Life," with which we have already dealt, "We belong to God." Should every-

---

46. *CO* 6.600; cf. George H. Williams, *The Radical Reformation* (Philadelphia: Westminster, 1962), pp. 603f.
47. See *Institution,* pp. 17f.

one declare himself openly, whether or not anybody ask him about his faith? Only those called thereto should preach openly, but everyone should witness according to his gifts, inviting his neighbor to join in true worship and Christian instruction. Since we have no definite rule for all, let every man ask our Lord to direct him in true wisdom to his duty, and then let him do it with all his power.

The chief question to which Calvin addressed himself in this tract is this: "Should a truly Christian man go to mass when he is among the papists? Should he worship images, relics, and suchlike ceremonies? A prior question which must be answered is: what is idolatry? Idolatry is of two sorts: first, when a man through a false fantasy conceived in his heart or spirit corrupts and perverts the spiritual balm of the one only God; second, when a man gives or transfers the honor which belongs to God only, to any creature." (Parenthetically, this would confirm our earlier postulation that the Romans passage underlying this view of idolatry is in fact the key verse that triggered Calvin's conversion.)

What duty do we owe God? Is it not enough to hold God in secret within our hearts? Calvin answered with a resounding no! God must be glorified in both our hearts and our bodies as well, for the latter too are redeemed by Jesus' blood. Therefore, we must not prostrate our bodies, which are the very temple of the Holy Spirit, before an idol. When we kneel before an idol we derogate God's majesty. All this is, once more, the familiar call to holiness before the all-holy God.

But can we really label the mass as pagan idolatry? Surely, though it may be corrupt, it is still men's intention by it to worship God and not a humanly devised idol; consequently, such calling upon God's name, though perhaps idolatrous, is not perilous, is it? This argument did not impress Calvin. He responded: If you go about worshiping God in a perverse and unlawful manner, you are worshiping an idol.

What then about the practice of the mass in Calvin's own day? One does not condemn all papal rites, but only those that are completely bad. No evangelical Christian can submit to daily mass, for this is manifest idolatry. What then about high mass? Is this not better since it is a memorial of the Lord's Supper? No, this is a corruption of the Lord's Supper and as such is idolatrous; also the priestly absolution that follows is a violation of God's authority.

Calvin then sketched the cultic acts that mark the daily life of an unreformed Christian, from birth to death, labeling them abominations to be avoided by faithful believers. But still a crowd of excuses for conformity to such practices must be dealt with. Of course it is wrong to participate in these rites, but if one does them out of fear of men, is this not a light fault? Surely far worse crimes than this are committed! Calvin replied that such hypocrisy is no light fault, for it runs clean counter to God's requirement that man sanctify and consecrate himself to God—both in body and in spirit, but the spirit as chief takes the principal place.

Another excuse: What good would come of it if everyone declared he would serve God purely? To this Calvin rejoined: If it pleases God, the faithful man will undergo persecution, flight, prison, banishment, and even death itself.

Still another excuse: Suppose everyone wished to leave idolatry; then all the countries under Antichrist's reign would be deprived of the faithful. Having thus departed, where could they settle, since the regions where God is purely called upon cannot absorb any more population? To this Calvin replied: If this happened, our Lord would provide for His faithful in some way—either convert the hearts of the princes and magistrates, moving them to put down idolatry and establish the true worship of God, or at least soften them so they would not force the faithful to defile themselves against their consciences or would not act cruelly against them.

The supply of excuses is not yet exhausted. If those capable of following the gospel take themselves away, how, if the seed is removed, can the doctrine of the gospel be multiplied? Calvin's answer is sharp: If all who have been given knowledge of the truth did but half their duty, there would not be one corner of the world not filled with it. Lack of courage is the fault. Have faith that if one man moves away, God will raise up four in his place.

The final excuse is a taunt thrown at Calvin: It is very well for you to talk from your safe place! If you were in our place, you would do as we do! Calvin answered: I speak as my conscience prompts, without boasting. If I were in a place where I thought I could not avoid idolatry without danger, I would pray the Lord to strengthen me and give me constancy to prefer His glory over my own life.

After a call to martyrdom, Calvin gave his final advice to evangelical Christians. If you live in a land where you cannot worship purely, go into exile if you can. If you cannot flee, abstain from idolatry while purely worshiping God in private. But suppose one has not the strength or constancy or is held back by parents, family, or the like. As far as your infirmity permits, follow the surest and soundest counsel. Insofar as you depart from the right way out of fear of men, confess your sin to God. Try daily to be sorry in order that you may obtain God's mercy. Then ask your Father to draw you out of bondage or to establish a right form of the church throughout the world so you can duly honor Him.

Thus do these tracts pastorally apply *pietas* to the troubled, perplexed lives of those who longed to work out the renewal that had already touched their hearts. It has been said that Calvin is a theologian for hard times. Though too often curtained over by affluence, the church is living in a hard time. All the forces contrary to a truly Reformed faith that stood in the way in the sixteenth century have their late-twentieth-century counterpart. Lukewarm Nicodemites and learned scoffers are in the very bosom of the church, and — I may say — the seminaries. It will not take much imagination to find the category of obstacle-makers to which each of us in our failure to follow Christ belongs. Deny self! Follow God! Bear your cross! Let the hope of the life to come give meaning for your present life. What excuses do we give for not following this way of *pietas*?

12

Calvin
and the Church

G. S. M. Walker

"For all his abhorrence of Rome, he was after his manner as good a Churchman as any Pope."[1] Such, whether it be intended to express approval or the reverse, seems to be a sound judgment on Calvin's churchmanship. To a liberal like Grosclaude,[2] it was indeed his chief fault that he could not rid himself entirely of Roman ideas: that he continued to regard the church as depository and dispenser of the means of grace, rather than as a free association of like-minded believers. Unity and universality were lost in the general turmoil of the Reformation; but that outcome was the direct opposite of what this allegedly "devil-worshipping genius"[3] had intended; for Calvin stressed, more strongly than any other Reformer, the catholicity of the *Una Sancta*. And if the ideal of a free church in a free state has grown on Calvinist soil,[4] Calvin himself would have repudiated such a deduction from his doctrine of the crown rights of the Redeemer. His entire object was to bring human life in its totality under common obedience to God in Christ.

For this purpose, he discerned that the Reformed church must retain the medieval attributes of unity, authority, and catholicity. Nothing less would suffice to withstand the rampant individualism of the radical Reformers on the one hand, and on the other to oppose

Reprinted from *Scottish Journal of Theology* 16 (1963): 371–89. Used by permission of the Scottish Academic Press.

1. R. N. Carew Hunt, *Calvin* (1933), p. 136.
2. C. Grosclaude, *Exposition et critique de l' ecclésiologie de Calvin* (1896), p. 8.
3. Hoffman Nickerson, *The Loss of Unity* (1961), chap. 11.
4. B. B. Warfield, *John Calvin: The Man and His Work* (1909), p. 15.

the absolutism of the Renaissance state. His objective was what Barth[5] has called a "Protestant Catholicity," or in the words of Imbart de la Tour,[6] "a new catholicism solely founded on the Word of God." And the latter author continues: "What Calvin sought to restore, in the midst of protestantism and to some extent in opposition to it, was the catholic idea of universality and authority."

Hence came his stress on the church's indefeasible permanence. "Moreover we must assert this principle, that there has been no time since creation when God did not have His Church upon earth, nor will there, up to the ending of the world, be a time when He does not have it, as He Himself declares."[7] Its outward form may disappear,[8] but the "everlasting continuance of the Church" is founded on Christ's eternal reign.[9] Israel in the old dispensation was a true church, possessing sacraments of real efficacy. Calvin rejects the scholastic view that those ordinances merely prefigured grace without conferring it;[10] although in our day the *manducatio* is now *substantialis,* nonetheless "the Holy Spirit . . . was (then) active in such a way that Christ's flesh, not yet created, should be efficacious in them" as well.[11] Indeed, even before the incarnation, Christ had united Himself with His ancient people, thus foreshadowing not only the church's deliverance, but also the sufferings of His own incarnate life.[12]

On such principles, Calvin was bound to regard his work as one of restoration and not innovation. When from his deathbed he charged the ministers of Geneva to resist change, "since all changes are dangerous and sometimes harmful,"[13] this was not a case of the conservative beadle's advice to his young successor, "remember, aye resist improvements." Even if a Reformed church must be in some sense *semper reformanda,* there is nonetheless, to Calvin's mind, an eternal pattern which, once recovered, requires only to be fixed. His admiration for the patristic period, *ante papatum* as he puts it, was as unbounded as that of any Anglican. Not only does he model his organization expressly on the second century.[14] Not only does he refer

5. J. Moltmann, ed., *Calvin-Studien* 1959 (1960), p. 71.

6. P. Imbart de la Tour, *Les Origines de la Réforme* (1935), vol. 4, pp. 52–53.

7. *Institutio* (1536), chap. 2 (*OS* 1.87).

8. *Inst.* Praefatio.

9. Ibid., 2.15.3.

10. *Comm. on 1 Cor.* 10:3.

11. Ibid., 10:4.

12. R. S. Wallace, *Calvin's Doctrine of the Word and Sacraments* (1953), p. 155. I owe a number of references to this book.

13. B. J. Kidd, *Documents Illustrative of the Continental Reformation* (1911), p. 650.

14. J. Mackinnon, *Calvin and the Reformation* (1936), p. 80.

to the Fathers at almost every turn. The extent to which his spirit was steeped in early Christian literature appears in more unconscious moments, as when, in discussing the true mode of fasting, he makes an unacknowledged reference to the works of Cassian.[15] And when he has to meet Castellio's objections to the Song of Songs, he takes no other ground than "the perpetual consensus of the Universal Church."[16]

"Therefore," runs the preface to his first theological work, the *Psychopannychia*,[17] "this is the chief point in preserving charity, that our faith should remain holy and entire." The *Ordonnances Ecclésiastiques*[18] arise out of the question, "what must be restored from antiquity?" And the letter to Sadoleto assures its recipient that "we strive for nothing else than the restoration of the Church to its primitive splendor."[19] Calvin recognized in practice that the New Testament, though perpetually normative for doctrine, cannot be the ordinary norm of organization. For the church, in later ages, must be content with the local ministry of pastors and teachers, since apostles, prophets, and evangelists have now ceased unless it should please God to raise them up again.[20] Such extraordinary offices may be revived at a special period of crisis, and Calvin believed[21] that the vocation of himself and of his colleagues belonged to this abnormal though divine type. But the regular ministry must conform to the threefold order of early catholicism, which is itself of scriptural authority.[22] In agreement with Jerome,[23] the development of monarchical episcopacy is to be explained as the creation of a president for the presbyteral college; even the appearance of metropolitans and patriarchs can be accepted, provided that their function is only to preside.[24] At the same time, the

15. *Inst.* 4.12.18; cf. Cassian, *Inst.* 5.23.
16. Kidd, *Documents,* p. 635.
17. Ibid., p. 528.
18. J. S. Whale, *The Protestant Tradition* (1955), p. 130; no reference given.
19. *OS* 1.466.
20. *Inst.* 4.3.4.
21. "The charge which the Lord gave us has been altogether extraordinary when He employed our work to restore the churches" (letter to the King of Poland, 5 Dec. 1554, in *CO* 15.335).
22. *Inst.* 4.4.1. His own fourfold order is produced by dividing bishops into pastors and doctors (ibid., 4.3.4 and 8); ordination is a sacrament (ibid., 4.14.20, 19.28), for which imposition of hands is desirable but not essential (Kidd, *Documents,* p. 592; *Inst.* 4.3.16).
23. Ibid., 4.4.2; cf. *Comm. on Titus* 1:5 ("we learn from this passage that there was not then such equality among the ministers that none had some authority and counsel above the others").
24. *Inst.* 4.4.4; writing to King Sigismund (*CO* 15.332ff.) Calvin is ready to allow an archbishop and bishops, but purely as presidents of the Polish church courts.

parity of pastors, on which Cyprian[25] so strongly insisted, must by all means be preserved, lest any individual should arrogate to himself the "sole bishopric"[26] of Christ. And the practice of the primitive church must also be copied in the election, or at least approval,[27] of ministers by popular vote.

However, the chapter of the *Institutes*[28] which thus commends the organization of the early church is followed by seven other chapters containing a violent attack upon the papacy. It is vital for Calvin to prove that the Roman obedience is no true church of Christ, because it would be our inescapable duty to submit to Rome if she were entitled to that appellation.[29] Disagreement on matters which are not fundamental cannot justify schism.[30] The fundamentals of Christianity are these: "that God is One, that Christ is God and the Son of God, that our salvation depends upon God's mercy and so forth,"[31] or more pointedly, the worship of one God, invoked in the name of Christ, together with faith in Christ for our salvation, and a ministry that is not quite corrupt.[32] Christ is the sole foundation,[33] and anything which obscures Christ tends by that very fact to destroy the church. God does indeed employ the "vicarious ministry"[34] of men. But when an individual man usurps the divine throne, when a real absence of the church's Head is proclaimed by the appointment of a supreme terres-

25. *Inst.* 4.11.6. At the Colloquy of Worms in 1540 Calvin said, "I am quite sure that the Lord willed to remove from the Church not only all ambition, but also all pre-eminence (*praefecturam*). . . . He instituted apostles, prophets, teachers, without any mention of a primacy. It is thus certain that Christ did not wish there to be one" (see E. Doumergue, *Jean Calvin: Les hommes et les choses de son temps* (1902), vol. 2, p. 613).

26. *Inst.* 4.2.6; cf. *Comm. on Eph.* 4:11.

27. Against Cyprian's desire for popular election, Calvin quotes Virgil(!), *Aen.* 2.39, on the contrary passions of the crowd (*OS* 1.214); he was genuinely afraid of radical democracy, and "under the theoretical forms of election, it was a system of co-option that Calvin established" (Imbart de la Tour, *Réforme* 4, p. 107; on the next page he points out that Calvin's system of appointment was parallel to that of Roman canon law prior to the Decretals).

28. *Inst.* 4.4.

29. Ibid., 4.2.10; this explains, if it does not excuse, the vehemence of his vituperation.

30. Ibid., 4.1.12 and 16; cf. A. Mitchell Hunter, *The Teaching of Calvin* (1950), p. 158.

31. *Inst.* 4.1.12. The Apostles' Creed is of course treated, throughout the *Institutes*, as a "brief and simple summary of Christianity."

32. *Comm. on 1 Cor.* 1:2.

33. "Christ is the one and only foundation of the Church" (*Comm. on 1 Cor.* 3:11); "Christ is actually the foundation on which the Church is built by the preaching of doctrine" (*Comm. on Eph.* 2:20).

34. *Inst.* 4.3.1.

trial Vicar, and when the Eucharist is exalted into competition with the sacrifice of Calvary, then the form of the church as Christ's body is obliterated and entirely lost. A mere succession, which is not a succession in apostolic doctrine,[35] confers no title to authority, for Caiaphas was after all in direct descent from Aaron.[36] And the corruption of the papal communion is worse than anything which occurred in Israel.[37] Since the power of the keys depends upon the Word of God, Rome in rejecting that Word has renounced her ecclesiastical jurisdiction.[38] Her tyranny,[39] her abuse of discipline,[40] her Judaistic ceremonies,[41] coupled with "that supreme climax of all abominations the Mass,"[42] have so displaced Christ that He is no longer allowed to reign, and so perverted her own structure that she is now no more a church.

Nonetheless, Rome has retained the organic continuity of valid baptism, together with certain other vestiges, as the sign of a perpetual covenant.[43] The voice of God cannot be entirely stifled, and the opportunity of returning to her former status remains open; though she has ceased corporately to be the church, local churches may survive[44] under her dominion. For despite her aberrations, Rome always intends to be Christ's body, whereas the Anabaptists reject the very possibility of a church as Calvin understands it. These "frantic spirits"[45] who condemn infant baptism, these "Catabaptists and other monstrous lewd men,"[46] are the Donatists, Cathari, and Novatianists[47] of modern times. They are schismatics on principle, and by denying the institutional aspect of Christianity they are in fact denying the priority of grace. The whole radical Reformation is a diabolical attempt to remove the glory of God and the confidence of Christians for their children.[48] Calvin was conscious of deliberately occupying a *via media,* not only

35. Ibid., 4.2.2. "In what else does succession consist, except in perpetuity of doctrine?" (CO 35.611).
36. *Inst.* 4.2.
37. Ibid., 4.2.
38. Ibid., 4.2.
39. Ibid., 4.5 and 9.
40. Ibid., 4.11.7.
41. Ibid., 4.10.11 and 19.26.
42. "Epistola de fugiendis impiorum illicitis sacris" (1537), in OS 1.289.
43. *Inst.* 4.2.11; Roman baptism is valid if administered by a priest; if by a woman it is a "grievous sin" (4.15.22; cf. CO 11.625).
44. *Inst.* 4.2.12.
45. Ibid., 4.16.1.
46. Ibid., Praefatio.
47. Ibid., 4.1.13 and 23.
48. Ibid., 4.16.32.

between Luther and Zwingli on the limited question of the sacraments,[49] but also on the much wider controversy between Rome and Anabaptism. To his mind, the propriety of baptizing infants[50] marked the crucial difference between church and sect.

What then is this church of Christ, so permanent in God's design, so easily obscured by man's inventions? It is the bride of Christ, the spouse of God, His edifice, plantation, dwelling-place, or temple.[51] It is the object of a special providence, the "workshop" of God, the sanctuary where He resides as Father of His family.[52] More especially, the church is the mother of all the godly, showing her maternal care by gathering God's children to her bosom;[53] her motherhood is parallel to the divine Fatherhood, and "there is no other entry into life, unless she conceive us in her womb, bring us forth and nurse us, and finally keep us under her own care and discipline until, having put off our mortal flesh, we shall be like to angels."[54] With an even wider sweep, the church is defined as "the universal number of the elect, whether they be angels or men";[55] in Calvin's mind,[56] it is virtually identified with the communion of saints, whether in heaven or on earth. As a community, it is frequently compared in Scripture[57] to a commonwealth or family. Hence its function is to educate mankind: "We see those two things 'children of the Church' and 'taught of God' are united in such a manner that they cannot be God's disciples who refuse to be taught in the Church."[58] But above all, the church is the sole place of reconciliation. "Apart from the Body of Christ and the fellowship of the godly, there can be no hope of reconciliation with God. Hence in the creed we profess to believe the Catholic Church and the forgiveness of sins. . . . Hence also, an open departure from the Church is an open renouncement of eternal salvation."[59]

49. See the studied moderation of the "Petit Traicté de la Saincte Cène" (1541), especially OS 1.527ff.

50. Doumergue, *Jean Calvin,* vol. 5, p. 336.

51. References in Moltmann, *Calvin-Studien,* p. 134.

52. J. K. S. Reid, trans., *Concerning the Eternal Predestination of God* (1961), pp. 164–65.

53. *Inst.* 4.1.1.

54. Ibid., 4.1.4; cf. *Comm. on Gal.* 4:26 ("whoever refuses to be a child of the Church vainly desires to have God as Father; for it is only by the ministry of the Church that God begets and nourishes children"). But after birth there must be growth, and Calvin condemns the "popish system" under which the people are kept "in absolute infancy" (*Comm. on Eph.* 4:14).

55. *Institutio* (1536), chap. 2 (OS 1.86).

56. Doumergue, *Jean Calvin,* vol. 5, p. 8, n. 5; *Inst.* 4.1.3.

57. *Comm. on Eph.* 2:19.

58. *Comm. on Isa.* 54:13.

59. Ibid., 33:24; cf. *Inst.* 4.1.20.

There is a highly significant passage in the Genevan Catechism of 1545.[60] "What is the Church? The body and society of the faithful, whom God has predestined to eternal life. Is this point also essential to faith? Yes indeed, unless we wish to make void the death of Christ, and count as nothing all that has been so far said. For this is the one effect of it all, that there should be a Church." The culminating purpose of the divine economy, the product of Christ's passion, is a continuing mystical body of which He is the Head. Not without reason did Calvin devote about one-third of the *Institutes,* in their final form, to the doctrine of the church. For to him that subject is intimately intertwined with Christology,[61] and neither church nor predestination can be understood apart from Christ. Hence too the sacraments, of which Christ is "the matter or substance,"[62] are treated as a part of ecclesiology and not dogmatics.

Troeltsch[63] regards this union of the members with their Head as a "surrender to the electing and renewing will of God," or as God's activity in the believer, who is "absorbed into the active and effectual spirit of Christ." He denies that this involves a mystical or substantial union. But Calvin argues[64] that "we are then really united to the Body of Christ, when His death brings forth in us its fruit . . . inasmuch as grafting designates not only a conformity of example, but a secret union by which we are joined to Him . . . we not only derive the vigor and nourishment of life from Christ, but we also pass from our own to His nature." This does not imply that we are immediately made perfect in holiness. One of Calvin's objections to the Anabaptists was that they would not tolerate a partially imperfect church,[65] and he insists that all Christians must pray daily for forgiveness,[66] so that in this life "it is enough if every day brings some nearer to others, and all nearer to Christ."[67] But "Christ adorns the Church His bride with

60. Chap. 15 (*OS* 2.88–89).
61. Cf. John Macpherson, *Doctrine of the Church in Scottish Theology* (1903), p. 2 ("the studies which these divines prosecuted were christological rather than ecclesiastical; when they argued about the Church it was in order to exalt Christ").
62. *Inst.* 4.14.16 and 17.11. Christ remains the substance although the wicked fail to receive Him (*Comm. on 1 Cor.* 10:5), just as God's Word remains His Word even if it is not obeyed (*Inst.* 4.14.7).
63. E. Troeltsch, *The Social Teaching of the Christian Churches* (ET 1931), vol. 2, p. 584.
64. *Comm. on Rom.* 6:3 and 5.
65. *Comm. on 1 Cor.* 1:2 ("it is a dangerous temptation to think there is no Church, where perfect purity is lacking").
66. *Inst.* 4.1.23.
67. *Comm. on Eph.* 4:13.

holiness as a proof of His regard,"[68] and it is our part to strive after perfection. Troeltsch is perfectly correct in pointing to the activism of Calvin's thought;[69] it is based on the concept of God as active Will, going back behind the Scotist school to Jehovah of the Old Testament. "In conflict and in labor the individual takes up the task of the sanctification of the world, always with the certainty, however, that he will not lose himself in the life of the world . . . election consists in being strengthened to perform actions of this kind . . . the Church is not merely an organ of (personal) salvation . . . it ought to prove itself effective in the Christianizing of the community."[70]

Because the church as an institution is prior to the individual as a saved soul, Calvin refuses to lay much emphasis on personal salvation. When Cardinal Sadoleto suggested that Rome could provide the safest road to heaven, Calvin replied: "It is extremely untheological to give a man such an addiction to himself, that you do not commend to him a zeal for God's glory as his principle of life. For we were born in the first instance for God and not ourselves. . . . It is certainly the part of a Christian man to look higher than seeking and securing salvation for his own soul."[71] Admittedly the glory of God is closely concerned with man's salvation, and on our part fulfilment of the heavenly calling is second only to the hallowing of His name. But Calvin's interest in predestination is so impersonal that he has almost, though not quite, reached the position of those New England ministers who asked their ordinands if they were willing to be damned for the greater glory of God. It may be recalled that his own armorial device was a flaming heart offered on an open hand, with the motto "I give my heart to the Lord in sacrifice."[72]

"Let us mark well," he says in one of his sermons,[73] "what this word Christianity means: its meaning is to be members of the Son of God." In the first edition of the *Institutes,* the church as the body *of Christ* is connected closely with the effects of predestination *in Christ;* later editions begin to separate the two themes, because the church is regarded still more as an institution, and so as a *corpus mixtum,* through its involvement with the world.[74] But even in its institutional

68. Ibid., 5:27.

69. Troeltsch, *Social Teaching of the Christian Churches,* p. 586.

70. Ibid., pp. 588, 591.

71. *OS* 1.463–64.

72. Calvin thought that every true pastor must have his heart thus offered (*CO* 27.482), and for those who served in France these were no idle words.

73. Sermon on 2 Tim. 2:19.

74. E. Buess, "Prädestination und Kirche in Calvins Institutio," in *Theologische Zeitschrift* 12 (1956): 347–61.

aspect, it remains a miracle of grace, and to the end the principle of
extra ecclesiam nulla salus[75] stands firm. Indeed, the more the stress
that Calvin lays upon predestination, the more does he assert a corresponding significance for the church. Ideally, as the object of faith,
it is a mystical or invisible body; but in its pragmatic nature, it is a
visible religious corporation. The two aspects of the one church can
be distinguished as two eccentric but overlapping circles. Part of the
elect fall outside the sphere of the visible community since, unlike
Lutherans and Romanists, Calvin holds that even baptism is not essential to salvation.[76] Again, part of the visible membership falls outside the sphere of election, since chaff is mingled with the wheat.[77]
But these two aspects are "neither separated nor confounded,"[78] and
they are constantly striving to converge. To be effective, the spiritual
communion of saints must be embodied in institutional forms; and
the institution, by prayer and self-discipline, must ever seek to conform itself to the ideal. Though the corporation cannot be identified
with the body, the one is an incarnation of the other.

Strange as it may perhaps seem, this doctrine is derived from Calvin's emphasis on the Old Testament. The history of the patriarchal
families, and the prophetic concern for national life as a whole, provide
its biblical justification. It is founded on a federal theology which, as
Lecerf[79] remarks, goes back behind Cocceius to Calvin himself. But
whereas the former thinks in terms of a personal covenant between
man and God, Calvin asserts that God deals, not so much with isolated individuals, as with people in community. Natural groupings, by
families and nations, are embraced in His design. The idea of a "house-
church" was not unknown to Calvin; "What a wonderful thing to be
put on record," he writes,[80] "that the name 'church' is applied to a
single family, and yet it is fitting that all the families of believers
should be organized in such a way as to be so many little churches."
Hence the children of believers possess a federal holiness, and a title

75. "Those who wish to become partakers of so great a benefit must be a part of
Israel, that is of the Church, out of which there can be neither salvation nor truth"
(*Comm. on Isa.* 49:7); "by nature we are aliens from the Kingdom of God" (ibid.,
49:21).

76. *Inst.* 4.14.14 and 15.22; cf. Hunter, *Teaching of Calvin,* p. 155. But "by ne-
glecting baptism (when available) we are excluded from salvation, and in this sense
I acknowledge that it is necessary" (*Comm. on John* 3:5), so that disregard of the
sacraments amounts to "neglect of the whole gospel, for we must not separate those
things which the Lord has commanded us to join" (*Comm. on Isa.* 7:12).

77. *Inst.* 4.12.

78. A. Lecerf, *Études Calvinistes* (1949), p. 56.

79. Ibid., p. 58.

80. *Comm. on 1 Cor.* 16:19.

to baptism may even by derived from remote grandparents.[81] Because God "not only receives each of us individually into His favor, but also herein associates with us our offspring by a sort of hereditary right,"[82] therefore "the children of the godly are born the children of the Church, and are accounted members of Christ from the womb."[83]

The nation, no less than the family, can be a part of the Christian organism. When Geneva accepted the Reformation, its general council resolved "to live in this holy evangelical law and Word of God."[84] But that vague promise was not enough for Calvin. Recalling the pacts made in Israel under Josiah and Asa,[85] he asked the magistrates to impose on every citizen a personal Confession of Faith, "which is the right beginning of a Church." It was to be regarded as a once-for-all act of corporate covenant with God, and those who refused to accept it should be banished from the Christian commonwealth thus formed. In fact the scheme was defeated by an alliance of libertines with reactionaries. But Calvin's ideal remained that of a society in which citizenship was equated with church-membership. Not that he identified church and state, for his long struggle to secure the right of excommunication is sufficient proof that he distinguished sharply between the spiritual and temporal powers. He refused, however, to secularize the state, because it has the same divine origin and purpose as the church,[86] and "in protecting public morality it acts as the guardian of God's honor."[87] As Doumergue[88] puts it, "at this epoch a particular faith involves a particular form of civic life."

It is because the church embraces communities as well as individuals that a distinction must be drawn between its visible and invisible aspects. There is a general vocation, from which "none is excluded,"[89] producing a *Volkskirche* or territorial establishment. And there is a special election, from which unbelievers exclude themselves, producing a gathered fellowship of saints. But the latter depends upon the former: "although the common election be not effectual in all, yet it may set open a gate for the special elect."[90] And in practice Calvin

81. Letter to John Knox, 7 Nov. 1559, on baptizing the children of idolaters or excommunicates; see Hunter, *Teaching of Calvin*, p. 178.

82. *Comm. on Ps.* 103:17.

83. *Comm. on Acts* 8:37.

84. Kidd, *Documents*, p. 519.

85. Doumergue, *Jean Calvin*, vol. 2, pp. 236, 239.

86. Imbart de la Tour, *Les Origines de la Réforme* (1935), vol. 4, p. 109.

87. R. N. Carew Hunt, *Calvin* (1933), pp. 136–37; magistrates are "God's vicars" (1537 Confession of Faith, chap. 21, in Kidd, *Documents*, p. 571; cf. *Inst.* 4.20.4).

88. Doumergue, *Jean Calvin*, vol. 2, p. 249.

89. *Comm. on John* 3:16.

90. *Comm. on Acts* 3:25.

finds an adequate proof of election in sincere church-membership. "Do you wish to know whether you are elect? Look upon yourself in Jesus Christ. . . . When we receive this testimony of salvation which is given us through the Gospel, thereby we recognize and are assured that God has chosen us."[91] Admittedly, God alone knows those that are His. Although we can be sure of our own state of grace "if we have communion with Christ," yet in the case of others "it is not our part to separate elect from reprobate."[92] But for practical purposes, the only charitable judgment is to recognize as children of God all those who profess the Christian faith, live the Christian life, and participate in the Christian sacraments.[93] New England Calvinists substituted for the last of these a conscious experience of conversion. To Calvin conversion is relatively unimportant,[94] and he gives as the outward proofs of election the three marks or notes which serve to define the church itself. Doctrine, life, and sacramental worship provide surer indications in the case of churches than they can do in that of individuals,[95] because the Word and sacraments must always bear some fruit in any congregation.[96] But for the individual, active churchmanship is an adequate testimony of being saved. Calvin makes no mention of predestination in his children's catechism,[97] and that catechism is addressed to all the baptized. His formula of absolution is addressed to every penitent sinner.[98] "Let each of you humble himself before God and believe that the heavenly Father wills to be merciful to him in Jesus Christ; to all those who thus repent and seek Jesus Christ for their salvation, I pronounce absolution in the name of the Father, the Son, and the Holy Ghost."[99] The circle of election is strained to the utmost in seeking to embrace the whole circle of the church.

Calvin's doctrine of predestination, so harsh when isolated, must be tempered by reference to his doctrine of the church. Neither can be understood apart from the other, and both must be interpreted in Christ. Whatever may have happened in later Calvinism, it is false to say that Calvin himself destroyed the Augustinian synthesis of church

91. CO 8.114.
92. *Institutio* (1536), chap. 2 (OS 1.88).
93. Ibid. (p. 89); cf. *Inst.* 4.1.8.
94. He was notoriously reticent about his own conversion, and I know of no passage in which he makes an experience of it essential to salvation. Repentance and faith, on the other hand, are constant exercises of the Christian life.
95. *Inst.* 4.1.9.
96. Ibid., 4.1.10.
97. Hunter, *Teaching of Calvin*, p. 297.
98. Lecerf, *Études Calvinistes*, p. 35.
99. CO 6.174, n. 4; OS 2.19; the formula occurs in his Strasbourg liturgy, freely adapted from Bucer's German mass.

and grace. On the contrary, he regards the visible church as a token of God's goodness to creation, and of His covenant with all mankind. Its scope is as wide as the universal "sacraments"[100] of the rainbow and the tree of life; its existence witnesses to the general *sensus religionis* of humanity;[101] its mission is to Christianize the world. But Calvin strikes a proper balance between collectivism and particularity. If the visible church maintains the continuity of a religious institution, the church invisible guarantees the rights of each individual believer. The former concept makes Calvinism "a school of order and of social life"; the latter makes it "an invincible fortress where personal faith finds a refuge against the tyranny of men."[102] It is this twofold character, combining the ideals of a free church with those of an establishment, that has rendered Calvinism at once so prone to divide and at the same time so fertile in reunion.

Because the church is in Christ,[103] its *unity* is both commanded and given in Him. "Without Christ . . . the whole world is a shapeless chaos and frightful confusion. We are brought into actual unity by Christ alone."[104] It may be that in practice, as Professor McEwen[105] has suggested, Knox laid more stress than Calvin did upon the unitive effect of the sacrament; but in theory, Calvin asserted with equal emphasis that through the Eucharist "we are forged into one body with Christ,"[106] and quoting Augustine's description of it as "the bond of charity," he went on to say that Christ, "by giving Himself to us" in this sacrament, "makes us to be all one in Him."[107] However, Calvin is careful to remember that the church is not constituted merely by a blind sacramental participation. It is founded upon Christ in His totality, as the Truth of God no less than as the Bread of Life. Apart from the preached word of promise[108] sacraments become devoid of mean-

100. *Inst.* 4.14.18.

101. B. B. Warfield, *Calvin and Calvinism* (1931), p. 37.

102. Lecerf, *Études Calvinistes*, p. 68; for what precedes see pp. 55–56.

103. "But because Paul calls the Church 'Christ' this verse is full of rare comfort. For Christ invests us with this honor that He wishes to be discerned and recognized, not only in His own Person, but also in His members" (*Comm. on 1 Cor.* 12:12).

104. *Comm. on Eph.* 1:10; cf. ibid., 4:6 ("Christ cannot be divided. Faith cannot be rent. There are not various baptisms, but one which is common to all. God cannot cease to be one and unchangeable. It cannot but be our duty to cherish holy unity, which is bound by so many ties"), and *Comm. on 1 Cor.* 1:12 ("the unity of the Church rests mainly on this one thing, that we all depend on Christ alone").

105. J. S. McEwen, *The Faith of John Knox* (1961), pp. 56–57; on p. 53 he misinterprets Calvin's teaching on baptism, and then transfers it to the Eucharist.

106. *Inst.* 4.17.2.

107. Ibid., 4.17.38.

108. Ibid., 4.14.4 and 17.39.

ing. And if "Christ is actually the foundation on which the Church is built," it is built "by the preaching of doctrine,"[109] in such a way that "we must look for no other bond of union than the pure truth of God."[110] It follows that unity is impossible apart from truth, for the very reason that truth is Christ and Christ is not divided. "Indeed it is certain that we ought to disregard the whole world, and to embrace only the truth of God; for it is a hundred times better to renounce the society of all mortals and union with them, than to withdraw ourselves from God; but when God shows Himself our leader, the prophet teaches that we ought mutually to stretch forth our hand and unitedly to follow Him."[111] While thus allowing a sort of escape clause for the individual conscience, Calvin nonetheless uses the strongest possible language to condemn the sin of schism. "Strangers who separate from the Church can look for nothing else than to rot in their own malediction."[112] "Nothing is more formidable than to be rejected from God's flock. For no safety is to be hoped for, except as God gather us into one body under one Head. . . . Christ will not and cannot be torn from His Church, with which He is joined by an indissoluble knot. . . . Hence, unless we cultivate unity with the faithful, we see that we are cut off from Christ."[113] Only "traitors and deserters" abandon the Word and sacraments, and as "a denial of God and Christ"[114] "departure from the Church is always damnable."[115] Because Christ cannot be divided, there can be no other church than the one which is His body,[116] and therefore "the most important principle of our religion is this, that we should be in concord among ourselves."[117] "For only Christ ought to rule in the Church," and "He reigns in our midst only when He is the means of binding us together in an inviolable union."[118]

Again, because the church is in Christ, its *authority* derives from Him. "The Lord governs His Church with His Word as with a scep-

109. *Comm. on Eph.* 2:20.
110. Letter to Bullinger, 12 March 1540, quoted in Moltmann, *Calvin-Studien,* p. 74.
111. *Comm. on Zech.* 8:23.
112. *Comm. on Isa.* 33:24.
113. *Comm. on Ezek.* 13:9.
114. *Inst.* 4.1.10.
115. Ibid., 4.1.4. Much more could be quoted on the same lines, e.g. *Comm. on Heb.* 10:26 ("such as forsake the Church . . . wholly alienate themselves from Christ").
116. *Institutio* (1536), chap. 2 (*OS* 1.86); *Inst.* 4.1.2.
117. *Comm. on 1 Cor.* 1:10.
118. Ibid., 1:13.

ter,"[119] He instructs us as our "only Schoolmaster,"[120] and under the guidance of the Holy Spirit, the Bible in both Testaments provides the church's sole ultimate rule.[121] Councils can have no independent authority, but must themselves be judged by Scripture, however useful they may be in practice as a means of determining and deciding controversies.[122] Nonetheless, the authoritative divine Word is communicated ministerially by preaching, so that "those who reject or despise this ministry offer insult and rebellion to Christ its Author."[123] It is in compassion for our human weakness that God chooses to address us through the lips of weak and fallible men. But in virtue of his office, the minister speaks "not otherwise than as God Himself."[124] The authority of pastors and doctors depends on fidelity to their commission, so that "whatever authority is exercised in the Church ought to be subjected to this rule . . . that men blend nothing of their own, but only define what is right according to the Word of the Lord."[125] Subject to this proviso, the faithful minister is commissioned to "constrain the world's glory, pomp, and excellence to give place and obey the majesty of the Word; lay its commandments upon all from the greatest to the least; edify Christ's household, demolish the reign of Satan; feed the sheep, kill the wolves, instruct and exhort the docile; confute, repress, and conquer rebels — but all in the Word of God."[126]

Such was the high credential which Calvin assigned to the ministry of preaching. It "penetrates the consciences of men," making them "see Christ crucified,"[127] in such a way as to render a visible crucifix superfluous;[128] it replaces the elevation of the host, so that attendance at sermon is more profitable than non-communicating attendance at mass. But Calvin was far from sharing Luther's naïve confidence that preaching alone could achieve everything. Looking back on his first

119. Ibid., 4:20; cf. *Inst.* 4.2.4.

120. *Inst.* 4.8.1.

121. Ibid., 4.8.8.

122. Ibid., 4.8.10, 9.9, and 9.13.

123. *Comm. on Eph.* 4:11; cf. *Inst.* 4.3.2, and the sermon on Deut. 10:8–11 in *CO* 27.27–28 ("when there are no ministers, no men appointed to teach the people, what remains? Only a horrid confusion").

124. *Inst.* 4.1.5. The pastor, as a humble servant of the Word, is God's ambassador and mouth, to be received as an angel and as Christ Himself (*Comm. on Gal.* 4:14), and the pulpit is "the sacred throne of Jesus Christ" ("De scandalis," in *Opuscules,* p. 1187).

125. *Comm. on Hag.* 2:10–14.

126. *OS* 1.414; the passage appears in *Institutio* (1536) and in the Genevan Catechism of 1537.

127. *Comm. on Gal.* 3:1.

128. *Inst.* 1.11.7.

arrival at Geneva, he remarked "there were sermons and that was all."[129] When the number of sermons in the three parish churches rose to seventeen each week,[130] it might have been considered fully adequate. But "whatever may be the opinion of others," Calvin wrote in his French Catechism,[131] "we ourselves do not consider our functions to be so strictly limited that, once we have preached a sermon, our task is finished and we have no more to do but rest. We must take care, much more directly and vigilantly, for those whose blood will be demanded of us, if they perish through our neglect." Though doctrine is "as it were the soul which gives life and vigor to the body,"[132] yet the Christian organism remains incomplete without a nervous system, and "discipline and correction of manners must be considered as the nerves."[133]

Hence the church cannot be defined solely with reference to the Word and sacraments; discipline must be added as the third characteristic note or mark. Inquisitorial and humorless[134] though it may sometimes have been, the Genevan regime was at least a form of self-discipline, collectively imposed,[135] from which no one was exempt. Meeting with opposition and ridicule from the start, it eventually became so acceptable that, in December 1557,[136] the town council was moved to copy the Venerable Company by instituting a quarterly session for mutual criticism. Calvin constantly urged the exercise of patience and mildness,[137] with a "zeal for God" devoid of personal "passions and vengeances."[138] "Each," he said,[139] "should begin with himself. If then I wish to be a good judge of my neighbors to judge their faults, I must know my own and condemn them first." He did no more than develop a system of discipline which existed already in

129. "On preschoit et puis c'est tout" (from his farewell address in Kidd, *Documents*, p. 649).

130. J. Mackinnon, *Calvin and the Reformation* (1936), p. 78.

131. *CO* 5.319; Latin text in *OS* 1.428.

132. "Supplex exhortatio ad Caesarem Carolum quintum" (1543), in *Opuscules*, p. 508.

133. Letter to Somerset, 22 Oct. 1548, in *CO* 13.89; cf. *Inst.* 4.12.1.

134. Details in Mackinnon, *Calvin and the Reformation*, pp. 90ff. and 171; Hunter, *Teaching of Calvin*, pp. 208ff. and 225–26; Doumergue, *Jean Calvin*, vol. 5, p. 328.

135. "There is nothing in greater opposition to the discipline of Christ than tyranny; and the door is wide open to it, if all the power is surrendered to one man" (*Comm. on 1 Cor.* 5:4); "the apostles have transmitted to us a contrary practice" (letter of 27 Aug. 1554 in Hunter, *Teaching of Calvin*, p. 226); cf. *Inst.* 4.11.6.

136. Mackinnon, *Calvin and the Reformation*, p. 163.

137. *Institutio* (1536), chap. 2 (*OS* 1.91); *Inst.* 4.12.8.

138. *CO* 26.553.

139. Ibid., 54.562.

Switzerland.[140] His main achievement was to separate ecclesiastical
from civil jurisdiction, not only because the church as Christ's kingdom must be autonomous,[141] but also because the purpose of her
censures is the amendment of the sinner.[142] Yet the court which inflicted excommunication had a predominantly lay membership,[143] and
this supreme penalty was imposed only as a last resort. The power
of the keys is properly "an embassage of reconciliation,"[144] exercised
not only in all the public ordinances of the church, but also privately
by way of admonition and ghostly counsel, by catechizing and by
regular pastoral visitation,[145] and even by a modified form of the
confessional. When in exile at Strasbourg, Calvin asked his congregation to consult him individually before communicating, and he told
Farel that "he did not think it desirable to abolish confession, unless
it was replaced by what he had just attempted."[146] Although he rejected confirmation from the number of the sacraments, he considered
it proper as a matter of discipline that children should make a public
profession of faith at the age of ten,[147] and he wished this to be sealed
by imposition of hands as "a fitting climax to the catechism."[148] Before
the Lord's Supper could be celebrated, every effort must be made to
secure mutual amity and good-will throughout the neighborhood. The
old Fathers may on occasion have been too severe,[149] but in general
the somewhat rigid discipline of early catholicism was so "holy and
healthful"[150] that it ought to be restored.

Yet again, because the church is in Christ, its *catholicity* is embraced through Him. This does not only mean that it extends throughout all ages and through all the world. Its influence must also be
ubiquitous in the concerns of human life; the scope of its interests
must be as catholic as those of mankind to which it ministers. Calvin's

140. Doumergue, *Jean Calvin,* vol. 2, pp. 223–24.
141. "The spiritual Kingdom of Christ and civil government are entirely distinct"
(*Inst.* 4.20.1).
142. Ibid., 4.11.3.
143. The twelve elders annually appointed by the Small Council are most often
called "comys ou députez par la Seygneurie" (Doumergue, *Jean Calvin,* vol. 5, pp. 170
and 185); cf. Moltmann, *Calvin-Studien,* p. 165, for the responsible place assigned
by Calvin to the laity.
144. *Inst.* 4.1.22.
145. Cf. Hunter, *Teaching of Calvin,* p. 208; J. L. Ainslie, *Doctrines of Ministerial
Order* (1940), pp. 59–60.
146. Doumergue, *Jean Calvin,* vol. 2, pp. 412–13; cf. *Inst.* 3.4.12 and 14 (on the
benefits of private absolution).
147. *Inst.* 4.19.13.
148. Doumergue, *Jean Calvin,* vol. 5, p. 364.
149. *Inst.* 4.12.8.
150. Ibid., 4.19.14.

educational policy made his university an international center of scholarship, with a curriculum to which Jesuits paid the compliment of imitation.[151] At the elementary level, poor children and orphans were provided with free education in the city school.[152] A sort of health service was instituted when Calvin secured the appointment, at public expense, of a physician to attend the poor.[153] In order to check unemployment, he persuaded the council to open a silk factory, and with the purpose of promoting trade, he sanctioned loans at a moderate rate of interest on terms which guarded carefully against abuse.[154] Unlike Luther, who in practice handed poor relief over to the state, Calvin believed that social welfare is properly a concern of the church. It was the consistory, and not the town council, which in 1557[155] sent two of its members to see that the streets of Geneva were kept clean, that chimneys were swept, that fires were not lighted in unsafe places, and that nurses did not sleep with babies in their beds. No one was allowed to be ill for three days without informing his minister, and regular religious services were provided in the prisons.[156] The singing of metrical psalms, some composed by Calvin himself, was comparable to the use of popular folk-music in the liturgy of today. And thus, in its impact upon public life, the Reformed ministry became at least as pervasive as the medieval priesthood had been. Here Calvin's great triumph lay in his revival of the primitive diaconate. An office which during the Middle Ages had degenerated into a mere liturgical adjunct was restored by him to its original function of caring for the sick and poor,[157] and this was the sole sphere of ministry in which he was prepared to find a place for women.[158] If Calvin foreshadowed the Tractarians in his demand for spiritual autonomy, he also anticipated the Christian Socialists through his interest in social welfare.[159]

In one respect he shared the blindness of many of his contemporaries. At a time when Roman missionaries were making a spectacular advance in three continents, he was inclined to leave the heathen to

151. F. W. Kampschulte, *Johann Calvin* (1899), vol. 2, pp. 337–40.

152. Doumergue, *Jean Calvin,* vol. 5, p. 258.

153. Ibid., p. 259; Calvin regretted that the doctor's salary was paid by the state rather than the church.

154. Mackinnon, *Calvin and the Reformation,* p. 276.

155. Hunter, *Teaching of Calvin,* p. 192 note.

156. Kidd, *Documents,* pp. 599–600.

157. Doumergue, *Jean Calvin,* vol. 5, pp. 233ff.

158. Ibid., p. 301. *Inst.* 4.3.9 distinguishes two sorts of deacons, financial agents and welfare workers, the latter of which may include women.

159. Both Newman and Maurice had some personal experience of Calvinism; echoes of it can be traced in their writings, and this common background may help to explain the readiness of later Anglo-Catholics to adopt the "social gospel."

the uncovenanted mercies of God. Reasons of geography and politics combined to hinder missionary work by Protestants; but in 1555 Calvin did appoint two ministers to accompany Coligny's abortive expedition to Brazil,[160] thus initiating the sole foreign mission which non-Romanists attempted in this period.

Otherwise, his outlook was surprisingly modern. It has been said[161] that "because of its very origin Calvinism is an ecumenical movement." Whereas Lutherans and Anglicans drew together into national churches, the followers of Calvin formed an international alliance, reaching out into many lands from the small city of Geneva, and occupying a central position in their churchmanship. Indeed, it is inaccurate to speak of Calvinism at all because, through his efforts for unity, Calvin secured something greater than a merely personal following. He aimed with considerable success at restoring a Reformed but catholic church. Holy communion was so important to him that he desired a weekly or at least frequent celebration.[162] His liturgy is not so far removed from traditional patterns as its bare simplicity might at first suggest.[163] The Apostles' Creed was regularly used by him in public worship, for which he recommended an "appointed form"[164] allowing reasonable flexibility; and without requiring a stronger constraint than that imposed by Scripture,[165] he approved of kneeling for public prayer,[166] together with due observance of decency and order,[167] τὸ πρέπον,[168] in sacred things. He criticized Hooper's refusal to wear episcopal vestments,[169] and to a refugee congregation at Wesel he wrote,[170] "None of us through dislike of a candle or chasuble would wish to separate from the body of the Church." To Cranmer's proposals for a council he replied:[171] "I wish indeed it could be brought about that men of learning and authority from the different churches might meet somewhere, and after thoroughly discussing the

160. Hunter, *Teaching of Calvin*, pp. 159–60.
161. Quoted from O. Noordmans in Moltmann, *Calvin-Studien*, p. 64.
162. *Inst.* 4.17.43–44.
163. Lecerf, *Études Calvinistes*, pp. 46–48.
164. *Inst.* 4.10.27.
165. "The Lord allows us freedom in regard to outward rites, in order that we may not think His worship is confined to those things . . . however . . . He has restricted the freedom . . . in such a way that it is only from His Word that we can make up our minds about what is right" (*Comm. on 1 Cor.* 14:40).
166. *Inst.* 4.10.30.
167. Ibid., 4.10.27.
168. *Comm. on 1 Cor.* 11:2.
169. Letter to Bullinger, March 1551, *CO* 14.74ff.
170. *CO* 15.79–80; and "Lettres Françaises" 1, pp. 420ff.
171. Letter of April 1552, *CO* 14.312ff.; and "Zürich Letters" 1, pp. 21ff.

various articles, should by a unanimous decision hand down to posterity some certain rule of faith . . . drawn up according to Scripture in order to unite widely severed churches." For such a purpose he added that he himself would be ready to cross ten seas. And in a memorandum of 1560[172] he envisaged a really ecumenical council, over which the pope would be welcome to preside on condition that he accepted the authority of Scripture.

Catholicism and Calvinism, according to Hume Brown,[173] are the only two absolute types of Christianity. It would be more accurate to say that there are two types of catholicity, one Roman, one Reformed. They stand in fundamental opposition because of a certain fundamental likeness, for Geneva offered to Rome an alternative which was ultimate and in itself complete. A partial synthesis was indeed achieved by Canterbury, but at the price of creating parties which finally sundered the religious unity of England. And the Anglican genius is rather of the Byzantine type; primarily a way of worship, of ὀρθὴ δόξα, it can become almost a department of the state. Calvin stood closer to the Latin tradition of churchmanship, and on the formal basis of *sola Scriptura,* he sought to realize at least some ideals of the great medieval popes.

172. *CO* 18.286.
173. Hume Brown, *John Knox* (1895), p. 252.

13

The Preached Word as the Word of God

Ronald S. Wallace

Preaching as the Word of God

Calvin takes note of the fact that, in communicating His Word to the children of Israel, God did not normally allow His voice to sound as thunder directly from heaven upon the ears of the assembled people. Usually when He had a word to speak He spoke it through the medium of a prophet, whose speech, however, in the act of speaking, God so closely identified with His own Word that it may be said the mouth of the prophet was the mouth of God Himself. In this case man's speech can really become God's Word in the event of its being communicated to those who are intended to hear it. "The Word *goeth out of the mouth* of God in such a manner that it likewise *goeth out of the mouth* of men; for God does not speak openly from heaven but employs men as his instruments."[1] Commenting on the power of Haggai's word to stir up the people of his day to begin the work of building the temple, Calvin says, "The people received not what they heard from the mouth of mortal men, otherwise than if the majesty of God had openly appeared. For there was no ocular view of God given; but the message of the prophet obtained as much power as though God descended from heaven, and had given manifest tokens of His presence. We may then conclude from these words, that the glory of God

Reprinted from *Calvin's Doctrine of the Word and Sacrament* (Edinburgh: Oliver and Boyd, 1953), pp. 82–95. Used by permission.
    1. *Comm. on Isa.* 55:11 (*CR* 37.291). "Sic egreditur verbum ex ore Dei, ut simul ex ore hominum egrediatur. Nec enim loquitur palam e coelo Deus, sed hominibus tanquam organis utitur."

so shines in His Word, that we ought to be so much affected by it, whenever He speaks by His servants, as though He were nigh to us, face to face."[2]

Today the Word of God is normally heard by men in a similar form, through the word of a man, a preacher of the gospel, called and appointed by God to this task. The task of the preacher of the Word is to expound the Scripture in the midst of the worshipping church, preaching in the expectancy that God will do, through his frail human word, what He did through the Word of His prophets of old, that God by His grace will cause the word that goes out of the mouth of man to become also a Word that proceeds from God Himself, with all the power and efficacy of the Word of the Creator and Redeemer. The word preached by man can become "God speaking." "The Word of God is not distinguished from the word of the prophet."[3] "God does not wish to be heard but by the voice of His ministers."[4]

The task of preaching must therefore be undertaken, and the word of the preacher should be heard, in the expectancy that Christ the Mediator will come and give His presence where the gospel is preached, and cause men to hear His voice through the voice of the minister. On John 10:4, "They know His voice," Calvin says, "Though he speaks here of ministers, yet instead of wishing that they should be *heard* he wishes that God should be *heard* speaking by them."[5] "This ought to add no small reverence to the Gospel, since we ought not so much to consider men as speaking to us, as Christ by His own mouth; for at the time when He promised to publish God's name to men, He had ceased to be in the world; it was not, however, to no purpose that He claimed this office as His own; for He really performs it by His disciples."[6] Christ is the sower who goes forth to sow, in the gospel parable, but this does not mean that the parables of sowing do not at the same time refer also to the sowing of the Word by the ordinary preacher. "When Christ says not that ministers of the Word sow, but that He alone sows, this is not without meaning: for though this

2. *Comm. on Hag.* 1:12 (*CR* 44.95). "Tantundem efficaciae obtinuit prophetae legatio, ac si Deus e coelo descendens dedisset manifesta signa praesentiae suae. Ergo colligere ex his verbis oportet, sic fulgere Dei gloriam in eius verbo, ut perinde affici nos deceat quoties loquitur per servos suos, ac si facie ad faciem nobis esset propinquus."

3. *Comm. on Hag.* 1:12 (*CR* 44.94). "Neque enim hic sermo Dei a prophetae verbis discernitur."

4. *Comm. on Isa.* 50:10 (*CR* 37.224).

5. *Comm. on John* 10:4 (*CR* 47.237). "Deum per ipsos loquentem vult audire."

6. *Comm. on Heb.* 2:11 (*CR* 55.29). "Quod non parum addere debet reverentiae Evangelio: si quidem non tam homines ipsos loqui reputandum est, quam Christum ipsorum ore. . . . Vere hoc per discipulos suos praestitit."

cannot be supposed to be restricted to His person, yet as He makes use of our exertions and employs us as His instruments for cultivating His field, so that He alone acts by us and in us, He justly claims for Himself what is in some respects common to His ministers. Let us therefore remember that the Gospel is preached not only by Christ's command, but by His authority and direction; in short, that we are only in His hand, and that He alone is the author of the work."[7] "Among the many noble endowments with which God has adorned the human race, one of the most remarkable is, that He deigns to consecrate the mouths and tongues of men to His service, making His own voice to be heard in them."[8]

Preaching as a Sign of the Presence of God

"Words are nothing else but signs."[9] Through the preaching of the Word by His ministers, Christ therefore gives His sacramental presence in the midst of His church, imparts to men the grace which the Word promises, and establishes His kingdom over the hearts of His hearers. The preaching of the Word by a minister is the gracious form behind which God in coming near to men veils that in Himself which man cannot bear to behold directly. "He consults our weakness in being pleased to address us after the manner of men by means of interpreters, that He may thus allure us to Himself, instead of driving us away by His thunder. How well this familiar mode of teaching (*familiaris docendi ratio*) is suited to us, all the godly are aware, from the dread with which the divine majesty justly inspires them."[10] "When the prophet says *by the breath of His lips,* this must not be limited to the person of Christ; for it refers to the Word which is preached by His ministers. Christ acts by them in such a manner (*sic enim Chris-*

7. *Comm. on Matt.* 13:37 (*CR* 45.369). "Porro quod Christus non verbi ministros seminare dicit, sed se unum, ratione non caret: quamvis enim ad eius personam hoc restringi minime conveniat, quia tamen nostra opera sic utitur, et ad culturam agri sui tanquam instrumenta nos adhibet, ut per nos solus et in nobis agat, merito sibi vindicat, quod eius ministris quodammodo commune est. Meminerimus ergo, non solum Christi mandato praedicari evangelium sed eius auspiciis et ductu, ut sumus tanquam eius manus, ipse autem unicus operis autor."
8. *Inst.* 4.1.5. "Dignatur ora et linguas hominum sibi consecrare, ut in illis sua vox personet."
9. *Inst.* 4.14.26. "Nihil aliud sunt verba quam signa"; cf. *Comm. on Gen.* 9:12, where Calvin speaks of Word and sacrament together as a "vocal sign."
10. *Inst.* 4.1.5. Cf. sermon on Eph. 4:11–14 (*CR* 51.565). "Quand l'Evangile nous est presché, c'est autant comme si Dieu descendoit à nous, quand il s'accommode ainsi à nostre petitesse."

tus in illis agit) that He wishes their *mouth* to be reckoned as His *mouth,* and their *lips* as His *lips.* "[11]

Christ, therefore, uses the preached word as a means of revelation and self-communication in much the same way as He uses the other signs of His presence and grace in His historic acts of revelation. Thus Calvin can refer to preaching as a token of the presence of God, and as a means whereby He comes near to us. "The Lord is said to 'come' when He gives any token of His presence. He approaches by the preaching of the Word, and He approaches also by various benefits which He bestows upon us."[12] In another place he takes note of the fact that Paul (in Rom. 10:8) equates God's being *near* to the preaching of the gospel.[13] Preaching is the means whereby the gifts of Christ are conveyed to us. "The voice which is in itself mortal, is made an instrument to communicate eternal life."[14] "God has ordained His Word as the instrument by which Jesus Christ, with all His graces, is dispensed to us."[15]

Preaching as the Instrument of Christ's Rule

Preaching is, moreover, a means whereby Christ establishes His rule in the hearts of His people. On the verse, "He hath placed in my mouth a sharp sword," Calvin says, "Christ hath therefore been appointed by the Father, not to rule, after the manner of princes, by the force of arms, and by surrounding Himself with other external defenses, to make Himself an object of terror to His people; but His whole authority consists in doctrine, in the preaching of which He wishes to be sought and acknowledged."[16] David ruled over his earthly kingdom by a golden scepter and sword of iron, but "how Christ designs to rule in His Church, we know; for the scepter of His kingdom is the

11. *Comm. on Isa.* 11:4 (*CR* 36.240).
12. *Comm. on Isa.* 50:2 (*CR* 37.216–17).
13. *Comm. on Isa.* 55:6 (*CR* 37.288); cf. sermon on Deut. 4:6–10 (*CR* 26.132). "Quand nous venons au sermon . . . nous ne pouvons point recevoir un seul mot qui nous soit publié et annoncé en son nom, que sa Maiesté ne soit presente, et que nous ne soyons devant lui."
14. *Comm. on 1 Peter* 1:25 (*CR* 55.231). "Vox quae per se mortua est, vitae aeternae sit organum."
15. *OS* 1.505. "Comme instrument, par lequel Jesus Christ, avec toutes ses grâces nois soit dispensé."
16. *Comm. on Isa.* 49:2 (*CR* 37.191). "Totum eius imperium consistit in doctrina, in cuius praedicatione quaeri atque agnosci vult."

Gospel."[17] "Christ does not otherwise rule among us than by the doctrine of the Gospel."[18]

Calvin does not stop even here in his assessment of the function of preaching. He makes the final claim that preaching is such a mighty instrument in the hand of the Lord that through its means not only does Christ create and uphold and rule His church, but also in a hidden way directs the whole course of history and creates the disturbance amongst the nations that is to bring about the consummation of His eternal purpose. Preaching is the *banner which shall stand for an ensign to the peoples.* "We know that this was fulfilled by the preaching of the gospel, and indeed was more illustrious than if Christ had soared above the clouds."[19] Preaching establishes the kingdom of God far and wide wherever the disciples of Jesus go and proclaim His Word. Replying to the apostles' question about the manner and time of the coming of the kingdom, Jesus simply turned their thoughts towards their appointed task of preaching the gospel. "For hereby He meant to drive out of His disciples the fond and false imagination which they had conceived of a terrestrial Kingdom, because He shows them briefly, that the Kingdom consists in the preaching of the Gospel. . . . They heard that Christ reigns whenever He subdues the world to Himself by the preaching of the Gospel."[20]

Preaching is not only the scepter by which Christ rules within His church but also the sword in the hand of the church by which secretly and unknown even to itself the church rules or brings judgment amongst the nations. "As to the Church collective, the sword now put in our hands is of another kind, that of the Word and Spirit, that we may slay for a sacrifice to God those who formerly were enemies, or again deliver them over to everlasting destruction unless they repent (Eph. 6:7). For what Isaiah predicted of Christ extends to all who are His members. 'He shall smite the wicked with the Word of His mouth and shall slay them with the breath of His lips' (Isa. 11:4)."[21] Thus

17. *Comm. on Hos.* 1:11 (*CR* 42.221).

18. *Comm. on Mic.* 4:3 (*CR* 43.348); cf. *Comm. on Ezek.* 17:24 (*CR* 40.420); *Comm. on Isa.* 11:4 (*CR* 36.238). In his sermon on Deut. 7:5-8 (*CR* 26.514-16), Calvin shows that through the preached Word the church is continually called, sanctified, reformed, and held together in unity.

19. *Comm. on Isa.* 11:10 (*CR* 36.244).

20. *Comm. on Acts* 1:8 (*CR* 48.10). "Hac enim voce falsam de regno terreno imaginationem excutere voluit discipulis: quia breviter significat, in evangelii praedicatione consistere. . . . Audiunt tunc regnare Christum, ubi per evangelii doctrinam sibi mundum subiugat."

21. *Comm. on Ps.* 149:9 (*CR* 32.440). "Quantum ad totum ecclesiae corpus spectat; alius nunc gladius nobis datur in manum, verbi scilicet, ac spiritus, quo mactemus Deo in sacrificium qui prius fuerant hostes: vel etiam quo eos tradamus

Calvin applies many of the Old Testament prophecies of the rule of the Messiah amongst the nations to the preacher of the Word, for he regards Christ as acting in this world mainly through the instrument of the preached Word. "This is why Jesus Christ spoke so often of the Gospel, and called it the Kingdom of God. For unless we adhere to it, we are rebels against God, and are banished from all His benefits. For we cannot participate in these until we are reformed. . . . In fact, since apart from this the Devil dominates everything, on account of which he is also called the 'King of this World,' so when Jesus Christ causes His Gospel to be preached in a country, it is as if He said, 'I want to rule over you and be your King.' "[22]

Calvin claims for preaching even the function of renewing the whole fallen creation. He gives his views on this matter in his application of Isaiah 51:16, "That I may plant the heavens," that is, restore all things to proper order. "Heaven and earth are said to be restored by the doctrine of salvation; because *in Christ,* as Paul says, *are collected all things that are either in heaven or earth.* . . . Since, therefore, the whole face of the world is disfigured . . . there are good grounds for saying that godly teachers renovate the world. . . . Thus, the *heavens* are said to be *planted and the earth to be founded* when the Lord establishes the Church by the Word."[23]

The Preached Word Effective to Accomplish Its Commands and Promises

Calvin has such an exalted view of the importance of preaching in the church and world that he regards the Word of God as always mighty in power to effect what God promises or commands, even though that Word may be uttered through the frail human words of the preacher. God's Word cannot be divorced from His action. "He calls God true, not only because He is ready to stand faithfully by His promises, but also because whatsoever He says in words He fulfils the same in deed; for He so speaks that His command immediately becomes His act."[24] Isaac blessed Jacob "as the authorized interpreter

---

in aeternum exitium nisi resipiscant." Cf. his sermon on Job 4:7–11 (*CR* 33.195). "Il ne faut point que Dieu ait grand equippage quand il est question de reprimer ceux qui sont ainsi revesches . . . qu'il souffle seulement, et voilà tout abbatu . . . ses ennemis sont confondus par sa simple Parole qui est comme un souffle."

22. Sermon on Acts 1:1–4 (*CR* 48.598).

23. *Comm. on Isa.* 51:16 (*CR* 37.237). "Coelum et terra salutis doctrina instaurari dicantur: quoniam in Christo colliguntur omnia, quae aut in coelis aut in terra sunt, ut etiam ait Paulus . . . Ergo quum horribilis dissipatio totam mundi speciem deformet, non abs re dicuntur pii doctores mundum renovare, ac si Deus eorum manu coelum et terram de integro formaret."

of God, and the instrument employed by the Holy Spirit." He later found out that he had been deceived, but he could not go back on the word of blessing he had spoken, for it had been God's Word and had been efficacious in bringing into being what had been promised. "Behold I have made him lord," said Isaac. "He claims a certain fire and efficacy for his benediction," says Calvin in his comment, and then he adds, "In this way *they* are said to remit sins, who are only the messengers and interpreters of free forgiveness."[25]

Thus when God speaks through the mouth of the preacher offering forgiveness, those who hear the Word in faith are there and then really absolved from their sins, for the Word effects what it declares. "Christ puts forth His power in the ministry which He has instituted, in such a manner that it is made evident that it was not instituted in vain . . . for He is not separated from the minister, but on the contrary His power is declared efficacious in the minister."[26] "Christ through our instrumentality illuminates the minds of men, renews their hearts, and in short regenerates them wholly."[27] "I will hear what God the Lord will speak, for He will speak peace to His people," says the psalmist, and Calvin comments, "The Psalmist might have spoken more plainly of divine providence, as for example 'I will look to what God will do,' but as the benefits bestowed upon the Church flow from the divine promises he makes mention of God's *mouth* rather than of His *hand*."[28] "The voice of God is . . . living and conjoined with effect";[29] "a powerful instrument for communicating strength";[30] "nothing that has come out of God's holy mouth can fail in its effect."[31]

Calvin seldom refers to the preaching of the gospel without speaking of it in such exalted language and without exhorting his readers to prize beyond all other gifts of God to the church this incomparable

---

24. *Comm. on Rom.* 3:4 (*CR* 49.48). "Deum veracem dicit non modo quia bona fide stare promissis paratus sit, sed quoniam opere implet quidquid loquitur: siquidem dicit, ut imperium mox quoque fiat opus."

25. *Comm. on Gen.* 27:37 (*CR* 23.381). "Iterum notanda est loquutio qua suae benedictioni Isaac certam vim et effectum asserit, ac si in eius voce inclusum fuisset imperium. . . . Sic remittere peccata dicuntur, qui tantum gratuitae veniae nuncii sunt ac interpretes."

26. *Comm. on 1 Cor.* 3:7 (*CR* 49.351). "Sic in ministerio a se instituto potentiam suam exserit Christus, ut appareat, non frustra fuisse institutum . . . neque enim ipse separatur a ministro, sed potius vis eius in ministro efficax praedicatur."

27. *Comm. on 2 Cor.* 3:6 (*CR* 50.40). "Christus per nos mentes illuminat, renovat corda, totos denique homines regenerat."

28. *Comm. on Ps.* 85:9 (*CR* 31.788).

29. *Comm. on 1 Thess.* 1:4 (*CR* 52.142). "Vivam et cum effectu coniunctam." Calvin in this context speaks of "spiritualem doctrinae energiam."

30. *Comm. on Isa.* 35:4 (*CR* 36.592). "Nisi enim efficax esset organum huic vigori inspirando."

31. *Comm. on Isa.* 34:16 (*CR* 36.588).

treasure set in our midst by the grace of God, for it is the Word which is *able to save* the human soul. "It is a high eulogy on heavenly truth, that we obtain through it a sure salvation; and this is added, that we may learn to seek and love and magnify the Word as a treasure that is incomparable."[32] For, he reminds us, "The Gospel is not preached that it may only be heard by us, but that it may as a seed of immortal life, altogether reform our hearts,"[33] and "as often then as God's fatherly love towards us is preached, let us know that there is given to us ground for true joy, that with peaceable consciences we may be certain of our salvation."[34]

The Preached Word Effective Only in the Freedom and Power of the Holy Spirit

It must be emphasized, however, in this discussion on the preached Word of God, that the word of the preacher can become the Word of God only through a sovereign and free act of the Holy Spirit, by whose power alone preaching can be effective. "Saving is not ascribed to the word, as if salvation is conveyed by the external sound of the voice, or as if the office of saving is taken away from God and transferred elsewhere."[35] "The work of the Spirit, then, is joined to the Word of God. But a distinction is made, that we may know that the external word is of no avail by itself, unless animated by the power of the Spirit. . . . All power of action, then, resides in the Spirit Himself (*resident igitur penes ipsum spiritum omnis agendi virtus*), and thus all power ought to be entirely referred to God alone."[36] "The whole power of ministers is included in the Word — but in such a way, nevertheless, that Christ must always remain Lord and Master."[37] Preaching may thus fail to be the Word of God. The act may remain on a merely human level throughout, in which case the preacher with all his eloquence and skill and fervor will accomplish nothing. When Paul calls himself a minister of the Spirit "he does not mean by this that the grace of the Holy Spirit and His influence were tied to his preach-

32. *Comm. on James* 1:21 (*CR* 55.394).
33. *Comm. on 1 Peter* 1:23 (*CR* 55.229).
34. *Comm. on John* 15:11 (*CR* 47.345).
35. *Comm. on James* 1:21 (*CR* 55.394). "Non in hunc finem, servandi vis sermoni adscribitur, quasi aut salus in externo vocis sonitu inclusa foret, aut servandi munus Deo ablatum, alio transferretur."
36. *Comm. on Ezek.* 2:2 (*CR* 40.62).
37. *Comm. on 2 Cor.* 10:8 (*CR* 50.118). "Tota ministrorum potestas in verbo est inclusa, ut semper nihilominus maneat Christus solus Dominus et Magister."

ing so that he could whenever he pleased breathe forth the Spirit along with the utterance of the voice. . . . It is one thing for Christ to connect His influence with a man's doctrine (*adiungere suam virtutem*), and quite another for the man's doctrine to have such efficacy of itself. We are then, *ministers of the Spirit*, not as if we held Him enclosed (*inclusum*) within us, or as it were captive (*captivum*), not as if we could at our pleasure confer His grace upon all."[38] "God sometimes connects Himself with His servants and sometimes separates Himself from them: . . . He never resigns to them His own office."[39] "When God separates Himself from His ministers, nothing remains in them."[40]

The Relationship Between Man's Speech and God's Word

In the event of God's "connecting Himself" thus with the preacher, to make his act of speaking the effective Word of the Lord, a relationship is set up between the human act of the preacher and the divine action of grace which we may call a sacramental union. The nature of this relationship can be . . . fully [explored only in a discussion] of sacraments. . . . However, these points may be noted: when God graciously comes to give His presence and power along with the human word, there is the closest identity between the divine and human actions. "The Word of God is not distinguished from the words of the prophet."[41] "He is not separated from the minister."[42] "God Himself who is the author is conjoined with the instrument, and the Spirit's influence with man's labor."[43] So close is this identity that the preacher can actually be called a *minister of the Spirit* and his work spoken of in the most exalted terms.[44] Indeed it may legitimately be said that it is the preacher who effects what is really effected by God. But even when all this happens there must remain at the same time the sharpest distinction between what is divine and what is human in this mysterious event. "We require to distinguish . . . we must set the Lord on

38. *Comm. on 2 Cor.* 3:6 (*CR* 50.40). "Non intelligit, gratiam spiritus sancti ac vim suae praedicationi esse alligatam: ut quoties libuerit, una cum voce spiritum e gutture proferat."

39. *Comm. on Mal.* 4:6 (*CR* 44.497). "Aliquando coniungit se Deus cum servis suis: aliquando autem ab illis se separat. Dum se coniungit, transfert ad eos quod apud ipsum tamen residere non desinit. Neque enim suas partes illis resignat."

40. Ibid.; cf. also *Inst.* 4.1.6.

41. *Comm. on Hag.* 1:12 (*CR* 44.94).

42. *Comm. on 1 Cor.* 3:7 (*CR* 49.351).

43. *Comm. on 1 Cor.* 9:1 (*CR* 49.438). "Deus ipse autor cum instrumento, et vis spiritus cum hominis opera coniungitur."

44. *Comm. on 1 Cor.* 3:7 (*CR* 49.350).

one side and the minister on the other. We must view the minister as one that is a servant, not a master — an instrument, not the hand; and in short as man, not God."[45]

The Preached Word Effective to Condemn Where It Is Not Received in Faith

It must be emphasized that when the Word of God comes through preaching its effectiveness does not depend on the receptiveness of the hearer (though the nature of its effect may be so determined). As against those who dissolved the mystery of God's activity in preaching into a purely internal subjective effect in the hearts of the hearers Calvin says, "Delirious and even dangerous are those notions, that though the internal word is efficacious, yet that which proceeds from the mouth of man is lifeless and destitute of all power. I indeed admit that the power does not proceed from the tongue of man, nor exists in mere sound, but that the whole power is to be ascribed altogether to the Holy Spirit; there is, however, nothing to hinder the Spirit from putting forth His power in the word preached."[46] "The wickedness and depravity of men do not make the Word to lose its own nature."[47] The power is thus in the Word quite apart from the receptive hearing. "Though the Word of God does not always exert its power on man, yet it is in a manner included in itself (*in se inclusam*), as though He had said, 'If anyone thinks that the air is beaten by an empty sound when the Word of God is preached, he is greatly mistaken, for it is a living thing and full of hidden power (*occultae energiae*), which leaves nothing in man untouched.' "[48] Thus the true preaching of the Word of God, if it does not find a willing response through faith in the hearer, can, instead of bringing blessing and salvation, rouse within men the opposite effect and harden the heart instead of blessing it.

Calvin in his own day had the accusation thrown at him that Christian preaching made the world worse rather than better. He grimly admits a truth that lies in the reproach[49] and gives us the warning: "All who shall labor faithfully in the ministry of the Word will be laid under the necessity of meeting with the same result. We too have

45. Ibid. "Ministrum considerat ut est servus non dominus: ut est organum non manus: ut denique homo est, non Deus." Cf. the sermon on Luke 1:16–18 (*CR* 46.39).
46. *Comm. on Heb.* 4:12 (*CR* 55.51).
47. *Comm. on Matt.* 13:19 (*CR* 45.364).
48. *Comm. on Heb.* 4:12 (*CR* 55.50).
49. Cf. *Comm. on Matt.* 21:45 (*CR* 45.598).

experienced it more than we could have wished. . . . We ought indeed to be deeply grieved when success does not attend our exertions. A part of the blame we ought even to lay on ourselves . . . yet . . . the truth must always be heard from our lips, even though there be no ears to receive it . . . for it is enough for us that we labor faithfully for the glory of God . . . and the sound of our voice is not ineffectual, when it renders the world without excuse. . . . That our faith may not fail, we ought to employ this support, that the office of teaching was enjoined upon Isaiah, on the condition that, in scattering the seed of life, it should yield nothing but death; and that this is not merely a narrative of what once happened, but a prediction of the future kingdom of Christ."[50]

This hardening of the heart against the Word Calvin attributes to the satanic reaction to the inevitable advance of the kingdom of Christ through the preaching of the Word. "Although the elect of God are reduced to submission by means of the Gospel, nevertheless on the other hand we see that the enemies of truth become more proud and more rebellious, so that the world is plunged into conflict, as experience today shows. For while there was no preached Gospel, all the world was without care and at rest. There was little to argue or dispute about. Why? The devil reigned without any question. But since our Lord Jesus Christ has appeared with the pure doctrine of the Gospel see how much closer the skirmishes have become!"[51]

The Twofold Effect of the Preached Word

Thus preaching has a twofold effect. It can either soften or harden the heart. It can either save or condemn the hearer. "The Gospel is never preached in vain, but has invariably an effect, either for life or death."[52] "As the Word is efficacious for the salvation of believers, so it is abundantly efficacious for the condemning of the wicked."[53] Calvin regards Jesus' word to Peter, "whatsoever thou shalt bind on earth shall be bound in heaven, and whatsoever thou shalt loose on earth shall be loosed in heaven," as referring to the office of preaching. "The comparison of the keys is very properly applied to the office of teaching. . . . We know that there is no other way in which the gate of life

50. *Comm. on Isa.* 6:10 (*CR* 35.136).
51. Sermon on Acts 2:1–4 (*CR* 48.629). Cf. the sermon on 1 Tim. 2:3–5 (*CR* 53.155).
52. *Comm. on 2 Cor.* 2:15 (*CR* 50.34). "Nunquam frustra praedicatur quin valeat aut in vitam aut in mortem."
53. *Comm. on Isa.* 55:11 (*CR* 37.292).

is opened to us than by the Word of God; and hence it follows that the key is placed, as it were, in the hands of the ministers of the Word. . . . As there are many who are . . . guilty of wickedly rejecting the deliverance offered them . . . the power and authority to *bind* is . . . granted to ministers of the Gospel."[54] Calvin is, however, careful to add when he speaks in this strain that this negative effect "does not belong to the nature of the Gospel but is accidental."[55] "The doctrine of the Gospel has in its own nature a tendency to edification — not to destruction. For as to its destroying, that comes from something apart from itself — from the fault of mankind."[56] We must thus "always distinguish between the proper office of the Gospel, and the accidental one (so to speak) which must be imputed to the depravity of mankind, to which it is owing, that life to them is turned into death."[57]

Thus it is that it is a fearful thing for men to be confronted with the grace of God offered through the preaching of the Word. Grace can so easily be made by man's decision to show its other side, which is judgment, and can indeed be turned into its very opposite. Through the preaching of the Word the judgment of the world is continually proceeding. In giving their inescapable decision about the Word as it comes through the preacher, men are giving their eternal decision about God. Since the Word is the scepter of Christ's kingdom "it cannot be rejected without treating Him with open contempt. . . . No crime is more offensive to God than contempt of His Word."[58] "The reprobate . . . though not softened, set up a brazen and an iron heart against God's Word, yet . . . are . . . restrained by their own guilt. They indeed laugh but it is a sardonic laugh; for they inwardly feel that they are, as it were, slain; they make evasions in various ways so as not to come before God's tribunal; but though unwilling they are yet dragged there by this very Word which they arrogantly deride; so that they may be fitly compared to furious dogs, which bite and claw the chain by which they are bound and yet can do nothing — they still remain fast bound."[59]

It may be added, in closing, that this twofold effect, which is so

---

54. *Comm. on Matt.* 16:19 (*CR* 45.475). Cf. the sermon on Deut. 4:6–10 (*CR* 26.132). "Quand il veut que sa parolle nous soit preschee, c'est autant comme s'il nous appelloit à soy, et que nous fussions devant son throne, comparoissans là chacun pour soy, afin de rendre compte comme devant nostre Iuge."

55. *Comm. on Matt.* 16:19 (*CR* 45.475).

56. *Comm. on 2 Cor.* 10:8 (*CR* 50.118–19).

57. *Comm. on 2 Cor.* 2:15 (*CR* 50.34). "Semper ergo distinguendum est proprium evangelii officium ab accidentali (ut ita loquar)."

58. *Comm. on Matt.* 10:14 (*CR* 45.279).

59. *Comm. on Heb.* 4:12 (*CR* 55.50).

characteristic of the true Word of God, can act even on its negative side for the benefit of the church and for the spiritual health of the believer. It is through the Word's producing this violent reaction of offense in the hearts of those who are hardened that the life of the church is partly cleansed and those who are not Christ's sheep are by their own choice warded off from the fold. "The pastor ought to have two voices: one for gathering the sheep; and another for warding off and driving away wolves and thieves. The Scripture supplies him with the means of doing both."[60] Moreover, the believer himself must continually be assisted to mortify in himself those natural tendencies that run continually so counter to the Word of God. This mortification is effected by the Word of God, which, even in the heart of the children of God, can slay and subdue and cast out what is evil. . . . "There is a certain vivifying killing of the soul"[61] which continually slays the children of God in order that continually, under the Word of God, they may rise to new life.

---

60. *Comm. on Titus* 1:9 (*CR* 52.412). "Duplex esse vox pastoris debet; altera ovibus colligendis, altera arcendis fugandisque lupis et furibus. Utramque facultatem scriptura suppeditat."

61. *Comm. on Heb.* 4:12 (*CR* 55.50–51). "Est enim (ut diximus) vivifica quaedam occisio animae, quae fit per evangelium."

14

The Sacraments[1]

Wilhelm Niesel

Whereas the fifth article of the *Augustana* reads: "To win such faith God has instituted the order of preaching and has given the gospel and sacraments as means by which He imparts the gift of the Holy Ghost,"[2] Calvin begins his doctrine of the church with the observation that God has instituted "shepherds and teachers in order to instruct His servants by their words" and then continues in characteristic fashion: "Above all He has instituted the sacraments, of which we know in fact that they are efficacious means of grace — means of maintaining and consolidating our faith."[3] The administration of the sacraments is not simply placed in the hands of the pastors as something ancillary to preaching (despite the fact that Calvin re-

Reprinted from *The Theology of Calvin,* trans. Harold Knight. First published in Great Britain in 1956 by Lutterworth Press. Published in the U.S.A. in 1956 by The Westminster Press. Used by permission.

1. Joachim Beckmann, *Vom Sakrament bei Calvin: Die Sakramentslehre Calvins in ihren Beziehungen zu Augustin* (Tübingen, 1926); D. J. Groot, "Het effect van het gebuik der sacramenten voor ongeloovigen volgens Calvijn," *Vox Theol.* 7, pp. 144–49; Jean de Saussure, "La notion réformée des sacrements," *Bull. de la Soc. de l'Hist. du protest. français* 84 (1935): 243–65; W. Boudriot, "Calvins Tauflehre im Licht der katholischen Sakramentslehre," *Ref. Kirchenztg.* 80 (1930): 153f.; Alfred de Quervain, "Der theologische Gehalt von Calvins Taufformular," *Ref. Kirchenztg.* 84 (1934): 261–63; W. Boudriot, "Calvins Abendmahlslehre," *Ref. Kirchenztg.* 79 (1929): 90ff.; Wilhelm Niesel, *Calvins Lehre vom Abendmahl,* 2nd ed. (Munich, 1935); idem, "Das Calvinische Anliegen in der Abendmahlslehre," *Ref. Kirchenztg.* 82 (1932): 49–51; E. Pache, "La sainte cène selon Calvin," *Rev. de Théol. et de Phil.,* n.s. 24 (1936): 179–201; Ernst Pfisterer, "Calvins Stellung zum Krankenabendmahl," *Ref. Kirchenztg.* 85 (1935): 268.

2. *Die Bekenntnisschr. d. ev. luth. Kirche* (Göttingen, 1930), p. 57. I; see esp. Lat. text, "institutum est ministerium docendi evangelii et porrigendi sacramenta."

3. *Inst.* 4.1.1.

gards them alone as having authority to administer the same)[4] but they are stressed as something of particular importance. The focus of church life, that upon which the act of worship depends, is not simply the Word of God proceeding from human lips, but also and above all the sacrament in its objective reality independent of man. Whereas the Word can and must be preached to individuals also, the celebration of the sacrament requires absolutely the presence and the participation of the congregation.[5] It is an act of worship in which the whole community engages, even though the distribution of the sacred elements is entrusted to the servant of the Word alone. Calvin regards the church as essentially a Eucharistic fellowship. "It is certain that a church cannot be regarded as well ordered and governed if the holy meal instituted by our Lord is not often celebrated and well attended."[6]

The Meaning of the Rite

Seeing that Calvin lays such emphasis on the sacrament, we must at once ask what he means by the rite. It is a "token of divine grace towards us confirmed by an outward sign."[7] Hence the Eucharist does not consist only of its earthly species. Rather its fundamental nature is determined by the divine word of promise spoken by Christ when He instituted the service. His word alone lifts the sacramental tokens out of the mass of earthly things which form our material environment. He declares to us for what purpose He has set aside the elements of water, bread, and wine.[8] In themselves and apart from the divine promise of grace these signs mean nothing. No efficacy is inherent in them as such by which they might acquire for us sacramental significance and be of use.[9] In fact it must be said: "If the visible symbols are offered without the Word, they are not only powerless and dead but even harmful jugglery."[10] "What meaning could it have if the whole assembly of the faithful were to pour out a little bread and wine without proclaiming aloud that heavenly truth which says that the flesh of Christ is meat indeed and His blood drink indeed?"[11] Let us

---

4. *Inst.* 4.3.4. It is typical of Calvin's strict idea of the ministry that he definitely disallows baptism by private persons or women (*CR* 45.822). Baptism by women is invalid: *CR* 17.453; 10a.54; cf. 11.625, 706.
5. See *CR* 15.265, and next note.
6. *Inst.* 4.17.43–44.
7. *Inst.* 4.14.1.
8. *Inst.* 4.17.11.
9. *Inst.* 4.14.3.
10. *CR* 9.21.
11. *CR* 9.21ff.

recollect the fact that today Christ reveals His will through the words spoken by men. Thus it is not sufficient that in the celebration of the sacrament His words should be read out. The latter must be interpreted in a sermon,[12] for only the real preaching of the divine promises "leads the people as it were by the hand to those heavenly places which the symbols shadow forth and whither they are intended to guide us."[13] For faith — and just in this connection Calvin stresses the point — comes by preaching.[14] When the promise of God rings out, when a voice from heaven is really heard, when God Himself speaks to man, then faith is made steady, comforted, and strengthened.[15] Thus the certitude of salvation is not grounded in the sacraments in so far as by these we mean earthly signs and tokens.[16] The Word of God alone is the foundation of our faith.[17]

But what is the purpose of outward signs if the Word itself secures our salvation? "Because our faith is slender and weak, it is soon shaken, tottering unsteadily, and finally falls if it is not supported on every side and held upright in every possible way. And so in this respect the merciful Lord according to His unfathomable goodness adjusts Himself to our mode of apprehension: since we are fleshly and ever creep on the earth, cling to the things of sense and think of nothing spiritual, far less understand it, He is not vexed to lead us to Himself precisely by means of these earthly elements, and even holds before us in the things of flesh a mirror of spiritual values."[18] God knows that we are not naturally inclined to seek Him, and hence He confronts us in this earthly world here below which we love so much. Not only does He call us by His Word but He offers us as media tangible, palpable things. In speaking His Word He claims for Himself our faculty of hearing, but through sacramental signs He claims also our other senses,[19] so that we cannot possibly escape His gift. We have seen that in the human word of preaching God condescends to us sinners. In the Eucharist His merciful condescension to the measure of our everyday realities attains its utmost extent. If we refuse His gift in the face of such kindness we are piling a very heavy load of guilt upon ourselves.[20]

12. *Inst.* 4.14.4.
13. Ibid.
14. *Inst.* 4.14.5.
15. *OS* 1.137.
16. *CR* 7.693, 702; 12.728.
17. *Inst.* 4.14.6.
18. *Inst.* 4.14.3; *CR* 6.114; 28.251.
19. *CR* 46.679.
20. Ibid.

These earthly elements — so we have understood — are like a mirror in which we see reflected spiritual values. They have this advantage over the Word that as in plastic art they hold before our very eyes the promises of God.[21] Water, bread, and wine are tokens, figures, and symbols, of what is promised to us in the Word.[22] Of course this does not mean that they should induce in us a mood of pious contemplation. During the celebration of the sacrament they are not merely visible; they are put into operation and in that process exert their due effect upon us. These symbols have a specific purpose. They express to us the promises in such a tangible way that we are as certain of them as if they were before our very eyes.[23] Their role is to seal for us and to make effectual within us God's promise of grace and salvation.[24] Hence Calvin compares the sacramental signs with a seal affixed to an original document in order to confirm its contents.[25] The elements render valid for us and make effective this divine promise.[26] Thus, strictly speaking, we should not say that the tokens authorize and make effectual the promise itself. "The truth of God is sufficiently firm and assured in itself not to require confirmation from any other source than its own authority."[27] It is not the Word of God which in itself requires the service of these earthly things, but *we* need them in view of our ignorance and dullness and weakness. The sacramental signs must plastically represent to us what the words say, in order to arouse in us effective belief.

From this it is clear that the earthly tokens do not possess any intrinsic value. It is not the case that alongside the proclamation of the Word there is another mode of proclamation by signs. Rather it is that from the start the signs gather all their value from their vital connection with the divine promise. They are nothing more than appendices to the Word,[28] or, as Calvin says in commenting on Augustine, "visible words."[29] Their purpose is in the service of the Word to preach the same thing as the latter.

The sacraments have this appointed part to play and it must not be denied. Their task is not simply "to maintain faith but also to increase it." Of course it must be noted that they do not fulfil this

21. *Inst.* 4.14.5.
22. *Inst.* 4.17.1, 11.
23. *Inst.* 4.17.1.
24. *Inst.* 4.17.4; 14.2.
25. *Inst.* 4.14.5.
26. *Inst.* 4.14.3; *CR* 20.423f.
27. *Inst.* 4.14.3.
28. Ibid.
29. *Inst.* 4.14.6.

purpose by means of any power residing within them. In comparison with the divine grace imparted to us they are nothing more nor less than "instrumental causes."[30]

It is just here that Calvin joins issue with the Reformers of Zurich and their friends. Zwingli refused to entertain the notion that faith receives anything through the sacraments. He thought that such a doctrine violated the honor of God and implied a false view of faith. The Holy Spirit alone can generate faith, and it will not do to connect the reality of the Spirit with material things. As far as man is concerned he has everything if he has faith. But if he does not believe, the sacraments cannot help him.[31] Zwingli thinks that the Lord's Supper has merely the significance of enabling the believing congregation through the use of the signs to remember vividly the saving work of God, to confess its faith thereby and vow to pursue a Christian manner of life.[32]

Calvin, of course, admitted that faith is the proper effect of the Holy Spirit. "But instead of the one benefit wrought by God on our behalf which they praise we count precisely three: For first, the Lord teaches and instructs us by His Word; then He confirms our faith through the sacraments; and finally He sheds into our hearts the light of the Holy Spirit, and so opens them to the power of Word and sacrament."[33] We are dependent on this regular channel of hearing and instruction,[34] and are referred to the sacraments which the Lord has instituted for our soul's health,[35] although it is undeniable that God retains the freedom to accomplish His saving work towards man if it so pleases Him without any of these means. This freedom of God does not give us permission to wait for secret inspirations of the Holy Spirit.[36] We must hold fast to the means by which Christ wills to be present with us today. In this connection it is wrong altogether to reject the sacraments as means of grace. Calvin pointed out to Bullinger that "the word of man too is an instrument of God for the promotion of our salvation, although in itself it is just as dead as the sacramental sign."[37] The human word of the preacher as such has no advantage over the earthly element. Neither can it intrinsically help

30. *CR* 7.494.
31. *CR Zwingli* 3.760ff.
32. See my essay "Zwinglis 'spätere' Sakramentsanschauung," *Theol. Blätter* 11 (1932): 12ff.
33. *Inst.* 4.14.8.
34. *CR* 46.679.
35. *CR* 9.29; 15.227.
36. *CR* 9.29.
37. *CR* 7.704.

us. The word of man is an instrument of God in so far as it testifies
to the one Word, and the sacrament is a means of grace inasmuch as
it expresses the word of promise and seals it for us,[38] and both chan-
nels can be of any avail to us only if the Holy Spirit makes them
effectual within us.

But if the revelation of God in flesh implies that Christ wills to act
towards us today through word and sacramental sign, then the second
objection of the Zwinglians falls to the ground. There is no such thing
as a faith that in itself is firm and complete. Faith is utterly dependent
on the word of preaching and the use of the sacraments. Apart from
the means of grace it would not arise within us and remain alive; for
in this world it is threatened on all sides. Calvin reminds us of the
word: "Lord, I believe, help Thou mine unbelief,"[39] and says that the
fact that we are all sinners is sufficient proof of the imperfection of
our faith.[40] Placed as we are in the midst of the temptations and
assaults of this world, we need too just those sacramental means of
grace which God has given us which confirm for us the favor of God
and "in this way support, maintain, consolidate, and increase our
faith."[41]

The Operation of the Sacraments

Having discussed the meaning of the sacraments as expressed in
the words of promise, we must now turn to consider the nature and
effect of the sacraments themselves as implied in the word of promise
and sealed by the signs. Here we come to the heart of the Calvinistic
doctrine of the sacraments, and are faced by the question whether the
sacraments really convey a gift to us or whether they merely exercise
an effect upon our faith — as has mostly been supposed. Anyone who
has the remotest idea of Calvin's teaching about our appropriation of
salvation must know straight away how he answers this question:
"In proportion as by the ministry of the sacraments the true knowledge
of Christ is implanted, strengthened, and increased in us, and in proportion as we attain perfect fellowship with Himself and enjoy the
benefit of His gifts, so is their effect upon us."[42] The operation of the
sacraments depends entirely on the fact that they bring us into relationship with Christ and bind us to Him. For Calvin believes that all

38. Ibid.
39. *Inst.* 4.14.7.
40. Ibid.
41. Ibid.
42. *Inst.* 4.14.16.

spiritual effects have their ground in the one Mediator, and thus can be experienced by us only in so far as we stand in vital relationship with Him.[43]

But this insight does not flow only from the whole system of Calvinistic doctrine; it springs above all from the words of promise which are joined to the sacraments. If in the Last Supper we are told that we must take the body of the Lord, then in fact this means that the Lord is really our Lord; and if we are further told that we must eat it, it means that He becomes fully one with us. The Word of the Lord cannot deceive us falsely. What God says takes effect. Because in the Last Supper a promise of God is declared, we must know that what is promised us will really be conveyed to us "not otherwise than if Christ Himself were present to our view and taken in our hands."[44]

The same applies to the sacramental signs themselves. God does not intend to deceive in them either.[45] Because it is the Lord who has given them to us they are completely different from all other signs in this world. For example, bread and wine do not symbolize to us the presence of Christ as the picture of a man brings the latter visually before us.[46] The material species do not merely suggest to us the spiritual reality in order to strengthen our assurance and faith; they also effectually convey it to us. If the breaking of bread is intended to show forth plainly that we are made participants in the body of Christ, we must not doubt that the Lord truly bestows on us His body.[47] If He causes the visible token to be presented to us, then He gives us also His living body. We are made to share no less truly in His life than in the bread which is put in our mouths.[48] By the symbols of bread and wine the real presence of Christ is conveyed to us.[49] They are not the thing represented, and must be carefully distinguished from the latter; but they are instruments and organs by which the Lord gives us His body and His blood.[50]

Just as certainly as the words and the species of the Lord's Supper do not promise us an accession of vaguely conceived spiritual strength, but rather certify to us our communion with the body and blood of Jesus Christ, so the substance of the meal is the crucified and risen Christ, or "His body and His blood with which He perfected His

43. *OS* 1.507.
44. *Inst.* 4.17.3.
45. *Inst.* 4.17.10; *CR* 12.728.
46. *CR* 49.486.
47. *Inst.* 4.17.10.
48. *CR* 49.486ff.
49. *Inst.* 4.17.11; *CR* 9.30, 182, 195; 29.226.
50. *OS* 508; *CR* 9.17ff.

obedience in order to win righteousness for us."[51] The gift of the Lord's Supper is not therefore the spirit of Christ or His divine nature. Nor does it consist in His human nature as such, but in His humanity in so far as it was given over to death for our sakes.[52] There lies the crux of the matter. The crucified body would, of course, avail us nothing if Christ had not thereby overcome death and passed into eternal glory. For us Jesus Christ is forever the two things — the Crucified and the Risen One. Our salvation depends upon the fact that He is both. But in this connection Calvin avoids speaking of the heavenly or glorified body of Christ.[53] What is in question in the Eucharist is not the imparting of a heavenly substance but communion with the Mediator. This is what Calvin is concerned to express, whether he speaks of the body of the Son of God delivered up for us, or whether in allusion to the Gospel of John he speaks of the flesh of Christ in which for us lies embodied eternal life, so that we have not to seek it in some remote sphere but can find it quite near to us, nearer than hands and feet.[54] Through the Eucharist we truly receive the body and the blood of Christ, and grow with Him into one body, so that He dwells in us and we in Him.[55]

This recognition is the living heart of the Eucharistic doctrine which Calvin develops in the framework of his revelational theology. If anyone supposes that Calvin made such statements only in order to be at one with the Lutherans, let him read what he writes, about the sacramental teaching of à Lasko, to someone like Vermigli to whom he really did not need to prove that his own view of the presence of Christ in the Eucharist was beyond suspicion. In this letter he deplores the fact that the arguments of à Lasko always end up in the assertion " 'that the natural body of Christ is not given us to eat.' As though we could gain life from any other source than the natural body of Christ."[56] If we did not gain communion with the God revealed in flesh, then all would be in vain. With reminiscences of the New Testament, Calvin describes this communion by means of various metaphorical expressions, all of which are meant to express the closeness of the union between Christ and His own. He even compares the communion between Christ and ourselves to the unity of the divine

51. *OS* 5.354; 7.21.
52. *CR* 9.9ff., 188ff.
53. Once in debate with Sadolet: *Inst.* 4.17.11.
54. *Inst.* 4.17.8.
55. *OS* 1.509; *CR* 49.487; 12.728; *Inst.* 4.17.11.
56. *CR* 15.388.

Son with the Father.[57] So important to him is the fact that the whole Christ in His spiritual and also in His bodily reality becomes our own.[58]

For the sake of clarity in exposition we have so far spoken only of the substance and theme of the Lord's Supper, but must now add that for Calvin what is issue in baptism is equally the reality of the same Jesus Christ. "Baptism is the sign of our adoption, of our reception into the communion of the church, so that incorporated in the body of Christ we may be numbered among the children of God."[59] Calvin mentions three gifts which are imparted to us in baptism: forgiveness of our sins, our dying and rising again with Christ, and our communion with the Lord Himself;[60] but the first two of these gifts depend wholly upon the third.

Baptism is symbolical of the fact that we are incorporated in the body of Christ. Christ is the real Subject of baptism.[61] This is the correct view of the matter, although Christ Himself commanded us to baptize in the name of the Father, the Son, and the Holy Ghost. For inasmuch as "we receive the mercy of the Father and the grace of the Spirit only through Christ Himself, we rightly describe Him as the real aim and end of baptism."[62] It is for this reason that according to Calvin the New Testament at times speaks of baptism in the name of Christ alone. "If we wish to summarize the power and inspiration of baptism we name Christ alone."[63]

To sum up: "Christ is the matter or rather the life-blood of all the sacraments."[64] In this respect we must keep well in view the fact that not only the spirit but also the very body of Christ is promised us and must be bestowed upon us through the sacraments. "Although they direct our faith to the whole Christ and not to a mere part of Christ, yet they also teach us that the cause of our righteousness and salvation lies in His flesh; not that a mere man could make us just and spiritually alive, but that it has pleased God to reveal in the Mediator what in Himself lay unfathomably concealed."[65]

57. *CR* 9.31.
58. *Inst.* 4.17.9.
59. *Inst.* 4.15.1.
60. *Inst.* 4.15.1, 5–6.
61. *Inst.* 4.15.6; *CR* 6.119; 9.718; 48.600; 51.407.
62. *CR* 49.318.
63. Ibid.
64. *Inst.* 4.14.16; *CR* 5.437; 6.114; 9.718, 728; 29.414. For the idea of "substance," see Niesel, *Calvins Lehre vom Abendmahl,* pp. 50f.
65. *Inst.* 3.11.9; *CR* 10a.159.

The Effect of the Sacraments

When through the sacraments we attain communion with the Mediator we receive everything which He has gained on our behalf. "We receive a share in the body and blood of Christ, that He may dwell in us and we in Him, and that thus we may enjoy all the benefits of His passion."[66] It must not be overlooked that from Christ who has performed His saving work for us there flows out upon us a decisive effect. We must now consider this in order to give a complete representation of the spiritual reality of the sacraments.

"Baptism testifies to us that we are purified and cleansed, the Eucharist that we are redeemed. The water symbolizes for us the washing away of sins, the blood the satisfaction wrought to redeem us from sin. We find both in Christ who, as John says, came with water and with blood; that means, to cleanse and to ransom."[67] The language of the symbols speaks to us not only about the theme and the meaning of the sacraments but also about the fruit which they are to bear in us. In virtue of the divine institution there exists an analogy between the earthly sign and the thing symbolized in regard to the effect which the sacraments exert upon us.[68] By the water of baptism we are meant to experience that in Jesus Christ we obtain the forgiveness of our sins, by the offering of bread and wine that the body and blood of Christ feed and sustain in us true life.[69]

All this is implied too in the words of promise which are uttered when the sacraments are celebrated. The words of the Eucharist make especially clear to us that Christ did not receive and sacrifice His human body for His own advantage but for our salvation.[70] Hence Calvin, following Luther, says: "It must be carefully noted that the most conspicuous, indeed almost the whole power of the sacrament resides in these words: 'which is given for you,' 'which is shed for you.' For otherwise it would be of no avail that the body and the blood of the Lord should be administered, had they not once for all been sacrificed for our redemption and salvation."[71] Calvin's view of our communion with Christ is far removed from all mysticism of being. The sacraments do not effect our union with divinity as such, but with the Mediator, and we thereby attain the salvation which He has

---

66. *CR* 12.728; *Inst.* 4.17.11; *CR* 9.81, 165.
67. *Inst.* 4.14.21.
68. *Inst.* 4.17.3.
69. *Inst.* 4.17.3.
70. Ibid.
71. Ibid.

won for us by His suffering and death: "Redemption, righteousness, sanctification, and eternal life."[72]

Just as certainly as the question of the effect of the sacraments is not a subsidiary one, since the work of Christ may not be separated from His person, so it must also firmly be believed that "the benefits of Christ would not reach us if He were not from the start willing to bestow His life upon us."[73] He Himself in His person is the substance and the foundation of all other gifts.[74] Without the matter of the sacrament there is no effect, and apart from fellowship with the divine-human Jesus Christ there is no salvation.[75] This teaching discloses the roots of the whole theology of Calvin. If anyone supposes that he expounded such a sequence of ideas only in order to achieve unity with the Lutherans, then he has understood nothing of Calvin.

The Action of the Holy Spirit

The communion with Christ which is assured us and bestowed upon us through the sacraments remains a mystery which we cannot pierce by our understanding nor describe in human speech.[76] Hence Calvin refrained from answering the question how the sacraments can mediate such communion. But he could not ignore what Holy Scripture declares to us on the subject. He observed that the Scriptures always refer to the Holy Spirit in answer to the question how it is possible for us to be united with Christ.[77] The distance between ourselves and Christ, who has really overcome and departed from this world and now dwells in the world of eternity, can be overcome only by an act of God Himself. Such action is effected by the third person of the Holy Trinity, "by the secret and incomprehensible power of the Holy Spirit."[78] By the action of the Spirit Christ condescends to our level and at the same time lifts us up to Himself.[79] By the Spirit our hearts are opened to the penetrating power of Word and sacrament.[80] The Spirit links and unites us with Jesus Christ,[81] so that in body, mind, and soul we become His very own.[82]

72. *Inst.* 4.17.11.
73. Ibid.
74. *OS* 1.508.
75. *CR* 9.88.
76. *Inst.* 4.17.7, 9; *CR* 9.31.
77. *Inst.* 4.17.12; *CR* 16.678.
78. *CR* 16.677, 430.
79. *CR* 16.677; *Inst.* 4.17.24, 16.
80. *Inst.* 4.14.8.
81. *Inst.* 4.17.12, 24.
82. *Inst.* 4.17.12.

Only in this way is it possible that by the word of man and earthly elements we become sharers in the living reality of the Christ. This statement does not mean that Calvin wishes to render accessible to our human understanding the mode of Christ's self-communication to us.[83] The reference to the Holy Ghost is rather to be construed as the recognition of sheer divine miracle.[84]

His teaching is a protest against the idea of the inherence of Christ in the Eucharistic species as such, since it is legitimate to speak of Christ as becoming inherent for us only through word and sign and the power of the Holy Ghost. Two deviations of Lutheran sacramental doctrine are thus avoided.

Firstly: sign and gift of the sacrament are not confused. If we affirm, like the Lutherans, an inherence in the sacraments themselves of the reality they convey, we are violating the glory of the exalted Lord who has really overcome this our world.[85] But more important for Calvin is the fact that the true humanity of Christ is threatened if we suppose that Christ, invisibly omnipresent, corporeally indwells the bread and wine. Certainly the humanity of Christ enjoys pre-eminence through the resurrection[86] but assuredly not that immeasurability which the Lutherans ascribe to it in order to be able to maintain their Eucharistic doctrine.[87] For by glorification a body loses only those characteristics which arise from the corrupt and decadent state of this world, but not such as belong inseparably to its essential being.[88] If we describe the body of Christ in such a way as to cancel out the community between His body and ours, then we are endangering God's self-revelation in our flesh. Calvin said that he quarrelled with the Lutherans only on this ground. Because they substituted a reality of infinite extension for the flesh of Christ, he defended as against them "the truth of the human nature in which our salvation is grounded."[89]

We have already emphasized the fact that Calvin wished to see the symbol and the reality of the sacrament strictly distinguished but not separated from each other. We are bound to the sacraments in virtue of their divine institution. We do not indeed possess Christ in them, but the Holy Ghost bestows Christ upon us not otherwise than through

83. *CR* 16.678.
84. *Inst.* 4.17.24; *CR* 10a.157.
85. *Inst.* 4.17.19, 32.
86. *CR* 9.79f.
87. *CR* 16.429, 677.
88. *CR* 14.333; *Inst.* 4.17.24.
89. *CR* 9.208; 16.678.

Word and sacramental sign. In the church, which gathers around Word and sacrament, we stand face to face with the divine decision upon us. We may not seek it elsewhere because we have no promise that we shall find and receive Christ elsewhere.

It must, of course, be observed that the connection between sign and reality which Calvin asserts is not only nonspatial but also non-temporal in our sense of the words.[90] When the sacramental rite is completed, at that moment the sacramental gift is imparted, as certainly as God is true and His Word and sign do not lie. But the connection of sign and thing signified is grounded solely in the Holy Ghost.[91] The expression "at that moment," as far as this connection is concerned, implies a divine reality. The divine moment in which the Holy Ghost fulfils His action of rendering effectual to us the ministry of the signs is not interchangeable with the earthly moment of the completion of the sacramental rite. The divine moment can — humanly speaking — be situated before or after the celebration of the sacrament.[92] Also it outlasts this action.[93]

Secondly, Calvin objects to the idea of a natural physical assimilation of the life-giving reality of the sacrament by the communicants. If a spatio-physical connection exists between the reality and the sacrament which embodies it, the same connection necessarily exists also between the reality and the sign on the one hand and the communicant on the other. The latter is implied in the former. In that case the reception of the body and blood of Christ takes place through the mouth in physical fashion[94] and a fusion of the underlying reality of the Eucharist with the communicants is an unavoidable thought. But this idea must be rejected;[95] for everything depends on this — that if Jesus Christ the God-man is to help us, then in His union with us He must remain what He is. In spite of the emphasis which Calvin places on the communion of the whole Christ with us, he is strictly concerned to note that there must be a distinction between Christ and ourselves. Hence he says: "It is enough for us that Christ out of the substance of His flesh brings life to our souls, indeed pours out His own life into us, although the flesh of Christ itself does not enter into us."[96]

Let us note well that Calvin contrasts this point with the assertion

90. *CR* 7.704; 9.29.
91. *CR* 48.180.
92. *CR* 9.118.
93. *CR* 9.232ff.
94. *CR* 9.187, 183; *Inst.* 4.17.33.
95. *CR* 15.388; *Inst.* 4.17.32.
96. *Inst.* 4.17.32. Thus also is to be understood the passage in the first *Institutes* (*OS* 1.142) which does not appear in the later editions.

that the body of Christ is received directly by us through our mouth. He does not by any means intend in all this to cancel his fundamental thesis that we really receive through the Eucharist the true body and blood of Christ. But it is just that we receive it by the agency of the Holy Ghost, which means that we are united with Christ but not fused with Him. The Holy Spirit guides us and preserves us as an integral personality. The fellowship with the divine which He procures is real fellowship and not fusion. "Christ in His body is far from us, but by His Spirit He dwells within us and draws us upwards to Himself in the heavens in such wise that He pours out upon us the life-giving power of His flesh."[97] Christ is the gift of God to us and not a given power of which we can avail ourselves as we please. After His ascension He is not simply there for us but He comes to His own as their Lord. This implies too that Calvin rejects the doctrine of the enjoyment of the body and blood of Christ by the unworthy. This doctrine is a necessary consequence of the idea that we receive Christ directly through our lips, and shows very plainly its untenability. What sort of Christ is that which in the opinion of the Lutherans even unbelievers receive through the Eucharist? Is He not a dead thing? But with Christ dwells always His life-giving Spirit.[98] If Christ is bestowed upon a man, it cannot be other than that at the very heart of this world of unbelief faith arises and goes on increasing. Because the living Lord in His sovereign ascendancy is the gift of the Eucharist, the saving effects of the rite cannot be separated from this gift. It is impossible that the unworthy should really receive Christ in the Eucharist.

This does not mean that the validity and efficacy of the sacrament are dependent upon man. What the words and the sacramental signs of the Lord declare to us is and remains true. "The Lord intends the bread as His body to be there for all."[99] "Christ with His gifts of grace is offered to all in the same way, and the truth of God remains unaffected by the unfaithfulness of men, so that the sacraments always retain their power."[100] In fact, Calvin can go so far as to say "that the body and blood of Christ are as truly given to the unworthy as to the elect faithful of God."[101] But when this happens to the godless, it is like rain pouring over a rock. The result of their hardness of heart is that divine grace does not penetrate their being. They are not worthy

97. *CR* 9.33.
98. *Inst.* 4.17.33.
99. *CR* 16.678.
100. *CR* 7.719; 49.74.
101. *Inst.* 4.17.33.

to receive so precious a gift.[102] In other words, Christ passes them by and does not cause His Spirit to move within them in the way in which it accomplishes its work on the elect of God, incorporating them into Christ. The doctrine of Calvin preserves the objectivity of the sacrament on which the Lutherans set so much store; but he distinguishes it from the objectivity of a thing[103] by exalting the sovereign freedom of the Lord who in Word and sign wills to bestow Himself upon us by the working of His Spirit. By the preaching of the gospel and the use of the sacraments the Holy Ghost as it were bridges the gulf between Jesus Christ and ourselves. Just as certainly as Calvin objects to a fusion of the sacramental gift with the communicants themselves, so here again he has no intention of teaching a reception which is not based on an inward spiritual relation. He wishes to distinguish but not to separate. If the Holy Spirit accomplishes His work, the receptive faculty of faith is created and strengthened in us:[104] for we ourselves are intrinsically incapable of receiving Jesus Christ into ourselves. Neither our soul nor our physical lips are capable of receiving the Lord who died and rose again for us. Christ Himself must by His Spirit open our hearts to His coming. This accessibility to Himself which He creates is called faith. But Calvin draws our attention to the fact that faith is not the reception of Christ, the eating and drinking of His body and blood itself.[105] Receiving the gift of Christ means not only that by the power of the Holy Spirit our hearts are turned towards Him, but that we receive life-giving fellowship with Him.[106] The Holy Spirit creates within us the relationship to Christ which we describe as faith, but He also crowns faith with that which consummates it.[107] The establishment of a relation between Christ and ourselves cannot take place apart from a relation at the deepest level of being. Our faith as such is always an empty vessel, but the Holy Spirit which creates and strengthens it through Word and sacrament imparts to it in so doing its true content: Jesus Christ. That content leaves no part of our being untouched. Body and soul we become united with Christ.[108]

Calvin said that he clung to his particular form of sacramental doctrine not from obstinacy but because he believed himself to be

102. *CR* 16.678; 7.719.
103. *Inst.* 4.17.33.
104. *Inst.* 4.14.7.
105. *Inst.* 4.17.5.
106. *Inst.* 4.17.5, 11; *CR* 9.75.
107. *Inst.* 4.17.5.
108. *Inst.* 4.17.12; *CR* 9.208.

bound by the authority of Scripture.[109] In defining his doctrine by contrast with that of the Lutherans he has no wish to cast doubt upon the fact that the Christ who died and rose again for us is the essential gift of the Eucharist. By his differentiations from the Lutheran doctrine he secures precisely the truth that the very body and blood of Jesus Christ are bestowed upon us in that sacred rite.

109. *CR* 16.430.

15

Calvin
and Civil Government

John T. McNeill

True wisdom, says John Calvin at the beginning of his *Institutes,* consists in the knowledge of God and of ourselves. God is to be known in His work of creation and redemption. He is revealed inadequately through nature and reason, adequately and authoritatively through the Scriptures, which are His authentic utterance. He is clothed with majesty and sovereign power, yet "he allures us to himself by his mercy." Man, enfeebled by sin, rises to his true life by God's undeserved grace, and finds his liberty in a voluntary obedience to God. Throughout his writings Calvin stresses his unwavering belief that the high Sovereign of the universe is also intimately present in the world of mankind. He sees God's hand in all historical events, and never doubts that in our personal affairs and choices we have "dealings with God" all the days of our life (*in tota vita negotium cum Deo*).

We cannot understand the political element in Calvin's teaching, any more than in the teaching of St. Paul or St. Augustine, without being aware that it hangs upon his scriptural conception of the relation of God to man and of the consequent obligation of man to man. He has numerous points in common both with Aquinas and with Marsiglio; but he is less indebted to Aristotle and more insistently scriptural than either of these contrasting medieval interpreters of government.

The dealings with God to which Calvin refers include far more than acts of worship and contemplation. The Calvinist piety embraces all the day-by-day concerns of life, in family and neighborhood, edu-

Reprinted from John Calvin, *On God and Political Duty,* ed. John T. McNeill, The Library of Liberal Arts (Indianapolis: Bobbs-Merrill, 1956), pp. vii–xxv. Used by permission.

cation and culture, business and politics. These are for Calvin realms of duty in which men ought so to act as to honor God and benefit their fellows. Calvin's awe-stricken consciousness of God carries with it no indifference to mundane matters. Rather it demands the most intense participation in the common affairs of men. If, in Aristotle's phrase, man is a "political animal," he is in Calvin's view not less but more political when he is motivated by religion. Calvin is repelled, and even appalled by the type of sectarian spirituality that would desert the sphere of politics as beneath the spiritual man's plane of living. More emphatically than most theologians, he calls for active and positive political behavior.

The Letter to Francis I

Calvin wrote no extended formal treatise on government. His utterances on the subject are incidental, but they represent a continuous, thoughtful interest in political matters. The [references we will discuss cover a] period of about twenty-five years. In the first of these he is addressing the greatest monarch of his time. In the last he is applying principles of political duty to a royal figure portrayed in an Old Testament book. He shows in the other selections political interests that go far beyond the topic of kingly authority and duty. His own age, and his immediate environment in Geneva, offered for consideration the phenomena of government by elective assemblies. Calvin is not so naive as to suppose that political salvation comes from the adoption of any mere structure of government, but his decided preference is for some type of government in which citizens in general share responsibility.

"Shakespeare loves a king," but Calvin rarely mentions one with admiration. It is true that in passages of his works he shows a high regard for biblical kings who are approved by the Scripture writers. His warmest praise of King David is associated, however, with his belief that David was the author of that matchless treasury of devotion, the Book of Psalms. His approach to contemporary kings was respectful but far from subservient; he always assumes the role of a counsellor rather than of a mere suppliant. He wrote numerous letters to the crowned heads of nations and to others in positions of power, seeking to move them to adopt a tolerant attitude toward their Protestant subjects, or urging them to action in the reform of the church in their domains. The earliest and most notable of these is the letter to Francis I of France, which serves as an introduction to the *Institutes of the Christian Religion.* It was written in August 1535. The first edition of this work was then about to go to the Basel printer, Thomas Platter; it appeared in March of the following year.

The letter offers a defense of the French Protestant minority, then subjected to persecution, against the charges of heresy and sedition. Early in the document we come upon statements of Calvin's fundamental ideas concerning the duties of kings, and in fact of all who bear rule. It belongs to true royalty for a king to acknowledge himself "the minister of God." Where the glory of God is not the end of government there is no legitimate sovereignty, but usurpation. The kingship of Christ is over all earthly dominion. One is reminded here of a celebrated passage in Augustine's *City of God* (5.24), oft quoted by medieval authors and known as the "Mirror of Princes," where the great African Father observes that in the Christian view those emperors are happy who "make their power the handmaid of God's majesty."

The significance of this letter lies not only in its vehement defense of the cause to which Calvin was attached and assertion of its right to the king's recognition, but also in the fact that the young scholar ventured thus boldly to admonish the proud and absolute monarch of a great nation. Aroused by the sufferings of his fellow believers, Calvin charges with "falsehoods, artifices, and calumnies" the inspirers of persecution who have gained influence over the king. He derives his munitions from the arsenal of Scripture and from the writings of the church fathers. His attack is merciless; it is with no tolerant spirit that he demands toleration. By implication [Calvin denounces the king himself for] the policy of "extermination" which the government of France has apparently instituted. We do not know that Francis ever saw the letter; if he did, his policy was not affected by it. Calvin's passionate vehemence was less likely to be effective than a more moderate plea might have been. There were more prudent and balanced statements within the book itself in which we discern the outlines of his political doctrine. But the letter to Francis gave startling evidence that Calvin and his followers regarded all rulers as subject to criticism from the standpoint of scriptural religion.

[We turn now to two chapters from the final edition (1559) of the *Institutes* (3.19; 4:20).]

Christian Freedom

Substantially the first of these texts ["Christian Freedom"] is contained in the final chapter of the 1536 edition.[1] Calvin was about

1. Chapter 6, *"De libertate christiana, potestate ecclesiastica et politica administratione."* In Peter Barth's edition, *Joannis Calvini opera selecta* (*OS*), vol. 1 (Munich, 1926), this long chapter occupies pages 223–80.

twenty-six years old when he completed the writing of the first edition, but his thought was already so mature in this field that he found little occasion to alter or expand this passage in his later editions. The same statements hold for the second selection ["Civil Government"], with the qualification that considerable additional matter of some interest was introduced, chiefly in the last edition. The structure of the work as a whole was materially altered in the series of revisions, and it was extended to five times its original size. While in the first edition the two topics here treated were separated only by a section on "ecclesiastical power," they appear in separate books of the final edition, and the materials inserted between them comprise no less than twenty-five chapters. Moreover, these are now set in different main divisions of the treatise. Despite the fact that in the enlarged *Institutes* our two selections have been widely separated and placed under different general headings,[2] they still bear references to one another, and the student will do well to remember that in their original form the relationship between them was made obvious in the organization of the work.

In the chapter on liberty, Calvin is largely concerned with the topic of conscience. Man stands helpless before the divine law, since the law condemns all imperfections. From this unhappy state God calls men "with paternal gentleness" into the liberty of faith. Man's good actions arise in glad response to this call, as children respond to a kind father. All the good works of the patriarchs referred to in the Epistle to the Hebrews are there said to be done through faith. It is important that we should be aware that we have liberty of choice with regard to external matters of the class of *adiaphora,* things morally indifferent. If this assurance is lacking, conscience may be entrapped into a course of meaningless cumulative self-punishment, and be led to despair. Yet for Calvin the things indifferent are not to be used in ways that escape moral restraint. Ivory and gold, music, good food and wine are to be enjoyed without excess and without pride or covetousness. Christian liberty is thus opposed both to unwholesome asceticism and to irresponsible indulgence. It requires that, like St. Paul, we shall know "how to be abased and how to abound," and that we avoid offending the scruples of others. It may involve, for example, abstinence from flesh on Fridays in deference to our neighbor's conscience.

2. Book 3 of this edition is entitled, "On the Manner of Receiving the Grace of Christ, the Benefits Which We Derive from It, and the Effects Which Follow It." Book 4, which concludes with the chapter "Civil Government," bears the title: "The True Church, and the Necessity of Our Union with Her, Being the Mother of All the Pious."

Thus conscience is by no means merely an individual matter; it must be exercised with consideration for other men's consciences, where no imperative duty is thereby infringed. On the other hand, we must not by yielding too much "fortify the conscience of our neighbor in sin." Calvin's rule is that we are to assert or restrict our liberty in accordance with charity and a due regard for the welfare of our neighbor (*studendum charitati et spectanda proximi aedificatio* [3.19.12]).

Calvin here introduces the question of obligation to political authority. He warns against the error of supposing that since the Christian's conscience is set free by faith, he may disregard this obligation. But man stands under a double government (*duplex in homine regimen* [3.19.15]): spiritual and political; these require to be separately considered. Calvin first examines in connection with "spiritual government" the meaning of the word *conscience,* "a kind of medium between God and man," which "places man before the Divine tribunal." He insists on the principle that conscience, in the strict sense of the term, is directed to God, not to human laws. The nature of obligation to public law and government concerns the relations among men on the temporal level, which are discussed later, in book 4, chapter 20.

The Duties of Magistracy

This chapter (4.20) is Calvin's most systematic statement on government, and summarizes his entire thought on the subject. Again he distinguishes the two realms, of the spiritual and the temporal, and confines the liberty of the gospel to the former. On the other hand, he protests against the notion that civil government is a polluted thing with which Christians have nothing to do. The political state has, indeed, functions directly connected with religion. It protects and supports the worship of God, promotes justice and peace, and is a necessary aid in our earthly pilgrimage toward heaven — as necessary as bread and water, light and air, and more excellent in that it makes possible the use of these, and secures higher blessings to men. Calvin is eloquent on the benefits of government in combatting offenses against religion, securing tranquility, safeguarding private property, promoting honesty and other virtues, and maintaining "a public form of religion among Christians and humanity among men."

The state is not free to dictate laws to the church, but is obligated to protect it. There is common ground here between Calvin and St.

Thomas Aquinas; but Calvin gives to the state as over against the church a somewhat larger sphere of action than did the medieval doctor, and in this approaches more nearly to the position of Dante in *De Monarchia,* if not to that of a Marsiglio in the *Defensor Pacis.* Marsiglio has been regarded (though I believe unjustly) as a prophet of secularism. Certainly Calvin is not that. In his warm admiration for political government, he does not for a moment regard it as a realm of mere secularity. It is God-given, a "benevolent provision" for man's good, and for it men should give God thanks. The function of the magistrate is a "sacred ministry," and to regard it as incompatible with religion is an insult to God. Calvin has here in mind the Anabaptists and other enthusiastic groups. When he wrote, the fanatical experiment of the Münster Anabaptists had very recently come to a tragic close.

Calvin insists on applying this teaching to all sorts of political rulers. Paul, writing under the least satisfactory kind of government, which is "by one man" and accompanied by a "common servitude," states that "there is no power but of God." It is evident that Calvin regards even non-Christian governments and governors as divinely authorized and worthy of obedience. A state may be well constituted though it "neglects the polity of Moses" and rests upon the common law of nations. Yet he is addressing Christian rulers and subjects of professedly Christian states, and is of course primarily concerned with politics in a Christian setting.

Magistrates are the guardians of the laws, and their very making and enforcement of law are "presided over" by God. Theirs is a holy calling, "the most sacred and honorable" of all. In a powerful passage it is pointed out that their realization of this should induce them to pursue zealously clemency, justice, and other virtues becoming to their office. Calvin admonishes them as "vicegerents of God" to avoid bribery, to defend good men from injury, to aid the oppressed, vindicate the innocent, and justly to mete out punishment and reward. They are obligated where necessary to suppress violence by force. The commandment not to kill does not bind the justice of God of which they are executors. But there must not be undue severity. No equitable sentence is pronounced without mercy, yet an ill-advised lenity toward violent men may prove cruelty to the many who become their victims. By the same principle, a war of defense against a ruthless aggressor may become a necessary duty, though only when every peaceable effort has failed. Against this necessity frontier garrisons, foreign alliances, and military preparations are legitimate precautionary measures.

Calvin realizes that government requires revenues and taxation. These funds are not the ruler's private incomes but belong to the people; they are in fact the very blood of the people and should be used in their behalf as a sacred trust, and not collected with rapacity or wasted in luxury.

Calvin on Law

The treatment of the duties of magistracy is followed by a discussion of public law. Calvin, a doctor of law, was at home in this field, but he restrains himself from a lengthy disquisition and handles the topic succinctly, with primary reference to the Old Testament. He follows the traditional distinction of the "moral, ceremonial, and judicial" aspects of the Mosaic law, of which the first only is of perpetual authority. The judicial law supplied a political constitution with rules of equity and justice by which men might dwell together in peace. The ceremonial law aided piety in the childhood stage of the development of the Jewish nation. Valuable as these were, they were of passing necessity. Only the moral law endures without change. It is summarized in the Ten Commandments, and in the commandment of love (Lev. 19:18; Deut. 6:5; Matt. 22:37–39). Nations are free to adopt such laws as they may find expedient, without regard to the political constitution, or judicial law, of ancient Israel, but always on the principles of the moral law and "the perpetual rule of love."

At many points in his other writings Calvin has touched upon the topic of natural law and equity, but his references here to this vital theme are disappointingly compressed. In his *Commentary on Romans* (1:21–22; 2:14–15) he affirms that God has set in all men's minds a knowledge of Himself — "his eternity, power, goodness, truth, righteousness, and mercy." Gentiles, though they have in large degree disregarded these intimations of a divine natural morality, have nevertheless, "without a monitor," devised laws which reflect it.

It is beyond doubt that there are naturally inborn (*ingenitas*) in the minds of men certain conceptions of justice and uprightness, which the Greeks call "anticipations" (προλήψεις). They have therefore a law without the law [and] are not altogether lacking in knowledge of right and equity. [St. Paul] has set nature over against the written law, understanding that for the Gentiles a natural light of justice shines, which supplies the place of the law by which the Jews are instructed; so that they are "a law unto themselves."[3]

In an earlier passage of the *Institutes,* Calvin gives an extended treatment of the moral law as expressed in the Ten Commandments. He there refers to that "interior law . . . imprinted on the heart of everyone," which in some sense conveys the teaching of the Commandments. The inner monitor that expresses this is conscience, which ever and anon arouses us from moral sleep. The written moral law of the Bible is given by God to attest and clarify the precepts of natural law, and fix them in the memory (2.8.1).

In the present context we have a variant expression of the same teaching. Calvin's words are:

> Now since it is a fact that the Law of God which we call "moral" is nothing else than a testimony of the natural law and of that conscience which has been engraven by God in the minds of men, the entire scheme (*ratio*) of this equity has been prescribed in it. [4.20.16]

Thus Calvin adopts, and clearly enunciates, the traditional view that a primal natural law has been imparted by God to all men, and that the scriptural Commandments bear witness to it (*naturalis legis testimonium*). All such laws as men may frame in accordance with the natural law, however they may diverge from those of other states, and from the Jewish law, are to be approved. The laws of Moses were not all intended for all nations; they took account of the "peculiar circumstances" of the Hebrew people. The Commandments are, so to speak, a divine transcription for the Jewish people of the natural law that has always and everywhere been lodged in men's hearts, and properly governs all enacted laws.[4]

In general Calvin identifies natural law with equity. He seems to think of equity not in the technical sense of the human modification, in given circumstances, of the letter of a written code, but in the popular sense of common justice. Equity is natural, and hence "the same for all mankind"; and all laws should "have equity for their end." It is noteworthy that both Luther and Melanchthon, who were not trained in law, use the technical language and make equity a "mitigation" of the *summum ius,* the limit of the law, while Calvin,

---

3. In this article, the translations of quotations from Calvin's works are by the writer.

4. For further evidence see the present writer's article, "Natural Law in the Teaching of the Reformers," *The Journal of Religion* 26 (1946): 179ff.

the trained lawyer, avoids a definition of the term and gives it a sense
virtually as inclusive as that of natural law itself. He leaves us, however, in no doubt of his desire to emphasize the normative authority
of natural in relation to positive law. In all this Calvin has no notion
of modern secular interpretations of natural law. It is a part of the
divine endowment of the natural man, impaired indeed, but not obliterated by sin, evident in common concepts of justice and in the inner
voice of conscience.

Calvin's affirmation of law, on this basis, is accompanied by a
justification of participation in its judicial processes. An injured person has the right to claim its protection, and bring his cause before
the courts. The magistrate in legal judgments exercises "a holy gift of
God," and litigation is to be sought without feelings of revenge or
enmity. St. Paul asserted his rights as a Roman citizen, and his rebuke
of the Christians of Corinth (1 Cor. 6) was designed to check their
spirit of dissension and covetousness. Again he invokes the rule of
charity, which is not necessarily violated when we defend our property.

The Duty of Obedience

Calvin lays emphasis repeatedly upon the duty of obedience to
magistrates as vicegerents of God. So far as the individual citizen is
concerned, this rule of obedience applies even to tyrannical rulers who
seem to be in no sense representatives of God. An impious king is
thought of as a scourge visited upon a people in punishment for sin,
yet he too possesses a divine authority. Old Testament passages are
adduced here: Jeremiah represents God as calling Nebuchadnezzar
"my servant" and commanding the people to serve him and live, though
in fact he was "a pestilent and cruel tyrant." Under a wicked ruler we
are not to rebel, but to consider our own sins, and implore the help
of God. This is not futile, for God does intervene to lay tyrants low,
sometimes raising up leaders who are His appointed instruments of
revolution even when they know it not. "Let princes hear and fear!"

[A passage] from the *Commentary on Romans* (1539) accords with
these views. The magistrate in punishment exercises the vengeance of
God against the violation of His Commandments. Calvin remarks that
no "private man" may seize the reins of government from the appointed ruler. [Calvin] applies to government the principle of charity,
which is the fulfillment of the law. To induce anarchy is to violate
charity; obedience to magistrates is a great part of charity.

But we create a wholly false impression of Calvin's political ideas
if we give sole attention to his exhortations to obedience. It will be

observed that in commenting on Romans 13:1, he stresses the point that Paul speaks of the "higher," not of the "highest" power. The ruler has no authority that contends with God's. Calvin frequently reminds us that "we must obey God rather than men" (Acts 5:29). In the last edition of the *Institutes* he reinforces this argument (in the final paragraph of the work) by fresh Bible texts: according to Daniel 6:22–23 (Vulgate) the king has abrogated (*abrogaverit*) his authority by raising his hand against God; and Hosea 5:11 condemns the submissive obedience of the Israelites to the decrees of Jeroboam II enjoining idolatry. God does not resign His right to mortals when He makes them rulers.

Nor does Calvin deprive subjects of all right of resistance. The classical passage here is in the *Institutes* 4.20.31, which is in all editions of the work. So far as private persons are concerned, they are never permitted to resist. But if there are magistrates whose constitutional function is the protection of the people against the license of kings (*populares magistratus ad moderandam regum libidinem*), such as the ephors of Sparta, the Roman tribunes, or the demarchs of Athens, or, perhaps with such power as is exercised by the meetings of the Three Estates in the several modern kingdoms, it is not only their right but their duty to oppose the king's violence and cruelty. It would be "nefarious perfidy" for them to fail in this duty, and thus to "betray the liberty of the people."

How should we understand these references to the ancient popular magistrates and to the estates in modern realms? Calvin introduces his reference to the latter with the word *perhaps*. This may suggest that he hesitated to regard them, or, at least, to regard all of them, as functioning like the ephors for the protection of the people against tyranny. He was doubtless aware that the classes of ancient magistrates here mentioned were all elected by popular vote. This was not uniformly the case in the membership of the estates; in some nations it was hardly the case at all. If he possessed detailed knowledge of the estates or parliaments of England, Scotland, Sweden, Denmark, Norway, Poland, Bohemia, Hungary, and Spain, of the diets of the Swiss Confederation and the imperial diets of Germany, he would observe wide differences among them in constitution and function, and in potentiality for defense against monarchical absolutism or tyranny. But Calvin would have in mind primarily his native France, and he could not fail to be aware that the French estates had not even met since three years before his own birth. During his lifetime, any expectation that the Three Estates would redeem France from absolutism was faint indeed. His "perhaps" may be, in relation to France, an expression of doubt regarding the very survival of the institution. Yet it is noteworthy that in all these European organs of quasi representative government he saw at least the possibility of some guarantee of liberty and security for the people. His words were, in fact, an invitation to these bodies to play the role of the ephors and check the irresponsible arrogance of kings.

This emphatic and suggestive passage opened a path for writers like Francis Hotman and the authors of the *Vindiciae contra Tyrannos* who a few years after Calvin's death would frame doctrines of resistance that were to be vastly influential in the practical world. It also gave suggestions to the British seventeenth-century political prophets, Rutherford, Sydney, and Locke. It was not less but more influential in that it came as a concession at the end of a discussion that is anxiously conservative.

The Ideal Form of Government

That Calvin was hostile to monarchy as a form of government has been affirmed and denied by equally competent scholars.[5] At times he refuses to choose among the forms of government, and he avoids any blanket denunciation of the royal office. The piety of some Bible kings would exclude that. He has, as we saw, a high ideal for the behavior of kings. Good government under a king is for him a possibility. Yet the fact is that he is habitually severe in his judgment of the kings of history and of his own time. This characteristic is most marked after the inception of the severe persecutions of Henry II in France and of Mary in England, but no express connection with these matters appears in his treatment. Denunciations of bad kings who come to notice in the commentaries readily and frequently lead to expressions of unqualified disparagement of kings in general. Calvin's sermons on Job (1554) and on Deuteronomy (1554–55) offer numerous instances of this. We [might also mention] his Lectures on Daniel, a work of his later years (1561).

The Book of Daniel, a story of heroic fidelity and divine deliverance, lent itself to treatment by the spokesman and counsellor of the harassed minority of Protestants in France; and Calvin devotes sixty-six lectures to its twelve chapters. The work bears a dedicatory epistle to the pious in France, in which Daniel's "memorable example of incred-

5. In the pages that follow in this essay a few sentences are taken from my article, "The Democratic Element in Calvin's Thought," *Church History* 18 (1949): 153–71, and there is a further indebtedness to the materials of that paper. For permission to use these I am indebted to Professor Matthew Spinka, chairman of the editorial board of *Church History.*

ible constancy" is held before them, along with "the goodness of God at the close of this tragedy."

In these lectures we may sometimes discern an allegory of French affairs of the times. Nebuchadnezzar wishes to have in his kingdom no dissident religious minority. He is blinded by pride: "And to this day we see with what arrogance all earthly monarchs conduct themselves." His officers obey his edicts, since they have no religion but that of their fathers (Lecture 13). Daniel, Calvin notes, presents in the Babylonian kings a description of the greatness of a royal power exercised not because it is lawful, but by tacit consent of subjects who dare not murmur. Belshazzar fails to learn from the punishment of Nebuchadnezzar's pride (Lecture 25).

It is Darius who is the type of royal incapacity and misgovernment, yet he is not so bad as modern kings. His initial recognition of virtue in Daniel suggests that "we ought to weep over the heartlessness of kings in these days, who proudly despise God's gift in all good men." We see how unworthy of their power kings usually are. Their favorites are flatterers, panders, and buffoons (Lecture 27). Darius yields to the counsels of evil and designing nobles. At each stage of his moral downfall Calvin generalizes on modern kings. "If one could uncover the hearts of kings, he would find hardly one in a hundred who does not despise everything divine" (Lecture 18). Yielding to wicked persuasion, kings become slaves of their own servants: a prisoner in a dungeon is freer than they. "Thus slaves rule the kingdoms of the world" (Lecture 19). When one has perused many such passages, it is difficult to accept the judgment of those who hold that the Reformer has no hostility toward the monarchical form of government. A growing revulsion toward kingship itself seems to be involved in his persistent, and often sweeping, denunciation of kings.

On the other hand it is manifest that Calvin is anxious to avoid the language of political revolution. He quotes "Honor the King," and observes that it is vain for those who have no part in determining the form of government to dispute about it. Which form is advantageous will depend upon circumstances. But, in the 1543 edition of the *Institutes* he introduced, following this neutral statement, the flat assertion that "aristocracy, or aristocracy tempered by democracy, far excels all other forms." He retained this phrase in the 1559 edition, supporting it on the ground that justice, rectitude, and discernment are rare in kings. He then adds:

> The vice or inadequacy of men thus renders it safer and more tolerable that many (*plures*) hold the sway (*gubernacula*), so that they may mutually be helpers to each other, teach and admonish one another,

and if one asserts himself unfairly, the many may be censors and masters, repressing his wilfulness (*libidinem*).[6]

Thus Calvin clearly takes his stand upon a plural magistracy as contrasted with a monarchy. There is safety in numbers, who can check the ambition of anyone disposed to seek domination. This, it may be noted, is a reversal of the view of St. Thomas Aquinas, who in *The Governance of Princes* argues for monarchy from the principle of unity (chap. 2), and from the judgment, supported by the example of ancient Rome, that government by the many more often turns into tyranny than does government by one (chap. 5). In Geneva the scriptural principle of mutual admonition, or "fraternal correction" (cf. 2 Thess. 3:15), in which Calvin sees a safeguard against arrogance, was incorporated into the constitution of the church. Moreover, in 1557, Calvin induced the Little Council, the chief organ of civil government, to adopt the practice of a quarterly meeting for mutual criticism "in fraternal charity"; the proceedings of this session were kept secret.

There are other passages that guide us to an understanding of these concise sentences from the *Institutes*. On Romans 13:4 he notes that rulers are "obligated to God and to men." On Micah 5:5 he finds authorization for the popular election of rulers. He takes the word *shepherds* there in the sense of political rulers, and observes:

> For the condition of the people most to be desired is that in which they create their shepherds by general vote (*communibus suffragiis*). For when anyone by force usurps the supreme power, that is tyranny. And where men are born to kingship, this does not seem to be in accordance with liberty. Hence the prophet says: we shall set up princes for ourselves; that is, the Lord will not only give the Church freedom to breathe, but also institute a definite and well-ordered government, and establish this upon the common suffrages of all. [CO 43.374]

The system here clearly favored is one that rests upon popular election, which is also thought of as the work of God. Without the slightest sense of incongruity, the theocratic and democratic principles are drawn together. The blend of aristocracy and democracy that he recommends as superior to all other forms of government should be

6. *Inst.* 4.20.8.

thought of in the light of this. When he speaks of aristocracy as "the rule of the principal persons" he is in all probability not thinking of any hereditary ruling caste. He sees liberty infringed when kings are born to kingship, and we may assume that the "principal persons" are not such by inheritance, but through the recognition of their qualities by their fellows. It would be perilous, however, to press this point too far. Where a hereditary nobility exists it has some actual authority and influence which ought to be brought to bear for good government, and thus entails a specific responsibility. Calvin would have agreed with John Knox — whose political attitude was in general more revolutionary than his — when that Reformer writes:

> To bridle the fury and rage of princes in free kingdoms and realms . . . it pertains to the nobility, sworn and born to be councillors of the same, and also to the barons and people, whose votes and consent are to be required in all great and weighty matters of the commonwealth.

The Government of Geneva

Calvin became a citizen of Geneva only after his completion of the last edition of the *Institutes*. He had already committed himself to views consonant with membership in a republic, and had helped to reshape the constitution and laws of the city. The system of government was that of a conservative democracy. Calvin's word for democracy (*politia*) came to him from past ages with suggestions of disorderliness and anarchy which he largely retained, and which in many European minds still attach to the word *democracy* itself. He is cautious, therefore, in his use of the term. But his "aristocracy-democracy" formula is not only consistent with a republican order of government, but in fact conducive to it. In the commentaries he frequently expresses warm praise of liberty, and this is sometimes associated with the right of the people to elect their rulers. Twice in the homilies on First Samuel he refers to liberty as an "inestimable good" (*CO* 29.544; 30.185); the same language is used in the *Commentary on Jeremiah* (39.178); and in a reference to Deuteronomy 24:7, liberty is characterized as "more than the half of life" (24.628). These sentences from his sermons on Deuteronomy indicate his wholehearted approval of the elective principle:

> When [in the days of the judges] God gave such a privilege to the Jews, he ratified thereby his adoption and gave proof that he had chosen them for his inheritance, and that he desired that their con-

dition should be better and more excellent than that of their neighbors, where there were kings and princes but no liberty. . . . If we have the liberty to choose judges and magistrates, since this is an excellent gift, let it be preserved and let us use it in good conscience. . . . If we argue about human governments we can say that to be in a free state is much better than to be under a prince. [Disputes of this sort are unprofitable, but:] It is much more endurable to have rulers who are chosen and elected . . . and who acknowledge themselves subject to the laws, than to have a prince who gives utterance without reason. Let those to whom God has given liberty and freedom (*franchise*) use it . . . as a singular benefit and a treasure that cannot be prized enough. [27.410–11; 458–60]

Thus the priceless boon of liberty is to be cherished and defended; but it is not to be sought by violent revolution, and not to be expressed in ways that escape the bounds of law.

Calvin's idea of good government is concisely stated:

I readily acknowledge that no kind of government is more happy than this, where liberty is regulated with becoming moderation and properly established on a durable basis (*ad diuturnitatem*).[7]

In February, 1560, on the eve of an election, he addressed the General Assembly of citizens, urging them "to choose [their magistrates] with a pure conscience, without regard to anything but the honor and glory of God, for the safety and defense of the republic." Thus theocracy and democracy were easily and naturally associated in his teaching, and impressed by him upon the city-state that was the special sphere of his activity, in which he sought to establish, according to his pattern, a regulated and enduring liberty.

To our modern minds, in Calvin's Geneva the "regulation" outweighed the "liberty." It is idle to estimate the experiment by modern standards; but, at any rate, under the system of governing elective councils, and of annual elections, the constitutional means of revision were maintained. Calvin was no modern man, and he was not writing in the interests of secular conceptions of democracy. Government was for him concerned with what we call the "rights of man" only in relation to scriptural concepts of God, the moral law, and "the perpetual rule of love." But from these presuppositions he reached certain viewpoints that have leavened political theory in modern liberal states.

7. *Inst.* 4.20.8.

16

Church and Society
The Difficulty of Sheathing Swords

W. Fred Graham

Calvin's Geneva was a city with all the problems of its age. It had to deal with heretics and confessed spreaders of the plague, but also with chickens that left droppings in church and a cemetery too close and therefore too offensive;[1] with chimneyless and privyless houses, and nurses who endangered the lives of infants by sleeping with them;[2] with serious problems of defense against Savoy, and the constant problems of getting enough wheat to feed the people.

In that city the stature of Calvin grew as the years went on. Nothing seems to have been beneath his notice, and no duty too trivial for the Council to ask his advice. In addition to being chief pastor, lecturer at the college, and ofttimes law codifier, and in addition to his voluminous correspondence, his ecumenical, apologetical, and polemical efforts, and his diplomatic concerns, the little world of Geneva continually called for his best efforts. It was Calvin who complained to the Consistory about the high cost of dying, when the undertakers — following their practice of eating and drinking at the expense of the

Reprinted from *The Constructive Revolutionary: John Calvin and His Socio-Economic Impact* (Richmond: John Knox, 1971), pp. 157–73; 235–37. Used by permission.

1. CO 21.648. 10 September 1556: "Raymond Chauvet, minister, warns the *Seigneurie* that the dead are interred so close to the houses that there is a great stench, and that one named Mouroz has a chicken coop of which the chickens make ordures in church" — *Registres du Conseil* (the unpublished minutes of the city Council), vol. 52, fol. 302.

2. Amédée Roget, *Histoire du peuple de Genève depuis la réforme jusqu'à l'escalade,* 7 vols. (Geneva: J. Jullien, 1870–1883), vol. 5, pp. 56f.

relatives of the deceased — ate and drank a poor man's supper.[3] At a
period when he was involved in renewal of the federation with Berne,
but also devastated by the adultery of his sister-in-law with his own
servant, he and three members of the Council were appointed a commission to examine a new invention that was supposed to make stoves,
furnaces, ovens, and fireplaces heat at half the expense.[4] From furnace
examiner he must needs turn to literary criticism, to decide whether
a *cantique* written by young Michel Roset to celebrate the renewal of
the alliance was worth presentation. Roset's thrill at being involved
in the alliance negotiations at the age of twenty-six must have been
immeasurably heightened by hearing his work praised by Calvin, who
"found it beautiful and elegant in poetry, sense, substance, and
understanding."[5]

But in more serious matters Calvin was also available. . . . It was
he whose advice finally proved acceptable to the city when it had to
decide how far to help Lyons in defense of Reformation in 1562, when
the city of Geneva felt threatened as well. No wonder the Council
refused to allow him to travel to France to take part in the Poissy
negotiations unless "some notable hostages" were received in return![6]

As Monter puts it: "In Genevan history, all roads lead eventually
to Calvin."[7] His ability to distinguish the spiritual and the temporal
was uncommon for his day; his refusal to allow the spiritual be subject
to the temporal was uncommon to Protestantism in his day; his ability
to suffuse the temporal with the values of the spiritual without robbing
the former of its identity is instructive for our day.

But not everything was well in the permeation of Calvin's thought
into Genevan politics and society. We shall survey briefly the actual
relationship between the Genevan church and the political arm, and
then criticize the harshness that too often reflects badly on Calvin's
influence at this critical point in his practice of Christian ministry.

The Church in Politics

. . . The theoretical separation of church and state existed for Calvin
more in theory than in practice. By his words Calvin expressed an

3. CO 21.781. 18 June 1562 — *Registres du Consistoire* (the minutes of the
Consistory).
4. Roget, *Histoire,* vol. 5, p. 58. "The common measure of humanity was decid-
edly not made for this exceptional person."
5. CO 21.682. 28 December 1557 — *Registres du Conseil,* vol. 54, fol. 25. See
also Roget, *Histoire,* vol. 5, pp. 90 – 91.
6. CO 21.754 – 55. Although there is little likelihood that the Queen Mother
wanted Calvin in France.
7. E. William Monter, *Studies in Genevan Government, 1536 – 1605* (Geneva:
Droz, 1964), p. 118.

ideal of separation; by his practice it is quite clear that separation for Calvin did not mean what it does for most Americans today.

> The gospel is not to change the administration [*polices*] of the world, and to make laws which pertain to the temporal state. It is very true that Kings, Princes, and Magistrates ought always to consult the mouth of God and to conform themselves to His Word; but our Lord has given them liberty to make the laws which they know to be proper and useful by the rule which is committed to them.[8]

. . . However, Calvin fought for the church's right to enforce its discipline on its members in such a way that city officials feared it was usurping the liberty of the magistrates. We would expect the line to be very hard to define and to see Calvin and the other pastors constantly stepping into the political circle both as individuals and as representatives of the church in Geneva.

Nothing illuminates better Calvin's insistence that as individuals the pastors have full political duties and privileges than his argument when the Perrinists denied the pastors their right to vote. All the city's clergy except Calvin were received into the *bourgeoisie* when they were sworn into office, and this carried with it the right to vote in the General Council. The Perrinists, as part of their war against overzealous pastors, took from them the right to attend or vote, citing the practice of the priests in Roman Catholic days. But Calvin argued that they were not priests, that unlike them the pastors did not wish to be exempt from temporal judges, and therefore the comparison was faulty.[9] He lost the argument, . . . but his point was clear.

Calvin's own involvement is pointed up in his efforts to maintain the federation with Berne. This alliance was absolutely necessary to Geneva's independence, and in both instances when it was essential that it be renewed despite Berne's dislike of Geneva's internal affairs, Calvin was picked to help in the negotiations. In 1541 the deposed "Artichauds" were the friends of Berne, and Calvin was enemy, therefore, to both. Yet he worked patiently in the political arena and wins praise from the balanced Roget.[10] The second negotiations were even more difficult, for they stretched over a several-year period immediately after the fall of the Perrinists and their flight to the protection of Berne. [At that time Geneva was dependent on Calvin's efforts.] The final renewal agreement had little in it of religious matters, but

8. *CO* 51.797.
9. *CO* 21.536–37. 28 February 1553 — *Registres du Conseil,* vol. 47, fol. 29. Priests were subject only to the ecclesiastical courts.
10. Roget, *Histoire,* vol. 2, p. 109.

dealt with the defense of Geneva against aggressors, the inviolability of the two cities from molestation (here the Word of God is named, however, as a cause for which some outsider might attempt such molestation), the adjudication of differences between the cities, imprisonment for debts of citizens of the two, and other matters mainly economic and contractual in nature.[11] How many pastors would involve themselves in such grubby bargaining when there are "spiritual" matters in plenty to take care of? But Calvin subjected himself to the political arm, worked with all the legal knowledge he had learned from his early training, and labored to effect a "perpetual alliance" firm enough to continue long after he was gone. The only extra pay he would accept from the city was the gift of wine.

The real problem here is not to find evidence that the church under Calvin's leadership meddled in the political arena, but to ascertain whether Calvin considered the church to be *over* the magistrate in any way reminiscent of the medieval Pope Boniface's bull *Unam Sanctam,* where "temporal authority [is] subject to spiritual."[12] He did not, of course. This is evident from his concern that kings, princes, and magistrates have the freedom to rule as God has given them liberty to do so. Even Eugene Choisy, . . . who described the Calvinistic regime as a "theocracy," makes clear that this did not mean the domination of the church over the state, or the clergy over the political government. But it did mean for Calvin a vast, all-encompassing concern for the way the government handled its affairs. Calvin was an almost thoroughgoing secularist in the sense that he understood the gospel to be irrevocably concerned with the world. And the magistrate who did not "consult the mouth of God and conform . . . to His Word"

11. *Les Sources du droit du Canton de Genève,* ed. Émile Rivoire and Victor van Berchem (Aarau: H. R. Sauerländer, 1933), vol. 3, pp. 64–73.

12. *Documents of the Christian Church,* ed. Henry Bettenson (London: Oxford University, 1963), p. 160. Writes Boniface VIII in 1302: "And we learn from the words of the Gospel that in this Church and in her power are two swords, the spiritual and the temporal. For when the apostles said, 'Behold, here' (that is, in the Church, since it was the apostles who spoke) 'are two swords'—the Lord did not reply, 'It is too much,' but 'It is enough.' Truly he who denies that the temporal sword is in the power of Peter, misunderstands the words of the Lord, 'Put up thy sword into the sheath.' Both are in the power of the Church, the spiritual sword and the material. But the latter is to be used for the Church, the former by her; the former by the priest, the latter by kings and captains but at the will and by the permission of the priest. The one sword, then, should be under the other, and temporal authority subject to spiritual. For when the apostle says 'there is no power but of God, and the powers that be are ordained by God' they would not be so ordained were not one sword made subject to the other. . . ."

would find that the mouth of God (here, Calvin!) was giving advice anyway.

It may be that this concern for the world was overparticular. Berthold Haller, reformer and chief pastor in Berne, wrote in 1554, just when Calvin's trials were hardest: "I do not know any one among us [ministers at Berne] who accuse Calvin of heresy. But the truth is that some of ours love him very little because he seems to be mixed up in too many affairs."[13] But Choisy admitted that much of the concern for morals and decency on the part of the church, i.e., by the Consistory, was commendable:

> It intervenes in order to re-establish peace and unity in families, in order to recall individuals to their duty; it takes in hand with a commendable energy reforms favorable to the small and the weak; it sends for and censures the lazy and the idle, the fathers and creditors who are too harsh; it shows itself without mercy for usurers, monopolizers, and speculators, for merchants who defraud their clients. It combats the rudeness of the mores of the time, the brutality of men, the negligence in the care given to the ill. . . . It interdicts the Supper to "scandalous" persons, that is to say, those guilty of lying, fraud, or bad conduct.[14]

The theoretical separation, then, was honored in a sense: the pastors did not try to make laws. But they tried to influence the making and enforcing of good laws — laws of all kinds pertaining to the lives of men — and certainly at times stepped over that hazy boundary between concern and domination that is always difficult to delineate. Too many problems that another age might consider political or economic seemed to Calvin and the other pastors to be religious. And their influence . . . was brought to bear directly upon the Councils of Geneva.

Peter's Sword in Caesar's Hand

The marks of the true church for Luther were the right preaching of the Word and the administration of the dominical sacraments (baptism and the Supper). To these marks the radical Reformers added a third, that of godly discipline within the redeemed community. This led the radicals, such as Menno Simons, to develop intricate and rather

13. Quoted by Roget, *Histoire,* vol. 4, p. 181n.
14. Eugène Choisy, *La Théocratie à Genève au temps de Calvin* (Geneva: J.-G. Fick, 1897), pp. 244–45.

legalistic guidelines and procedures whereby the church could exercise excommunication (or the ban) and thereby keep the church pure. It was a fateful decision when Calvin chose to include this godly discipline as the third mark of the church. The other two major branches of the Reformation—Lutheran and Anglican—did not do so. Had Calvinism been confined to little pockets of godly piety, as with the Anabaptists, then the problems this raised would have been self-contained, producing stability and purpose within the redeemed community. But Calvin understood church and state to be coterminous, the church to be concerned for the whole of life. So the inclusion of godly discipline optimally would be accepted by the total society. This is what is really meant by the term *theocracy.*

But if all society is governed by this discipline, as well as by the ordinary legalities that all societies must maintain, then the ecclesiastical sword (discipline) must be wielded by the police arm of the state. This did not mean in Geneva, as it did with Pope Boniface two and a quarter centuries earlier, that the church controlled the state, but only that in certain cases ecclesiastical censure required state punishment. Nor is this entirely strange to modern secular man, for the modern state still punishes adulteries, fornications, desertions, and other "consistorial" matters if they endanger the common good.

But in Geneva the church's call for the use of the secular sword was often quite shrill, not only when seen in retrospect but even by contemporaries. The long process of dismissing de Ecclesia from the ministry is an illustration. The discussion between the Company of Pastors and Council over that sad figure ran on for exactly four years, the pastors wanting to dismiss their wife-beating, heretical, insolent, incorrigible, usurious brother; the Council either unconvinced or unable to fire him. And when it was all over, Pierre Viret, in Lausanne, informed the brethren that, unknown to them, the Council gave de Ecclesia a good recommendation to the burghers of Berne. The secular officials simply refused to wield the sword, and since the church-state entente was such that the church's discipline was merely verbal, ecclesiastical discipline did not happen.[15]

If the church's weakness is exposed in the affair of Pastor Philip, its strength is exhibited in another strange situation. For in the affair of names not to be given children at baptism, church pressure caused the state to exercise its authority in an area clearly removed from its

15. Roget, *Histoire,* vol. 2, pp. 258–59n. See *CO* 21.448–50, 509, 535, 540–41; see also *Registres de la Compagnie des Pasteurs de Genève au temps de Calvin,* ed. Robert M. Kingdon and Jean François Bergier (Geneva: Droz, 1962, 1964), vol. 1, pp. 47, 56–57, 76, 132, 144, 148, 160.

rightful province (although modern secular France continues to make such ludicrous prohibitions). It all began because too many babies were being named after St. Claude, a local saint, and therefore the name of an *jdole*. Calvin came to the Council twice late in August 1546 over this problem, getting nowhere. Then a ruckus broke loose at St. Gervais when one of the pastors refused to baptize a child "Claude" and insisted on naming him Abraham. Finally, after Calvin had wearied the Council to death with the matter, *Messieurs* proclaimed an edict prohibiting the use of certain names: idols, such as Claude and Mama; the three kings (presumably Caspar, Melchior, and Balthazar); names of offices, such as Baptiste, Iuge, Evangeliste; names pertaining to deity, such as Dieu le filz, Espeoir, Emanuel, Saulveur, or Jesus; inept or absurd names, Sepulchre, Croix, Typhaine, Nouel, Pasques, Pentecoste, Toussainctz, Dimenche, Chrestien (because common to all); names with bad sounds, such as Comin, Mermet, Sermet, or Allemande; double names; or corrupted names, such as Tyvan or Tevenot for Estienne, or Monet in place of Simon.[16]

Of course, many of these names might well have been refused by the ministers. To name a child Sepulchre or God-the-Son is to do him no favor. But for *Messieurs* to pass an ordinance prohibiting names — some, like Claude and Balthasar, belonging to Councilmen — strikes us as ridiculous, and evidently struck the Council the same way. Here ecclesiastical influence was exerted in a farcical, if not hurtful, manner.

Human Solidarity and the Rights of the Individual

For the past one hundred years mankind has found itself torn between two un-Christian theories of man, Marxist collectivism and radical individualism. Propagandists for both views rival each other in the denatured rationalism of their respective anthropologies. Neither view, whether expressed by a Lenin or a Robert Welch, has room for the obligation to love one's neighbor, which was preached (if often broken) by the church in the Middle Ages and preached (if often broken) by the pastors of Geneva. The partially reconstituted human life of man — in Calvin's theology — must be a life in loving community. In discussing the Supper, Calvin wrote:

We shall benefit very much from the sacrament if this thought is impressed and engraved upon our minds: that none of the brethren can be injured, despised, rejected, abused, or in any way offended by

16. *CO* 10a.48 — "Projet d'Ordonnance sur les Noms de Baptême."

us, without at the same time, injuring, despising, and abusing Christ by the wrongs we do; that we cannot disagree with our brethren without at the same time disagreeing with Christ; that we cannot love Christ without loving him in the brethren; that we ought to take the same care of our brethren's bodies as we take of our own; for they are members of our body; and that, as no part of our body is touched by any feeling of pain which is not spread among all the rest, so we ought not to allow a brother to be affected by any evil, without being touched with compassion for him.[17]

In order to preserve a degree of purity in the church, the body of Christ, that body — though bound together by the love of God — must exercise internal discipline. Calvin's discussion of that discipline is really quite moderate. He called for private admonitions for smaller or private sins, public admonitions for notorious sins, and excommunication for "flagitious and enormous crimes." Excommunication was practiced for three ends: that God be not dishonored by numbering with the body of Christ such "foul and decaying members"; that the good be not corrupted by constant association with the wicked; and that those censured be led to repentance. The last-mentioned end means that the excommunicated brother, though now a stranger to Christ, is still, paradoxically, a brother, else "there is danger lest we soon slide down from discipline to butchery."[18]

So far, so good. We know from Calvin's preaching that he tried to reform Geneva from the pulpit, but we also recognize that private admonitions were his way of dealing with smaller sins. The public admonitions sometimes got out of hand, as when he called the Council a "Council of the devil" from the pulpit — but it is easy to recognize the temptation. Excommunications seem to have been handled much as he said.

The problem arises at this point: for many sinners the way led straight from the ecclesiastical censure of the Consistory (made up . . . of Council members and preachers) to state punishment inflicted by the Council. Often the punishment was written directly into the church ordinances.[19] And this welding of ecclesiastical censure and the temporal sword was part and parcel of Calvin's view of the duty of the magistrate:

17. *Inst.* 4.17.38.
18. *Inst.* 4.12.1–13.
19. Not the 1541 Ecclesiastical Ordinances for the city, but the "Ordinances for the Supervision of Churches in the Country" specify the fines for missing worship, midwives who baptize, persons who "spin wildly in the dance," and other sins. See *Calvin: Theological Treatises,* trans. and ed. J. K. S. Reid (Philadelphia: Westminster, 1954), pp. 76–82.

Yet civil government has as its appointed end, so long as we live among men, to cherish and protect the outward worship of God, to defend sound doctrine of piety and the position of the church, to adjust our life to the society of men, to form our social behavior to civil righteousness, to reconcile us with one another, and to promote general peace and tranquillity. . . .

Let no man be disturbed that I now commit to civil government the duty of rightly establishing religion, which I seem above to have put outside of human decision. For, when I approve of a civil administration that aims to prevent the true religion which is contained in God's law from being openly and with public sacrilege violated and defiled with impunity, I do not here, any more than before, allow men to make laws according to their own decision concerning religion and the worship of God.[20]

What often happened in practice was that the human solidarity which men have in Christ, and which is expressed in the church, was defended and pursued in such a manner that the rights of the individual in Geneva were ignored. . . . Generally the church's pursuit of the common weal was beneficial. [But] sometimes privacy was violated, the weak were browbeaten and at times physically beaten, and brutality was promoted and condoned in the name of religious and civil harmony. The tension between society and the individual is always likely to tip; in Geneva it sometimes tipped over and distributed horror on the individual.

It is one thing to admonish in private for private sins. It is another to play peeping Tom to catch persons in private peccadilloes. We can sympathize with one Jean Guidon who, on 10 May 1553, was brought before the Consistory for swearing by the body of God and making a ruckus in his home. M. Jean declared ". . . that it was neither fair nor honest to go along the rooftops in order to see what people are doing, and that if he had had a crossbow or a blowtube [*sarbacane*] he would have dislodged those so well informed about what goes on in his house."[21]

This amusing practice proved quite deadly in the affair of Jaques Gruet. On 28 June 1547, someone had attached a note to the pulpit at St. Pierre's. Aimed primarily at Pastor Abel Poupin, who had been particularly vitriolic in Consistory hearings with the Favre family, it was addressed to "fat belly and your companions." The note warned

20. *Inst.* 4.20.3.
21. Roget, *Histoire,* vol. 3, p. 282, digs this one from the still unpublished *Registres du Consistoire.*

them to leave the city, referred to them as "fucking renegade priests," and threatened them with the fate of an ecclesiastic who was killed in the riots preceding independence.[22] The author of the note was thought to be Jaques Gruet, *bon vivant* and freethinker. He was arrested, and confessed under threat of torture that he had composed the document, though it was not in his handwriting. Then his quarters were searched, and books and papers showing his heretical views came to light. Among other items to anger Calvin and/or the Council: he spoke well of the pope, but referred to Calvin as *abuseur, ambitieux, fier, glorieux, pertinax*; he wrote, concerning Moses, "That horned one says much and proves nothing," and "all laws, both divine and human, have been made by the caprice of men"; he objected to officers of justice investigating the private lives of individuals; and worst, from the magistrates' point of view, was a letter in which he advised a Frenchman to write to Francis I (*du grand Turc*) to come to close the mouth of Calvin. The letter was treason, or close to it, but Gruet argued that it was not meant seriously, and it had not been sent, anyway. Imprisoned the day the note was found, he was tried before the Council daily from 2 July for three weeks. It is interesting that the Consistory had nothing to do with this trial, though part of the charge was heresy. Less than a month after his incarceration he was sentenced to death for blasphemy and rebellion, "in the name of the Father, of the Son, and of the Holy Spirit. Amen."[23]

The public, then, was protected, but not the individual. His house was searched. Every confession he made was extracted either by torture or by the threat of torture. The verdict was already in, and he had only to confess his crimes and to be put away. Thus the solidarity of the human community required the blood of the one who threatened that community. It is difficult, of course, to abstain from imposing modern ideas upon the Reformer and the magistrates of Geneva. They did, after all, live in the sixteenth century. And they did develop a siege mentality, not surprisingly. But there was nothing in the arrest, trial, and beheading of Jaques Gruet to give us reason to think that any regard whatsoever was had for his rights as a man.

It could be argued that a deplorable lack of private morality in that

22. French translation of the patois placard is found in Roget, *Histoire,* vol. 2, p. 290.
23. Roget, *Histoire,* vol. 2, pp. 289–312, discusses the trial at some length, as well as the letters written by Calvin which refer to it. Gruet seems to have been a freethinker in a frivolous way, immoral and resentful of authority, but not deep enough to have been called a heretic or dangerous enough to be convicted of lèse majesté.

day justified some of the extreme measures taken. Extracts from the *Registres du Conseil* prior to the Reformation indicate that the priests and monks of Catholic days were constantly getting into trouble because of prostitutes and lewd women.[24] Some of the early Protestant pastors fared no better, Simon Moreaux being deposed in 1545, the next year two losing their posts together for attending the baths "nud a nud" with one Huguenne and her sister, and Jean Fabri being removed for suspicion as late as 1556.[25] The absence of public disapproval is well illustrated by the case of the *lieutenant de justice,* Jean Ami Curtet, who was tried and imprisoned for fornication, degraded from office, and compelled to seek pardon from the Two Hundred in 1536. Six months later he was elected first syndic, the highest post in Geneva![26]

But there was more to the defense of public solidarity than simply chaotic moral conditions. One could, I think, say that the authorities went out of their way to search for dissenters. A case in point was that of the card-manufacturer Pierre Ameaux in 1545. Ameaux was a member of the Small Council who complained to a private gathering in his home that Calvin was an evil man, only a Picard, and had preached false doctrine.[27] The Council duly examined the evidence — brought in by an informer at the private gathering — and decided Ameaux should pay a fine and, with bared head and torch in hand, kneel to the ground and confess his sins. But this did not placate Calvin, who wanted a harsher sentence imposed upon one who could call his ministry into question. Before the whole quarrel was over, the Council was split into two factions; the original prosecutor, Claude Roset (Michel's father), resigned his task in disgust at the overzealousness; the Consistory made protracted statements in favor of Calvin; a riot took place in St. Gervais; pastor Henri de la Mare was cashiered for friendship with Ameaux; and the unlucky card-

24. Antoine Froment, "Extracts," in *Les Actes et gestes merveilleux de la Cité de Genève,* ed. Gustave Revilliod (Geneva: J.-G. Fick, 1864), pp. c–cv.

25. For Moreaux, *CO* 21.350–54; for Champereaux and Megret, ibid., p. 367; for Fabri, *Registres de la Compagnie des Pasteurs,* vol. 2, p. 66.

26. Herbert D. Foster, "Geneva Before Calvin," in *Collected Papers of Herbert D. Foster* (privately published, 1929), p. 19 (first printed in *American Historical Review* 8 [1903]). Roget appends to the end of each of his seven volumes the names of councilors and pastors, and we see that Curtet served on the Small Council every year but one from 1537 to the end of Roget's work in 1567. He was first syndic again in 1541, 1545, 1552, 1556 (the first election after the Perrinist defeat), 1561, and 1565.

27. *CO* 21.368. 26 January 1546. "Lon a revelle que Ameaux a diest que M. Calvin estoyt meschant homme et nestoyt que un picard et preschoyt faulce doctrine" — *Registres du Conseil,* vol. 40, fol. 359.

manufacturer spent more than two months in prison, lost his office, and had to make a complete tour around the city in a shirt, with head bared, carrying a lighted torch, and then kneel to the ground, confessing to libel. He also had to pay the expenses of the trial.[28] Christian love simply departed in this sad affair as Calvin pressed rigorously for civic solidarity, which could be guaranteed only if dissent was put down severely. One reads the account even today with shame and sorrow.

There is evidence that the Consistory did not always perform its task with moderation. In the drawn-out affair between the Favre family and the Consistory, the Council had to counsel both sides to have more care for their language. Pastor Abel Poupin was picked out pointedly and warned not "to use what he uses against those who are called to the Consistory."[29] Since he had called François Favre a dog, it is no surprise that Favre's daughter referred to Poupin as a "fat loin of a French pig" and nearly rode him down with her horse when he was fleeing to the family estates in Bernese-controlled territory to avoid prison. The next day the Council made a special resolution to the effect that people should be treated more graciously in Consistory meetings. Thus suspicion arises that in practice Calvin's views concerning private and public admonition really amounted to something only a few steps removed from an inquisition. However, it must be admitted that in the case of the Favres, they probably got everything they were asking for.

Calvin's instincts were for the good of the public, but too often the good of the individual — which must be protected if in the long run the public is to benefit — was not protected. If anything, Calvin himself was harder on the wrongdoer than were others in the Genevan community. An example of this occurred in 1563 when Jacques de St. Mortier was arrested for embezzlement and theft and would not confess. The Council gave the case to five judges, one of them Calvin, whose office does not make clear how he came to be involved in this bit of judiciary or magistracy. The other four judges concluded that the offender should be whipped, but Calvin that he should be put to death! The Council, still perplexed, sent him to the crane (*grue*) and then released him after this torture, although he never confessed. Cal-

28. The Annals are full of this trial — CO 21.368–77. Roget, *Histoire,* vol. 2, pp. 207–23, gives a good account and tells us something of Ameaux's later citations before the Consistory, which give some evidence that Ameaux neglected public worship but conducted services in his own home.

29. CO 21.499. 21 March 1547 — *Registres du Conseil,* vol. 42, fol. 63.

vin was sure of his guilt despite lack of proof and would have sacrificed the individual for the sake of the community.[30]

However, in at least two instances Calvin tried to intervene to secure better conditions for prisoners and easier death for the condemned. In the Servetus case, as everyone knows, Calvin wished for death, then burning. Nine years earlier, on 9 March 1545, Calvin had come to the Council pleading for better treatment for prisoners convicted of spreading the plague by smearing excretion from infected bodies upon doorposts. The whole story sounds like witchcraft trials where people actually believed they had sold their own souls to the devil. Anyway, the executioner was asked to make sure those being burned were already dead. A small thing, perhaps, but of some consequence at a time of fear and horror at the plague and those convicted of spreading it (*empoysonneurs*) from house to house.[31]

Sixteenth-century Geneva was probably not made a more merciful state because of the influence of Calvin. In some ways, it does not seem to have been the aim to treat prisoners badly. Jailing was common, many councilors having seen the inside of L'Evêché themselves, and generally the treatment there must have been fairly good by medieval standards. The Council kept strict surveillance over the man and woman in charge. But the common method of third-degree interrogation was torture, pure and simple, and there is no hint that Calvin ever tried to protect the individual from this trial. Punishments often were rude and cruel also. In addition to public whippings, tongues were pierced and ears trimmed, people were branded with the mark of the *Seigneurie,* and at times burning was done in effigy.[32]

All of the items mentioned in this section are part of the material taught in humanities classes or reviewed without understanding by

30. Roget, *Histoire,* vol. 7, p. 42. Roget gives a résumé of a number of instances in 1563 where cases tried before the Council, probably first tried in Consistory, had penalties affixed after consultation with Calvin. Most likely the reason was not his position as pastor, but his legal knowledge. Examples: two arsonists were burned in effigy, whipped, and imprisoned four years; upon the advice of Calvin a woman oft tried for *impudicité* was given two hours in the stocks in addition to six days in jail; upon the advice of Calvin a man who pushed his mother-in-law against a door was put to the *collier;* a bigamous woman was whipped publicly; on the other hand, it was due to Calvin's advice that a young scholar who stole from his father was released because the father had not initiated a complaint. Roget adds: "Could not Calvin, hampered by illness and overworked, have transferred to others these magisterial concerns in criminal matters, quite sterile and having little connection with tasks of a minister of the gospel?" (pp. 43–44).

31. *CO* 21.348. 9 March 1545 — *Registres du Conseil,* vol. 40, fol. 42v.

32. See, for example, Roget, *Histoire,* vol. 6, pp. 194–95. The hot pincers used on the *empoysonneurs* in 1545 seem not to have been used again.

a Stefan Zweig. They are dished up as if Calvin contributed nothing to Protestantism, but simply brought the Inquisition into the Reformation. This . . . is simply not so. These conditions had long existed everywhere. But they do show the Reformer in a bad light precisely because his theory was weighted toward love and justice. They serve, perhaps, as warnings (if we need any) that even the common good must be protected with discretion, that evildoers must be tried justly and punished mercifully, that the public weal does not demand individual woe. Or, as C. S. Lewis has said somewhere: It takes a saint to make an inquisitor. That is, you have to care more about good and evil than most of us do to want to take extreme measures against evil.

Calvin's Political Blinders

Before we leave the subject of the church and the sword of the magistrate, we should say a word about the one instance when Calvin's religious convictions caused political blindness and outright injustice. It should be said at first, however, that such was not always the case. As he looked afar, Calvin could see quite clearly the earthen vessels God had raised up to foster and protect the Reformation. He had no delusions about the strength or morals of the Prince de Condé, for example, nor about King Anthony of Navarre (father of Henry of Navarre, Henry IV), who for a time espoused the Huguenot cause. One simply cannot imagine Calvin allowing a Philip of Hesse to con him into permitting bigamy.

. . . [On] the evening of 16 May 1555 a riot broke out in the streets of Geneva, which was interpreted by the majority of the Council to have been an attempted coup d'état [by the Perrinists]. There was almost no evidence for that charge, and in the surrounding cantons opposition to the executions and the flight of the more fortunate almost amounted to a storm. Haller wrote to Bullinger that "Calvin is blamed now by those who, up till now, were always his supporters." Later, he wrote that one could hardly find one person in a hundred to speak well of Calvin. François Hotman wrote from Basel that "Calvin isn't spoken of here any better than in Paris." And Musculus from the same city lamented: "The hatred around here for our well-loved brother Calvin increases every day."[33]

Calvin's response to these calumnies, contained in a long letter to Bullinger (to whom the other letters were addressed), is certainly disappointing. He avers he was not present at the tortures, which he describes as quite light, and defends this barbarity by saying:

33. Roget, *Histoire,* vol. 4, pp. 321–22.

But it was quite natural to do this; without that they would have denied everything, being encouraged by their adherents. The judges were not able to allow that they deny the plot, since it was evident.[34]

Here, as later with the embezzler, Calvin presumed the guilt of the accused. The trial was quite unnecessary under such a judiciary. That there was a plot at all is denied by more balanced scholars such as Roget and Williston Walker. As the latter says,

... the facts speak too clearly against the existence of any well-planned conspiracy to overturn the Genevan government to make that interpretation tenable.

Of Calvin's assurance that it was a plot to overthrow the magistrates, he writes,

There is no reason to doubt that Calvin and most of his sympathisers sincerely believed that the affair was a deep-laid plot. He thought no good of Perrin, and Vandel. Their work was, and had long been, in his judgment one hostile to God. But it was a very convenient belief, also, in the existing political situation.[35]

Indeed it was a convenient belief. The usually perspicacious Calvin, who cared not for the appearances put up by men, was in this case certain that Perrin had troops waiting to attack. Despite the fact that only one man received a stone on the ear, the whole city was presumed to have narrowly escaped assault. Dislike for the silly, comical, pugnacious, infuriating *comique Caesar* and his friends turned Calvin's judgment to nonsense in this affair. The common weal, the solidarity of the community, had to be protected.

Conclusion: The Saint and the State

If the attempt to impose a godly discipline for the sake of the common good sometimes resulted in evil for the individual rather than good, this does not mean that the Calvinist understanding of the dynamic relationship between church and state was in the long run bad. There is something very positive to be said about the way Genevan politics became saturated with moral considerations. To understand public office as a charge, to view politics as a conscientious and con-

34. Ibid., p. 323 — from CO 15.830.
35. Williston Walker, *John Calvin: The Organiser of Reformed Protestantism, 1509 – 1564* (New York: Putnam, 1906), pp. 352 – 53.

tinuous labor, is far from bad doctrine.[36] Historians with a penchant for the medieval have long regarded the ability of Calvinists to over-turn such social traditions as the divine right of Stuart kings and to dispense with other traditional social structures as an evil which has denatured modern social existence. Revolutionaries know better. Me-dieval society was largely one where common men were nonpartici-pants. "Calvinism taught previously passive men the styles and methods of political activity and enabled them successfully to claim the right of participation in that on-going system of political action that is the modern state."[37] Rising nations and tribes everywhere to-day are claiming precisely this right to participate politically which Calvinist concern for the total community taught Genevans in the middle of the sixteenth century.

Franklin H. Littell, whose sympathies in the Reformation period lie with the radicals, not the Calvinists, argues that in Germany under Hitler the active resistance to Nazism was largely Calvinist because the Reformed tradition of lay initiative was better equipped to cope with persecution than were the "pyramided church structures" of Ger-man Lutheranism.[38] Here again is evident a responsibility for society fostered by the Calvinist insistence that the will of God must extend to the total community.

These short paragraphs are not meant in any way to mitigate the evils we saw earlier in this chapter. Instead, they are meant to show that the Calvinist position inculcated an involvement in the political order, for better and for worse. It was in no sense pacifist or with-drawn from the total society. Calvinists were instead active and ag-gressive, and participated in that revolutionary ferment — so little understood by many who lived in the midst of it — which was even in the sixteenth century changing the physiognomy and psychology of northern and western Europe.

36. See, for example, Michael Walzer, *The Revolution of the Saints: A Study in the Origins of Radical Politics* (Cambridge, Mass.: Harvard University, 1965), p. 2 *et passim.*

37. Ibid., p. 18.

38. Compare Littell's *Anabaptist View of the Church* (Boston: Starr King, 1952, 1958) and his monograph on American church history, *From State Church to Plu-ralism* (Garden City, N.Y.: Doubleday, 1962), to see his Free Church sympathies. As far as the German situation is concerned, see Littell's *German Phoenix* (Garden City, N.Y.: Doubleday, 1960), pp. 10f. Although he substantiates his position that the Lutheran resistance to Hitler was largely passive, the Reformed active, we should be careful not to overstate this, when men like the Niemoellers, Hans Asmussen, and Dietrich Bonhoeffer represented the Lutheran side.

17

John Calvin
A Theologian
for an Age of Limits

Donald K. McKim

In the last decade, Western industrial nations have had to radically examine some previously unquestioned assumptions. Various crises have forced Western societies to look hard at goals and ideals which for the most part had been taken for granted. The assumption that we are living in a world of unlimited resources in which boundless growth and development are achievable is now untenable. Shortages of food, oil, and energy have made previous projections and policies unrealistic. Where before consumption of such commodities was of little concern to consumer economies thriving on full stomachs, mobility, and cheap power, now the prospect of future unavailabilities has made sensitive leaders nervous. Inflation is but one indicator that supplies in coming years may not keep pace with demands. Nonrenewable resources are irreplaceable. To use them as if there were no tomorrow may lead precisely to the point where indeed there is no tomorrow! Political tensions escalate when competition for available resources stiffens. With nuclear capabilities as they are, the fight for the world's resources is taking on an even more ominous shape. In short, coming to grips with a world of limits means shifts in priorities and lifestyles. No responsible person can believe that ever increasing consumption by an expanding world population will not eventually

A shortened version of this essay was delivered at the Fourth Colloquium on Calvin and Calvin Studies of the Calvin Studies Society at Calvin Theological Seminary in Grand Rapids, Michigan, on May 5, 1983.

bring us face to face with the limits of the world's resources. What will happen when that time arrives is anyone's guess.

Many contemporary Christians are focusing attention on issues related to the world's limits. Various groups are urging Christian action in the areas of world peace, elimination of hunger, justice, energy controls, and simpler lifestyles. They are calling us to do what we can to preserve the world and its people. In view of the poverty of much of the world, this challenge is directed particularly to us Americans. Christians of the United States have used the world's resources as intensively as has anyone. So appeals to this nation and its Christians to recognize that the world's resources are limited are especially apropos.

This challenge leads us to ask whether the Christian theological tradition has anything to say regarding our responsibilities as God's people living in an age of limits. Do biblical religion and theological reflection offer any insights pointing us toward appropriate lifestyles as twentieth-century American Christians? What, indeed, is the definition of a responsible Christian lifestyle, given who we are and what we have in a world where so many millions "have not"?

One source of help is the social teachings of the Protestant Reformer John Calvin (1509–1564). Calvin is often portrayed as an incurable pessimist about humanity, a dour predestinarian, or a crypto-capitalist. But beyond these mistaken caricatures, his writings are rich in theological insight. At its best, Calvin's theology has provided generations with a springboard for constructive involvement in human history. Moreover, his social teachings have offered no less significant insights into the Christian life than have his specifically theological formulations. Calvin spent his life as a pastor, preacher, and teacher dealing with others in a wide variety of social settings. Calvin's context and our own are, of course, vastly different. But an examination of his writings will disclose some fundamental aspects that are of the essence of the Christian life in any age, in any context. Our lives as twentieth-century American Christians are always under the scrutiny of the gospel of Jesus Christ. Calvin's perspectives will point us toward a more faithful living out of the biblical beliefs we claim to support.

Calvin's Middle Road

Before his death, Ford Lewis Battles, translator of Calvin's *Institutes* and one of the world's leading Calvin scholars, suggested that Calvin's 1559 *Institutes* can be summed up in terms of its "antithetical structure." Calvin steered "a *via media* between the Scylla of aberrant Romanism and the Charybdis of the radical tendencies of his time, whatever name he might give to them."[1] This means that "every fundamental notion of his thought is defined in a field of tension — a true middle between false extremes." As Calvin encountered beliefs with which he disagreed, he analyzed them and incorporated them (unconsciously, of course) into what we might call a spectrum. Battles saw the additions appearing in the post–1536 editions of the *Institutes* as castigations of positions inclining toward one or the other of the extremes on this spectrum and as an attempt to steer a middle course (see Figure 17.1).[2]

Figure 17.1

Spiritualist	Calvin	Papist
(including Anabaptist, Libertine, etc.)	*via media*	

Calvin regarded virtue (and hence true doctrines) as "a sort of means between extremes, of which the one tends to defect, the other to excess."[3] Thus, with respect to individual issues, his theological position was forged between "defect" on one end of the spectrum and "excess" on the other. For example, with respect to angels, while the Libertines held that angels do not exist (defect) and the Roman Catholics held that angels are to be worshiped (excess), Calvin steered a middle course: angels are one means of God's accommodating to feeble human capacity.[4]

In articulating his position on individual topics by means of this method, Calvin also made use of what we might call a true/false principle. Through successive dichotomies on the basis of this principle, Calvin arrived ever closer to the truth (his *via media* — see Figure 17.2).[5]

1. Ford Lewis Battles, *Calculus Fidei: Some Ruminations on the Structure of the Theology of John Calvin* (Grand Rapids: Calvin Theological Seminary, 1978), p. 2. Portions of this work are also published in *Calvinus Ecclesiae Doctor*, ed. W. H. Neuser (Kampen: Kok, 1979), pp. 85–110.
2. Battles, *Calculus Fidei*, p. 20.
3. John Calvin, *Commentary on Seneca's "De Clementia"* (2.4.1) — quoted in Battles, *Calculus Fidei*, p. 16.
4. Battles, *Calculus Fidei*, p. 33.
5. Ibid., p. 20. According to Battles, the successive dichotomies of the true/false principle "exemplify a concept of truth emergent from bondage to falsehood, or conversely, of the lie seeking to engulf truth; it is the notion of the false approaching the negation it truly is, and of the true (as perceived by divinely-aided man) approaching the infinite perfection of God, its beginning and its end" (p. 22).

Figure 17.2

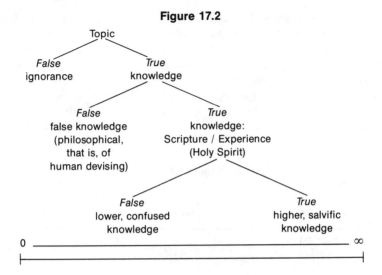

Note that the false positions approach the negation (0) they really are, while the true positions *approach* the infinity (∞) of God. This reminds Battles of the theory of limits in the field of mathematics:

> The Theory of Limits, on which modern mathematics, and as a corollary, all modern science and technology depend, is actually a secularized form of the Scriptural view of reality. Mathematics and Scripture both view the human grasp of reality as increasingly approximated to, but never identified with, the human symbols we use to represent reality. Even our system of numbers, when faced for example with defining the ratio of the side of a square to its hypotenuse, or of the circumference of a circle to its radius or diameter, cannot do more than approximate relationships given in the realm of creation.[6]

In this life, then, we can never arrive at complete truth. The limited nature of our human constructs or symbols of reality warns against the absolutizing of all human (theological) formulations.

Battles cautions us that the pathway to truth

> is fraught with turnings to either side, which to take is disaster. Faithful listening to Scripture prevents us from turning to either side. Truth, then, is an approaching, by man the created, under divine guidance, to the goal of God his Creator, Redeemer, and Judge.
> Our grasp of all Christian truth has this dynamic bipolarity — be-

6. Ibid., p. 44.

tween absence and presence, between nothing and infinity, between Creator and created — growing toward perfect comprehension but in this life not reaching it.

This movement toward the truth of God is seen in the agonizing effort to grasp the cardinal doctrines of our faith; the once dead but ever recurring heresies of the past clearly illustrate both the pitfalls of the search and the limits of the human mind in groping toward the truth.[7]

A Balanced Attitude Toward This World

Given Calvin's quest for the *via media,* it is no surprise that his teachings about proper Christian use of "the present life and its helps" begin by warning of a "double danger: mistaken strictness and mistaken laxity" (*Inst.* 3.10.1).[8] Calvin believed Scripture "duly informs us what is the right use of earthly benefits — a matter not to be neglected in the ordering of our life" (3.10.1). He saw the dangers of undue severity in those who would "fetter consciences more tightly than does the Word of the Lord." They would scarcely permit adding any food at all to plain bread and water. Calvin cited the example of Crates the Theban, who is said to have thrown all his goods into the sea, "for he thought that unless they were destroyed, they would destroy him."

On the other hand, Calvin was concerned about those who sought an excuse for "intemperance of the flesh in its use of external things." Such people refuse to be constrained by any limitations. They pave the way to "licentious indulgence." This lifestyle, too, Calvin firmly rejected. Thus he set himself against the "excess" of setting too many limits and the "defect" of having none at all.

Calvin did not intend to set precise legal formulas to bind consciences on these matters. This he believed was unbiblical. "But," he wrote, "inasmuch as Scripture gives general rules for lawful use, we ought surely to limit our use in accordance with them" (3.10.1).

Calvin takes a similar approach when he develops his doctrine of Christian freedom. He sees Christian freedom as consisting of three parts: (1) freedom from the law — the Christian is justified by God's mercy alone and not by his own works; (2) freedom of conscience — freed from the law's yoke, one obeys God's law willingly, as a response

7. Ibid., pp. 44–45.
8. John Calvin, *Institutes of the Christian Religion,* ed. John T. McNeill, trans. Ford Lewis Battles, Library of Christian Classics (Philadelphia: Westminster, 1960). All further references in the body of this essay are to this translation.

to grace, and not out of necessity; (3) freedom in "things indifferent" (*adiaphora*) (3.19.2–7). Here Battles notes the true/false principle at work (see Figure 17.3).[9]

Figure 17.3

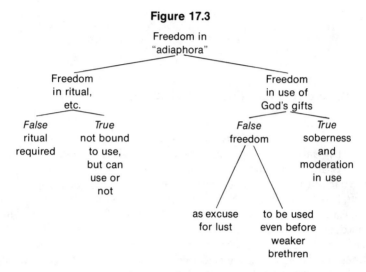

With respect to those matters on which no specific scriptural prescriptions have been given, Calvin argued that "we are not bound before God by any religious obligation preventing us from sometimes using them and other times not using them, indifferently" (3.19.7). Calvin was aware that sensitive consciences might be in serious doubt on certain matters and thus be in dire need of knowing the liberating power of the gospel with regard to these "things indifferent."

> If a man begins to doubt whether he may use linen for sheets, shirts, handkerchiefs, and napkins, he will afterward be uncertain also about hemp; finally doubt will even arise over tow. For he will turn over in his mind whether he can sup without napkins, or go without a handkerchief. If any man should consider daintier food unlawful, in the end he will not be at peace before God, when he eats either black bread or common victuals, while it occurs to him that he could sustain his body on even coarser foods. If he boggles at sweet wine, he will not with clear conscience drink even flat wine, and finally he will not dare touch water if sweeter and cleaner than other water. To sum up, he will come to the point of considering it wrong to step upon a straw across his path, as the saying goes. [3.19.7]

9. Battles, *Calculus Fidei,* p. 73 (table 14).

On the other hand, there are many who think that Christian freedom justifies their gluttony, luxury, and lusts (3.19.9). To strike a balance, Calvin affirmed that we are free to use God's gifts for God's purposes. We must realize that whatever we have is a gift from God. Accordingly, we should receive all blessings with an attitude of thanksgiving (3.19.8). As long as we realize that God is the source of our gifts and commit ourselves to using them for the purposes for which they were given, we may use them "with no scruple of conscience, no trouble of mind. With such confidence our minds will be at peace with him, and will recognize his liberality toward us."[10]

Calvin extended this freedom to use and enjoy earthly benefits into many realms. Food and drink are good gifts of a good God. Food was created by God "not only to provide for necessity but also for delight and good cheer" (3.10.2).[11] Clothing is meant not only for warmth, but also for "comeliness and decency." So too with such natural elements as grasses, trees, and fruits: "apart from their various uses, there is beauty of appearance and pleasantness of odor (Gen. 2:9)" (3.10.2). Calvin's sense of the aesthetic was also apparent when he commented on such things as wine, flowers, colors, gold, silver, and ivory. In short, did God not "render many things attractive to us, apart from their necessary use" (3.10.2)?

Thus Calvin displayed a genuine openness to the aesthetic dimensions of life. His broad cultural outlook included an appreciation for both the arts and science.[12] He recognized the good gifts of God and understood they are intended for the use and enjoyment of human beings. Accordingly, he emphasized that they must be used for the end or purpose for which they have been given: "for our good, not for our ruin" (3.10.2). Referring all these gifts to God as their source is, ultimately, the only check to preserve ourselves from perverting them. "All things," Calvin reminds us, "were created for us that we might recognize the Author and give thanks for his kindness toward us" (3.10.3). This attitude of thanksgiving preserves us from both excess and defect. When we fail to be thankful, either one of these dangers may arise. When we veer to either extreme, the true purpose of the

---

10. *Inst.* 3.19.8. See Ronald S. Wallace, *Calvin's Doctrine of the Christian Life* (Grand Rapids: Eerdmans, 1959), pp. 135ff.

11. See Wallace, *Calvin's Doctrine*, p. 137.

12. For Calvin on the arts and sciences see *Inst.* 1.11.12 and 2.2.12ff. and the notes in the Library of Christian Classics edition. Calvin's background in humanism is significant here.

gifts is not realized. Calvin comments graphically on the extreme of excess:

> Where is your thanksgiving if you so gorge yourself with banqueting or wine that you either become stupid or are rendered useless for the duties of piety and of your calling? Where is your recognition of God if your flesh boiling over with excessive abundance into vile lust infects the mind with its impurity so that you cannot discern anything that is right and honorable? Where is our gratefulness toward God for our clothing if in the sumptuousness of our apparel we both admire ourselves and despise others, if with its elegance and glitter we prepare ourselves for shameless conduct? [3.10.3]

The Issue of Wealth

Now that we have summarized Calvin's view of the proper Christian stance toward the world and the Christian's freedom to use, within limits, the provisions of the world, we must examine Calvin's position on the matter of wealth. This issue will be particularly instructive since the problems it poses are as real today as they were in the sixteenth century.

Calvin's Geneva, like all cities in all eras, displayed great economic disparities between the very rich and the very poor. Calvin had a cautious and suspicious attitude toward wealth. Although he without question saw material prosperity as a gift from God,[13] he strictly warned against the desire to amass a fortune. "It remains for us not greedily to strive after riches and honors — whether relying upon our own dexterity of wit or our own diligence, or depending upon the favor of men, or having confidence in vainly imagined fortune — but for us always to look to the Lord so that by his guidance we may be led to whatever lot he has provided" (3.7.9).

The mad rush for riches is exactly that, madness: "To covet wealth and honors, to strive for authority, to heap up riches, to gather together all those follies which seem to make for magnificence and pomp, our lust is mad, our desire boundless" (3.7.8). Those who covet such things delude themselves and reject the wisdom of Christ. Calvin is reminded of the Pharisees of old — entertaining a deep-rooted conviction "that riches were blessed and therefore that there was nothing better than to increase one's possessions by any method and to hold

---

13. See the citations in Wallace, *Calvin's Doctrine*, pp. 135ff. But Calvin did not accept the related view that poverty and misfortune are direct signs of God's disfavor. See W. Fred Graham, *The Constructive Revolutionary: John Calvin and His Socio-Economic Impact* (Richmond: John Knox, 1971), pp. 66–67.

tight to what one has got, they rejected as an absurd paradox whatever Christ said on the opposite side."[14] Those who strive after wealth actually scorn God when they dare pray the petition in the Lord's Prayer asking for daily bread:

> Those who, not content with daily bread but panting after countless things with unbridled desire, or sated with their abundance, or care-free in their piled-up riches, supplicate God with this prayer are but mocking him. For the first ones ask him what they do not wish to receive, indeed, what they utterly abominate — namely, mere daily bread — and as much as possible cover up before God their propensity to greed. . . . [3.20.44]

The danger is that possessions can become possessors and can indeed cause one to lose his soul; they can become like cords which strangle.[15] Calvin describes the "insatiable desire for possessions" as a "major plague."[16]

On the other side there stands the grim specter of poverty. Physical poverty was real enough in Geneva, a city that received a steady stream of refugees from all over Europe. Calvin's concern for the poor is evident in his theological writings and also in his actions on their behalf in Geneva.[17] In 1541 Calvin drafted the Church Ordinances that dealt with the "fourth order of ecclesiastical government, that is, the Deacons."[18] The diaconate was to handle money, administer the hospital, and distribute aid to the poor.[19]

In particular Calvin saw it as the duty of those blessed with material wealth to come to the aid of the poor:

> Those who have riches, whether inherited or won by their own industry and labor, are to remember that what is left over is meant not

14. *Comm. on Luke* 16:14 in *Calvin's New Testament Commentaries (CNTC)*, ed. David W. and Thomas F. Torrance (Grand Rapids: Eerdmans, 1959–1972), vol. 2, p. 114; cf. Ford Lewis Battles, "Against Luxury and Licence in Geneva," *Interpretation* 19 (1965): 182–202.

15. See Wallace, *Calvin's Doctrine,* pp. 127, 176; cf. *Inst.* 3.20.46.

16. *Comm. on Matt.* 6:19 (*CNTC* 1.215).

17. See Calvin's commentaries as cited in Graham, *Constructive Revolutionary,* chap. 4, "Wealth and Poverty"; and Robert M. Kingdon, "Social Welfare in Calvin's Geneva," *American Historical Review* 76 (1971): 50–69.

18. See *Calvin: Theological Treatises,* trans. and ed. J. K. S. Reid, Library of Christian Classics (Philadelphia: Westminster, 1954), pp. 64ff.

19. See Graham, *Constructive Revolutionary,* pp. 98ff.; and J. K. S. Reid, "Diakonia in the Thought of Calvin," in *Service in Christ: Essays Presented to Karl Barth on His 80th Birthday,* ed. James I. McCord and T. H. L. Parker (Grand Rapids: Eerdmans, 1966), pp. 101–09; cf. *Inst.* 4.3.9; 4.4.5.

for intemperance or luxury but for relieving the needs of the brethren.
. . . I acknowledge indeed that we are not bound to such an equality
as would make it wrong for the rich to live more elegantly than the
poor; but there must be such an equality that nobody starves and
nobody hordes his abundance at another's expense.[20]

The poor, in fact, serve a positive function in God's overall scheme of
things. As His *procureurs* or *receveurs,* they serve as a type of ba-
rometer of the faith and charity of the Christian community. "God
sends us the poor as his receivers. And although the alms are given
to mortal creatures, yet God accepts and approves them and puts
them to one's account, as if we had placed in his hands that which
we give to the poor."[21] But sadly, "there are many apparently liberal,
who yet do not feel for the miseries of their brothers."[22] In these
statements we find what has been called Calvin's "social and economic
ethic of concern."[23]

Calvin considered poverty a serious problem. It deprives people of
the material benefits of God's kindness that are meant to be shared
by all. But poverty can also be detrimental spiritually. For in the midst
of poverty, faith in God can go into eclipse. Just like the lust for
possessions (excess), poverty (defect) can cause one to forget God.
Commenting on the Lord's Prayer, Calvin notes that Christians are
subject to temptations on both ends of the scale:

> And these temptations are either from the right or from the left. From
> the right are, for example, riches, power, honors, which often dull
> men's keenness of sight by the glitter and seeming goodness they
> display, and allure with their blandishments, so that, captivated by
> such tricks and drunk with such sweetness, men forget their God.
> From the left are, for example, poverty, disgrace, contempt, afflictions,
> and the like. Thwarted by the hardship and difficulty of these, they
> become despondent in mind, cast away assurance and hope, and are
> at last completely estranged from God. [3.20.46]

Because of its physical and spiritual consequences, then, poverty must
be fought and alleviated. To fail to respond to this problem is to fall
short of God's desire for any society and seriously to misunderstand
God's commands in Scripture and the implications of the Christian
gospel.

20. *Comm. on 2 Cor.* 8:15 (*CNTC* 10.114).
21. Sermon 95 on Deut. 15:11–15 (*CO* 27.338). This translation is found in
Graham, *Constructive Revolutionary,* p. 69.
22. *Comm. on 1 John* 3:17 (*CNTC* 12.277).
23. Graham, *Constructive Revolutionary,* p. 70.

Now that we have taken a brief look at Calvin's stance on wealth and poverty, it remains for us to comment on a few related matters. Calvin's economic thought has, of course, been the topic of much scrutiny and debate.[24] Without entering the various arguments, we will make several points with regard to Calvin's general view of economic activity.

It is to be noted that Calvin was concerned with issues of commerce and economic justice. His theology was not disembodied, divorced from the realities of life where laborers and employers are often at odds over economic matters. Calvin realized that because of the nature of humanity and sinfulness all of our institutions and endeavors are to some extent motivated by self-interest, pride, and greed.[25] Yet his is a "world-affirming theology" in the sense that he sought to apply the gospel to all of life. That meant seeking the guidance of Scripture for the problems besetting humanity, particularly those besetting the citizens of Geneva. Thus Calvin as a theologian and pastor became involved in everyday matters as diverse as the "high cost of dying," hospitals, sumptuary laws, and the regulation of business and industry. Some today may not agree with or approve of Calvin's stands, but they must admit that he regarded no area as too secular to be of legitimate Christian concern.

This meant that Calvin dealt with the question of wages. For him, wages were a sign of the unmerited favor or grace of God. No one, before God, can lay claim to any rightful remuneration. As Calvin commented on the parable of the unprofitable servant: "God is not moved to render a reward by the worthiness of the works but by his free kindness."[26] Since no one is ultimately worth what is received, "for the employer to withhold from his worker what he owes is really to withhold from him what God pays to him."[27]

The guiding principle in all of this for Calvin was equity (*aequitas*). In determining what is equitable we must keep our minds on God and be guided by the norm in the gospel: "Do unto others as you would have them do unto you." Wages must be adequate for the support of life. In deciding an employee's wages the employer should ask: "If I were in his place, how would I want to be treated? I would want to

---

24. See the well-known work by Max Weber, *The Protestant Ethic and the Spirit of Capitalism,* rev. ed. (New York: Scribner's, 1977); and Robert S. Paul, "Weber and Calvinism: The Effects of a 'Calling,' " *Canadian Journal of Theology* 11 (1965): 25–41, as well as Graham, *Constructive Revolutionary,* chap. 11.

25. See *Inst.* 2.2–3.

26. *Comm. on Luke* 17:7 (*CNTC* 2.123); cf. André Biéler, *The Social Humanism of Calvin,* trans. Paul T. Fuhrmann (Richmond: John Knox, 1964), pp. 47ff.

27. Graham, *Constructive Revolutionary,* p. 83.

be supported."[28] On other issues as well, equity is "the prime principle for Calvin in understanding true justice."[29] Like other principles discussed earlier in this essay, equity marks a middle ground between too much and not enough. While no fixed formula for a just wage is set by Calvin, he does hold to this fundamental principle of equity, determined by the sensitive Christian conscience.

Prescriptions for the Christian Life

Calvin's writings offer several prescriptions as to how we might best live the Christian life in the midst of society. These prescriptions do not take the form of legalistic commandments, but rather point toward a stance, a mind-set, a lifestyle, that seeks to take seriously what it means to live as a Christian in the midst of a world or culture that has its own meanings and values.

Moderation

Calvin's theology, balanced as it was on the spectrum between defect and excess, takes practical shape when he urges moderation. This means curbing extravagant appetites and intemperances, fleeing from excesses, and bridling ourselves so "that we may not burn with an immoderate desire to grow rich or ambitiously pant after honors" (3.7.9). For Calvin this amounted to a rule of temperance which checked inordinate passions and desires for worldly comforts and pleasures.[30] These turn one's heart from God and choke true piety. Calvin urges instead that all should live, "whether slenderly, or moderately, or plentifully, so that [they] may remember God nourishes them to live, not to luxuriate" (3.19.9). As he struggled against poverty and warned against excessive possessions and profits, Calvin urged the *via media* of moderation.

In his preaching and biblical expositions, Calvin dealt with a number of excesses that corrupt culture and sear society. These range from gluttony, sexual vice, intemperate wine-drinking, and riches to civil litigations and war.[31] In the face of all these, Calvin urged moderation as "the chief virtue of believers."[32]

28. Sermon 95 on Deut. 15:11–15 (CO 27.347), as cited in Graham, *Constructive Revolutionary*, p. 85.

29. Ford Lewis Battles, "Notes on John Calvin, Justitia and the Old Testament Law," in *Intergerini Parietis Septum (Eph. 2:14)*, ed. Dikran Y. Hadidian (Pittsburgh: Pickwick, 1981), p. 32. On Calvin and usury see Graham, *Constructive Revolutionary*, pp. 87ff.; and Wallace, *Calvin's Doctrine*, p. 156.

30. See Wallace, *Calvin's Doctrine*, chap. 6; *Inst.* 3.19.9.

31. See Wallace, *Calvin's Doctrine*, pp. 171–78.

32. *Comm. on Rom.* 12:16 (CNTC 8.275).

Calvin called for moderation even in the midst of the trials and deprivations of life. It is important to have restraint when we are tempted to overindulge. But it is also important, according to Calvin, to cultivate moderation amid the afflictions to which all lives are subject. Thus he called for:

> the moderation of passion and grief in the face of adversity, insult, injury and every kind of care and anxiety, for it is fatally easy under such circumstances to indulge in our infirmity and allow ourselves to be carried away by our feelings and reactions beyond the bounds of all moderation. Indeed, the sorrows of life can carry us away into excess even more easily than the joys of life. We must "compose our mind to patience" by moderating even our grief.[33]

Correlatively, even zeal and ardor for the sake of the kingdom of God need this tempering of moderation. The fervor of our zeal must not be allowed to "exceed the bounds of reason and moderation."[34] The gift of prudence is needed so that our bold actions are not propelled headlong by rashness and recklessness (*témérité*), but tempered by wisdom and judgment.[35] Thus all spheres of Christian behavior need to be grounded in moderation.

Modesty

Related to the prescription of moderation is Calvin's concern for modesty. Most often this means avoiding lavish outward display and showing, at the same time, a willingness to honor, love, and serve others. As Calvin comments on Romans 12:10: "So modesty, by which each comes to honor others, best nourishes love."[36] Then again, he refers to humility as "the mother of modesty, the effect of which is that, yielding up our own right, we defer to others, and are not easily thrown into disorder."[37] This love is so genuine that there is no desire to indulge in "pomp and display" before others.[38] There is a careful scrutiny of one's manner and style of dress.

---

33. Wallace, *Calvin's Doctrine*, p. 182, citing Calvin's commentaries on 1 Thess. 5:16 (CO 52.174); Ps. 85:9 (CO 31.788); Ps. 39:2 (CO 31.396); and the sermon on Job 1:20–22 (CO 33.94).
34. *Comm. on Matt.* 26:51 (CO 45.730), cited in Wallace, *Calvin's Doctrine*, p. 145.
35. Sermon on 2 Sam. 2:22–23, p. 26, as cited in Wallace, *Calvin's Doctrine*, p. 185.
36. *Comm. on Rom.* 12:10 (CNTC 8.271).
37. *Comm. on Phil.* 2:3 (CNTC 11.245).
38. Sermon on 1 Tim. 6:9–11 (CO 26.329–30), as cited in Wallace, *Calvin's Doctrine*, p. 179.

Calvin extended his admonitions on "modesty and chastity" within the framework of the seventh commandment: "Thou shalt not commit adultery." He urged that husband and wife not engage in anything that is unworthy of the marriage. "For it is fitting that thus wedlock contracted in the Lord be recalled to measure and modesty so as not to wallow in extreme lewdness" (2.8.44). Calvin linked the themes of modest dress and chastity when he argued that God not only forbids fornication but also "does not permit us to seduce the modesty of another with wanton dress and obscene gestures and foul speech." For God "loathes all uncleanness, in whatever part of our soul or body it may appear." To drive the point home, Calvin concluded: "And lest there be any doubt, remember that God is here commanding modesty. If the Lord requires modesty of us, he condemns whatever opposes it" (2.8.44).

Calvin's general interpretation of the seventh commandment has both a negative and positive pole: "we should not become defiled with any filth or lustful intemperance of the flesh. To this corresponds the affirmative commandment that we chastely and continently regulate all parts of our life" (2.8.41). And once again, Calvin advocates the *via media*. His prescription of modesty is set within the context of defect and excess. Calvin recognizes celibacy as the exception rather than the rule for Christian life (see 2.8.42). It is "a special grace which the Lord bestows only upon certain men, in order to hold them more ready for his work" (2.8.43). Since Scripture openly declares that all are not able to "keep chastity in celibacy," God has instituted marriage for (among other purposes) the regulation of human sexual desire. God "requires purity and modesty of us" (2.8.43) and in marriage provides the way this prescription can be met. Calvin notes that "Paul defines modesty as 'purity of heart joined with chastity of body' " (2.8.43). Thus modesty has an inner dimension (intent) as well as an outward manifestation (temperance and chastity). According to Calvin, the modesty prescribed by God is both inner and outward. Through marriage humanity is provided the means by which a middle path between complete abstinence from sexual relations, possible only for the few given the gift of celibacy, and the excess of "defilement" and "lustful intemperance of the flesh" can be attained. This is the "modesty" of marriage. And even within wedlock itself, Calvin continues, let no one "admit anything at all that is unworthy of the honorableness and temperance of marriage" (2.8.44). If Calvin's comment on Romans 12:10 ("so modesty, by which each comes to honor others, best nourishes love") is normative, then within the marriage relationship modesty should be the controlling feature.

Meditation on the Future Life

Calvin's third prescription for Christians is meditation on the future life. Christians are called upon to meditate on the world to come while living in the tensions of this world. Calvin urges us to adopt the fundamental attitude of *contemptio mundi*. "Whatever kind of tribulation presses upon us, we must ever look to this end: to accustom ourselves to contempt for the present life and to be aroused thereby to meditate upon the future life" (3.9.1). The present life is full of vanities and allurements. "Stunned by the empty dazzlement of riches, power, and honors, [our minds] become so deadened that they can see no farther. The heart also, occupied with avarice, ambition, and lust, is so weighed down that it cannot rise up higher" (3.9.1). Yet God calls us "not to be captivated by such panderings" (3.9.2), but to come away from a "perverse love of this life" to a "desire for a better one" (3.9.4). This is the eternal life which God sets before us; He rescues us from "this boundless abyss of all evils and miseries" and leads us into "that blessed inheritance of his life and glory" (3.9.5). Thus the Christian life "strains towards a completion and fulfilment that belong to it only beyond death."[39]

Calvin speaks in the strongest possible terms about total renunciation of this world: "Indeed, there is no middle ground between these two: either the world must become worthless to us or hold us bound by intemperate love of it" (3.9.2). Further, "if the earthly life be compared with the heavenly, it is doubtless to be at once despised and trampled under foot" (3.9.4). Yet Calvin goes on to qualify this by explaining that the earthly life "is never to be hated except in so far as it holds us subject to sin; although not even hatred of that condition may ever properly be turned against life itself" (3.9.4). For "this life, however crammed with infinite miseries it may be, is still rightly to be counted among those blessings of God which are not to be spurned" (3.9.3).

What Calvin is advocating here is that Christians be fully involved in the present world — they should accept God's good gifts with thankfulness and be active in all spheres of human endeavor — yet manifest an outlook oriented primarily toward the future:

We must remember to distinguish between the blessings of the present and those of the future. For in this world God blesses us in such a way as to give us a mere foretaste of His kindness, and by that taste

39. Wallace, *Calvin's Doctrine*, p. 88; see chap. 4: "Meditation on the Future or Heavenly Life."

to entice us to desire heavenly blessings with which we may be satisfied. That is why the blessings of this present life are not only mixed
but almost destroyed by very many afflictions, for it is not good for
us to have abundance here lest we should begin to luxuriate in it.[40]

This life, insofar as it entraps us in sin, is to be hated. At the same
time good gifts are to be accepted with gratitude and Christians are
to be involved in the world — but always with an eye toward the coming kingdom of heaven.

In this sense the Christian stance which Calvin urges is a *via media.* Christians are to live midway between the "brutish love of this
world" (3.9.1) characteristic of the sinful self and the final perfection
and blessedness which the saints will achieve in the kingdom of God
(3.9.6). What separates godly people from the worldly is "their opposite attitudes to this present world and to that beyond."[41] Meditation on the future life will give meaning to all the good gifts received
in the present. It is in the present, in the tension between living in
this world and looking to the next, that this *meditatio futurae vitae*
takes place.

Theologian for an Age of Limits

What do Calvin's theological method of reaching for the truth of
God that lies between the false limits of defect and excess, his attitude
toward the world and the problems of social life (particularly the
disparity between wealth and poverty), and his prescriptions for
Christian living have to say to this contemporary age of limits?

Calvin's Theological Method

Calvin's theological method itself is suggestive. Not only does it
offer a model for theological reflection, but it also gives us a certain
warning. By recognizing that all human statements can only approximate the truth (the only ultimate Truth being God Himself), it warns
against the absolutizing of theological positions. Our language as well
as our theological reflection is limited. We cannot make statements
which exhaust the truth; nor can our doctrinal formulas, being limited
statements, claim to be identical with the realities to which they point.

40. *Comm. on 1 Tim.* 4:8 (*CNTC* 10.244); cf. *Inst.* 3.9.3; Thomas F. Torrance,
Kingdom and Church (Fair Lawn, N.J.: Essential Books, 1956), p. 121.
41. Wallace, *Calvin's Doctrine,* p. 129, citing Calvin's *Comm. on Ps.* 119:132.
Wallace notes that Calvin employs the term *contemptio* (in *contemptio mundi*) as the
opposite of *meditatio* (in *meditatio futurae vitae*).

In this connection it is most helpful to see that Calvin's own theology seeks to approximate as closely as possible the revelation of the truth of God which he found in Holy Scripture. But his was a theology within limits. As investigation has shown, his positions invariably reside at some midpoint between those with whom he was in dialogue — between their defects and excesses on the theological spectrum.

This insight into Calvin's method takes practical hold when we examine his views about the world and the Christian in the world. For it is most significant that just as intellectual and theological perceptions are framed within a context of limits, so also proper human behavior under God is set within a context of limits. Recognizing that, in matters of behavior, there are problems inherent in both extremes (defect and excess), the Christian adapts his lifestyle accordingly. Thus intellectually, theologically, and behaviorally, the Christian lives within limits.

The importance of this on the global scale is that in view of limited resources (e.g., food, energy) the only approach to living that can insure a continued future is that of people who recognize and are willing to adapt to the limited resources of the world community. Only those who are willing to come to grips with a world of limits by living a life and adopting attitudes that work within these limits offer hope. Calvin's recognition of the existence and nature of limits and his consequent call for balanced attitudes can help us in the twentieth century realize that Christian life, as well as Christian theology, must be carefully carved out in responsible ways that take the matter of limits seriously.

Calvin on the Issue of Wealth and Poverty

As this study has shown with regard to selected social problems, Calvin constantly warned against the dangers of excess. With regard to both possessions and profits Calvin cautioned that excesses can be corrosive. They can seduce one from a proper detachment from the things of this world toward a mistaken bold confidence that possessions and profits are all that need to be sought in life. Calvin did not deny that there is a legitimate use of worldly possessions, and he also sanctioned commerce and economic activities. Yet these are to serve a greater end. They are not to be without restraint. For they must ultimately be turned by the Christian to the service of God. Note what Calvin has to say about the writer of the twenty-third Psalm, who, while the Lord provided him a table furnished with "good things," kept his mind on the fact that he was going to dwell in the house of the Lord forever:

He valued all the comforts of the flesh only in proportion as they served to enable him to live to God. . . . It is therefore certain that the mind of David, by the aid of the temporal prosperity which he enjoyed, was elevated to the hope of the everlasting inheritance.[42]

We should view earthly enrichments in the light of our eternal destiny and use them for the purposes of God. Calvin had this in mind when he spoke of stewardship: "We are the stewards of everything God has conferred on us by which we are able to help our neighbor, and are required to render account of our stewardship. Moreover, the only right stewardship is that which is tested by the rule of love" (3.7.5). Eschatology and ethics are intimately interrelated.

This is why Calvin is so conscious of the dangers of inordinate desires and excess in possessions and profits. In a cogent passage in the *Institutes* he warns against allowing the gift to obscure the Giver:

Where is your recognition of God if your flesh boiling over with excessive abundance into vile lust infects the mind with its impurity so that you cannot discern anything that is right and honorable? . . . Clearly, leave to abuse God's gifts must be somewhat curbed, and Paul's rule is confirmed: that we should "make no provision for the flesh, to gratify its desires" [Rom. 13:14], for if we yield too much to these, they boil up without measure or control. [3.10.3]

On the other hand, Calvin was equally anxious to find remedies for the defects in social situations. His concern for the poor and particularly for the refugees in his own city of Geneva took special theological shape in his understanding of the role of deacons in the church.[43] Calvin believed the diaconate should be "a lay ministry devoted solely to aiding the poor."[44] Scripture, in his view, authorizes two kinds of deacons: those who collect alms for the poor and those who distribute them. In a sermon on 1 Timothy, he used the terms *hospitaliers* and *procureurs* of the poor, the exact terms for those charged with these tasks by the city government of Geneva.[45] Whatever Calvin's rela-

42. *Comm. on Ps.* 23:5–6 (*CO* 31.242–43), cited in Wallace, *Calvin's Doctrine,* p. 127.

43. See *Inst.* 4.3.9; 4.4.5; 4.5.15; 4.19.32; and Reid, "Diakonia in the Thought of Calvin."

44. Kingdon, "Social Welfare," p. 60.

45. Ibid., p. 60. Kingdon suggests Geneva may have influenced Calvin here more than Calvin influenced Geneva. His study of those who became *hospitaliers* and *procureurs* of the Geneva hospital indicates that "the great majority and the most active of them were especially devoted to Calvin's leadership" (p. 64).

tionships were to institutions such as the General Hospital and whatever amount of promotion he personally gave to the *Bourse française* (a fund to aid refugees who wished to establish residency in Geneva), it can rightly be said that "Calvin was neither indifferent to the needs of the poor nor unwilling to enter politics to advance a cause he valued. He simply selected with care the particular arenas in which he deployed his formidable energies."[46] Calvin's activities rested ultimately on his views that stressed the solidarity of humankind, love as the ethic for Christian social and economic practices, and the right of the state to interfere in business practices in order to foster a decent standard of human life.[47] Such views propelled the Christian church to seek relief and even a cure for poverty.

Calvin's Prescriptions for Christian Living

Calvin's prescriptions for Christian living, which, as we have seen, are set within a context of excess and defect, also have application to the contemporary scene. The dangers of excess are constantly with us. They are intensified now in a world pushing against its limited resources for human survival. Those in wealthy nations with high standards of living must take seriously Calvin's warnings against the dangers of luxuries, not only from the perspective of how one's eternal destiny is affected, but also from the standpoint that we live in a world of limited natural resources. To use them with no thought of restraint or of future generations is irresponsible and sinful. To amass more and more for self, while others have less and less, is not only uncharitable but flies in the face of Calvin's concern that all persons have enough to survive (equity). Thus along with an avoidance of excess, Christians in a world of limits must have an equal discomfort over the lacks endured by the world's poor. This discomfort should goad them to action. The resources of God must be shared. In a world of limited resources, we must propose and implement more-equitable means of distributing them.

Calvin's prescriptions for the Christian are moderation, modesty, and meditation on the future life. Each, as seen above, is the *via media* between extremes. They call us to receive God's good gifts thankfully and employ those gifts for God's purposes. They call us to curb our appetites and do away with "uncontrolled desire, . . . immoderate prodigality, . . . vanity and arrogance," so we may "with a clean conscience cleanly use God's gifts," remembering all the while that "God nourishes [us] to live, not to luxuriate" (3.19.9).

---

46. Ibid., p. 64.
47. See Graham, *Constructive Revolutionary*, p. 76, and the whole of chap. 4.

Moderation and modesty mean we will so temper our living as to reflect our realization that we are parts of a global community in which all people share the problem of diminishing resources. We will be willing and active in using our material possessions for the sake of those with less. In following a moderate and modest lifestyle, we will make do with the least possible for ourselves so that others might have enough. As Calvin commented on Ezekiel 18:7, God has united humanity "in the bonds of mutual society; hence they must mutually perform good offices for each other. Here, then, it is required of the rich to succor the poor, and to offer bread to the hungry."[48] "Scripture calls us to resign ourselves and all our possessions to the Lord's will, and to yield to him the desires of our hearts to be tamed and subjugated" (3.7.8). Thus while making moderate use of what we have, we will also fulfil our obligation to give and share. All this is possible only because Christians have renounced ultimate claim on their lives (self-denial; see 3.7) in light of the claim of God in Jesus Christ.

Meditation on the future life which has been promised us in Christ will help us set priorities for life here and now. Christians labor in the midst of the complexities of present-day society, struggling with the problems inherent in a world of limits, yet knowing that "in the Lord their labor is not in vain" (1 Cor. 15:58). It is this hope in God, amidst even turbulent issues, which "encourages believers at the start, and sustains them later on, so that they do not fall out of the race."[49]

---

48. *Comm. on Ezek.* 18:7, as cited in Wallace, *Calvin's Doctrine,* p. 153.
49. *Comm. on 1 Cor.* 15:58 (*CNTC* 9.347–48).

18

Eschatology and History
A Look at Calvin's Eschatological Vision

David E. Holwerda

Calvin has never been famous for his eschatology. Yet political and economic historians have frequently emphasized Calvin's revolutionary understanding of history. In fact, there are those who believe that the two most influential revolutionaries of the modern world have been John Calvin and Karl Marx.[1] Whether one agrees with that estimation or not, historians do agree that the Protestant Reformation restored a sense of dynamism and purpose in history, and provided its adherents with a fresh interpretation of the past and a vivid sense of historical destiny. The key figure in this development was John Calvin.[2]

However, is it possible to hold a revolutionary view of history without having, implicitly or explicitly, an equally significant eschatology? Of course, one can hold eschatological beliefs concerning life after death and the return of Christ without seeing any significant relationship between history and eschatology. But is it possible for a Christian theologian to advocate a dynamic view of history without seeing a direct and positive relationship between history and eschatology?

Reprinted from *Exploring the Heritage of John Calvin,* ed. David E. Holwerda (Grand Rapids: Baker, 1976), pp. 110–39.

1. E.g., R. H. Tawney, *Religion and the Rise of Capitalism* (London: John Murray, 1960), pp. 111ff.

2. E. H. Harbison, "History and Destiny," *Theology Today* 21 (Jan. 1965): 395. See also his book *Christianity and History* (Princeton: Princeton University, 1964), chap. 12.

In the Middle Ages history was viewed as static, and eschatology was not really concerned with history.[3] Consequently, there was no sense of dynamic movement in history. There was the passing of time, but no essential change. At best, events were recorded as examples of timeless truths, not as signs of the times. History was static and so was the kingdom of God, for it was embedded in the permanent and unchangeable structure of the church. The Reformation challenged these static views of kingdom and history. The dynamic, active God of the Bible was rediscovered, and from that flowed the vision of history as constant change and meaningful turmoil until the final consummation of the kingdom.[4]

For those acquainted only with the characteristic theological face of Calvin, it must be noted that Calvin's theological thinking was deeply involved with the structures and realities of everyday life. W. F. Graham observes that

> for Calvin the real world was to be taken seriously, and for him the real world involved shoemakers, printers, and clockmakers, as well as farmers, scholars, knights, and clergymen. Calvin's world-affirming theology is quite apparent.[5]

More than any other in his time, Calvin attempted to see the relevance of the gospel for all areas of life. It is precisely here in Calvin's social and economic thought that Graham sees his revolutionary character, rather than in his more strictly theological positions. From this perspective Graham describes Calvin as "an almost thoroughgoing secularist in the sense that he understood the gospel to be irrevocably concerned with the world."[6] The evidence supplied by Graham demonstrates conclusively that Calvin was a constructive revolutionary, but the relationship between Calvin's revolutionary social and economic ideas and his theological perspective is left unanswered.[7]

3. The notable exception was Joachim of Floris (1131–1202), who attempted to revive an eschatological perspective on history, but whose views were considered heretical. See K. Löwith, *Meaning in History* (Chicago: University of Chicago, 1949), chap. 8.

4. Harbison, "History and Destiny," pp. 396ff. See also T. F. Torrance, "The Eschatology of the Reformation," *Eschatology* (Edinburgh: Oliver and Boyd, 1957), pp. 37ff.

5. W. F. Graham, *The Constructive Revolutionary: John Calvin and His Socio-Economic Impact* (Richmond: John Knox, 1971), p. 79.

6. Ibid., p. 160.

7. See also A. Biéler, *The Social Humanism of Calvin* (Richmond: John Knox, 1964).

Traditionally the theological taproot for Calvin's historical dynamism is found either in his doctrine of the sovereignty of God[8] or in his doctrine of predestination.[9] Both of these doctrines are essentially the same. Calvin's God is not the "empty, idle" God of the scholastics, but a "watchful, effective, active sort, engaged in ceaseless activity." He is the omnipotent and sovereign God because "governing heaven and earth by his providence, he so regulates all things that nothing takes place without his deliberation."[10] This same sovereign God who determines all things by His will calls men to effective obedience in the world. Thus the life of the elect is created by God's redemptive purpose in the world, and their task becomes one of obediently advancing the kingdom of God in the world.

Without a doubt Calvin's view of the sovereignty of God and of His predetermining will gives considerable impetus to his view of history. This is what I call the "push-view" of history. God is pushing history toward its destiny, like the great stone in Daniel cut from the mountain by no human hand, rolling down and crushing the kingdoms of the world until finally there stands the sovereign kingdom of God which will never be destroyed. Calvin was filled with this vision of the sovereign God controlling human history and destiny. But this is not the only source of his historical dynamism.

There is another taproot for Calvin's historical perspective, one generally overlooked in the past but today beginning to receive its due emphasis. Calvin held not only a "push-view" of history, but also a "pull-view" of history. There is a new reality at work drawing and pulling us into the future. Since Christ appeared "there is nothing left for the faithful," says Calvin, "except to look foward to His second coming with minds alert."[11] For Calvin, the predetermining will of God has been revealed and accomplished in the person and work of Christ. Now after Christ's ascension to heaven, this new reality draws believers upward and forward toward the culmination of human history and the consummation of the kingdom of God.[12] Calvin's escha-

---

8. W. S. Reid, "The Genevan Revolutionary," *Evangelical Quarterly* 32 (1960): 75-78.

9. Harbison, "History and Destiny," pp. 402ff.

10. *Inst.* 1.16.3.

11. *Comm. on 1 Peter* 4:7.

12. Although W. F. Graham makes little reference to Calvin's theological perspective, several of his statements suggest an eschatological source for Calvin's historical perspective. For example, "Luther leaned toward the medieval idea of God present at holy times in holy places. He understood history to be nearing its end, and waited in anticipation for the imminent divine disclosure. Calvin pointed toward the future and had little need for holy times or places. His God was dynamic, futuristic,

tological vision is indispensable for a proper understanding of his dynamic view of human history.[13]

Why was this taproot not stressed in the past? Probably because the positions Calvin adopts on specific eschatological doctrines are quite traditional. Naturally Calvin argued against Roman Catholic speculation about purgatory and the location of paradise, and he vigorously opposed the fanatical belief that the kingdom of God could be established by violence (as attempted in Münster in 1534). Still his eschatology remained a rather moderate, nonspeculative, middle-of-the-road position, containing no creative reformulation of the church's eschatology. At least such is the case when one focuses on *specific* doctrines, such as the intermediate state, resurrection, return of Christ, judgment, and the future kingdom of God.

In addition, there are elements in Calvin's theology that create problems for the thesis that his eschatology contributes significantly to his historical dynamism. One such element is his meditation on the future life coupled with his doctrine of the immortality of the soul. To some interpreters this seems to short-circuit any real concern for historical destiny or for the cosmic sweep of biblical eschatology.[14] Another problem stems from Calvin's stress on the unity of the Testaments. Some believe that this leads Calvin to a position where there are no longer any real differences created within the history of God's people,[15] and that the only significant moments are eternal and transcendent.[16]

Therefore, in order to establish the thesis that Calvin's eschatological vision contributed significantly to his revolutionary stance, it will be necessary, first of all, to examine the problem areas mentioned above.

---

concerned for human obedience in the present" (*Constructive Revolutionary,* p. 208; see also pp. 54–56). If this is so, perhaps it would be fruitful to argue that Calvin's occasional "overuse" of government to achieve the demands of the gospel lay in his failure to consistently distinguish the eschatological reordering of man and society, which occurs in Christ, from the political reordering appropriate to human government. In a chapter on "Success and Failure," Graham argues, however, that this was caused by a failure in Christology. That may be the case, but I am not convinced.

13. Torrance, "Eschatology of the Reformation," pp. 39ff. Where Calvin's view of the sovereignty of God is separated from eschatology, the possibility arises of transforming that sovereignty into a rigid determinism which destroys all human responsibility for history.

14. E.g., H. Quistorp, *Calvin's Doctrine of the Last Things* (London: Lutterworth, 1955), pp. 12–13; J. P. Martin, *The Last Judgment: In Protestant Theology from Orthodoxy to Ritschl* (Grand Rapids: Eerdmans, 1963), pp. 4, 12.

15. H. H. Wolf, *Die Einheit des Bundes* (Neukirchen Kreis Moers, 1958), chap. 6.

16. L. G. M. Alting Geusau, quoted in I. J. Hesselink, "Calvin and Heilsgeschichte," *Oikonomia* (Hamburg: Bergstedt, 1967), p. 164.

Meditation on the Future Life and Immortality of the Soul

Sometimes it seems that for Calvin the death of the individual is the dividing line between time and eternity, the present and the future life. Death appears to be the key eschatological event because through death the immortal soul enters into the perfection of the future kingdom. The entire eschatological perspective seems to be removed from the plane of history and to be exhausted in its application to individual destiny.

For example, how should the following words of Calvin be understood?

> If heaven is our homeland, what else is the earth but our place of exile? If departure from the world is entry into life, what else is the world but a sepulchre? . . . If to be freed from the body is to be released into perfect freedom, what else is the body but a prison? If to enjoy the presence of God is the summit of happiness, is not to be without this, misery? . . . Therefore, if the earthly life be compared with the heavenly, it is doubtless to be at once despised and trampled under foot.[17]

Does Calvin advocate a world-flight which seeks the freedom of the soul apart from the body? Does his "contempt for the present life"[18] make death the key eschatological event? Is Calvin's eschatology more Greek than biblical?

Calvin did hold to what is essentially a philosophical doctrine of the immortality of the soul. But like most of the early church fathers, Calvin modified the Platonic doctrine by means of the doctrine of creation.[19] The soul is not immortal in and of itself. Immortality is a gift of God and the life of the soul is continually dependent on the grace and will of God. If God's grace were withdrawn, the soul would be but a passing breath. Nevertheless, the immortality of the soul was very important to Calvin. He found it useful for articulating important perspectives on life and death, and for constructing theological or philosophical refutations of opposing positions.

The doctrine of the immortality of the soul was especially important in Calvin's first theological writing, the *Psychopannychia*. This work

17. *Inst.* 3.9.4.
18. *Inst.* 3.9.1.
19. See H. A. Wolfson, "Immortality and Resurrection in the Philosophy of the Church Fathers," in *Immortality and Resurrection,* ed. K. Stendahl (New York: Macmillan, 1965), pp. 57–58; and Wilhelm Niesel, *The Theology of Calvin* (Philadelphia: Westminster, 1956), p. 66.

was devoted to a refutation of the position of some Anabaptists who held to the doctrine of soul-sleep between death and final resurrection. In this work Calvin expresses himself, as he continues to do later in the *Institutes,* in terms of a dichotomy of body and soul.

> If the body is the prison of the soul, if the earthly habitation is a kind of fetters, what is the state of the soul when set free from this prison, when loosed from these fetters?[20]

Calvin followed the doctrine of creationism, which holds that the soul is a direct creation of God. Consequently, the soul is considered to be a substance independent of the body. And it is primarily in the soul that one finds the image of God.

Calvin's thought on the preeminence of the soul is complex.[21] On the one hand, it is rooted in creation. Calvin can say that without any doubt "man was made for meditation upon the heavenly life."[22] Since the first man had an immortal soul which "was not derived from the earth at all,"[23] it is the chief activity of the soul to aspire to heaven. Nonetheless, under the impact of Paul's teaching in 1 Corinthians 15, Calvin can still suggest that there was something insufficient about man's created condition. Even though Adam possessed an immortal soul, "he yet smacked of the earth, from which his body had its origin, and on which he had been set to live."[24] In fact, Calvin can go so far as to say that

> the state of man was not perfected in the person of Adam; but it is a peculiar benefit conferred by Christ, that we may be renewed to a life which is *celestial,* whereas before the fall of Adam, man's life was only *earthly,* seeing it had no firm and settled constancy.[25]

Therefore, on the other hand, the preeminence of the soul is ultimately rooted in redemption. For in comparison with the life we have in Adam and the immortality of the soul which we share with him by virtue of our created nature, the life which we receive in Christ is far superior.

20. "Psychopannychia," in *Tracts and Treatises in Defense of the Reformed Faith* (Grand Rapids: Eerdmans, 1958), p. 443.

21. For an excellent discussion of this issue, see Quistorp, *Calvin's Doctrine,* chap. 2.

22. *Inst.* 1.15.6.

23. *Comm. on 1 Cor.* 15:47.

24. Ibid.

25. *Comm. on Gen.* 2:7.

Christ . . . has brought us the life-giving Spirit from heaven, in order that He might regenerate us into a life that is better and higher than that on earth. In short, our life in this world we owe to Adam, as branches to the root; Christ, on the other hand, is the originator and source of the life of heaven.[26]

Calvin believed that the soul can die only a spiritual death, that is, it can be the recipient of the judgment of God with all that that entails for human life. But the believer has been born anew by the Spirit of God, and in his soul is being constantly transformed into the image of Christ. So for reasons of both creation and redemption the teaching of soul-sleep made no sense to Calvin.

If they (souls) always increase till they see God, and pass from that increase to the vision of God, on what ground do these men bury them in drunken slumber and deep sloth?[27]

One senses that Calvin's anthropology is inclined toward a basic dichotomy between body and soul, earth and heaven. In fact, these dichotomies are essentially the same. As far as heaven is from the earth, so far removed is the heavenly soul from the earthly body.[28] Thus part of Calvin's eschatological vision seems to proceed as follows: since the soul is the nobler part of man[29] and eternal life (or the kingdom of God) has already begun in it, the life of the body or earthly life should be despised[30] and death should be desired.[31]

If this were the whole of Calvin's perspective, the thesis that eschatology contributes significantly to his historical dynamism would fall flat on its face. The entire dynamic of the Christian life would then be reduced to the quest of the soul seeking its origin in heaven and in God. It would be exclusively individualistic, ignoring the cosmic sweep of biblical eschatology. But this is not all that Calvin says. In fact, in his letter to Cardinal Sadolet, Calvin explicitly rejects the view which reduces the Christian life to the quest of the soul seeking its salvation in heaven.[32] Although Calvin's anthropology may create some

26. *Comm. on 1 Cor.* 15:47.
27. Calvin, "Psychopannychia," p. 441.
28. Ibid., p. 444. "Had they a particle of sense they would not prattle thus absurdly about the soul, but would make all the difference between a celestial soul and an earthly body, that there is between heaven and earth."
29. *Inst.* 1.15.2.
30. *Inst.* 3.9.1.
31. *Inst.* 3.9.5.
32. Reply to Cardinal Sadolet's Letter, *Tracts and Treatises on the Reformation of the Church* (Grand Rapids: Eerdmans, 1958), pp. 33–34.

tensions within his attempt to do justice to history and the cosmos, we will see that Calvin does not allow his anthropology to cancel a genuine appreciation for the eschatological dynamic of human history and of the renewal of the creation.

Eschatology and Meditation on the Future Life

The doctrine of the immortality of the soul clearly makes an impact upon Calvin's meditation on the future life. But it is not the basis for that meditation, neither does it constitute the central or even one of the most important perspectives. When Calvin's meditation on the future life is carefully read in the context of his entire discussion of the Christian life,[33] the most fundamental and pervasive perspective is clearly eschatological.[34]

For Calvin, the Christian life is a life lived in imitation of Christ. Christ "has been set before us as an example, whose pattern we ought to express in our life."[35] The Christian life will be characterized, therefore, by self-denial. We deny ourselves because we belong to God.

> We are God's: let us therefore live for him and die for him. We are God's: let his wisdom and will therefore rule all our actions. We are God's: let all the parts of our life accordingly strive toward him as our only lawful goal.[36]

But this striving toward God as our goal must be understood in connection with the eschatological motive of "our blessed hope."

> For, as Christ our Redeemer once appeared, so in his final coming he will show the fruit of salvation brought forth by him. In this way he scatters all the allurements that becloud us and prevent us from aspiring as we ought to heavenly glory. Nay, he teaches us to travel as pilgrims in this world that our celestial heritage may not perish or pass away.[37]

These comments of Calvin conclude a section devoted to the exhortation found in Titus 2:11–14, where Christians are urged "to live sober, upright, and godly lives in this world, awaiting our blessed

33. *Inst.* 3.6–10.
34. Niesel asserts that "all other points with regard to the origin of Calvin's *meditatio vitae futurae* should be subordinated to this insight," viz., that Calvin gave "his arguments about the imitation of Christ an eschatological bearing" (*Theology of Calvin,* p. 149, n. 3).
35. *Inst.* 3.6.3.
36. *Inst.* 3.7.1.
37. *Inst.* 3.7.3.

hope, the appearing of the glory of our great God and Savior Jesus Christ."

There is an additional element in Calvin's understanding of self-denial as imitation of Christ which is extremely important. Self-denial means bearing the cross. Calvin's description of life under the cross frequently strikes Christians who live in times of peace and prosperity as too gloomy, too negative toward the joys of life. Even those who claim Calvin as a spiritual father feel a bit depressed by this theme in Calvin, and consequently fail to appreciate its full significance. But unless the theme of cross-bearing as descriptive of the Christian life is given its full significance, one cannot understand Calvin's concept of unworldliness and contempt for this present life. In other words, one will miss the basic eschatology behind Calvin's vision.

If Christians are to reflect the pattern of Christ in their lives, each must bear his own cross.

> For whomever the Lord has adopted and deemed worthy of his fellowship ought to prepare themselves for a hard, toilsome, and unquiet life, crammed with very many and various kinds of evil. It is the Heavenly Father's will thus to exercise them so as to put his own children to a definite test. Beginning with Christ, his first-born, he follows this plan with all his children.[38]

Cross-bearing is absolutely essential to lead the believer to trust in God's power, to develop patience and obedience, to allow him to experience the faithfulness of God, and to create within him hope for the future. In addition, to suffer persecution for righteousness' sake is an "honor God bestows upon us in thus furnishing us with the special badge of his soldiery."[39] But whatever shape the cross may take and for whatever reason it is borne, it always entails sorrow, grief, bitterness, and pain. Although the bitterness of the cross is "tempered with spiritual joy," spiritual joy does not cancel sorrow, grief, and suffering.

This discussion of self-denial and cross-bearing is the immediate context for Calvin's meditation on the future life. He begins his discussion with this sentence:

> Whatever kind of tribulation presses upon us, we must look to this end: to accustom ourselves to contempt for the present life and to be aroused thereby to meditate upon the future life.[40]

38. *Inst.* 3.8.1.
39. *Inst.* 3.8.7.
40. *Inst.* 3.9.1.

Because this life is nothing but struggle, the thought of the crown that awaits the believer causes him to raise his eyes to heaven.

> For this we must believe: that the mind is never seriously aroused to desire and ponder the life to come unless it be previously imbued with contempt for the present life.[41]

Calvin's reasons for advocating contempt for the present life are not rooted primarily in a body-soul dichotomy, but are to be found rather in a contrast between the present life under the cross and the future life of the heavenly kingdom.

Yet, no matter how often one is reminded that the phrase "contempt for the present life" must be understood as part of an eschatological contrast, the phrase still seems far too negative for Calvin. If he intended it seriously, how could he ever attempt to participate meaningfully in this life? Why would Calvin vigorously throw himself into the struggles and turmoils of his time, if he advocated contempt for this present life?

We need to be reminded that the phrase did not originate with Calvin. He borrowed it from the devotional literature of his time, although he used it in a significantly different way. L. J. Richard, a Roman Catholic theologian, has compared Calvin's understanding of "contempt" with that advocated in the devotional literature of the Middle Ages. The classic example is Thomas à Kempis's *On the Imitation of Christ and Contempt for the World*. The full title of that work is important. The imitation of Christ entails contempt for this world or this present life. Although there are many formal similarities between Calvin's view of the Christian life and that of à Kempis — for example, imitation of Christ, self-denial, and cross-bearing — there is a decisive difference in their understanding of contempt for the world.

Thomas à Kempis's idea of contempt is a very literal one. It means simply to avoid, shun, or reject the world. Richard summarizes this view as follows: "The *Imitatione Christi* projects the image of a pilgrim who pays no heed to the things around him that he may offer his entire attention to the other world, which is eternal."[42] The Christian is preoccupied with his interior life. "There is very little interest in the apostolate of a service of God and the world."[43]

Calvin's view of contempt for the world, however, does not lead to

---

41. Ibid.

42. L. J. Richard, *The Spirituality of John Calvin* (Atlanta: John Knox, 1974), p. 176.

43. Ibid., p. 29.

a withdrawal from the world. Immediately after speaking of contempt, Calvin urges gratitude for earthly life. In spite of the fact that it is "crammed with infinite miseries," this life is a blessing of God in which we already begin "to taste the sweetness of the divine generosity in order to whet our hope and desire to seek after the full revelation of this."[44] Although like à Kempis, Calvin uses the biblical imagery of Christian life as a pilgrimage toward the heavenly kingdom, it is a pilgrimage in which one must use the world as God intends.[45] So Calvin does not advocate a rejection of the present life as such.[46] Contempt means only a rejection of what is evil, and a recognition that true life must be sought in Christ. Since Christ is in heaven, Christians must seek their life in heaven and in the future, not on earth and in the present. Or from another perspective, "believers ought to lead a heavenly life in this world."[47] The Christian pilgrimage has important consequences for the world.[48]

Hence the perspectives that dominate Calvin's meditation on the future life are eschatological in nature. His entire outlook is determined by the believer's relationship to the ascended Lord.

However, since Calvin believes that one enters the peace of the kingdom already at death, his belief in the immortality of the soul plays an important role in his understanding of the future life. Accordingly, Calvin can speak of this future life as "eternity after death," "heavenly immortality," "immortality to come," or "heavenly kingdom." Nonetheless, for Calvin this future, immortal, or heavenly life may never be divorced from the final eschatological reality of the return of Christ and the resurrection of the dead.[49]

Even though H. Quistorp believes that Calvin's perspective on the position of the soul after death in its relationship to the final resurrection lands Calvin in a contradiction, he nevertheless stresses that for Calvin the soul "does not perish nor sleep in death but in so far as it is born again in Christ already enjoys heavenly peace in the expectation of the resurrection of the body, which will bring in consummate blessedness."[50]

44. *Inst.* 3.9.3.
45. *Inst.* 3.10.1.
46. Quistorp asserts that Calvin's "aspiration towards heavenly life cannot . . . imply any flight from the world but rather impels us already in this world to live another kind of life" (*Calvin's Doctrine,* p. 43).
47. *Comm. on Phil.* 3:20.
48. Richard, *Spirituality of John Calvin,* chap. 6.
49. *Inst.* 3.9.5–6.
50. Quistorp, *Calvin's Doctrine,* pp. 81–82. See also pp. 87–92.

Calvin did not allow his belief in the immortality of the soul to negate the biblical eschatological hope.

> We would certainly agree that the correct exposition of Scripture is that the life of the soul without hope of resurrection will be a mere dream. God does not promise souls the survival of death, glory complete and immediate, and enjoyment of blessedness, but delays the fulfillment of their hope to the last day. . . . Scripture informs us that the life of the spirit depends on the hope of resurrection, and to this souls released from the body look with expectancy. Whoever destroys the resurrection is also depriving souls of immortality.[51]

Earlier it was pointed out that Calvin modified the classic view of the immortality of the soul by means of the biblical doctrine of creation. In the above quotation it is further modified by the doctrine of the resurrection of the body. Although Calvin advocates the preeminence of the soul over the body, he frequently corrects his own onesidedness by affirming that for man the body is essential in both creation and redemption.

Commenting on Peter's phrase "the salvation of your souls," Calvin finds it necessary to say something about the body. "The body is not excluded from participation in glory in so far as it is connected to the soul." The soul is clearly preeminent, and because it is immortal "salvation is properly ascribed to it."[52] Yet when Calvin addresses himself self-consciously to this matter, he relates immortality ultimately to the resurrection of the body. As quoted above, "whoever destroys the resurrection is also depriving souls of immortality." And in more general terms Calvin affirms that

> it is a dangerous piece of scoffing when they cast doubt on the resurrection of the last day, because if this is taken away nothing is left of the Gospel, the power of Christ is drained away, and all religion is destroyed. Satan directly attacks the throat of the Church when he destroys faith in the return of Christ.[53]

Because of his biblical sensitivities, and because Christian life is life in Christ, Calvin refuses to allow his eschatological vision to be

---

51. *Comm. on Matt.* 22:23. See also *Comm. on Isa.* 26:19, and *Inst.* 3.6.3. It is important to note that for Calvin meditation on the future life and meditation on the resurrection are synonymous: "Accordingly, he alone has fully profited in the gospel who has accustomed himself to continual meditation upon the blessed resurrection" (*Inst.* 3.25.1).

52. *Comm. on 1 Peter* 1:9.

53. *Comm. on 1 Peter* 3:4.

determined simply by the philosophical doctrine of the immortality of the soul. It is one of the factors which may at times loom large (especially in the discussion of the intervening state between death and resurrection), but the most important perspective governing Calvin's vision of the Christian person in life and death continues to be the eschatological one. Life in Christ is for Calvin basically an eschatological reality.[54]

Eschatology and Jesus Christ

Jesus Christ stands at the center of Calvin's perspective on the Christian life. Everything said about self-denial, cross-bearing, and contempt for this life, as well as everything Calvin says about the history of the world and its future, is determined by the person and work of Jesus Christ. Calvin makes no attempt to speculate directly about world history as such, because its meaning and future are determined by the redemption accomplished by Christ.[55]

The advent of Christ, including His death and resurrection, is for Calvin the decisive point at which the renewal of the world has occurred. Sin brought disorder into the world, but the death of Christ restored all things to order. Listen to Calvin's remarkable comment on John 13:31:

> For in the cross of Christ, as in a splendid theater, the incomparable goodness of God is set before the whole world. The glory of God shines, indeed, in all creatures on high and below, but never more brightly than in the cross, in which there was a wonderful change of things — the condemnation of all men was manifested, sin blotted out, salvation restored to men; in short, the whole world was renewed and all things restored to order.[56]

A similarly striking comment is found in his interpretation of the phrase "now is the judgment of the world."

54. Quistorp describes Calvin's perspective as fully eschatological in the biblical-Pauline sense, i.e., "a *theologia crucis* demanding sheer faith in the hidden glory of Christ and His kingdom and also at the same time a lively hope of its future manifestation" (*Calvin's Doctrine*, p. 11). And commenting on Calvin's stress on death and immortality, Quistorp argues that "it is the Christological foundation of his eschatology and whole theology which prevented Calvin from lapsing into a certain philosophy of death to which he perhaps was inclined" (ibid., p. 47).

55. See H. Berger, *Calvins Geschichtsauffassung* (Zurich: Zwingli, 1955), pp. 92ff. T. F. Torrance asserts that the Reformers "taught that the earthly future is divinely governed through the mission of the Church" ("Eschatology of the Reformation," p. 39).

56. *Comm. on John* 13:31.

The word *judgment* is taken as "reformation" by some and "condem-nation" by others. I agree rather with the former, who expound it that the world must be restored to due order. For the Hebrew word *mish-pat* which is translated as *judgment* means a well-ordered constitu-tion. Now we know that outside Christ there is nothing but confusion in the world. And although Christ had already begun to set up the kingdom of God, it was His death that was the true beginning of a properly-ordered state and the complete restoration of the world.[57]

The advent of Christ, His death and resurrection, is for Calvin the eschatological turning point of world history. At that moment the renovation of the world — all that was necessary for the reordering of the disordered world — was completed in Jesus Christ. There can be no other event of such decisive significance for human history and the life of the cosmos. Every subsequent event can have meaning only in relationship to that "renovation of the world which took place at the advent of Christ."[58]

To highlight these remarkable statements, it will be useful to intro-duce briefly the contemporary dispute as to whether or not Calvin's eschatological perspective fits the history-of-salvation mold. The cen-tral reason for the dispute will be obvious to anyone who has ever read Calvin's discussion of the similarities and differences between the Old and New Testaments. His stress on unity is so emphatic that there seems to be no essential difference between the two Testaments. "In substance and reality," says Calvin, "the two are really one and the same."[59]

Consequently, H. H. Wolf, for example, argues correctly that for Calvin there is only a difference in the administration of the covenants, not in their substance. There is only a difference as to how we par-ticipate in Christ, not as to the content of that participation. The promise and the salvation enjoyed are the same; only the mode of participation differs. The Old Testament saints participated by means of a more obscure and hidden promise, whereas the New Testament saints participate by means of a more clearly revealed promise. But in both cases, what is promised is basically a future reality, even though in both cases there is already a certain distribution of these future gifts. And even though the advent of Christ distinguishes the two Testaments, His kingdom even now remains basically a future reality for which we still hope. Thus both the Old and New Testament people of God live by promise, both meditate on the future life, and

57. *Comm. on John* 12:31.
58. *Comm. on Gen.* 17:7.
59. *Inst.* 2.10.2.

both already share in what is promised because the promises of God are sure. The fact that the New Testament people see the reality more clearly is only a relative difference, not a substantial or essential one.[60] Therefore, Wolf concludes that there can be no genuine history-of-salvation development in Calvin's eschatological vision. For if such a development actually existed in Calvin's theology, Wolf asserts that the unity and identity of the covenants in their substance and reality would be threatened.[61]

However, does a genuine history-of-salvation development require that there be no unity or identity in the substance of the covenants? Doesn't Wolf confuse participation in the promise (which in substance is always the same for Calvin because there is only one covenant) with the history that actualizes what is promised?

Calvin is fond of the metaphor of the sun and its light, using it to explain various mysteries, including that of the relationship between the Testaments. Concerning the position of the Old Testament saints, Calvin declares:

> Faith was not yet revealed; not that the fathers lacked light altogether but that they had less light than we. . . . However much darkness there might be under the law, the fathers were not ignorant of the road they had to take. The dawn may not be as bright as noonday, but it is sufficient for making a journey, and travellers do not wait until the sun is up. Their portion of light was like the dawn; it could keep them safe from all error and guide them to everlasting blessedness.[62]

The metaphor of the sun and its rays, of dawn and noonday, is a metaphor stressing unity and continuity. The light of dawn and noonday is in substance the same light. Yet when that metaphor is used to explain the differences in the history of salvation, it is clear that a decisive event in history distinguishes the dawn from the noonday. The two conditions can be neither equated nor reversed. Consequently, in explaining the meaning of the word *gospel,* Calvin affirms:

> Thus a distinction is set between the promises which held the hopes of the faithful in suspense, and this glad news, wherein God testifies that He has brought to pass that event which before He had made the object of hope.[63]

60. Wolf, *Die Einheit,* chap. 6.
61. Ibid., p. 64.
62. *Comm. on Gal.* 3:23.
63. Preface to *Comm. on the Harmony of the Gospels,* vol. 1, p. xi.

That "event which before He had made the object of hope" is for Calvin the advent of Christ in which the whole world was renewed and all things restored to order. Thus within the essential unity of the covenants Calvin expresses a sensitivity to a history-of-salvation perspective.[64] A decisively new event has occurred which establishes all the promises and determines the whole of human existence. The goal of history and creation, previously announced by the prophets and participated in by hope, has entered history in order to move it toward its destiny.

Although the renovation of the whole world has already occurred in Christ, the world has not yet arrived at that destiny. The actual, visible renewal of all things is still in the process of completion.[65] Until Satan's kingdom is wiped out, the right ordering of all things cannot actually be set up in the world. This tension between the goal already achieved in Christ and the destiny still to be achieved dominates Calvin's eschatological perspective. As we will see shortly, this tension provides him with a basic principle for interpreting prophecy. It leads him to assert again and again that the words of Scripture which seem to point to a victory that is momentary and final, actually point to a victory which is not limited to any short period of time. For example, the casting out of Satan on the cross continues to be "the remarkable effect of Christ's death which appears *daily.*"[66]

Because of this tension between the goal achieved in the advent of Christ and the destiny to be achieved at His return, and because Christ is now in heaven, the ascended Christ dominates Calvin's thinking about eschatology.

> Ascension goes along with resurrection. Therefore, if we are members of Christ, we must ascend into heaven, because when He had been raised from the dead, He was received up into heaven, that He might draw us up with Him.[67]

Calvin's so-called unworldliness is in actuality a seeking for renewal and life in Christ who is now in heaven. Meditation on the future life is not a rejection of this created world in favor of another heavenly world unrelated to this one, but it is always a seeking of

---

64. See Berger, *Calvin's Geschichtsauffassung,* pp. 99–103; Hesselink, "Calvin and Heilsgeschichte."

65. *Comm. on Acts* 3:21.

66. *Comm. on John* 12:31.

67. *Comm. on Col.* 3:1.

Christ in whom the renovation of this world has occurred.[68] "We must seek Christ nowhere else but in heaven, while we wait the final restoration of all things."[69]

The ascended Christ holds together advent and return. Seeking the ascended Christ in heaven may never be separated, therefore, from an eager anticipation of His return. Since the perfected kingdom is already complete in Him, the Christian is always waiting for the final, visible restoration of all things. And since the present life of the believer is "buried under the ignominy of the cross and various distresses" and "differs nothing from death,"[70] he is always looking for the revelation of the life that is now hidden. For Calvin, the "principle" governing the Christian life is "that from the time when Christ once appeared, there is nothing left for the faithful except to look forward to His second coming with minds alert."[71]

The ascended Christ, who incorporates within Himself both advent and return, stands at the center of Calvin's eschatological vision.

Prophecy and Eschatology

Unless one understands how significantly the ascended Christ dominates Calvin's eschatological perspective, his handling of specific prophecies can be rather exasperating. Calvin always seems to believe that the particular prophecy in question is not exhausted in a single, momentary fulfillment in time. Almost all prophecies appear to be fulfilled on a continuum. Calvin knows this, of course, because of the Christ who incorporates within Himself both advent and return: both the fulfillment already completed and the fulfillment that will one day be fully revealed.

Calvin's characteristic handling of prophecy is seen, for example, in his interpretation of Isaiah 26:19, "thy dead shall live, their bodies shall rise." He faults both rabbinic and Christian interpreters: the rabbis for thinking it would be fulfilled in the Messiah's first coming, and the Christian interpreters for limiting it to the last judgment. Calvin says that "the Prophet includes the whole reign of Christ from the beginning to the end." In other words, Calvin interprets this prophecy in the light of its fulfillment in Christ. Christ has already made

68. "*Heaven, heavenly,* refer as a rule in Calvin's thought not to some empyrean realm but to the new or celestial condition of God's creation" (Torrance, "Eschatology of the Reformation," p. 59, n. 1).
69. *Comm. on Acts* 3:21. See also *Inst.* 3.6.3.
70. *Comm. on Col.* 3:3.
71. *Comm. on 1 Peter* 4:7.

believers alive, and yet they do not "literally" or "fully" live until the resurrection.

> Believers, by fleeing to God, obtain life in the midst of afflictions, and even in death itself; but because they have in prospect that day of the resurrection, they are not said literally to live till that day when they shall be free from all pain and corruption, and shall obtain perfect life; and, indeed, Paul justly argues, that it would be a subversion of order, were they to enjoy life till the appearance of Christ, who is the source of their life.[72]

How does Calvin know that these words in Isaiah are not restricted to a final, single event in history but rather embrace the whole reign of Christ? Calvin replies:

> For, although we begin to receive the fruit of this consolation when we are admitted into the Church, yet we shall not enjoy it fully till that last day of the resurrection is come, when all things shall be most completely restored; and on this account it is called "the day of restitution."[73]

A prophecy can contain only what as a matter of fact has happened and will happen in Christ. Thus every prophecy announcing final victory receives a twofold fulfillment in the advent and return of Christ. And the eschatological existence of believers living between these times participates in both the identity and the distinctiveness of these two events; that is, believers share in the already completed, yet hidden, renovation of the world which someday will become fully visible.

The prophecy in Daniel 7:27, concerning the kingdom and the dominion which will be given to the people of God, is handled by Calvin in precisely the same manner. The dominion of the saints under heaven began already "when Christ ushered in his kingdom by the promulgation of his Gospel." The prophet announces the commencement of Christ's kingdom in the first preaching of the gospel, but he also goes further to draw "a magnificent picture of Christ's reign embracing its final completion." Again we meet Calvin's principle for interpreting the prophets:

> I may here remark again, and impress upon the memory what I have frequently touched upon, namely, the custom of the Prophets, in treat-

72. *Comm. on Isa.* 26:19.
73. Ibid.

ing of Christ's kingdom, to extend their meaning further than its first beginnings; and they do this while they dwell upon its commencement.[74]

Advent and return, commencement and completion — both are intended by the prophet. But notice the stress on commencement. For Calvin this is always the starting point in the interpretation of prophecies because already in the advent of Christ prophecies find their fulfillment. And even when a prophecy points to a final future event in the eyes of most interpreters, Calvin usually insists that it is already being fulfilled.

For example, Matthew 24:27 — "For as the lightning comes from the east and shines as far as the west, so will be the coming of the Son of Man" — is interpreted by Calvin as a promise that Jesus will suddenly extend the borders of His kingdom to the farthest ends of the earth. But this is not simply a promise to be fulfilled at a future date; rather it has already been fulfilled in the spread of the gospel.

The wonderful rapidity with which the Gospel flew out to every region of the globe was a shining testimony to the divine power. It could not be the result of human industry that the light of the Gospel should flash like lightning and reach from one corner of the world to the other extreme: it is sound commendation of the heavenly glory that Christ presents.[75]

Calvin knows that fulfillment has occurred and therefore is occurring and will occur. He knows that Christ has come and therefore is coming and will come. His entire perspective, focused on the ascended and presently reigning Christ, moves between the two poles of advent and return.

Calvin's rejection of an earthly millennial kingdom flows naturally from this fundamental perspective. The millennial belief assumes that Christ will reign visibly on the not-yet-renewed earth for a limited period of time. But Calvin believes that the perfected kingdom already exists in Christ, that it is eternal and includes the renovation of the world. Consequently, Christ's visible appearance can mean only the final revelation of the perfected kingdom. A temporally limited messianic kingdom on a nonrenewed earth struck Calvin as a childish

74. *Comm. on Dan.* 7:27.
75. *Comm. on Matt.* 24:27.

fantasy[76] similar to the teaching of the rabbis.[77] Until Christ's return on the day of the general resurrection, Calvin believed that "God rules in the world only by His Gospel."[78] Between advent and return, Christ's kingdom is visible only to the eyes of faith.

From this perspective also one other characteristic of Calvin's interpretation of prophecy becomes intelligible. Since the poles of prophecy are advent and return, with fulfillment occurring on a continuum moving from one pole to the other, prophecy cannot be used as the basis for calculating the time of Christ's return. Attempts to predict the time violate not only the express teaching of Jesus but also the very nature of prophecy itself. The time references in prophecy are intended, according to Calvin, to elicit hope and patience, not to give specific dates and time frames.

The Kingdoms of Christ and Antichrist

The various perspectives in Calvin's basic eschatological outlook, which have been discussed above, come together in his discussion of the Antichrist. This discussion reveals Calvin's refusal to calculate or even guess at the time of Christ's return, his basic anti-apocalyptic bias, and his continual weaving together of eschatological themes with the themes of history and Christian existence.

The central text for this discussion is 2 Thessalonians 2:3, "Let no one deceive you in any way; for that day will not come, unless the rebellion comes first, and the man of lawlessness is revealed." The apostle Paul is correcting the erroneous impression of some early Christians that the day of the Lord had come.

Because this teaching of Paul "corresponds in every respect" to the words of Jesus in Matthew 24 and 25, Calvin moves back and forth from Paul to Jesus to establish his interpretation. Even though the day of the Lord is at hand, it is not now. "It is at hand in regard to God," says Calvin, "with whom one day is as a thousand years."[79] In addition, Calvin believed that the sin of man could delay and upset

---

76. "This fiction is too puerile to need or deserve refutation" (*Inst.* 3.25.5).

77. See *Comm. on Dan.* 7:27 for Calvin's dispute with the position of Rabbi Abarbinel. All the Reformers rejected chiliasm as a kind of Jewish heresy. For example, the Second Helvetic Confession of 1566: "We further condemn Jewish dreams that there will be a golden age on earth before the Day of Judgment, and that the pious, having subdued all their godless enemies, will possess all the kingdoms of the earth" (chap. 11, sec. 14).

78. *Comm. on Rom.* 14:11.

79. *Comm. on 2 Thess.* 2:2.

the arrival of the kingdom, even though it could not finally prevent its coming.[80] For these reasons, only false prophets calculate a speedy advent. The Lord Himself wants believers to "keep in constant watch for Him in such a way as not to limit Him in any way to a particular time."[81]

Unlike Luther, Calvin did not speak about the time of Christ's return.[82] Instead he believed that the eschatological discourses of Jesus and Paul point to a "protracted conflict" for the church on earth. Consequently, the basic thrust of eschatological teaching is not to produce calculation, but patience and hope.

> In short, the preaching of the gospel is like sowing seed. We must patiently wait for the time of harvest. It is wrong to be soft and effeminate, and have our enthusiasm crushed by winter's frost, snow clouds or adverse seasons.[83]

Evils in the world should lead the faithful to "equip themselves with patience for a long stretch."[84]

The perfected kingdom of Christ is in heaven and must be sought there. There is no way of dragging it to earth prematurely, nor of jumping immediately into the rest of the blessed. The perfected kingdom is possessed only in hope. And the promise that it will be fully disclosed one day is given precisely to establish believers in that hope lest they be overwhelmed by the ensuing chaos. The church in history is a suffering church, a church long tested with hard and wearisome temptations.

> Not that the glory and majesty of Christ's Kingdom will only appear at His final coming, but that the completion is delayed till that point — the completion of those things that started at the resurrection, of which God gave His people only a taste, to lead them further along on the road of hope and patience.[85]

80. *Comm. on Matt.* 24:4.
81. *Comm. on 2 Thess.* 2:2.
82. Luther cherished several hopes about the return of Christ. He hoped that Christ would come in his own lifetime, that at least it would not be delayed over one hundred years, and he was rather certain that the day of judgment would not be absent three hundred years hence. Cf. R. V. Vinglas, "An Investigation into the Eschatological Teaching of Martin Luther and John Calvin" (diss., S.D.A. Theological Seminary, Washington D.C., 1948), pp. 35–40.
83. *Comm. on Matt.* 24:4.
84. *Comm. on Matt.* 24:6.
85. *Comm. on Matt.* 24:29.

The basic intention of the eschatological discourses is to "keep the minds of the faithful in suspense to the last day." Believers may not attempt to hurry on to triumph ahead of time. Instead they should so hope and look for the day of Christ's coming that "yet no one should dare ask when it will come." They must walk by faith without knowing the times with certainty, and they must wait for the final revelation with patience. "Beware then," Calvin warns, "not to worry more than the Lord over details of time."[86]

The kingdom of Christ has a history in time, and so does the kingdom of the Antichrist. Neither kingdom is limited to a single moment in human history. Both kingdoms in their coming and in their ruling affect human history over a very long period of time.

The coming of these two kingdoms is interrelated. The final coming of Christ cannot occur until there are a general apostasy and the rule of Antichrist in the church. But before there can be apostasy, there must be the universal proclamation of the gospel. The term *apostate* refers only to "those who have previously enlisted in the service of Christ and His Gospel." Therefore, the defection can take place only "when the world has been brought under the rule of Christ."[87]

Calvin's understanding of that "which is restraining" the revelation of the Antichrist corresponds to his interpretation of the "falling away." In distinction from the common medieval belief that the Roman Empire was the restraining force (which Calvin accepted as historical fact but not as Paul's intention), Calvin understands the restraining force to be the necessary spread of the gospel through every part of the world. The general apostasy could not occur until the gospel had been proclaimed to the nations. Therefore, the "gracious invitation to salvation was first in order of precedence." In fact, the one is, at least in part, for the sake of the other. Calvin affirms that God's grace was offered to all "in order that men's impiety might be more fully attested and condemned." The coming of the Antichrist is thus punishment for the rejection of the gospel.[88]

If such is Calvin's understanding of that which restrains, how could he identify the papacy as the Antichrist? Did Calvin believe that the gospel had already been proclaimed to the nations? Yes, he did. Even though he was aware that in his day some remote nations had "not even the faintest word of Christ," he did not find Jesus' words in Matthew 24:14 to be an insuperable obstacle to his position. With regard to Jesus' affirmation that the gospel would be preached

86. *Comm. on Matt.* 24:29, 36.
87. *Comm. on 2 Thess.* 2:3.
88. *Comm. on 2 Thess.* 2:5–6, 10.

throughout the whole world to all nations before the end would come, Calvin did not believe that Jesus was talking of "individual tracts of land or fixing any particular time but only affirming that the Gospel . . . would be published to the furtherest ends of the earth before the last day of His coming."[89] For Calvin, that had already happened essentially through the ministry of the first apostles. The gospel had been proclaimed to the nations, the universal church had come into being, and now a general apostasy had occurred in the church. The necessary conditions for the arrival of the Antichrist had made their appearance.

The Antichrist was not equated with a particular pope, for he was not considered to be a single individual. Instead, the Antichrist was viewed by Calvin as a succession of individuals, or more accurately, as a kingdom controlled by Satan. This kingdom was not limited to the papacy because anyone who led believers from the truth was a part of that kingdom, including Mohammed. Yet since the papacy ruled in the church and there usurped powers belonging only to God, the papacy was in particular the vicar of Satan.[90]

If then Calvin believed that the gospel had been proclaimed to the nations, the apostasy had occurred, and the Antichrist had come, did he conclude that the end of history was near at hand? No, he did not. Here again Calvin's characteristic eschatological perspective controls his understanding. For example, Calvin interprets Paul's prophecy that the Lord Jesus will slay the Antichrist "with the breath of his mouth and destroy him by his appearing and his coming" as referring only to the manner of his destruction, not to the time. Calvin admits that it seems that these words of 2 Thessalonians 2:8 refer to the final appearing of Christ when He will come as judge from heaven. Yet he holds that it is by no means certain that this reference should be restricted to the final appearance of Christ. For "Paul does not think that Christ will accomplish this in a single moment."[91]

Calvin discovers two perspectives in this prophecy concerning the slaying of the Antichrist. Obviously, the Antichrist will be "completely and utterly" destroyed when the final day has come. But in addition — and this is the most distinctive element in Calvin's perspective — Paul is also predicting that

in the meantime Christ will scatter the darkness in which Antichrist will reign by the rays which He will emit before His coming, just as

89. *Comm. on Matt.* 24:14.
90. *Comm. on 2 Thess.* 2:3–4.
91. *Comm. on 2 Thess.* 2:8.

the sun, before becoming visible to us, chases away the darkness of the night with its bright light.[92]

Thus Calvin develops his eschatological vision along historical lines. Since the breath of the Lord's mouth is simply His Word, the victory of Christ over Antichrist is already occurring and can be seen in history. True and sound doctrine is destined "at all times to be victorious over all the devices of Satan." At the same time, the preaching of true and sound doctrine is "Christ's coming to us."[93] Hence through its proclamation of the gospel, the church is already effecting in history the dawning of that future day of the return of Christ. The Reformation itself, with all the turmoil and commotion that accompanied it, was seen as a manifestation of the eschatological movement in history through which the kingdom of God comes.

Life Between the Times

Life between advent and return is thus determined by the ongoing conflict between the kingdom of Christ and the kingdom of Satan or Antichrist. Calvin's interpretation of the eschatological defeat of Antichrist as an ongoing process imparts a vigorous dynamic to his view of the task of the church in the world. Believers may not sit and wait, because the great eschatological events are not limited to the final moment of human history. Eschatological events contain for Calvin both the element of finality and of process. At the end Christ will come and "fully and completely" overthrow evil. But meanwhile through the proclamation of the Word there is an anticipatory, continual defeating of Satan and Antichrist. Consequently, believers are called to "fight hard under Christ, equipped with spiritual armor."[94]

Warfare is the shape of the church's life between the times. Believers must participate in Christ's continual war against His enemies because until the last day Christ "has no peaceful possession of His

92. Ibid.
93. Ibid.
94. *Comm. on 2 Thess.* 2:8–10. E. C. Rust summarizes the impact of eschatology on Calvin's view of history as follows: "For Calvin, this era is no tension-filled waiting period prior to the final consummation. *Armageddon* is now in process, and, although Calvin emphasized the ultimate triumph, he saw the Church as now actively engaged with the powers of darkness. Here we have a *dynamic approach* which sees the Church waging war to transform the realm of historical existence more into the likeness of the Father's will in Christ. God is building His kingdom in this world, and through the history of this world, and all must not be left to the end" (*Towards a Theological Understanding of History* [New York: Oxford, 1963], p. 250).

kingdom."[95] Consequently, Calvin's view of the Christian life is active and dynamic. Believers are soldiers waging active warfare against Christ's enemies in order to establish the reign of God on earth,[96] and the organization of the church is essentially organization for battle.[97] The battle is waged with patience and hope because the outcome is sure. The Word of the gospel contains such "divine and incredible power" that it can and will with violence cast down the prince of the world, for "at the thunder of the gospel Satan fell down like a lightning flash." Characteristically Calvin applies this word of Jesus in Luke 10:18 not only to the final defeat of Satan but to "the whole course of the Gospel." "We cannot doubt," says Calvin, "that whenever He raises up faithful teachers He will give success to their work."[98]

There is nothing speculative about Calvin's eschatology. He was "no conjurer in numerical calculations." Specific numbers in Daniel and Revelation had to be interpreted figuratively. Through them God promises His elect some moderation, some shortening of the days; but the precise point of termination remains hidden in the secret counsel of God.[99] And the signs of the times cannot be added up like dates on a calendar. The point of all such prophecies is patience and persistence. Calvin's eschatological vision is in essence a call for decision and obedient action here and now.[100] Because the final victory is already occurring in the present defeats suffered by the Antichrist, the kingdom of God is already being established in the world. Such present victories anticipate and lead to the final victory of Christ over Antichrist. The church and its activity are an essential part of the eschatological movement of history from advent to return.

Is there any real progress in establishing the kingdom between the times? Calvin spoke of progress.[101] He said that "the Kingdom of God increases, stage upon stage, to the end of the world."[102] But this increase or progress of the kingdom was not for Calvin a kind of

95. Comm. on Heb. 2:8.
96. "It is a work of immense difficulty to establish the heavenly reign of God upon earth because of the obstacles Satan erects" (letter to Nicholas Radziwill, Letters of John Calvin [New York: Burt Franklin Reprints, 1972], 3:135).
97. Denn die organisation der calvinischen Gemeinde ist Kampforganisation" (Berger, Calvins Geschichtsauffassung, p. 166).
98. Comm. on Luke 10:18.
99. Comm. on Dan. 7:25.
100. See Berger, Calvins Geschichtsauffassung, p. 77.
101. "Zeal for daily progress is not enjoined upon us in vain, for it never goes so well with human affairs that the filthiness of vices is shaken and washed away, and full integrity flowers and grows. But its fullness is delayed to the final coming of Christ" (Inst. 3.20.42).
102. Comm. on Matt. 6:10.

evolutionary growth by which the kingdom of God gradually and progressively displaces the disordered structures of the world. Calvin was under no delusion concerning the elimination of evil prior to the return of Christ. He never became falsely optimistic about a time in history in which the struggle against evil would be easier than in his own time. For Calvin believed that "the more pressingly God offers Himself to the world in the Gospel, and invites men into His Kingdom, the more boldly will wicked men belch forth the poison of their impiety."[103] Christian existence between the times will always be in the shape of a cross, "for it is in this way that God wills to spread his kingdom."[104]

Calvin's view of history is hopeful rather than optimistic, because he believed that the power of the kingdom of God would continually defeat the power of evil. But until that final return of Christ when God will be all in all, there will always be constant turmoil, conflict, and suffering. Calvin lived in a time when the church was under the cross. His commentary on Daniel, dedicated to the persecuted church in France, clearly reflects his eschatological outlook. Calvin discovers that Daniel was already warning the people of God that

> the Church's state would not be tranquil even when the Messiah came. The sons of God should be militant to the end, and not hope for any fruit of their victory until the dead should rise again, and Christ himself should collect us into his own Celestial Kingdom.[105]

An Authentic Eschatology?

What is an authentic eschatology? In terms of the contemporary discussion, an authentic eschatological vision perceives history and eschatology as one. Eschatology concerns the dynamic of human history, the cosmic sweep of the rule of God involving the judgment and renewal of human life and all its structures. Eschatology is not concerned just with the final momentary events of history, but with the dynamic force moving at the core of human history here and now, giving history its meaning and its destiny.

Does Calvin's eschatological vision qualify? We have seen that Calvin did not allow his belief in the immortality of the soul to short-circuit his eschatological vision. His vision is focused on Christ who

103. *Comm. on 2 Peter* 3:3.
104. *Inst.* 3.20.42.
105. Preface to *Comm. on Dan.*

is in heaven. Yet this focus on heaven is not world-flight, for the Christ at the center is the One in whom the renovation of the world has occurred. Consequently, Calvin's eschatology leads to obedient action in which, through the promulgation of the gospel, the kingdom of God begins to occur here and now in the history of the world. Such a perspective seems to qualify as an authentic eschatology.

However, before a final answer can be given, there is an additional issue to be discussed. Although Calvin affirms that the kingdom of God manifests itself in history when God forces His enemies "all unwilling — with Satan at their head — to accept His authority, till all become His footstool,"[106] nevertheless, he sees the kingdom of God primarily in the renewal of individuals and the church. The kingdom of God is a spiritual reality manifesting itself at present in the "inward and spiritual renewing of the soul," or in a person being "reformed to the image of God by His Spirit."[107] From this perspective Calvin can say that the kingdom of God or of Christ means the same thing as the church of God.[108] Thus even when he is speaking of the presence of the kingdom of God, Calvin's focus is first of all on the renewal already occurring in the body of Christ.

Does this restrict Calvin's eschatological vision? Is his perspective more a philosophy of church history than an authentic eschatology? It is true that Calvin focuses on the church in history and makes almost all prophecies concerning the future apply to the present life of the church. But Calvin's understanding of the church is not parochial or even merely ecclesiastical. The history of salvation which becomes visible in the church contains within it the meaning of the history of the world. And the renewal manifesting itself in the body of Christ is the renewal that embraces the whole creation. Calvin would not understand the dichotomy expressed in the question above. The history of the church cannot be divorced from the history of the world. The destiny of the church cannot be divorced from the destiny of the world.

The kingdom of God, according to Calvin, is fundamentally the reordering of all things. "The opposite of the kingdom of God is complete disorder and confusion."[109] The mission of Christ is "to gather together out of a state of disorder those things which are in heaven

106. *Comm. on Matt.* 6:10.
107. *Comm. on Luke* 17:20; *Inst.* 3.20.42.
108. *Comm. on Amos* 9:13.
109. *Comm. on Matt.* 6:10.

and which are on earth."[110] We have seen that Calvin believed that the reordering of the whole creation has already taken place in the advent of Christ, especially in His death and resurrection. Following the biblical principle of the first-fruits, Calvin sees this reordering of all things occurring first of all in individuals and the church. There we can see "the beginnings of God's Kingdom, for we now begin to be reformed to the image of God by His Spirit so that the complete renewal of ourselves and the whole world may follow in its own time."[111]

Thus Calvin's focus on the renewal of the individual and the church imposes no restriction on his eschatological vision. He clearly understands the biblical teaching that man and the creation are in essence related to each other not only in origin but also in destiny. In a very remarkable comment Calvin affirms that the whole creation continues to function because of hope.

> From hope comes the swiftness of the sun, the moon, and all the stars in their constant course, the continued obedience of the earth in producing its fruits, the unwearied motion of the air, and the ready power of the water to flow. God has given to each its proper task, and has not simply given a precise command to do His will, but has at the same time inwardly implanted the hope of renewal.[112]

Eschatology makes the world go round! The whole machinery of creation, says Calvin, would have fallen out of gear after the fall of Adam were it not for this hope of renewal. Ever since that time the creation has been groaning age after age for the perfection that is still to come. Hence the creation should be an example for us who live by hope for only such a short period of time. "If the creatures have continued their groaning for so many ages, our softness or indolence will be inexcusable if we faint in the brief course of our shadowy life."[113] Man and the creation are companions in hope. But the beginnings of hope, or its first-fruits, are seen in believers who have been endowed with the Holy Spirit.[114]

110. *Comm. on Isa.* 11:6. See also *Comm. on Eph.* 1:10. For the significance of the restoration of order in Calvin's eschatology, see R. S. Wallace, *Calvin's Doctrine of the Christian Life* (Grand Rapids: Eerdmans, 1961), pp. 103–11; and B. C. Milner, *Calvin's Doctrine of the Church* (Leiden: Brill, 1970), chap. 2.

111. *Comm. on Luke* 17:20. Calvin also interprets Peter's statement about the elements being dissolved by fire as "renewal" of the elements rather than destruction. See *Comm. on 2 Peter* 3:10.

112. *Comm. on Rom.* 8:20.

113. *Comm. on Rom.* 8:22.

114. *Comm. on Rom.* 8:23.

Neither the believer nor the church exists or is saved apart from the world. But the eschatological reordering of the world occurs here and now — at least in its beginnings — in the believer and the church. Hence the destiny of the world becomes visible in the reordering which occurs in the body of Christ. Because that is so, because the restoration of man entails the restoration of order in the world, B. Milner can draw an important conclusion concerning the relationship of Calvin's political activism to his eschatology.

Calvin's political activism, then, may be traced directly to his conception of the church as that movement which stands at the frontier of history, beckoning the world toward its appointed destiny.[115]

Calvin's eschatological vision is cosmic in scope and contributes significantly to his dynamic view of history. For Calvin, eschatology and history are the same. One may disagree with his exegesis of specific passages, and ask whether his arguments against a millennial reign of Christ on earth are sufficient,[116] because it is the case that at times Calvin's basic perspective seems to override some of the exegetical details. Nonetheless, it cannot be disputed that Calvin's basic perspective stems from the core of biblical eschatology. His eschatology is an authentic eschatology of hope.[117]

Some Concluding Remarks

The creative thought of great teachers frequently contains a variety of tensions. Sometimes these tensions exist because such is the nature of truth. Sometimes they exist because of lack of clarity. For whatever reason they may exist in the thought of the teacher, these tensions are usually dissolved by their followers. Disciples find it difficult to keep up with their masters. They become selective and one-sided. Consequently, great traditions become narrow and rich traditions are impoverished.

Traditions developing in the wake of John Calvin have not done justice to his eschatology. Some of the fault lies with Calvin himself. His dynamic eschatological vision is articulated more clearly and

115. Milner, *Calvin's Doctrine,* p. 195.
116. H. Quistorp, for example, questions both (*Calvin's Doctrine,* pp. 115, 158–62).
117. Calvin's eschatology is thus characterized by Quistorp, *Calvin's Doctrine,* chap. 1 on "Hope," and T. F. Torrance, *Kingdom and Church* (Edinburgh: Oliver and Boyd, 1956), chap. 4, "The Eschatology of Hope: John Calvin."

forcefully in the appropriate biblical commentaries than it is in the *Institutes*. Although the positions developed in the *Institutes* are in complete harmony with the commentaries, they need the light of the commentaries to be fully appreciated. But since his followers have usually considered the *Institutes* to be an adequate summary of his thought, the essential nature of Calvin's eschatology has been easily overlooked.

However, it is not just a matter of not reading widely enough in Calvin. The tensions that exist in his thinking have contributed to one-sidedness in his followers. No one would dispute the fact that a kind of pietistic movement arose in the Calvinist tradition, making its appeal to Calvin's doctrine of the immortality of the soul and seeking its life in heaven. The movement became far more individualistic and otherworldly than Calvin ever was. It too focused on the Christ in heaven, but on a Christ divorced from the realities of world and cosmos. No longer was it the cosmic Christ in whom the reordering of the cosmos had already occurred, but rather a Christ who secured the life and destiny of the individual.[118] Calvin's meditation on the future life was read as though Calvin were Thomas à Kempis. Perhaps on this score, at least to a limited extent, Calvin can be appealed to against himself; but a close reading of the *Institutes*, in the light of the commentaries, clearly demonstrates that such a reading misses everything Calvin stood for.

Calvin has been called a theologian of the eternal decree, and that description is undoubtedly correct. The significance of the sovereignty of God, predestination, and the eternal decree can hardly be overemphasized; but it can be understood in a one-sided manner. Calvin did not separate the eternal decree from its content or from that which manifests and effectuates it in history. Calvin can say that "the eternal decree of God would be void unless the promised resurrection, which is the effect of that decree, were also certain."[119] Eternal decree and eschatology may not be separated. The eternal decree cannot be understood apart from the history of redemption which manifests and effectuates it.[120] But in parts of the Calvinist tradition the eternal decree

118. See C. R. Andrews, "A Baptist Looks Backward and Forward," *Theology Today* 13 (Jan. 1957): 507–20. Granting that Calvin was able to hold together the doctrine of the immortal soul and the consummation of the universe, Andrews asserts that Calvin's successors could not. "The corporate hope dimmed as the individual hope overspread it. This inner contradiction was to become a source of great weakness in the Reformed tradition, including English Independency" (p. 512).

119. *Comm. on Rom.* 8:23.

120. Note Calvin's assertion that "Christ, then, is the mirror wherein we must, and without self-deception may, contemplate our own election" (*Inst.* 3.24.5).

has been divorced from eschatology, and the result has been a kind of static, almost fatalistic determinism. History has been viewed as one great big push from behind, and the emphasis has fallen on the necessary action of God to the exclusion of any necessary action of Christians. The dynamic, active pulling into the future stemming from the renewal already possessed in hope has been a negligible ingredient in such traditions. Consequently, history has not been seen as an arena of eschatological happenings involving necessary Christian action; nor has the church been viewed, in Milner's words, as a movement standing "at the frontier of history beckoning the world to its destiny."

The threat of legalism, the nemesis of all Calvinist traditions, also stems from a failure in eschatological perspective. If obedience to the sovereign God, if conformity to the new order of God articulated in the law, is separated from the Christian's present participation in the reordering of all things already accomplished in Christ, the inevitable result is legalism. The law is then imposed only from the outside and obedience is at best external. For Calvin, obedience — even in the creation — is not only obedience to a command, but participation by hope in the new reality of the kingdom of God.

Finally, Calvin has acquired a justly deserved reputation as a social and political revolutionary. His slogan of establishing the kingdom of God on earth has had great appeal, and many of his followers have walked in his footsteps. Yet the use of that slogan in the contemporary scene populated by revolutionaries of various stripes can easily imply too much. That slogan can become captive to a kind of social Darwinism, promising a gradual but inexorably progressive development which will bring human society to a state of perfection — provided, of course, that Christians work hard enough and possess sufficient faith. Or that slogan can become captive to a radical revolutionary philosophy promising perfection as the inevitable result of the Marxist revolution — provided, of course, that a little transcendence is thrown in.

For Calvin, however, Christian action in establishing the kingdom may not be viewed apart from a proper eschatological perspective. The perfected kingdom is in Christ who is in heaven. Believers cannot by their actions drag that perfected kingdom to earth prematurely. What is experienced in the present and what is manifested through Christian action are only the beginnings of the kingdom of God. Calvin's eschatological vision tempered his revolutionary action. He was, in Graham's words, a constructive revolutionary.

Eschatology is an indispensable dimension of Christian thought and action. Without it the church becomes static, ineffective, and usually heretical. For eschatology contributes a compelling dynamic to Christian action and obedience. It also sets boundaries and gives direction to Christian thinking about God, salvation, and obedient action in the world. When the basic eschatological perspective of Scripture is minimized or lost, Christian thought becomes heretical and Christian social action merely secular. John Calvin provides a good example of the role biblical eschatology should play in Christian thought and life.